Defining
Global Justice

Defining Global Justice

The History of U.S. International Labor Standards Policy

Edward C. Lorenz

University of Notre Dame Press
Notre Dame, Indiana

Manufactured in the United States of America

Library of Congress Cataloging-in-Publication Data
Lorenz, Edward C.
Defining global justice : the history of U.S. international labor
standards policy / Edward C. Lorenz.
p.   cm.
Includes bibliographical references and index.
ISBN 0-268-02550-9 (cloth : alk. paper)
ISBN 0-268-02551-7 (pbk. : alk. paper)
1. International Labour Organisation—History.   2. Labor
policy—United States—History.   3. Industrial relations—United
States—History.   I. Title.
HD7801.L67   2001
331'.0973—dc21

                                                      2001001940

∞ *This book is printed on acid-free paper.*

Contents

Acknowledgments

As this book evolved during the past ten years, I incurred debts of gratitude to innumerable people and institutions. This study began as an investigation of the closing of the Amoskeag Mills in Manchester, New Hampshire. The economic restructuring and job loss that city experienced seemed relevant to other communities in which I had worked, such as Baltimore, St. Louis, and Detroit. Repeatedly in my studies of Manchester I encountered the name John Winant, who made a seemingly inexplicable transition from New Hampshire governor in the 1920s and early 1930s to head of the International Labor Organization (ILO). What seemed most remarkable was that his ILO leadership began in 1939, at which time I had believed the U.S. was too isolationist to join any arm of the League of Nations.

As I studied more about Winant, he became a portal into the world of international labor standards and the arcane history of American relations with the ILO. However, Winant did more than open a door. As I read his writings about labor standards and the ILO, I became convinced that the history of U.S. labor standards policy was not an esoteric subject, but one all those concerned with employment policy should understand. As I pushed this study back before Winant and then down to the end of the millennium, I learned it clarified both the weaknesses and the strengths common to all American policy making.

The U.S. can be exceptional in its failure to use social justice as a measure of policy effectiveness, yet the country can be equally unique in elevating concepts such as human rights and procedural equity to prominence. When and why can the U.S. be both so regressive and advanced? How can the U.S. be exceptionally transparent and doggedly committed to justice in some policy making, yet succumb to a process and outcomes fully distorted to serve the self-interests of the powerful and affluent?

The ILO policy process has helped identify answers to these questions. The relationship of the U.S. to the ILO shows the importance of guaranteeing a seat at the policy table to varied interests. Additionally, the history of the labor standards movement demonstrates the need and potential for those whose work includes the study of justice, such as clergy and attorneys, to intervene to restrain the pursuit of material self-interest. It provides a workable model for making the process function with restraint and integrity.

Staff of a number of libraries and archives helped greatly with this research. Because of Winant's tragic death, his papers are scattered as parts of other collections, including the Robert Bass Papers at the Baker Library of Dartmouth College and the Franklin D. Roosevelt Library in Hyde Park. Both institutions were welcoming, but especially the FDR Library, with which Alma College historically has had a fond relationship.

In the Washington area, Bill Creech at the U.S. Archives provided invaluable direction through the records of the Department of Labor and the National Recovery Administration, as did staff at the Library of Congress in the papers of Frank Knox and the National Consumers' League. John Shepherd at the Catholic University Archives helped with the papers of George Higgins and records from the National Catholic Welfare Conference. In Silver Spring, Lee Sayrs at the George Meany Archive offered guidance through their wealth of records of the International Affairs Department of the AFL-CIO, as did staff at the Reuther Library at Wayne State University.

Also outside Washington, Anne Engelhart at the Schlesinger Library at Radcliffe helped with the papers of Ethel Johnson and the Massachusetts Consumers' League. Thomas Rosko of the Seeley G. Mudd Manuscript Library at Princeton facilitated interlibrary loan use of the David Morse Papers. Likewise, staff of the Cincinnati Public Library helped with access, primarily by fax, to detailed information on William McGrath. Geir Gunersen at the Gerald R. Ford Library in Ann Arbor assisted not only with access to papers related to U.S. withdrawal from the ILO, but also directed me through resources available from other presidential libraries. Carol Ressler Lochman at the Hagley Museum and Library facilitated access to the records of the U.S. Chamber of Commerce. Finally, Kevin Cawley at the University of Notre Dame Archives guided me through records of the 1955 ILO conference held on the campus.

I was exceptionally honored to have time to spend with Msgr. George Higgins, who gave generously to discuss this project. He not only provided insight into several generations of participants in ILO policy making but suggested many additional contacts. He directed me to Stephen I. Schlossberg, who granted generously of his time to review recent ILO policy. Mahmood Monshipouri of Quinnipiac College, who jointly authored a paper on "The Ethical Dilemmas of Globalization and Liberalization," and others at the International Studies Association provided inspiration and criticism of the project. Likewise, participants in a panel at the American Society for Legal History on "Labor, Law and the State in the Interwar Period" offered many valuable comments, as did the editors at the *Seattle University Law Review*, who turned our papers into a symposium on labor law and the state.

Alma College offered continuing support for this project, authorizing several faculty small-grants and a recent Posey Award. Former Provost Leslie Brown; librarians and staff of the Monteith Library, including Peter Dollard, Priscilla Perkins, Larry Hall, and especially Arlene Nyman in Interlibrary Loans; our secretary, Barb Tripp; and innumerable others have helped. In the history department, Mike Yavenditti and M.J.J. Smith repeatedly reminded me of the need to balance the economic, social, intellectual, technological, and political perspectives in any research in the discipline. Burnie Davis, in political science, in addition to crucial computer help, reminded me of the need to define the long-term public interest. Liping Bu, Patrick Furlong, Sandy Hulme, and Marek Payerhin reminded me to take a global perspective. My student assistants of recent years: Julie Kellogg, Cindy Miller, Kristin Staton, and Cardell Johnson did essential detailed work. Students in a variety of other contexts, especially in the comparative policy course in Mexico, have asked insightful questions about the work and have inspired diligence in its completion.

Several anonymous reviewers have been extremely perceptive, asking needed questions, and suggesting structural improvements. John deRoo provided valuable editing. Ann Rice, Rebecca DeBoer, Barbara Hanrahan, and everyone else at Notre Dame Press have extended every assistance and support to the work.

Then there has been the interest, understanding, and stylistic advice from my family. Pete reviewed drafts of early chapters. Beth did extensive final editing. Steve, Dave, Karen, and Teresa accompanied me on research trips to Washington and New Hampshire. Their working-class grandparents, all of whom understood the fundamental need for labor rights and economic justice, provided a personal legacy which infuses this study. More recently, Karen and Erin have welcomed us on the final visits to archives and academic forums.

Mostly, of course, I am grateful to my wife, Marilyn. First, she has been the most persistent editor, reading multiple versions of the entire manuscript. Second, she has participated in innumerable late night discussions of hypotheses and evidence. Third, she has been with me on most research trips, as well as the service-learning classes in south Texas and Mexico that influenced the introduction. However, her most important role has been to be an inspiration for the effort to find out how to make sure justice is a factor in the policy process. For every hour I have given this work, she has given one, often at great sacrifice and always out of love.

Of course, all of the above contributed only help, guidance, and criticisms. They are responsible for many improvements, but none of the errors. Those are solely the author's responsibility. I only hope any value from this project overshadows its weaknesses and failures.

Introduction

On the Saturday afternoon before Mother's Day, my family and a group of my students from Michigan completed collecting samples as part of an environmental health assessment in Matamoros, Mexico. With our on-site work done, we stopped to help a family known to one of our hosts. They needed to move their home from decaying wooden supports to a foundation of cinder blocks. The shanty measured about twelve by twelve feet and had a dirt floor without running water or electricity. The neighborhood in which they lived had no normal public services—no paved roads, sewerage, or garbage collection, not even a formal community name. It had about ten thousand residents, who, under Mexican law, had staked out small plots of vacant land as their homesites. These were pioneers, much as millions of Americans before them, building something from nothing in a stark landscape.

Of course, this was hardly the idealized life of earlier American pioneers. Their dusty surroundings were not a pristine wilderness. The only pastoral feature of the setting was that the land had been farmed, before being occupied by the squatters. As a consequence of the exceptionally hot and dry spring season, dust blew constantly as we laid the foundation. A pickup stopped midway through the evening to offer drinking water. Hot from riding in the back of the truck, contained in a dusty plastic bottle, it nevertheless seemed like springwater in these surroundings. Geographically within an hour's walk of the U.S. city of Brownsville, Texas, the shanty and its owners remained worlds apart from earlier pioneers to the north. And, although the husband and wife worked among the thousands employed full-time by General Motors in the city, they could not legally gain access to the U.S., since they lacked the real "property," bank deposits, or other assets necessary to get a visa.

In contrast, it was a simple endeavor for us to cross the Rio Grande, as we did later that night. In order to preserve our samples, we needed a picnic cooler. The cheapest place to buy one was at Wal-Mart in Brownsville. Although it was ten o'clock at night, the Wal-Mart parking lot was filled with cars, many of which bore Mexican license plates.[1] As it was the eve of Mother's Day, the more established residents of Matamoros, those who could get entry cards, gladly waited in the long lines of traffic at customs to buy gifts at the symbol of American consumer culture. Of course, excepting the Mexican cars, many discount stores throughout the United States experienced the same shopping frenzy that evening.

Only a month later, national attention focused on a bitter strike by the United Auto Workers (UAW) in Flint, Michigan. As the strike spread beyond Flint, Ricardo Blazquez, the GM brake plant manager in Dayton, Ohio, pleaded with his union local to refuse to strike: "I am . . . concerned about the consequences a strike could have for [the survival of] our plants."[2] The UAW, refusing to be intimidated by such threats, ultimately halted all car production by General Motors in North America. The union's key grievance was movement of production both out of the country and to nonunion producers within the U.S. The strike became the longest in the auto industry in the last generation. To settle the dispute, the company promised not to close or sell the Flint or Dayton plants, but only during the following two years. Within days of the strike's end, the company announced that reorganization necessitated the closing of both plants after two years. GM no longer wanted to get its parts from high-cost facilities where workers received excellent wages. In order to keep car prices competitive, GM needed the freedom to shop around for parts for its cars, including buying more from Mexican plants.

Clearly GM, its union employees in the U.S., and those in Mexico had related problems. The challenge for neutral observers is to find an equitable policy that will address the needs of the company and both groups of workers. While no doubt benefitting personally from low-cost products, the workers in Flint and Dayton realized they would suffer more than they would benefit from the company's globalization. Yet, by moving jobs to Matamoros from Flint, Dayton, and other high-cost American cities, GM not only benefits with lower costs, but also provides jobs to desperate Mexicans. Cities such as Matamoros and Ciudad Juarez have mushroomed in population in the past few decades, due to the great numbers of people from the Mexican interior seeking jobs at the border assembly plants (*maquiladoras*). Likewise, the movement of production to the lowest-cost source has benefitted consumers throughout North America in the 1990s, as was reflected in the economic boom with minimal inflation that characterized the U.S. Except for the few disgruntled UAW members in Michigan, people seemed to be voting with their feet overwhelmingly in favor of the relentless cost reductions produced by the borderless global economy. In Mexico, large numbers walked into the border manufacturing plants to accept the low-wage jobs, and in both countries they also walked into their stores in droves to purchase the low-cost consumer goods produced by such plants.[3]

Are there any indicators that the strikers of Flint are not alone in their opposition to laissez-faire globalization of capital and trade? Looking north of the burgeoning Mexican border cities to the line dividing the two countries, several pieces of evidence can be found that raise questions about the support for such forms of globalization. First, there is the U.S. Border Patrol, with vehicles parked within line of sight to prevent undocumented crossings from the south. Stretching into the desert west of El Paso and east from San Diego, where the border is not a river, are massive fences inside U.S. territory to keep out the Mexicans. On the south side of the border there are no such controls, only staff of the Mexican agency to protect the rights of migrants heading north.[4] Throughout the borderland there are numerous other signs of the U.S. government effort to stop the flood of people attempting to cross from the south, such as military reservists helping the Immigration and Naturalization Service. To the south, retention data indicate that most Mexican *maquiladora* workers do not find the border factories a long-term place of employment.[5] Rather, such employment serves as a way station on the road to the promised land.[6]

Further evidence that globalization is not equally beneficial to people on both sides of the border comes from comparisons of Mexican shanty towns with their U.S. counterparts in south Texas. These *colonias* on both sides of the border are extremely poor communities, with limited public services and homes often built piecemeal by their owners. However, fundamental differences exist between U.S. *colonias* and those in Mexico. Poverty on the U.S. side of the border is characterized by a standard of living many times greater than that of shanty town residents across the Rio Grande.[7] Even to work at an American fast-food restaurant is to earn more in an hour than in a long day of work at a *maquiladora*. Moreover, when Americans leave work they can associate with others in a church, community organization, fraternal group, or union that can participate without inhibition in the public policy process, thereby assuring the people's opportunity to request or even demand better community services or more worker protections. Across the border, a different relationship exists between the *colonia* and the dominant political party, whether the old Institutional Revolutionary Party (PRI) or the newer National Action Party (PAN), which tends to circumscribe the freedom of association.[8]

Despite the rhetoric of the benefits of globalization, the contrasts between the two countries, particularly as concerns public policy making, became more stark at the end of the twentieth century. In Mexico, the rise of the neoliberals to control of government had made a mockery of the PRI's populist origins and revolutionary pretensions.[9] Worse for the poor, the institutions which would critique this trend, such as organized labor, the churches, and the professorate, remained under the thumb of the PRI and government bureaucrats. Mexico increasingly had a free economy with restrictions on the political participation of nonbusiness groups.[10] While change may come with the defeat of the PRI in 2000, the victorious PAN's commitment to economic liberalization seemed only slightly different from what had gone before, although proposals by Vincente Fox to open the border might undermine some of the extreme labor cost differences between the countries.[11] The positive policy consequence of the PAN triumph might come in the treatment of labor, the church, and other nongovernmental organizations, which if allowed independence might give the country as vibrant a civil society as the U.S.

In contrast to late-twentieth-century Mexico, the United States experienced a resurgence of policy participation by populist institutions. Especially in Texas, democratic empowerment undermined discrimination against Hispanics, weakening the system of patronage upon which the privileged position of the old border elite had been based. The success of the Texas Industrial Areas Foundation (IAF) in empowering the state's poor exemplified this trend. Based in the churches of average people—Hispanic and black, as well as white—IAF groups from Valley Interfaith along the lower Rio Grande to the El Paso Interreligious Sponsoring Organization at the other end of the border have proven that populist institutions can have an impact upon political decisions and the distribution of public resources.[12]

One of the most powerful empirical proofs of the increasing value many people place on the civil society in the U.S. are the numbers crossing to the northern side of the border. While it is difficult to determine the reasons for migration, it is helpful to note the relative merits of cultural, social, economic, and political factors. There is much anecdotal evidence that Mexicans do not find U.S. culture to be superior to their own.[13] In fact, the respect for family, the delicate balancing of indigenous and European cultures, and the blending of tradition with modernity have been features of Mexican culture that have made it a model for the world. Furthermore, many Mexican migrants are aware of this, as demonstrated by their reluctance to abandon ties to the homeland after migrating north.[14] Likewise, despite mythic tales of masses of Mexican women sneaking into the U.S. to deliver their babies as U.S. citizens, social services are not necessarily better for the poor on the north side of the border.[15] Access to public health services, housing, and primary schooling may be easier for the poor in the south and certainly is not dramatically different in the north. Finally, while no doubt very important, the economic motivation should not be seen as the preeminent one. While wages are far better north of the border, Mexicans do not need to come north for cheap consumer goods. Such goods are available to Mexicans on both sides of the border.[16]

Popular explanations of migration often minimize a factor that on closer examination seems to rival the economic—the pursuit of American civic life. Its absence is what fundamentally differentiates the opportunities for a CTM (Mexican Workers Confederation) member at GM's Deltronics plant in Matamoros, Tamaulipas, from those of a UAW member at the Dayton, Ohio, brake plant.[17] It is what also differentiates the political experiences of a parishioner at one of the churches affiliated with Valley Interfaith in the Diocese of Brownsville, Texas, from a communicant of a church in the Diocese of Matamoros. And, it is what may cause the policy involvement of an American political science professor to contrast markedly with that of a Mexican counterpart.[18] In each case, if an American dislikes public policies, an American can use American institutions to strengthen an individual voice of protest by merging it with that of others. The Mexican counterpart can try the same approach but is much more likely to be circumspect in criticizing the state, elite business leaders, and the leadership of the nongovernmental groups to which the person is affiliated. Thus, the attractiveness of the United States is not its general culture, with its anti-family values, individualism, and violence. It is not simply its laissez-faire consumerism and materialism. In fact, Mexico's problem is that it has come much closer to real laissez-faire than the U.S. Who could be more of a free economic actor than the worker building his shanty without any public help or regulation in southeast Matamoros? The attractiveness of the north side of the Rio Grande is its civic culture, particularly those civic procedures that allow the popular classes, that is average people, to speak out on public issues with some chance of being heard or, at a minimum, not harmed.[19]

A perennial problem of politics is maintaining the balance between justice and freedom, of allowing individuals to seek their interests without destroying opportunity and justice for all.[20] We must be perfectly clear about which citizens usually have guaranteed access to power. Except in the most extraordinary circumstances, it is people such as the GM executives in Flint, Dayton, and Matamoros, as in the past it was the slave owners in pharaoh's Egypt and the southern planters before the U.S. Civil War who were assured freedom and justice. The problem is that to maximize their income and comfort such people may be tempted to use the power that accompanies their wealth to take as much as possible from the less articulate, the poor, the minorities or aliens in their midst. Beginning at least with the Hebrew prophets, and continuing through the nineteenth-century abolitionists to modern labor standards advocates, good societies have been distinguished not by the material prosperity of their rich but by prophetic defenses of justice and freedom for all. Also, we must recall that prophets are not enough to make a good society. Moses and Harriet Beecher Stowe shared not only an aversion to the injustice of slavery, they also found support within powerful institutions.

Good societies need free institutions to speak for the outcasts and the vulnerable. Moses had God on his side. Stowe had the abolition movement, based especially in faith communities. They understood that prophets need institutional support. In colonial Mexico, the Spanish pitted a powerful church against a powerful civil elite—the priests in the mission against the *hacendados* and soldiers in the *presidio*.[21] The U.S. is exceptional in addressing this problem with minimal formal government involvement, instead doing so by protecting the right to establish a vigorous structure of free associations, especially religious, fraternal, professional, and educational ones, as a check on the corruption of public life by the privileged.

The U.S. system does not assume that elites always possess wisdom or practice altruism nor that any one church or social movement will always be right when it claims to define justice or good policy. In fact, the founders hoped we usually would be governed by benevolent sages drawn from a detached agrarian elite, clones of Washington and Jefferson. However, James Madison, the "father of the Constitution," knew that not all people were angels, and that elites could be blind to justice, instead greedily seeking only their self-interest.[22] He created a system that assumed neither elites nor other institutions, whether unions or universities, churches or corporations, would always seek the public good. Churches and colleges, unions and community groups can become bureaucratized monsters, as unresponsive to the needs of the popular classes as any business. They can even become tools of the elite; yet, they will be kept from always being so as long as there are many of them and the people can freely create others.

Despite the many well-defined weaknesses of the American system, these independent institutions have guided some remarkable reforms — reforms quite unpopular with many elites. Whether during the abolition movement or during the social crises arising from the industrial revolution, churches, colleges, labor organizations, and consumer movements, often working with concerned business leaders, served to provide a forum for critics of the injustices of the reigning political economy. Even when American elites harassed unions, fired troublesome professors, or withdrew donations from prophetic churches, some of the victimized institutions survived to nurture alternative perspectives. We must not overlook the likelihood that the migrants waiting in Matamoros and the workers striking in Flint sense this strength of America. They especially sense that this system somehow works to protect popular interests and, despite its failures, has done so in exceptional ways.

No case study makes this feature of American public life clearer than that of the international labor standards movement. It may be that changing international labor standards cannot do much to alter recent global economic trends. Regardless of standards, any mechanism for enforcing them, particularly through the bureaucratized or ossified ILO, may be inadequate. Debating those questions, however, misses an essential point about the modern labor standards movement. As former New York Senator Daniel Patrick Moynihan observed in his dissertation about the ILO, "The practicality of the idea of international labor legislation derives not so much from the fact that the assumptions on which it is based were true as that they were thought to be true."[23] For example, the authors of one recent study of the global economy concluded, "All over the world, people are being pitted against each other to see who will offer global corporations the lowest labor, social, and environmental costs. Their jobs are being moved to places with inferior wages, lower business taxes, and more freedom to pollute."[24] Innumerable American state officials share their perspective and seek to ease labor protections, such as worker compensation laws or unemployment insurance regulations, believing that to do so will attract business.[25] It is possible that businesses do not pick locations because of lower labor standards. Whether or not that is a fact, it is true that state officials reduce benefits to attract businesses, and it is a fact that workers lose benefits as a result of these changes.[26]

Consequently, it does not matter if international labor standards are necessary as symbols or enforceable law; their presence or absence influences policy decisions that impact the rights and protections of workers. The battle for labor standards provided a forum for populist elements in America, particularly in universities, labor unions, professions, and faith communities, to define alternative policy goals to American liberalism. Scholars, drawn from within the American elite, tend to see political economy in terms of what the historian Louis Hartz called "American Whiggery."[27] They may be conservative, they may be progressive, they may even be Marxist, but they all frame arguments about policy in the materialistic terms originated by liberals. The American labor standards debate, while regularly confined to those terms by the Whig elite, has been liberated from that at important times by the alternative populist vision that insists much of life must be kept free from markets — family relations, ethics, and the value of work. Specifically, the phrase that captures this populist vision in the field of labor standards is that "labor is not a commodity." That phrase is important, and its successful defense by labor and its allies teaches fundamental lessons about American popular and political culture.

The study of the American role in the international labor standards movement also contributes in at least four other major ways to an understanding of general American history and the American policy process. It clarifies the extent and nature of American exceptionalism, that is, the tendency for the United States to follow an especially distinctive or restrained social policy course compared to other industrial democracies. Second, because the policy demands of the labor standards movement have depended for nearly a century on a varied coalition of interest groups in America and abroad, it provides an excellent opportunity for a case study of the changing roles of such groups in America and internationally. Third, this group role provides an opportunity to study each type of group in detail, particularly women's organizations, labor unions, the consumer movement, business groups, professions, and churches. Finally, by reviewing the policy history, changing American support for international labor standards helps clarify major turning points in modern American intellectual, social, and economic history, as well as in American political development.

While many people throughout the world have played a pioneering role in the labor standards movement, the American policy process on remarkable occasions has brought forth the most courageous stands on labor injustices, requiring major public sacrifice. Recalling the abolition movement makes the uniqueness of the American process clear. Although the British, other Europeans, and the Canadians pioneered the modern abolition of slavery, none of them were doing so when, simultaneously, the most successful portion of their economy depended on it. None of them faced fighting a civil war at the cost of more than a half million lives in order to define the new labor standard.[28]

In the twentieth century, in a less dramatic yet still courageous way, the U.S. has taken the lead in the labor standards movement, particularly with the defense of free labor during the Cold War. Each of the twentieth-century efforts were consequences of the uniquely populist American policy process, as had been the abolition movement that finally brought under control the injustices of the post-Columbian global economic regime. Thus, the study of the American role in the international labor standards movement teaches not only much about the impact of that movement but important lessons about the much maligned American policy process, a process that may be better appreciated by the newest Americans sneaking across our southern border than by our social scientists. The newest Americans from Mexico certainly value it more than the old elites who so often wish to subvert it for their own profit.

If meaningful limits are to be applied to the contemporary re-creation of post-Columbian global labor exploitation, if justice is again to check individualism in the world economy, then we need to understand the American system and empower those groups that make it work well. For despite the academic criticisms of the American interest group process, it has been responsive to nonelite concerns. Likewise, while many students of social policy regularly lament American exceptionalism, by which they mean the extreme conservativism of the U.S. system, the study of labor standards reveals remarkable popular responsiveness. However, the history of the labor standards movement makes clear that the U.S. often muddles through, with self-interest trumping the pursuit of the public good. While the American system includes exceptional constitutional and cultural barriers that frequently doom the pursuit of rational policy, the valid critiques of the U.S. policy process should not blind scholars to its virtues and triumphs. We do a disservice to less articulate Americans, especially to the newest ones, if we cannot define the system's strengths. The study of the American role in the international movement for labor standards helps us to see the policy system more clearly, so that we might identify procedural and group reforms conducive to achieving exceptionally good policy.

ONE

The Exceptional Group Process

When opposition to the North American Free Trade Agreement (NAFTA) among traditionally Democratic labor leaders embarrassed the Clinton Administration in 1994, it used the seventy-fifth anniversary celebrations for the International Labor Organization (ILO) to demonstrate its sensitivity to the problem of globalization undermining labor standards. Speaking for the president, U.S. Trade Representative Mickey Kantor sounded like a leader of the 1998 Flint strikers or perhaps an astute Mexican migrant. He warned that international standards existed to prevent countries from gaining "comparative advantage . . . [from] low labor costs . . . created through illegitimate political suppression of wages and working conditions."[1] The founders of the labor standards movement a century earlier might have only changed Kantor's statement by replacing *illegitimate* with *immoral*.[2]

Although to the general public the ILO may be the most obscure U.N. affiliate, it is the international body with which the U.S. has had the longest and one of the most fascinating relationships. Begun in Europe, the labor standards movement rose to prominence on the expertise, dedication, and reputation of the American progressive elite. In the years before World War I they built a wide-ranging coalition to support the movement, from social welfare reformers and trade unionists to liberal businessmen and clergy. The Versailles Conference created the ILO in 1919. John Andrews, the head of one of the movement's leading interest groups, the American Association for Labor Legislation, noted in 1919 that "The wide appeal of uniform labor laws is doubtless based in large part upon the fact that such uniform minimum standards benefit humane employers as well as wage-earners."[3] Yet, as he wrote, the overall progressive movement as well as the labor standards coalition fell upon hard times. As with the general Versailles settlement, the U.S. abandoned the ILO after its birth. But unlike the other two international organizations created at Versailles, the League of Nations and the World Court, the U.S. reversed itself fifteen years later and joined the ILO.

From the start of U.S. involvement through the end of the twentieth century, the history of U.S. participation in the labor standards movement reveals the distinctive features of the American policy process, and the exceptional ideologies and political roles of groups within the country. For example, far more than in other industrial nations, middle-class, college-educated women in the U.S. greatly influenced social policy making. Likewise, the American churches played an exceptional role at key points in the policy debates. Organized labor came to the process with an ideology far less leftist and more populist than its European counterparts. Then there were the progressive business leaders, supporting reforms that it might be assumed decreased their own profits. Throughout the movement's history, but especially in the last quarter of the twentieth century, lawyers assumed a lead role in defining core labor standards. Finally, in the early years of the movement, American academic social scientists departed the ivory tower to play leadership roles.

As time passed, the role of such groups changed in the general policy process and in their support of labor standards. For example, women gained the vote and became simply a demographic group within the American electorate. Academics increasingly focused inwardly. A new type of business leader came to prominence after mid-century, with reputations built more on successful defense of capitalism than on concern with social stability. Once the U.S. joined the ILO, organized labor assumed the preeminent role in the country's participation in global labor rights policy making. While academics and women's groups lost interest in labor issues and business focused on labor control, the increasingly Americanized Catholic Church and attorneys schooled in human rights law joined with unions in filling the void.

The struggle for labor rights in the last century has been a barometer gauging the success of the American system in shaping international policies that provide minimum protection and some dignity for the least powerful people. The survival of child labor, exploitation of adult workers, payment of substandard wages, and various occupational health and safety problems, however, prove the movement has not fully succeeded. Yet, the creation of the International Labor Organization, the development of widely accepted minimal labor standards, the victory of free trade unions in eastern Europe during the Cold War, and the more recent campaign against sweatshops are remarkable triumphs of the movement and of the American role in the world. The history of labor rights teaches much about the U.S. policy process, the exceptionalism of America, the changes within the specific groups involved in the movement, and the means by which nonelites gain leadership in the policy process.

This study will focus on the role of interest groups and other institutions in the labor standards policy process. Inherently, it also will describe the changing policy preferences and roles of specific types of groups and institutions, especially business, organized labor, women's groups, academics, consumer organizations, the legal profession, and churches. In studying changes in such groups, the roles of leaders, their methods, and their impact will be analyzed. The study will outline the changes in American economic and social policy making in the twentieth century, helping to clarify the clear differences between eras and the factors contributing to transitions between eras. Most important, the review of the history of U.S. labor standards policy should answer questions arising from conflicting interpretations of the historical and normative role of nongovernmental organizations and interest groups in the public policy process.

INTEREST GROUPS AND INTERNATIONAL RELATIONS

The system of international relations that prevailed from the mid-seventeenth through the mid-twentieth century usually is named for the Peace of Westphalia, which ended the bloody Thirty Years War. Under the Westphalian system, nation-states were the prime actors in international relations. Essential to the functioning of the system, however, was a body of custom that the U.S. recognized as the law of nations—such as punishment of piracy, defining and protecting civilians during war, and, after the nineteenth century, the abolition of slavery.[4]

By 1900 this system seemed near perfection. The world was carved into empires or spheres of influence with such varied parts that each, ideally, could develop all major economic activities in a place that would be productive and profitable. No major multiempire war had taken place since the Congress of Vienna in 1815. Armies were professionally trained and led to follow the basic rules of war. Even slavery, which a century earlier had seemed a permanent feature of human society, had been banished from all major parts of the world. Then World War I shocked world leaders, especially those from the United States. The war had treated the entire population of each nation as the enemy. The empires, rather than being institutions to maximize economic efficiency, became the mechanisms that spread a regional conflict in southeast Europe around the globe. Finally, the rise of the Bolsheviks demonstrated that the global exploitation of industrial workers might have replaced slavery, warranting the destruction of governments that condoned it. These dramatic failures of the Westphalian system called for a transformation of the three-hundred-year-old global structure. At Versailles, President Wilson led the effort to chart a new global structure. Once the crisis of war faded, the victors could not find the will to launch a full revision. The creation of the ILO, as well as the League of Nations and the World Court, however, introduced new institutions that signaled the start of a transformation.

In the interwar period from 1919 to 1939, the world, and the United States specifically, witnessed a debate about the meaning of the First World War and Versailles, which laid the basis for the real transformation of the world system that resulted from World War II. While the era often is seen as one of American isolationism, in fact, the U.S. economy continued to be integrated into that of the world, and the U.S. participated in global politics as never before, from the Washington Naval Conference in 1921 through joining the ILO in 1934. The wartime economic planners completed the structure of global transformation in 1944, not only at Bretton Woods, but also with the simultaneous relaunching of the ILO at Philadelphia and the world agricultural conference.[5]

As the study of U.S. policy toward the ILO clarifies, the debates after Versailles until the end of the century pitted three alternative views of the post-Westphalian ideal. On the two extremes were theories that shared a deep distrust of world politics. There were realist advocates of freeing markets but retaining the nation-state as the primary policy maker. They hoped nation-states, other than the U.S., would become nearly powerless before private multinational corporations (MNCs). Realists dominated U.S. policy in the 1920s and often in the late twentieth century. In the U.S. context, realist fixation on minimal world government often seemed like isolationism. In fact, it simply was more international laissez-faire liberalism. On the other extreme, Marxists hoped to move the world to a worker paradise, beyond national states, in which withered states survived under the control of worker communities. To reach that ideal, a global totalitarian regime would first need to expropriate all private economic institutions. Of course, the United States overwhelmingly opposed this model, an opposition so intense that it often united the realists with supporters of a third model.[6]

Between these two antipolitical economic theories for replacing the Westphalian system was an overtly political economy model. It required the development of a number of specialized agreements among nations and the creation of institutions to implement those agreements. Unlike the free market or Marxist models, the political economy approach assumed the existence of multiple perspectives for addressing global needs. Replacing the previous reliance on nation-states to define multiple preferences, the political economy model recognized a host of nongovernmental organizations (NGOs) joining the nations to debate policy choices and to monitor policy implementation. Essentially, this model globalized the American pluralist policy process. Under this model, a world debate on a child labor policy or a global climate change treaty would cause the emergence of a multitude of NGOs endorsing alternative perspectives. Women's NGOs, religious institutions, various ethnic organizations, professional groups, and others would enter the policy arena and a compromise policy would evolve. While not necessarily the best policy, the compromise probably would not be the worst. Of course, the muddling through, inherent in the political economic model, appalled Marxists and the free market realists. Whenever they could, they sought to frustrate or destroy it.[7]

While a number of international institutions created after World War I reflect the political economic model, the ILO is the one with the longest history. The debates about the U.S. relationship with the ILO, therefore, provide a window into not simply the U.S. policy process, but into American attitudes toward the ideologies competing for the mind of the post-Westphalian world order. When the Marxist nations frustrated political economic pluralism at the ILO by sending delegations without real employer and labor representatives, the U.S. representatives rose in rebellion. Then the realists who dominated the U.S. foreign policy and business elite tried to ban pluralism in the world trading regime developed out of the Uruguay round of trade negotiations. They created a World Trade Organization (WTO) sanitized of any NGO involvement, concern with labor or environmental impacts, or ILO linkages. The rebellion against that extreme, which came in the 1990s, resulted in the U.S. supporting the ILO's right to be involved in global economic policy making, the need to define core labor standards, and specifically the assertion that labor remained more than a commodity.

THE DOMESTIC GROUP PROCESS

In addition to clarifying the international policy process, study of U.S. involvement in the ILO increases understanding of theories of domestic policy making. Nearly a half century ago political scientist David Truman described how the American interest group system distinguished U.S. democracy.[8] Subsequent studies by Robert Dahl and others seemed to verify his conclusions and found that the group process generally was a good one.[9] Other scholars disagreed. For example, E. E. Schattschneider noted that the U.S. system operated with a strong upper-class bias.[10] While not surprising to anyone aware of "the iron law of oligarchy,"[11] others saw the group process take on a new, more sinister form during the progressive era and especially after the New Deal. Both the number of groups and the amount of their policy expectations multiplied greatly. Theodore Lowi warned in 1969 that the contemporary group system may corrupt our political ideals as well as our political practices. He found a qualitative deterioration in the outcomes of the policy process when under intense group pressure.[12] Some scholars, such as Charles Lindblom, took a middle ground, finding the modern group system allowed for relatively good outcomes, what Lindblom called "muddling through."[13]

Lowi responded that the modern process prevented good planning and, most damning, blocked the achievement of justice. Coming out of the American South, Lowi knew whereof he spoke. For, the American South displayed most starkly the fundamental flaws of the American system, flaws that allowed a majority ethnic group to deny another its basic rights, retarding regional progress and imposing the starkest form of injustice. But while Schattschneider and Lowi called for procedural change to reemphasize public debate in setting policy over interest group bargaining, their solution seemed less prophetic than their diagnosis of the problems. The history of the labor standards movement, however, may suggest a method that has worked at key moments to bring some conception of justice to one of the least likely areas of American policy making.

Since the protection of labor rights historically has directly contradicted the interests of powerful pressure groups, from Southern planters meeting labor needs through international slave traders to global corporations working with totalitarian regimes, the periodic success of the labor rights movement shows the U.S. system can be made to define justice for all.[14] The successes of the labor standards movement after 1865 have proven that exceptional dedication and organization by political actors seeking justice can overcome the economic advantages of privileged elites.[15] The movement also shows the American empirical or pragmatic policy process at its best. Muddling through may work. The labor standards movement began with a focus on the local and state level and only turned to the nation and world after its experiences proved a nonglobal policy inadequate.

The movement's history also reveals that group participation in the policy process is not always motivated by an obvious or a consistent pursuit of simple self-interest. Many of the business and women leaders of the labor rights struggle had no self-interest in the outcome. Likewise, the process demonstrates that groups representing the poor, the good, or the wise, such as unions, churches, and academic societies, do not necessarily have benevolent motives. Rather, it shows that good policy results when civil society is marked by vigorous participation by citizen groups. Likewise, it proves leadership coming to the process with independent definitions of the public interest and justice can have remarkable success. Finally, it also indicates that special protections for the policy role of less affluent interests helps to assure their ability to be heard. The tripartite structure of the ILO is a good example of such a special protection.

Unlike other international organizations, the ILO has a representational system that gives interest groups a formal role in governance. This tripartite structure recognizes the right of organized labor and business to be heard in global labor standard setting. Thus, at the ILO governing body, each nation has four seats, but only two are appointed by the government. Both the major employer and leading worker organization appoint one delegate. When combined with the exceptional role of interest groups in the U.S., tripartism makes ILO policy making an especially fertile ground for understanding the limitations and possibilities inherent in the group policy process.

The ILO, like the United States, is an institution in which incremental changes in policy are the norm and often represent major achievements. While incrementalism can be an effective way of fine-tuning the policy process in the face of exceedingly diverse interests, structures prone to incrementalism must at times be changed fundamentally, especially when injustices are found. Studying U.S. policy toward the ILO and the ILO's responses to the U.S. policy process can provide multiple cases to evaluate methods for bringing significant reform to incremental systems.

Programs that seek social justice, such as the labor standards movement, are especially vulnerable to compromise under the incremental policy process. Fewer well-funded groups lobby for social justice than for the routine government decisions that benefit most people. Lowi has called these widely beneficial decisions "distributive policies." But, those decisions that may cause the majority or the elite to sacrifice for the good of a few, what he calls "redistributive policies," are both difficult to enact and implement.[16] With special interest groups increasingly dominating the policy process in America during the later twentieth century, debates

about justice for the poor face being converted, as most redistributive policies, into a quest for a bargain satisfying powerful groups. This may
appear insignificant when the issue is the location for a dam or a stadium;
it can seem sinister when the issue is the condemnation of forced labor in
a major trading partner. From the 1940s until the late 1980s, the U.S.
could not bring itself to ratify the ILO's forced labor convention, even
though we had fought a great war a century earlier to forbid such labor.

Policy making under the normal U.S. policy process is characterized
by concern with narrow benefits for the participating interests and, at best,
symbolic actions for the mass of the public.[17] An important consequence of
studying the history of interest group behavior related to the ILO is to understand the great changes in policy that have defined justice. These exceptions to the routine process do not prove the process always works but
rather demonstrate which combination of policy steps achieve justice and
which structures most facilitate that outcome. One of the best studies of the
ILO in its middle years, by Robert Cox, hinted at the importance of the exceptions to routine incrementalism. Cox described the ILO from the 1940s
to 1970s, when incrementalism based in consensual bargaining was the
norm. He called the ILO a limited monarchy, with all the antidemocratic
implications of such a label. He saw it inherently focused on satisfying only
the self-interest of a cozy network of bureaucratic staff, "individual [politi-
cal] actors," and international interest groups. In the early 1970s even
American business, while ostensibly anticommunist, gladly bargained
with the archenemy at the ILO. It saw that the organization helped nor-
malize relations with the "Communist bloc," a euphemism for ignoring de-
nials of labor rights in the East. Stable economic relations allowed for the
pursuit of economically profitable relations under detente. Cox sensed,
however, that this Faustian bargain, a classic incremental deal that satisfied
all interests at the expense of those banned from policy participation,
might be breaking down at the time he wrote. He saw "[The] structural possibility for change . . . [through] a major crisis between the participant sub-
system and some powerful force in its environment. Since June 1970 such a
crisis has arisen between the ILO and the United States. . . . Conceivably,
the crisis could mark the end of the political system."[18] In fact, the crisis did
bring significant change in the role of the ILO and ushered in one of its
great eras as a defender of human rights in Eastern Europe. But, he erred in
that the crisis did not come between the U.S. government and the ILO. It
came between U.S. labor and everyone else.

While not as glorious as the example of the 1970s, the ILO also took
upon itself major reforms of international labor standards earlier in its

history. On the earlier occasions, change seemed to arise from the vigor of a youthful bureaucracy and the special commitment of leaders. The study of the ILO policy process can show which of these structural differences should be repeated at other times to bring significant policy change.[19]

AMERICAN EXCEPTIONALISM

A common feature of comparative studies of American political culture is their emphasis on the exceptional structure and functioning of American society and its government. Typical is de Tocqueville's often-quoted statement that "Nothing is more striking to a European traveler in the United States than the absence of what we term the government, or the administration."[20] More recent students of exceptionalism focus on the less robust welfare state that developed in the United States. The U.S. has been at or near the end of the developed countries in adopting programs for universal health insurance, old-age pensions, and unemployment insurance.[21] This has been all the more remarkable given the more vigorous democracy that appeared in America at an early date. The picture of American exceptionalism is complex, as documented in Theda Skocpol's study of Civil War pensions; yet even she found the exception proved the rule that American policies, even when pioneering and nearly universal, have unique administrative structures and policy limitations.[22]

The experience with international labor standards generally reflects the pattern for other U.S. government social legislation. Swiss, German, French, and English leaders pioneered the creation of a mechanism for establishing international labor standards. The U.S. participated only minimally in the pre-Versailles labor standards movement. After the creation of the International Labor Organization in 1919, the U.S. was the only Allied power not to join. When the U.S. did become a member in 1934, it delayed paying its dues for a year. Then, from 1977 to 1980 the U.S. became the only democratic industrial nation to withdraw from the ILO. Earlier, various U.S. delegates and business organizations expressed concern that the ILO was one step on the way to "world government," an attitude perplexing to the delegates from our fellow democracies.[23]

The only exception to this pattern may have been the U.S. leadership in creating the International Labor Organization in 1919 and again during World War II, culminating in the Philadelphia Declaration, which rededicated the ILO in 1944. Yet, these exceptions do not depart greatly from the picture of American policy restraint. In 1919, the U.S. nearly boycotted the inaugural ILO conference, despite its being held in Washington. Similarly, at the start of World War II, while the U.S. helped rescue the bureaucracy from Europe, it would not host the organization, but forced it to move to McGill University in Montreal.

Social scientists have offered a number of explanations for this exceptionalism, including the unique socioeconomic development of the United States, the comparative weakness of labor and socialist movements, the ideology of the nation, the special role of organized interests—especially business interests—under American government, and the extensive limitations on state power and the related weakness of the administrative capacity of the American government.[24] While the experience with international labor standards does not categorically show which of these factors most explains exceptionalism, it sheds light on the nuanced interrelationship of these theories.

Although the United States experienced unprecedented economic growth in the late nineteenth century, becoming the first modern nation, vast regions of the U.S. remained rural. More so than developing regions of Western Europe, the country continued to have significant dependence on agriculture and extractive industries.[25] Until the end of the twentieth century, the northeast states remained the center of heavy industrialization. The U.S. never had the massive urban working class on the magnitude of England's during the first industrial revolution. The urban workers in the U.S. usually were the worker-consumers of the second industrial revolution.[26] Those who emphasize the socioeconomic explanation of exceptionalism find in these facts proof of their theory.

The ILO experience, however, complicates this explanation. In several congressional votes on ILO participation, members from rural southern and western states provided the core support for the ILO.[27] While these votes might be explained by party loyalty rather than socioeconomic conditions, other patterns of support make difficult the defense of the socioeconomic thesis. Not the least of these is the rather different approach to the ILO in Canada, which has quite similar socioeconomic indicators.[28] Yet, there is one correlation between socioeconomic conditions and ILO support in the U.S. that must give credibility to such an approach. Key support for American membership in the ILO came out of New England in the 1920s and 1930s, with its declining textile industry.[29] Because the remainder of the country experienced unprecedented economic hardship in the latter decade, the U.S. joined.[30]

The history of U.S. relations with the ILO likewise speaks to the theory that the vitality of socialist and organized labor movements explains comparative support for social protection.[31] The major ILO initiatives clearly came in periods when fear of leftist movements overshadowed policy making. Not only was European support for the ILO in 1919 driven by the specter of bolshevikism, but the U.S. had its own "Red Scare."[32] During the Great Depression, at the time of the decision to join, concern had resurfaced about the reemergence of a viable leftist party in America. Because labor unions flourished during both world wars, American support for the ILO can be interpreted as one reward for faithful wartime toil. When union membership declined in the 1920s and after 1980, U.S. interest in the ILO ran a parallel course. Yet, some key American decisions related to the ILO do not fit simply into this pattern. The 1919 rejection of ILO membership came before the 1920s decline in labor. What is exceptional in the U.S. is the unique philosophy and membership of organized labor.

Because of a variety of factors, American labor unions contrast greatly with those in other industrial nations. In the American federal system, in which courts played a fundamental role in defining economic relationships, American unions have been less confident than their European or Canadian counterparts that legislative protections of workers will prevail. Too often they have seen the courts declare legislated reforms unconstitutional. American unions came to rely more on contracts with employers and other voluntary agreements to produce results. Consequently, American union leaders placed much less stock than their foreign counterparts in the value of international labor laws as protections of minimal standards of employer behavior.[33]

More than most Western European trade unionists, American labor brought to their ILO work less hostility to religious faith and more concern with protection of freedom of association. Here they especially contrasted with trade union leadership in England and France.[34] It was only American labor, for example, that walked out of the ILO in the 1960s over suppression of freedom of association in Eastern Europe. It was American labor that walked out again in the 1970s to back the state of Israel, when the ILO admitted the Palestine Liberation Organization. And, repeatedly, labor leaders cooperated with Associated Jewish Charities, the Federal Council of Churches, and the National Catholic Welfare Conference on labor standards campaigns.

Certainly, church leaders served as intermediaries between labor and elite institutions. Yet, key labor leaders in America clearly identified with churches and a large number of the rank and file were members of faith communities. A distinctive feature of American labor and the churches was that membership heavily overlapped. Labor leaders did not just collaborate with churches as sympathetic elite institutions. Instead, American labor leaders could pressure churches to support the labor perspective. No incident could make this clearer than when George Meany met with the Catholic Apostolic Delegate and representatives of the bishops in Washington in the 1970s to settle policy differences. Meany came not as a member of one of two interest groups, but as a member of both. This special relationship between the unions and the churches in America is only one example of the ideological exceptionalism evident in the labor rights policy process.[35] Debates related to the ILO reveal the special balance in the U.S. between individualism and corporatism. The debates suggest that it is a mistake to see U.S. culture as only concerned with personal measures of success inherent in laissez-faire capitalism.[36] In fact, key segments of American society, including many church members, laborers, and women, to use representative demographic categories, support a balance in debates about social questions' concern with the community and the individual. For example, at the ILO, as well as in domestic policy debates, American labor insisted that "labor is not a commodity." The worker's value should not be set by a market. By giving meaning and dignity to life, work has intrinsic value. Likewise, the churches repeatedly introduced into ILO debates themes of community responsibility and even a rare defense in America of the "corporatism" common in other developed countries.[37] Especially during the progressive era, allies were found in the business community for "corporatist" solutions to the problems of industrialization. The National Civic Federation, for example, called for corporatist formal cooperation of business and labor and government in determining employment policy. While that effort faded after the first third of the century, it never completely disappeared from American business and had widespread support outside industry.

What the study of ILO policy does show regarding corporatism is the great growth within conservative business circles of nineteenth-century-style liberalism. After 1950, American business delegates at the ILO warned of creeping socialism, when everyone else saw bureaucratic inertia.[38] The change in American business is made clear when its ideology is compared to quite similar Canadian conservative thought. The Canadian employers, apparently maintaining their dual inheritance of English Tory noblesse oblige and French Catholic corporatism, did not join their American counterparts in the critique of the organization.[39] However, simply because American business largely abandoned cooperation does not mean the country did so. In fact, the battles with business gave special skills to American critics of laissez-faire, preparing them to attack all forms of deterministic materialism, whether capitalist or Marxist.

Consequently, the Americans brought a unique perspective to the tripartite representation scheme of the ILO. This was a structure potentially corporatist or pluralist. That is, delegates could approach the structure as one facilitating consensus or sharp ideological battles between conflicting interests. Since the 1950s, American delegates interpreted this structure in pluralist terms, being quite willing to engage in battle to win control of policy making. The walkouts from the ILO and refusal to pay required contributions reflect the problems American delegates have had with the more consensual, corporatist ILO process accepted by other nations. The remarkable success of the U.S. approach in changing the ILO after 1977 demonstrates the uniqueness of the American perspective and the vitality of the American interest group system. At the ILO the corrupting campaign finance component of the American pluralist system is absent and the distinctive populist aspects enhanced. The American interpretation of tripartism made U.S. business and labor powerful adversaries for the numerically dominant delegates from autocratic regimes.[40]

The American experience at the ILO also brings into focus the exceptional limitations on state power and administrative capacity in American government. At the establishment of the ILO in 1919, the U.S. played a key role in limiting the power of the organization relative to federal states. Federalism was a two-edged limitation on labor standards in the U.S. On the one hand, defenders of federalism did not want the central government to preempt state experimentation.[41] On the other, state discretion allowed any one state to frustrate labor standards in others by offering employers a haven from regulation. The story of the American decision to join the ILO in the 1930s is one of a desperate search for a solution to this "policy drag," where the least progressive state served as a check upon the more reformist.[42] Even after the U.S. Congress enacted rare national legislation, U.S. reformers faced the burden of judicial rejection of federal standards. One need only review the Department of Labor's *Labor Laws That Have Been Declared Unconstitutional* to gain an appreciation of the extent of the judicial barrier to national policy uniformity.[43] This barrier extended particularly to federal efforts to standardize the relationship of workers and employers, such as creation of a federal minimum wage or child labor standard.

To overcome policy drag and court rejection of national labor legislation, American promoters of labor standards first turned to the "interstate compact."[44] Yet, interstate compacts could not overcome the courts' opposition to restrictions on laissez-faire behavior and did not attract the interest of the regressive states, whose inclusion was needed. In the first year of the New Deal, reformers hoped that the corporatist procedures under the National Industrial Recovery Act (NIRA) might be the answer. Yet, immediately there were court challenges to the National Recovery Administration (NRA).[45]

The solution to these problems appeared in the form of the ILO. Its conventions established minimal standards that could be ratified as treaties, essentially enshrining them in the Constitution. The debates in the U.S. about the relationship of the ILO to the structure and functioning of American federalism, consequently, provide an excellent window from which to understand the exceptional social policy implications of the American federalism. Critics of the ILO insisted that, since the states were responsible for social policy, the U.S. government could not ratify most ILO standards. Only the individual states could do so. While other federal states, such as Canada, have had some of the same problems, they have been notably more receptive to the ILO. But this difference can be explained by the less obstructive role of courts in those system.[46] Here America clearly is unique, as it is in the role of powerful pressure groups in the policy process.[47]

THE PRESSURE GROUPS

The history of the labor rights movement exposes general trends in the American pressure group process and also shows important changes in the membership and ideologies of individual groups. Women's organizations, consumer groups, and academic social scientists played crucial parts in the start of the movement, but have been much less prominent since the 1930s, while the importance of the churches and attorneys has grown. Certain American business elites in the early twentieth century joined the backers of the movement; however, since the middle of the twentieth century, that leadership has declined greatly. These changes may reflect disturbing cultural changes, especially the narrow focus on self-interest and the pervasiveness of narcissism among modern American elites. Consistently the most important groups in the workers rights movement have been organized labor and the churches.

At several key points, labor acted in opposition to elites and not only formulated an agenda, but also achieved it. In doing so, American unions proved that the popular classes can develop their own distinctive policy choices and fight successfully for them. These triumphs teach that both conservative elites and Marxists are wrong when they assume popular movements need the direction of the intelligentsia.[48] Labor and its allies in the churches formulated their own goals for the movement, often rejecting material self-interest. Yet, major studies of the rise of pressure groups in the early twentieth century miss the nuanced differences between labor's objectives and those of its adversaries and even many of its allies.[49] Labor did not demand that international labor standards assure it a fairer share of the fruits of the market; it demanded exemption from the market. While critics might say that labor only wanted exemption so it could get wages above what the market would allow, that misreads the goals, since many of the expectations of labor related to nonmaterial rights and dignity. The study of the movement makes clear that the century spawned more than new ways to pursue self-interest. Rather, it shows how some populist elements, especially in unions and churches, organized exceptionally well to pressure the government to limit the intrusion of the liberal market into life and to define justice without reference to economic allocation of scarce resources.[50]

Organized Labor

The story of organized labor and labor standards has not been a linear tale of constant growth in influence and achievements. American organized labor came to the international labor standards movement only reluctantly in the early twentieth century. In the late nineteenth century, there were numerous fascinating links between American workers, leftist parties, and unions, with their foreign counterparts. Usually, the largest American labor groups were international only if they had Canadian members.[51] The largest permanent labor group, the American Federation of Labor, was too pragmatic to give great attention to issues beyond the local union level.[52] Partially as a result of the numerous judicial decisions overturning legislative victories on the state and national level, the AFL emphasized not laws but privately negotiated contractual agreements between its unions and employers to protect members' rights.[53]

That changed with the advent of the administration of Woodrow Wilson. The Clayton Act seemed to provide the ultimate protection for labor unions, exempting them from much judicial control by recognizing a long-held article of international labor faith: "labor is not a commodity."[54] Before the AFL could be disillusioned by court decisions undermining the Clayton protections, World War I brought unprecedented growth to the unions and access to the president.[55] While the war destroyed the radical opponents of the AFL, both in rival unions and the Socialist Party, it emboldened Samuel Gompers to devote time to world labor standards. The AFL endorsed the Fourteen Points and added its own demands for inclusion of labor at the Versailles Conference. At Versailles, Gompers became the patriarch of the ILO.

The fall from the triumph of Versailles to the 1920s came swiftly and returned the AFL leadership to a realistic assessment of the restrained nature of the American policy process. The dominance of courts and federal diversity had not been repealed at Paris. When the U.S. did join the ILO in the 1930s, labor had less hope for the organization. There also were divisions between the AFL and the upstart Congress of Industrial Organizations (CIO), and, worst, there were fundamental disagreements with foreign labor leaders sympathetic to the Soviet Union.[56] Post-World War II American economic dominance of the world also made the need for labor standards an academic theory, difficult to relate to the reality of most American workers. Major American employers did not seem to challenge worker rights or threaten incomes. Cost-of-living adjustments (COLAs) meant workers' lives only got better.[57] But American unions continued to bring to the ILO a special perspective. They might not have been radically leftist, and their unions were as bureaucratic as their corporate adversaries or the ILO itself, yet at their core, American unions could be populist organizations.[58] Their members and even leaders were from the working class, even if a prosperous one. They had not completely lost touch with the working class in their ethnic homelands or with other institutions, particularly the churches and synagogues, which often protected the workers in the American factory towns, as in Europe. These were the seeds for a confrontation with the complacent politicians and bureaucrats in Geneva and Washington, the business executives, third-world radicals, and Communist *apparatchiks*.

Especially during the administration of George Meany, the AFL-CIO became the chief thorn in the side of the ILO. Turning on the ILO for the twin sins of accommodating the "Godless communists" and the anti-Jewish PLO, the AFL walked out and demanded that the nation follow. At a time when the AFL-CIO was losing members, and when incomes began to stagnate, American labor regained interest in the ILO. Ignoring indifference and hostility from other groups, the AFL-CIO position on labor rights by the 1970s brought a remarkable change to a complacent international organization and contributed to the unraveling of Soviet suppression of labor rights and its control of Eastern Europe.[59]

Women's Organizations

Early American interest in the labor standards movement began with the revulsion of some elite women at employers' exploitation of working-class women. Seeking private and public policies that would protect women and children, this female elite included the best-known early advocates of labor standards, such as Florence Kelley, Alice Hamilton, Frances Perkins, Grace Abbott, and Mary Anderson. Abbott and Anderson lived long enough to serve as U.S. delegates to the ILO, and Perkins was the secretary of labor who led the U.S. into the organization in 1934. They each shared characteristics common to the women who led the creation of the maternalist welfare state.[60] College-educated, middle class, and often with graduate educations, seasoned in settlement houses, they successfully formed coalitions with women from different classes to fight for protections for the poorest working women.[61]

Historically, the involvement of women's groups in the quest for international labor standards is not a linear tale moving from less influence to more. It may be closer to a linear decline, or at best a cyclical pattern. After the first generations of reformers, women's role in the movement faded to near total absence in the late 1950s. As Carol Lubin's history of women and the ILO noted, although women staffed many senior ILO offices in the early years of U.S. membership, there were none between 1945 and 1988.[62] The organization moved away from women's protective legislation to legislation protecting men and women. While this change can be seen as a movement to complete equality, another interpretation would be that it reflected the indifference of the post–World War II culture to women workers. By the time the interest revived in the 1980s, cross-class coalitions to support the interests of working women had been replaced with upper-middle-class professional women's groups concerned more with glass ceilings than with protecting the freedom of association and the simple maternal rights of women staffing the assembly plants of the third world. Cross-class national or international organizations of women with real links to the grassroots have been neglected in favor of professional groups of lobbyists in national centers.[63] The same has been the case for organizations of men and women.

Professional Social Scientists

In contrast to the mixed roles of women's and labor organizations, the role of professional social scientists has followed a linear course. They have moved from extremely important, if not preeminent, in the creation and support for the movement, to being indifferent and irrelevant. A group of American social scientists, especially economists linked to the social gospel movement, such as Richard Ely, provided the nucleus for the American Association for Labor Legislation (AALL) that originally supported the international labor standards movement.[64] With labor largely indifferent and women's groups focusing on local and state labor standards, the members of the AALL and other economists, political scientists, and historians promoted the need for international labor standards and particularly the ILO. Especially important was a group associated with Ely, including Ely's student John R. Commons and Commons's disciple John Andrews. Even Ely's fellow Johns Hopkins associate Woodrow Wilson played an active scholarly role, as well as a political one, serving as a vice president of the AALL, even throughout his presidency.[65]

Equally important with Ely's AALL was an allied group from Columbia University led by historian James Shotwell. Shotwell not only helped draft the ILO section of the Versailles Treaty, he became the leading academic lobbyist for the movement in the early 1930s. To instruct members of Congress and the administrations he toured Washington, dropping off prepublication copies of his two-volume *The Origins of the International Labor Organization*.[66] His strategy worked.

After the success of U.S. membership in 1934, the academic role faded rapidly. Ely was dead and Commons was old. Shotwell had done his part. With Andrews's death in 1943, the AALL ended. The other professional academic organizations, which formerly had held joint conferences with the AALL, abandoned advocacy for more traditional academic scholarship. When Shotwell wrote a fortieth-anniversary essay in 1959 on the ILO's founding for the *Monthly Labor Review*, the role of social scientists as leaders of a cross-class coalition with labor and women had gone the way of cross-class feminists.[67] About a decade later, academics returned to writing a new labor history influenced by the upheavals of the 1960s, but then they had a broader concern. They wrote about workers, oppression, and struggle but not much about organized labor or the politics of international labor standards. When dealing with politics, labor defeats such as the Taft-Hartley Act received more attention than the old victories. Perhaps the approach fit the decline of labor unions that began about the same time, but it also paralleled the general demeaning of organized labor, which had never been popular among the American academic class.[68]

Business Interest Groups

While American business organizations on the national level began somewhat later than the national social science organizations, they did play a role in support of labor standards as they did in backing other progressive-era reforms.[69] However, progressive-era business groups were divided on the issue of labor standards. The U.S. Chamber of Commerce, only founded in 1912, was split on most issues, and the older National Association of Manufacturers (NAM) created in 1895 was radically antiunion. The major supportive organization was the National Civic Federation (NCF), established to reconcile business and labor after the Pullman Strike of 1894. It pioneered a corporatist tripartite approach to finding solutions to the social problems of industrialization.[70] Samuel Gompers was an NCF member, as were ex-presidents and leading academics. The lack of consensus on labor standards among business groups would continue throughout the century, as would the general pattern of support for international standards. For many years the chamber was officially friendly to the ILO, even inviting ILO officials to its meetings in the 1920s, when the U.S. was not formally an ILO member. By contrast, small businesses and those not competing in a world market seemed most hostile to protecting labor rights.

Once the crisis of the depression struck, many business leaders tolerated, if not welcomed, government coordination of the economy and the establishment of minimal labor standards. Industry had been experimenting during the 1920s with methods and institutions to stabilize competition. The judicial system became the major barrier to such innovation. Many business leaders agreed with labor that the courts acted foolishly in compelling laissez-faire competition and preventing planning and cooperation.[71] By the mid-1930s, leaders of devastated industries, such as New England textiles, supported the codification of labor standards. They hoped the NRA would provide the structure to assure standards and end unequal competition from southern mills.[72] It was fairly easy for such people to fix their gaze beyond the country and appreciate the international competitive pressures on their industry. Consequently, many cooperated with a 1937 ILO-sponsored World Textile Conference.[73]

In the post–World War II era, business attitudes toward the ILO changed. During the Eisenhower Administration, the U.S. Chamber of Commerce and National Association of Manufacturers selected delegates to the ILO who were critical of the organization's basic purposes. They filled business journals with critical reports.[74] But as labor became the leading ILO critic in the mid-1960s, business reconciled itself to the organization. So long as the ILO did not compel the U.S. to enforce standards that strengthened unions or provide unacceptable employee benefits, business could live with the group's symbolism. In fact, as American business became increasingly global, the ILO served as a useful forum that business could block from taking effective action. The ILO had been promoted at the close of the war as the solution to the labor-competitiveness problems of free trade. By the end of the century American business appreciated it as a meaningless cover for the adverse consequences of the unregulated global trading regime then being created.[75]

Consumer Groups

Before other groups in America focused on the issue of competitive labor standards, a few elite women in New York became concerned with the exploitation of women department store clerks. Realizing that there were competitive pressures that forced each store to get the most work for the least overhead cost, they tried to use consumer information to urge shoppers to patronize only stores that had acceptable minimal labor standards. The New York Consumers' League soon spread to other cities, the nation, and to several European countries, and it broadened its industrial focus beyond retail stores, especially to the garment industry. The league recognized that consumers needed to be aware of the conditions under which workers produced or processed a product. Market price and product quality should not be the sole determinants of which item to purchase. This early consumer movement realized that business owners were not the only or prime beneficiary of labor exploitation. Consumers seeking the lowest price might be the driving force behind reducing worker wages and worsening working conditions to the lowest common denominator.[76]

The consumer movement's interest in labor standards, as that of the women's groups with which it was intertwined, has followed a cyclical route, from pioneering and single-minded leadership to near indifference until showing renewed interest at the end of the twentieth century. The character and meaning of consumer groups has changed drastically, even though the oldest, the National Consumers' League, remains. The transition came after the passage of the Fair Labor Standards Act in 1938. That law enacted many of the early goals of the Consumers' League. Then in the early 1940s women workers achieved unprecedented opportunity under the wartime prosperity. Not surprisingly, consumerism came to mean assuring product quality and pricing fairness. The National Consumers' League, which tried to remain focused, saw its local and state branches close as it withered to a shadow of itself as a Washington lobbying office.[77] The consumer movement not only changed its focus, it forgot its origins.[78] One 1970s history of the movement erroneously traced its beginnings to an effort to protect postal customers from fraud. The same study misread the purpose of *The Jungle,* seeing it as a classic call for consumer protection from tainted meat. That had been the mistake of many of Upton Sinclair's contemporaries; yet a history of the era should not have ignored his primary concern with the need to improve the treatment of immigrant workers.[79] Another study from 1985 on *The Morality of Spending* missed the link between the progressive-era investigations of worker incomes and the need for labor standards, especially the minimum wage.[80] The modern consumer movement interprets modern consumer boycotts to protect laborers, such as those aimed at supporting farmworker rights, as events with no previous history.[81] In the late 1990s, the Consumers' League rediscovered its original purpose when it campaigned against imported rugs produced by child laborers; however, it continued to devote most of its effort to providing members with information on product safety, quality, and price.[82]

The prosperity of the postwar era severed the links between consumerism and social justice. Rather than promote policies that would subject consumers and businesses to the development and preservation of a just world order, the movement focused only on consumer needs. The consumer movement now helped individuals seek their advantage and personal protection in the loosely regulated free market. As for the workers, they also were consumers. Since individual consumers benefitted from cheaper prices, it benefitted consumers when multinational firms took advantage of the ungoverned global economy to seek the most unregulated and cheapest labor. Under the modern market economy, such behavior was beneficial because it delivered products to the consumer at the lowest price. Consumer ethics and wisdom now supported trade and labor deregulation.[83]

In addition to chronicling the evolution in the goals of the consumer movement, the history of international labor standards also reveals an important change in group structure. In the late twentieth century, many interest groups lost their grassroots base. Even organized labor, which inherently has many local members, became centralized and distant from the rank and file.[84] Groups perfected the professionalization of national headquarters and mass-mail fund-raising to the neglect of vigorous organizational life. While skillful central management can maintain such an organization for a long time, if not indefinitely, movements, whether among consumers, workers, or women, risk losing touch with their public when they neglect an active local base.[85] These groups stand in sharp contrast with the churches, which tend to maintain local congregational vigor. Hence the churches have played a unique advocacy role in the international labor standards movement.

Churches

The churches played a pioneering role in the development of modern labor standards, beginning with abolition. The nature of the role varied with each particular religious group, from the more congregational structure of Jewish communities to the international centralization of Roman Catholics. In the late nineteenth century, Catholics, Jews, and Protestants experienced their own version of a social gospel movement, which included concern with working conditions.[86] The efforts of Richard Ely and John R. Commons in establishing the American Association for Labor Legislation cannot be understood without appreciation of their Christian social philosophy.[87] Prophetic Jewish social justice teachings played a fundamental role in working out industrial protocols that set minimal labor standards in the garment trades.[88] Father John Ryan's defense of the "living wage" originated with Leo XIII's *Rerum Novarum*, and its legacy extended to Msgr. George Higgins's defense of the ILO in the 1950s.[89] Demonstrating the importance of the churches, groups such as the Consumers' League regularly included representative Protestant, Jewish, and Catholic clergy at meetings and on their boards of directors.

The churches helped launch the labor standards movement and increased their role during the twentieth century. The Catholic hierarchy both nationally and internationally, including the papacy, repeatedly became guardian angels of the ILO. At times, when the concept of international labor standards, or specifically the ILO, has been under attack by powerful interests, the churches have come to the defense. For example, in 1954, at the height of American criticism of communist admission to the ILO, Pope Pius XII granted an audience to the ILO governing body and praised its universality.[90] Again in the late 1970s, the churches intervened to defend the ILO first from American and then from Soviet attacks.

The church role in support of labor standards demonstrates both the special strengths and the difficult limitations of church involvement in the policy process. The churches have several special strengths that contrast to other groups. They have a committed and socially diverse popular base that both gives their position numerical backing and a tendency to be grounded in the experiences of a cross section of people. Except for some smaller denominations, the churches tend to be cross-class organizations that bridge some of the gap between rich and poor, rural and urban America. Finally, the churches have the stability to ensure that they will be involved in the policy process in the long run.[91]

At the same time, the churches face difficulty in the policy arena.[92] The very diversity of membership by class and region that provides some strength can also cause them to speak less clearly than small homogeneous organizations. Often, they speak with more than one official voice, as did the Catholic Church in the 1920s on the issue of federal regulation of child labor.[93] Particularly on social justice issues, pressure to favor the economic perspective of the more privileged members can quiet a church's voice. Despite these problems, the churches have done a consistently better job when addressing social justice than most other groups. One reason for this success is their frequent experience deflecting the pressures on their leaders coming from special economic interests.[94] One of the important lessons from the labor standards experience in the United States is the interest, ability, and impact of the churches to keep public policy debates reasonably focused on the needs of the least privileged.[95] That impact is too often ignored in analysis of the policy process and is a distinctive feature of the American system.[96]

While death and retirement are given features of human and organizational life, a key leadership challenge is maintaining continuity. Some institutions clearly have a better record of maintaining leadership stability than others, and here the churches have a great advantage. While often frustrating to their allies, the churches approached the social policy arena with the same timeless perspective they bring to their general survival. Pope Leo may have written about modern labor problems as "new things," but he did so by recalling the corporatist guild structure of the Middle Ages.[97] The AALL had no such continuity with the past. When communist entry into the ILO caused a crisis for American participants, the churches could take a long-term view that "this too shall pass." Church leaders stayed when labor and business walked out.[98] The churches, as labor, also profit from the strengths, and suffer from the inherent challenges, of living with local congregations. Whatever failures their leaders may encounter in dealing with the rank and file, they cannot allow them to disband, as happened with the Consumers' League. The leadership skills of church and union officials, therefore, may be the model for achieving responsible and just results from the incremental policy process in America and in international organizations.[99]

The Legal Profession

Much as with the role of churches, attorneys have become increasingly important in the labor standards movement. Like some religious leaders, a few lawyers assumed key leadership positions in the early movement. Florence Kelley at the Consumers' League held a law degree, and such future Supreme Court luminaries as Louis Brandeis and Felix Frankfurter worked with the domestic labor standards efforts before World War I. Nationally known attorneys such as Ernest Freund and Samuel McCune Lindsay played important roles in the Consumers' League effort to find a way around Supreme Court rejections of federal labor standards.[100] Lindsay worked long enough on the effort to lead the transition from a focus on interstate agreements to support for ILO membership. Then from 1948 to 1970, the American attorney David Morse headed the ILO.

In each case, these early attorneys filled their positions as individuals; there was not yet a general movement within the profession to monitor and formulate policies related to labor standards. However, that changed in the 1970s when the profession both launched a formal human rights organization and incorporated human rights training into some law schools. By the 1980s, the body of experience and publications related to human rights law mushroomed. Labor standard protections have become a subfield of this growing specialty.

The Lawyers Committee for Human Rights symbolized the institutionalization of human rights concerns within the legal profession. Established in 1978, the committee found support among leading law firms and hired a staff that would have been the envy of the Consumers' League at its height. Augmenting its full-time staff were innumerable pro bono contributions from attorneys in the U.S. and abroad. The committee produced a host of specific reports documenting human rights abuses in all corners of the world in the last quarter of the century. By 1999, Michael Posner, its executive director, emphasized a shift in its primary concern when he said, "Today the emerging issue is how do you hold private companies accountable for the treatment of their workers at a time when government control is ebbing all over the world."[101]

Defining Eras and Transitions

As the history of the labor standards movement reveals changes in interest groups and institutions in the United States, so it can help define major eras in the nation's modern history and mark the dates of fundamental transitions in intellectual, social, economic, and political development. The support for international labor standards has passed through five eras, each concluding with a defining institutional or policy change. Each era ended with unaddressed issues that threaten the effectiveness of its concluding institutional arrangements and decisions. The five eras generally correspond to those widely used to organize modern American history. This periodization is especially helpful in dating the most recent era and in relating more amorphous intellectual and social evolution to political and economic change.

The first era began in the late nineteenth century and continued into the first two decades of the twentieth. As social critics and reformers in both Europe and the United States perceived a linkage between economic growth and social problems, they sought to establish minimal national labor standards. However, the global economy that had already emerged in some industries placed a fundamental limitation on effective national labor standards. For example, if one country required employers to support comprehensive social insurance for their workers and others did not, its industry would have a major cost disadvantage in competing in the global marketplace. International labor standards could address the problem. Consequently, around 1890 a coalition emerged to confront the issue, made up of social scientists, political reformers, leaders of women's organizations, and some labor, business, and church leaders.[102] While they had a number of small successes in the first twenty-five years of work, World War I proved to be the catalyst that gained them wide support.[103] This era concluded with the Versailles Peace Conference, which created the ILO, as part of the League of Nations' system, to define and protect labor standards. Yet this organizational triumph masked major problems, not the least of which was the American decision not to join. This deprived the ILO of the cooperation of the world's greatest economic power and one with few national labor standards.

The second era began in 1920 and continued through the first half of the Great Depression. In the 1920s the U.S. publicly ignored the ILO, although key American reformers planted the seeds for later policy change. These reformers worked in response to the isolated but real economic problems of the "Roaring Twenties."[104] While the nation's economy boomed, some "sick sectors" existed, particularly in the New England textile industry. It experienced a disturbing decline, with massive numbers of mill closings and jobs migrating to lower-wage southern factories.[105] While the 1920s boom provided justification for the ideology of laissez-faire, the isolated economic problems of the decade taught many reform leaders the value of empirically based responses to problems. When the Great Crash led the rest of the nation and the world to question the ideology of the twenties, the reformers were prepared with a practical alternative.

In fact, the change from ideological to empirical policy making may be the most important legacy of the early 1930s.[106] In the case of labor standards, reformers tried a variety of solutions in a very short time. They began by establishing standards through interstate compacts. Then they used the NRA. There were efforts at national regulation culminating in the Fair Labor Standards Act. Simultaneously, they experimented with international agreements under the ILO. Beyond the immediate issue of labor standards, these alternatives provided the forums for renewed progressive-era debates about the proper mix of corporatism, individualism, and public regulation of market behavior. In keeping with the empirical approach of the era, the decision to join the ILO may be the era's conclusion, but it left in doubt the exact goals of American membership.

The third era began as the U.S. moved to control the international labor standards movement, first by selecting the director of the ILO and later by hosting the Philadelphia conference of 1944. At Philadelphia the U.S. defined the ILO's role, linking it to the postwar international economic regime.[107] As soon as the war ended, however, American leaders followed this apparent policy triumph with indecision. The former allies became Cold War enemies. The various factions of the domestic and international labor movement quarreled. The ILO had to fight for a place in the U.N. structure. Within a few years the wartime commitment to labor standard enforcement collapsed. Redefined consumerism and a renewed free trade movement helped Americans forget about any need for international labor protections.

By the early 1950s, the fourth, or Cold War, era had come to the ILO. Its divisions were complicated by the influx of developing nations at the end of the decade. Internal ILO splits made it difficult to address substantive labor standards issues, while American dominance of the world economy made the U.S. indifferent to them. This situation provided a fertile ground for shifting concern from empirical social policy experiments to ideological disagreements. The presence of Soviet ideologues and third world apologists did not help. The ILO did not focus on demonstrable labor problems upon which people of goodwill from a variety of perspectives could agree. Instead, the ILO divided into philosophical camps. This international trend flourished especially because of growing domestic disillusionment with American government. Factors as different as Vietnam, urban unrest, and Watergate contributed to a lack of confidence in public solutions to national problems.

The labor standards movement in the era also provided one of the finest proofs of the resilience of American institutions. Despite growing domestic division and union weakness, labor conducted a decade-long drive to demand more of the ILO. Labor insisted that labor standards were universal and necessary. Suppression of freedom of association in Eastern Europe or elsewhere was not a quaint sign of diversity. It was oppression. In 1975, labor forced the U.S. to give notice of withdrawal from the ILO and to follow through with the threat in 1977. The stand worked, and the ILO changed its focus to basic labor and human rights. While this change left unanswered the institution's role in regulating more complex labor standards, it did mark a reincarnation of the rigidly bureaucratic ILO.

The current, or fifth, era began in the early 1980s. The new ILO focus on human rights helped labor movements in Eastern Europe. However, it was not clear whether the ILO was prepared to address the free market ideology that dominated the leadership of the major industrial powers.[108] Fueled both by Cold War ideological battles and the disillusionment with major political institutions after the 1960s, laissez-faire had such a firm hold on economic policy making and the related economics profession that any regulatory effort, such as would come from a reinvigorated ILO, faced fundamental resistance. Except for unions and the churches and synagogues, major groups that formerly supported labor standards either embraced or resigned themselves to the impersonal laws of capitalism. Social scientists accepted the unregulated market, either explicitly, as did most economists, or implicitly, as did those who focused on various studies of group oppression or failed Marxism.[109] Consumer advocates worried about the price or the quality of products. They lost sight of their role in battling the exploitation of the laborer who produced their bargains. Business organizations gloried in "growing the economy." Women's groups retreated to worrying about the Equal Rights Amendment or the narrow concerns of the professional classes, including the rights of women to share in leadership of the economic world that so often exploited poor working-class females.[110] The only groups resisting the new *weltanschauung*, labor, attorneys, and the church, were subject to mockery similar to that reserved for the government agencies that enforced labor standards.[111]

The most recent era is too close to be fully assessed. There clearly are signs that it may conclude with a reinvigoration of the labor standards movement. The demise of the Cold War may undermine the ideological rigidity of recent policy debates. The continuing decline in lower-middle-class living standards in the United States, Canada, and some other democracies may reawaken populist demands for restraint on classical economics. It may yet restore power to labor and other institutions critical of the unrestrained pursuit of wealth. It already has spawned a large human rights law movement with a diverse base in a multitude of law schools and law firms. The fact that in the past few years the U.S. has ratified record numbers of ILO conventions, including substantive ones, indicates the labor standards regime may be reawakening.[112] Also, there has been an interesting concern about labor rights among some evangelicals, the fastest-growing segment of American Christianity.

If international labor standards matter, as they have in symbol if not in effective law, this study will remind us of why many Americans have devoted much thought and time to their development. In a large federal state, rhetorically committed to individualism and inherently distrustful of all things political, the quest by leaders as different as Florence Kelley, James Shotwell, John Winant, and George Higgins was destined to be a particularly frustrating one. Yet, they studied, experienced, thought, and prayed enough to believe the struggle was worth their effort. They created a movement that has had remarkable results, as well as endless frustrations. They gave us numerous examples of effective use of the domestic and international interest group process to achieve social justice. We would do well to learn why such brilliant people took on such a difficult task. As Senator Daniel Patrick Moynihan of New York warned at the end of the twentieth century, such supporters of international law provided "a legacy not to be frittered away by forgetfulness of our own past."[113]

The
Threads

The origins of the international labor standards movement have been traced to the work of reforming industrialists in Scotland and Alsace, a French surgeon, a Belgian penologist, an evangelical German minister, a Catholic bishop, a Swiss academic, and the Prussian "Iron Chancellor," Otto von Bismarck. In the United States, the start also can be attributed to varied sources, from the sister of the commander of the Civil War's first black regiment, to the founder of the American Economic Association, to the German exhibit at the St. Louis World's Fair, or the reaction to the closure of the world's largest textile mill. As with any complex international movement, it is not inconsistent to prove that each of these and many other individuals and events contributed significantly to the movement to codify minimal world standards of labor protection.

The movement had roots in Western nations that had significant industrial activity by the mid-nineteenth century. The United States lagged in concern, an exceptionalism noted by the first American observers of the movement. When trying to form a large American group, the American Association for Labor Legislation (AALL), to lobby for support of labor standards in 1908, Yale Professor Henry Farnum contrasted his work with that in Belgium, where the movement was content with a small membership. "To organize a society [there] for the purpose of advocating [labor standards] would be like organizing a society to enable rich people to take vacations."[1] Two years later, one of the vice presidents of the AALL, Samuel McCune Lindsay of Columbia University, observed, "The general backwardness of the United States, and even most of the individual states of the Union, in social legislation, as compared with the leading federal states of the world and notably with the nations of western Europe, is a matter of frequent comment."[2] Given such self-consciousness, the subsequent efforts to win American support for international labor standards provide an excellent case study of the defining features of the American policy process.

European Origins

One student of the international labor standard movement identified four phases in its history: advocacy by individuals, then by the international socialist movement, next by the international trade union movement, and finally government sponsorship.[3] This classification is problematic in that it ignores the roles of business leaders, academics, clergy, and women leaders throughout all phases. To understand the differences between the American policy process and that in Europe, it is necessary to review the role of each group. Significantly, many of the labor standards reformers of the nineteenth century had lived through, if not participated in, the ultimate labor standard campaign—the abolition movement.

While the study of abolition and the related struggle against the pervasive indentured servitude that replaced it are topics for other books, the outlines of opposition methods should be reviewed.[4] As scholars such as Nobel laureate Robert Fogel have emphasized, these reforms were not automatic consequences of natural or economic laws: "Slavery did not die because either divine Providence or 'events' ensure that evil systems cannot work. Its death was an act of 'econocide,' a political execution of an immoral system at its peak of economic success, incited by men ablaze with moral fervor."[5] Leaders of the abolition movement acted out of belief, not self-interest. While often noble, those intellectual motives include racist assumptions of superiority. At times, abolitionists backed the growth of European empires, which they hoped would spread European values, what Fogel calls the "new civility,"[6] to backward slaveholding societies. Their success against overwhelming odds fired the imaginations of a later generation of labor rights defenders. However, abolition did not directly translate into protection of the rights of other labor. A long tradition of servant responsibility to masters survived, which many did not want to abandon and which inhibited any movement for government protection of worker rights.[7]

Several famous industrialists played an early advocacy role in changing attitudes toward labor and ultimately starting a general labor standards movement. While they can be viewed simply as individuals, without organizational affiliation, their credibility clearly came from their business success. Among the most important were Robert Owen of Scotland and Alsatian Daniel Legrand. Both Owen and Legrand lived exceptional lives for industrialists, sharing plans for establishing model worker communities and engaging in labor reform activities. With extraordinary foresight, Owen approached the European international government system in 1818, meeting as the Congress of Aix-la-Chapelle, and proposed continental labor standards. Acting a century before the similar Versailles Conference created the ILO, he hoped the congress would assure that the coming era of peace would not degenerate into one of ruthless industrial competition driving down working conditions. England already had begun to protect child laborers from the worst health dangers on the job. Owen feared that without standardization, competitive pressures would undermine such pioneering legislation. Despite his awareness of the problem, Owen did not call for formal international labor legislation. He did take the opportunity of his visit to the Continent to compare notes with Legrand.[8]

Twelve years Owen's junior, Daniel Legrand eventually went further than the Scot in defining his goal as "international labor legislation." His initial support for national labor standards might be interpreted as one proof that the presence of radical movements stimulate social policy innovation, because Legrand's efforts originated after he observed the Revolution of 1830 in Paris.[9] In addition, he brought to the movement deeply held religious beliefs, nurtured in a devout Huguenot community. Legrand's life established a pattern for the movement, for both religious motivations and efforts to defuse worker radicalism marked subsequent labor standard campaigns.[10]

After nearly a decade of concern with the need for national French labor standards, Legrand became a proponent of international standards. And, he knew which standards needed to be implemented: public education, Sunday rest, old-age pensions, child-labor restrictions, excessive labor protections, and limitations on night work. For twenty years until his death in 1859, Legrand lobbied bureaucrats and statesmen throughout western Europe to pass such laws. He especially focused on the Swiss, English, and French governments as well as the various states in Germany and Italy to create joint legislation. On December 5, 1840, he appealed to the German customs union, saying, "Those who advocate giving free reign to the industrialist, even though his factory workers are subjected to all manner of abuses, maintain that his profit is derived from the last hour of the day's work. . . . Unquestionably, those hours that deprive . . . the worker of health, rest and the free development of his children's physical and moral faculties hang like a pall upon industry. They destroy the equilibrium between production and consumption."[11] The last objection would be emphasized later by the first consumer movement; however, most other supporters of labor standards ignored it because neither Legrand nor Owen had an organizational structure in the business community to support their pioneering insights.[12] By contrast, the working class had several organizations that presented collective insights into the need for labor standards. The International Workingmen's Association, or First International, founded in London in 1864, noted in its *Address to Working Men* the fundamental contrast between "the development of . . . industry and the growth of . . . commerce" and the continuing "misery of the working masses."[13] Furthermore, the International revealed worker awareness of the benefits of labor standards at its first congress in Geneva in 1866. The Geneva meeting showed both the important role Switzerland would play in the early labor standards movement and the diversity of the International. The delegates included both disciples of Marx from Germany and a large number of Christian trade unionists from Switzerland.[14]

The First International demonstrated both the interest of workers in labor standards and the difficulty of holding together the diverse representatives of the working class. The Geneva Congress specifically proposed international limits on hours of work, ranging from two hours for young children to a maximum of eight hours, limitations on night work for men and prohibitions of night work for women, and protections for the health of women workers. However, these early proposals came to nothing, as did the First International. Within a few years it declined due to factional strife between socialists, anarchists, and other factions within the labor movement. Nonetheless, it provided an example of working-class cooperation across national boundaries. Even a few Americans attended various congresses, and the International moved its headquarters to the U.S. before closing in 1876.[15]

The Second International, created in 1889, was a more stable organization than the first because it developed at the same time that a large number of socialist parties evolved in Europe. It focused on coordinating national socialist policy. Some of the major socialist parties, such as the German social democrats, rejected a reformist approach, which would have included imposing labor standards on capitalism. It preferred to replace the economic system with one of public ownership. Thus, working-class supporters of international labor standards had to go elsewhere to gain support for their agenda.[16]

It was practical trade unions, not socialist politicians, who nurtured working-class support for labor standards in the last decade of the nineteenth century. However, before the support could flower, unions had to link across national boundaries. Beginning with the leather workers, a number of unions had joined together across frontiers, forming "International Trade Secretariats." By 1901, at the request of the Danes, the national trade unions in each country formed federations or "trade centers." The "trade center" for the United States was the American Federation of Labor (AFL). In 1913, the trade center meetings became the formal International Federation of Trade Unions (IFTU), headquartered in Berlin. More focused on labor union rights and specific worker protections than the International, the IFTU provided a fertile ground for proposals for international labor legislation. With membership based in federations of unions in each nation, the IFTU proved that international interest groups needed a strong base in active grassroots organizations. Such a base assured group survival because the group's fate was not tied to a single local union. If some unions in a nation declined, others grew and took their places. Being based in the capital of a World War I belligerent proved to be the IFTU's major weakness, but it did survive wartime divisions and helped create the ILO.[17]

As indicated by the religious motivations of Daniel Legrand and the Christian trade unionist activity at the First International Congress at Geneva, religious leaders and institutions played an important, if ignored, role in developing support for international labor standards. Many who have chronicled the development of labor standards have emphasized the roles of government leaders, secular social reformers, academics, and labor and socialist leaders. Only a few have credited religious leaders. Yet, clergy, devout lay members, and religious institutions have had a key part in the movement in both Europe and the United States.[18] The two regions primarily differ in whether they had Protestant or Catholic leadership. In America, Protestant supporters of the social gospel predominated in the pre–World War labor standards movement, while in Europe Catholics were more numerous.

However, some Protestants, like Legrand, made significant contributions in Europe. These included Charles Hindley, a devout Moravian in England; a German evangelical minister, Christoph Hahn; and the German theologian Heinrich Thiersch. Each pushed the movement beyond individual advocacy. Thiersch might best be described as an academic who called for creation of a "Christian state."[19] Hindley, who prepared for a career as a minister in Ireland, returned to Lancashire to run his family's textile mill after his brother died. Hindley gradually came to reform as he saw the competitive pressures placed on conscientious mill owners by both ruthless domestic producers and by the threat of foreign competition. Because of Parliament's failure to pass meaningful Factory Acts, he eventually stood for election as a reform member. For the next two decades he defended labor legislation and proposed international standards.[20]

Hahn's experience, especially his acceptance of ecumenical co-operation in church welfare work, was repeated in America. In conjunction with his church, Hahn established a benevolent society to serve a variety of functions, from distributing Bibles to supporting local charities. In 1857, Hahn attended the first Congress of Benevolence, organized by a Belgian Catholic, Edouard Ducpetiaux. There he called:

> the attention of this assembly to the utility and even the necessity of an international law of industries. . . . An international labour law—these are the words of the highly esteemed manufacturer [Daniel Legrand] who writes, "An international labour law is the only possible solution to the great social problem of granting moral and material well-being to the working class without working a hardship upon the manufacturers and without fair competition between industries of different countries being transformed into a competition which cuts the throat of workers."[21]

At the Brussels congress and subsequent ones in the 1850s and 1860s, leaders of benevolent societies proposed specific international labor protections much like those of labor, including limiting hours of work, limitations on child labor, restrictions on night work for women and children, and a Sunday day of rest. The last point led the Evangelical Alliance to launch The International Federation for the Observance of Sunday in 1876, which not only found ecumenical support, but linked American and European reformers. At least three of the Federation's conferences took place in the U.S., twice in conjunction with the World's Fairs in Chicago and St. Louis.[22]

The Roman Catholic role in the European labor standards movement changed from marginal in the 1870s to decisive by the 1890s. The change corresponded to the election of Gioacchino Pecci to the papacy in 1878. A poet priest who had studied under Bishop Ketteler of Mainz, he had been an early backer of the movement. As Leo XIII, Pecci brought to the papacy a desire to reconcile church teachings to the needs of the global industrial economy. For thirteen years he was under pressure to respond in varying ways, from condemning socialism and capitalism to banning Catholic membership in labor unions. Conservatives in America urged him to condemn the AFL's predecessor, the Knights of Labor. The proposals of Catholic social reformers in Europe ranged from backing Christian socialism to a nostalgic effort to restore medieval guilds.[23]

The complex mix of radicalism and reaction, of innovation and confusion, came together in France with the work of Count Albert de Mun after the Franco-Prussian War. He organized Catholic Worker Circles to give a religious perspective to organized labor. In the Chamber of Deputies, de Mun demanded government sponsorship of international labor congresses. He warned, "Competition, once healthy and lawful, . . . has become savage and pitiless."[24] While some socialists supported him, he also received rightist backing when he blamed the decline in labor standards on the weakening influence of the Catholic Church. De Mun's economics bordered on socialism, yet they were more supportive of the medieval guild system or modern corporatism. While de Mun remained an isolated politician in France, his ideas of "Social Catholicism" influenced reformers who did not carry the exceptional historical burdens of the church in France.[25]

Particularly in Switzerland and Germany, social Catholicism evolved in ways that spawned commitment to international labor standards. In Switzerland, the bishop of Fribourg brought together followers of de Mun, supporters of a worker benevolent society created by Leo XIII, and German thinkers inspired by Bishop Ketteler. This Union of Fribourg supported the work of Kaspar Decurtins, a member of the Swiss National Council. Decurtins launched the successful modern labor standards movement in 1888 with a proposal, cosponsored by a socialist member, to call an international labor standards conference. The conference convened in Berlin in 1890 after the German emperor's enthusiastic endorsement. Reflecting Decurtins's perspective, the conference included representatives of the Vatican, as well as from the twelve major industrial nations in Europe.[26]

Within a year of the Berlin Conference, Leo XIII issued his encyclical *Rerum Novarum*, summarizing the church's position on the labor question. The letter placed the church in a middle ground, between socialism and capitalism. It moved the church far beyond its traditional support for charity to help the poor into a leadership role in support of social welfare reform. To the special relief of American Catholics, it endorsed labor unions and did not condemn the dying Knights of Labor.[27] The letter came too late to restore dwindling church support among the working classes in Europe, and it did little to ease the existing conflict with secular socialists. However, it did place the church irrevocably on the side of labor protections and undermined the belief among Catholic conservatives that their faith should bless their economic enterprise and their wealth.[28] More important, *Rerum Novarum* justified and encouraged subsequent generations of church leaders to adopt labor standards and later the ILO as a special province of the church.[29]

While the efforts of the European Catholic Church in the movement contrasted with the U.S. Protestant leadership, women's organizations on the Continent contributed little, especially in contrast to the pivotal role played by women in the U.S. This difference lends support to those historians who emphasize an exceptional women's role in U.S. reform movements. When present, European women's support for labor standards can be traced to the initiative of the American Consumers' League movement. Despite having originated in London, that movement flowered in the U.S. and wilted when transplanted back across the ocean. As Maud Nathan observed in 1926, "The ideals and principles of the Consumers' League originally came to us from England, but tradition and conservatism are forces against which it is difficult to battle and the League languished in the country which gave it birth. In 1899, it was practically nonexistent."[30]

In contrast to women's movements in Europe, academics from the Continent not only led American counterparts into an interest in international labor standards, but European academics also sustained the movement during the entire period down to World War I. One of the first to support the movement was Louis Rene Villerme. A surgeon in Napoleon's army, he abandoned medicine for social research in the new fields of political economy, statistics, penology, and public health. In the 1830s, the *Institut de France* commissioned him to study conditions in the textile industry. After seven years of research, he produced a two-volume study documenting the terrible working conditions in the mills. He published a preliminary version in *Annales d'Hygiene Publique* in 1837, describing the competitive constraints on manufacturers who wanted to improve working conditions. Villerme was not a politician or activist. Rather, he set an example as a concerned scholar, whose careful documentation of social conditions promoted reform without partisan involvement.[31]

A number of other early social scientists worked in the labor standards movement, such as Jerome Adolphe Blanqui, J. C. Bluntschli, Karl Brater, Lorenz von Stein, and Louis Wolowski.[32] Blanqui had been one of the first of the new French economists to stress the limits to laissez-faire theory. His school held, "To produce wealth is not enough; it must be equitably distributed."[33] Recognizing the impact of the economic changes of the nineteenth century, Blanqui coined the term *industrial revolution*.[34] That revolution and the terrifying political revolutions of the era caused him and his compatriot Louis Wolowski to seek social reform.[35] Johann Bluntschli and Karl Brater helped found political science in order to study the proper role of the state in the new industrial era.[36] In 1848, von Stein, a zealous free trader, realized the need for labor standards if trade liberalization were to be fair. He became fascinated with the work of utopian socialists, while seeking a humane form of liberalism.[37]

The teachings and writings of this group of political economists laid the groundwork for the next generation of social scientists who, at the turn of the century, created an institutional base for the academic pursuit of labor standards. That generation inherited a profound concern with what they labeled "the social question"; that is, the possibility of more revolutions if the industrial exploitation of workers continued or worsened.

The most influential of these social scientists was a group of German economists associated with the Social Policy Association (*Verein für Sozialpolitik*): Adolph Wagner, Gustav Schmoller, and Lujo Brentano.[38] They created the association in 1872 to promote scholarly discussion and to advise governments of the social question. All three criticized the classical English economists and their doctrine of laissez-faire. Bringing historical and ethical considerations to economics, the Social Policy Association saw a need for labor standards.[39]

The final steps in forming an academic organization to promote labor standards began at the International Congress of Civil Social Reformers in 1897 at Brussels. Schmoller and Brentano, along with Heinrich Herkner, a younger member of the Social Policy Association, attended as did academics from other countries, including Eugen von Phillippovich of the University of Vienna, Ernest Mahaim of the University of Liege, and Stephen Bauer of the University of Basel, the latter recently a visiting professor at the University of Chicago. After much debate, they called for the creation of an International Bureau for the Protection of Labor. In the spring of 1899, the Germans took the lead in forming a local chapter of the bureau. They urged academics and social reformers in other countries to do likewise and meet the next year at the Paris World's Fair. At the exposition, the United States had representatives, including noted labor statistician Carroll D. Wright of the U.S. Department of Labor. Jane Addams and Richard Ely were American observers. This group created the International Association for Labor Legislation (IALL) and a permanent

International Labor Office in Basel, directed by Stephen Bauer. They committed the IALL to protect "working people in general, and in particular . . . children and women, the limitation of the hours of adult male workers, Sunday rest, intervals for rest, and [the regulation of] dangerous industries." While one of their purposes, "to facilitate the study of labor legislation," was clearly academic, others, such as "to secure the convocation of international congresses on labor legislation," were political.[40] Through the Paris exposition, the IALL increased American support for international standards. Richard Ely of the University of Wisconsin had studied in Germany under the historical economists who established the Association.[41] He now returned to the United States with Addams and Wright to form an American chapter. The actual work on that would not be completed until another World's Fair in St. Louis in 1904, but more than any other European labor standards development of the era, the IALL influenced Americans. Even the U.S. government agreed to provide a modest contribution to support the International Labor Office.

In addition to being the most influential organization among Americans, the IALL was instrumental in gaining the most specific achievements in the pre–World War I labor standards movement. The Basel office arranged for the Swiss government to serve as its diplomatic front. When the IALL identified issues requiring formal international deliberations, the Swiss Confederation invited nations to participate. In 1906, the IALL arranged the first major "diplomatic conference" in Bern, which approved the first two "Labor Conventions," one prohibiting night work for women and the other prohibiting the use of white phosphorous in matches. The IALL role in the conference extended beyond simply lobbying for the conference; it sponsored research and preliminary meetings of national labor experts to prepare draft conventions for the diplomats. After initially slow ratification by the European powers, both conventions received wide support. Even the U.S. accepted the white phosphorus ban through a backdoor procedure of imposing a prohibitive tax on the matches. In 1913, the IALL had prepared two more conventions, one restricting the hours of work of children and women, and a second prohibiting night work for children; however, the outbreak of World War I prevented the opening of the diplomatic conference scheduled for September 1914.[42]

The remarkable success of the IALL's experts in developing a new form of international law resulted from several factors important, then and now, to meaningful public policy. First, the Association included in its membership some of the most renowned social scientists and social reformers. Drawn from the elite universities of the West, they deserved special respect and had access to the policy makers in their home nations.[43] Second, the IALL developed a network of national affiliate organizations, some with branches below the national level. Thus, it cultivated its grassroots, as successful interest groups must do if they are to remain aware of current policy needs.[44] Finally, the association used empirical research to support its demands on the international community. The data provided by the IALL limited the options of political leaders and allowed for effective policy choices. The association's data did not predetermine specific results, but it did restrict vague or endless discussion of "problems."[45]

The success of the IALL demonstrated the need for academics in social reform. Their achievements may have hinged upon the fear of the growing socialist and labor movements and may have benefitted from the groundwork lain by religious leaders and an earlier generation of individual reformers; nevertheless, those facts do not diminish the indispensable role played by the academics associated with the German Social Policy Association and the international reformers linked to the IALL. While the academics came to reform for a variety of reasons, including uneasiness about the crassness of modern global capitalism, the reasons for their acts do not diminish the clarity of their research nor their identification of fundamental social problems.

Another factor in their success was the political structure and traditions in which they worked. The European states and Canada were more receptive to the IALL's conventions than the United States. While not all states quickly ratified the white phosphorous convention, only the United States went through the complex process of addressing this problem through a tax. The U.S. did not even attempt to implement the other convention, which limited the night work of women. As a federal state, the U.S. government position was that it could not impose a basic labor protection such as restricting the work of women.[46] The ratification of labor conventions, because it forced each state to consider the same proposals at approximately the same time, thus served as one of the best subjects for defining the extent of American policy exceptionalism. Beginning in 1890, diverging responses to labor standards exposed the differences in political philosophy and structure that were to distinguish America from its fellow developed countries.

After the Swiss in the 1880s launched the effort to bring European diplomats together to standardize labor legislation, Germany provided the venue in 1890 in Berlin for the first International Labor Conference. A variety of factors led Germany to pioneer the development of public sickness and old-age insurance in the 1870s and 1880s. These included the fear of growing socialism among the working class; a mix of religious motives, not the least being a desire to placate the once-persecuted Catholics; the traditional German role of the paternalistic state; the implementation of the theories of the anti-laissez-faire German economic school; and the response to the successful lobbying activity by well-organized German academics.[47] Chancellor Otto von Bismarck opposed the kaiser's desire to host the conference, which contributed to the split between the two men and Bismarck's dismissal. That is not to say Bismarck opposed international labor standards. There is evidence he supported such standards in bilateral treaties as early as 1871. He simply saw an international labor conference as impractical.[48]

While the details of the conference's agenda and proceedings have been treated elsewhere and are not the subject of this study, a few of its features differentiate it from later American international labor policy making. First, the United States did not participate in the conference, despite being one of the top three industrial powers in the world. Also, in contrast to many American labor standards meetings, the conference notably excluded women, who played a minor role in European labor reforms. Finally, the conference provided a special forum for the Vatican, which sent a bishop to present the church's views. While the conference set an impressive example of bringing together diplomats from throughout Europe to consider the "social question," the failure to enact specific international agreements led to major changes in the strategy of movement leaders and to a fifteen-year break in formal diplomatic meetings on the issue. When representatives of the powers reconvened in Bern in 1905 and 1906, academic experts from the IALL had done empirical groundwork for their deliberations. While the churches continued to play a major role in the movement, after 1890 it was in the background, not as one of the deliberators. By 1905, the U.S. participated on a limited basis in the international deliberations. The American labor standards movement sprang partially from such European sources, but it also evolved from distinctively American women's organizations, influenced by the unique American labor movement and the special role of religion in American public life.

AMERICAN ORIGINS

The Consumers' League

Comparing American participation in the early labor standards movement with that in Europe demonstrates a number of exceptional features of American society, culture, and America's policy process. While the social scientists had deep European roots, no Continental parallel existed for the female-led Consumers' League, which teamed with the academics as equal partners in creating the American branch of the IALL. Another difference in the U.S. was the comparatively cautious approach of organized labor to the cause. The more practical American labor movement came last to the labor standards cause, but when it did, it acted as a public interest group more than a class, demanding inclusion in the full policy process not as a special interest on the periphery of policy making. Likewise, the involvement of churches differed in the U.S., being more ecumenical and popularly based than those in Europe. Clergy guided the members of their congregations to participate in the populist policy process rather than speaking ex-cathedra. Consequently, the churches helped sustain the grassroots character of American involvement.

As with much of the American effort, the Consumers' League copied an English organization that had preceded it. Yet, the American league quickly overshadowed its foreign counterparts. To a great extent the league's history is a history of the power of organized women in the United States to influence the policy process. Distinctly American women leaders headed the league, with their Calvinist religious backgrounds, some educated in Europe, indelibly changed by experiences during the Civil War, nurtured as leaders of a variety of postwar charitable institutions, and with extensive personal experience with the working class.

The movement began quietly, when Alice Woodbridge, a young employee of a New York department store, sought help in improving the working conditions of the "counter girls." An active member of the city's Working Women's Society, she launched a study of the terrible conditions and low wages experienced by women in the stores. In 1890 she approached Josephine Shaw Lowell with her findings of worker exploitation, particularly, unhealthy restrooms and lunchrooms, absence of breaks during the workday, even the removal of chairs so employees could not sit. Lowell, a former Freedmen's Bureau volunteer, and the sister and widow of Civil War heroes, brought the prestige of two of America's leading abolitionist families to the cause. She not only publicized Woodbridge's complaints but organized an institutional solution—the Consumers' League.[49]

Lowell already had demonstrated her loyalty to the family's reform commitment by serving with the U.S. Sanitary Commission. With the end of the war, she became the chief fund-raiser for the Freedmen's Bureau in New York. Later she worked with the new Charities Organization Society. In 1876, Governor Samuel Tilden appointed her to the State

Board of Charities, the first woman to serve in such a position. For many years, she led the charities movement, urging the competent administration of charities and encouraging the needy to return to useful work as soon as possible after receiving help. Gradually, however, she came to think that the poor primarily needed assistance because of general economic problems and not because of their own weaknesses. She was an outspoken critic of employer exploitation of workers and political exploitation by bosses and the spoils system. She became a leader of municipal and civil service reform, she supported organized labor, especially during the Homestead Strike, and even joined the Anti-Imperialist League. In the midst of these activities, she met Alice Woodbridge and agreed to organize one more reform meeting.

Josephine Lowell knew how to get important people to meetings and to keep them involved. Before she sponsored the general meeting to hear Woodbridge's report, she turned to Dr. Mary Putnam Jacobi for help. Dr. Jacobi had a background much like Lowell, including Massachusetts religious reform roots, though in Jacobi's case from Baptist Calvinism, not Lowell's Unitarianism. Later in life, however, Jacobi embraced a creedless ethical cultural belief close to Lowell's. Daughter of publisher G. P. Putnam, Jacobi had an exceptional education in the private and public schools of New York, and earned a degree in pharmacy and then medicine in the 1860s. Like Lowell, she worked in military hospitals during the war and helped treat freedmen at Port Royal, South Carolina. Later she traveled to France for advanced medical education, beginning there her writings about medical education, pathology, physiology, and pediatrics, winning in 1876 Harvard's Boylston Prize for an essay on women's health. She won admission to numerous medical societies, only being denied entry into the New York Obstetrical Society. Not that she did not have relevant experience, as well as exceptional training, for in 1873 she married fellow physician Abraham Jacobi, and subsequently bore three children.[50]

Mary and Abraham were an exceptional pair of physicians and reformers. He had been a German revolutionary in 1848, and, like their friend Carl Schurz, had been imprisoned briefly. After escaping and coming to the U.S., Abraham practiced medicine in the tenement districts of New York and led infant mortality control campaigns.[51] Mary became an expert in environmental health. The two were involved in civil service reform, a movement led by Schurz. Mary was an active suffrage supporter, addressing the New York Constitutional Convention in 1894 and later founding the League for Political Education to campaign for it. Lowell naturally turned to Jacobi for support, since Woodbridge's study documented many health threats in the eating areas and restrooms of New York's department stores.

In a pattern to be often repeated when the labor standards movement needed help, Lowell and Jacobi depended on clergy as well as on other women leaders to organize a crowd to hear Woodbridge's report. On May 6, 1890, a mass meeting assembled at a hall in lower Manhattan. To chair the gathering they selected Everett Wheeler, a Harvard-educated attorney and recent chairman of the New York Civil Service Commission. A devout Episcopalian and son-in-law of Johns Hopkins President Daniel Coit Gilman, he brought both religious and educational credentials to the platform. Two years earlier he had written *Wages and Tariffs*, a book directly related to the general international labor standards movement.[52] He would continue to write economic, history, and religious books. Lowell and Jacobi formed an ecumenical group of clergy to address each danger arising from current store employment practices. The Reverend William Reed Huntington, a fellow Episcopalian and Harvard graduate, spoke on the dangers of long hours of work. Baptist minister William Faunce, future president of Brown University and of the World Peace Foundation, author of books on the social gospel, spoke on the absence of sanitary standards in the stores. Other clergy included Father Thomas Ducey, a Catholic municipal reform leader; Rev. George Alexander, a leading Presbyterian, later to head Union College and chair the Council of Reformed Churches in America; and Rabbi Frederic de Sola Mendes, founder of the *American Hebrew*, leader of Reformed Judaism, and member of the Central Conference of American Rabbis.[53] Following the preparatory speeches of these clergy, Alice Woodbridge read an abbreviated version of her report to the audience. When she ended, they endorsed several resolutions calling for a public health investigation of store sanitation, legislation to limit hours of work, and, most important, "That a committee be appointed to assist the Working Women's Society in making a list which shall keep shoppers informed of such shops as deal justly with their employees."[54]

This resolution expressed the core principal behind the Consumers' League. The responsible consumer, only willing to purchase products made by methods that did not exploit workers or sold in stores that treated employees well, would protect the labor standards of the poorest workers. Consumers' League attorney Josephine Goldmark declared that the league organized a third party, the consumer, to mediate the relationship between employers and workers. The first president of the league,

John Graham Brooks, identified the moral dilemma faced by the consumer: "To buy a sweated garment is to have someone work for you under sweated conditions as definitely as if she were in your own employ."[55] In addition to the desire to end worker exploitation, Lowell, Jacobi, and the other leaders of the Consumers' League made four fundamental assumptions that brought success. First, the organizers brought a confidence to the movement that it was wrong for the powerful to exploit the weak. Their vision of justice was not clouded by qualms about the businessman being hurt by low profit margins or the consumer needing the lowest price. Like Lowell and Jacobi, they came from traditions that when confronted with injustice, named it, and sought to stop it.[56]

Newton Baker, a later league leader, as well as secretary of war for President Wilson, introduced a book on the league, combining this moral certitude with the second key assumption: consumer responsibility. He noted, "[The league] assumed, and rightly, that the American consumer would not willingly profit by the cheapness of wares where that cheapness resulted from oppression and injustice."[57] The perception of consumer responsibility had been suggested earlier in the labor standards movement, but never made so central. In 1831 wool manufacturers in England had warned when Parliament considered a bill to restrict hours of work and prohibit child labor that one "negative" consequence would be to "raise the price of goods to consumers."[58] Supporters of the law willingly accepted that consequence. A few years later during the debates about slavery, defenders of that institution used the argument that enslavement was justified by its benefits for consumers. An English traveler in the South, Robert Russell, from the country that processed much southern cotton for the world's consumers, explicitly made this argument. He found slavery "a necessary evil attending upon the great good of cheap cotton."[59]

This defense frightened critics of slavery. They lacked confidence that consumers would support abolition if it meant rising costs. Frederick Law Olmsted, a leading Northern critic of slavery, devoted a chapter in his *Cotton Kingdom* to contradict Russell's argument.[60] More important than Olmsted's esoteric computations was his fear of the argument. One wonders if Olmsted would have become a supporter of slavery if it were efficient. The allies of labor standards increasingly confronted similar thinking. The only defense was ethics, not economics. As the French political-economist and politician Louis Wolowski observed in his 1868 lectures on child labor in manufacturing, "If it were true that men were compelled to crush pitilessly those whose weaknesses should serve as a safeguard . . . it would be time to resort to an international entente to halt so grievous a traffic, just as it has halted that abominable scandal, the slave trade."[61] Perhaps because of their involvement in the abolition movement and the Civil War, the early leaders of the Consumers' League confronted this issue explicitly. As they said in the second and third articles of the league's 1891 constitution:

> (2) That the responsibility for some of the worst evils from which wage-earners suffer rests with the consumers, who persist in buying in the cheapest market, regardless of how cheapness is brought about.
> (3) That it is, therefore, the duty of consumers to find out under what conditions the articles which they purchase are produced, and to insist that these conditions shall be at least decent, and consistent with a respectable existence on the part of the workers.[62]

This constitutional commitment is the most important contribution of the Consumers' League to the labor standards movement. It recognized more clearly than most earlier and many later leaders the real beneficiaries of labor exploitation. In an equally significant insight, they asserted, "Recognizing the fact that the majority of employers are virtually helpless to improve conditions as to hours and wages, unless sustained by public opinion, by law, and by the action of consumers, the Consumers' League declares its object to be to ameliorate the condition of . . . women and children . . . by patronizing . . . only such houses as approach the 'Standards of a Fair House,' as adopted by the league."[63] Absolving employers of responsibility and dismissing the possibility of voluntary employer-initiated labor reform were remarkable insights. But, could the league influence numerous consumers? Having participated in the destruction of the slave power, the reformers assumed consumers would do their "duty" and refrain from supporting exploitation once it was made clear to them.

A third characteristic of the Consumers' League approach that gave strength to their arguments was their use of detailed studies of working conditions, as in the case of Woodbridge's report. The motto of the league, as Baker proudly recalled in the 1920s, captured this strength: "Investigate, record, agitate."[64] When the league decided to move beyond New York and the initial study by Alice Woodbridge, it recruited exceptional investigators. For example, in 1896 the Boston League recruited a remarkable young Canadian who had studied at the University of Chicago and lived at Hull House, Mackenzie King, the future prime minister. This began a special relationship between King and the labor standards movement. He represented Canada at some of the later IALL conferences. When the ILO's staff had to flee Geneva in 1940 as Hitler's armies surrounded Switzerland, King welcomed it to Canada, while the Americans, out of fear of stirring up isolationists, denied it a home.[65]

To lend credibility to the work of the League's young researchers, Lowell, Jacobi, and their associates recruited an elite academic advisory board. When they established the National Consumers' League in 1898, they secured the support of a half dozen academic leaders in the social sciences, all with highly respected German graduate educations, most with German Ph.D.'s, and all acquainted with the work of the Social Policy Association. Arthur Hadley, president of Yale, topped the list. With a Ph.D. from Berlin, Hadley brought a combination of economic skill, concern with labor, and moral consciousness to the League. He had written books on economics, citizenship, and *Standards of Public Morality*.[66] Of the others, Edwin R. A. Seligman achieved the greatest distinction, concluding his career in the 1920s by editing the magisterial *Encyclopedia of the Social Sciences*.[67] Seligman was joined on the advisory group by a close associate, Henry C. Adams of the University of Michigan, with whom he had developed the field of public finance and with whom he had worked on defending progressive taxation.[68] From the University of Chicago, the Consumers' League recruited Charles R. Henderson, one of the founders of sociology and a Leipzig Ph.D. More than the others, Henderson brought formal religious training to the league, being an ordained Baptist minister and having come to Chicago as chaplain and professor. Throughout his career he merged sociological study with theology, serving as editor of both *The American Journal of Sociology* and *The American Journal of Theology* while he worked with the league.[69] Joining them were two graduates of the University of Halle, Jeremiah Jenks and Samuel McCune Lindsay.

Jenks from Cornell University had a remarkable career bridging academic and public service, including residing as president of the American Economic Association and the National Council on Religion in Higher Education as well as advising the World War I Council of National Defense. He served on innumerable other government advisory panels in the U.S., Mexico, England, and Holland. His books included such studies as *The Trust Problem*, *The Personal Problems of Boys Who Work*, and, from his religious life, *Jesus' Principles of Living*.[70]

Lindsay, of the University of Pennsylvania, was the youngest member of the group and the one who lived long enough to most influence the ILO. Like Jenks, he had conducted research for the U.S. Industrial Commission. His service to academia and the public included being president of the American Academy of Political and Social Science, the American affiliate of the IALL, and of the National Child Labor Committee. His books included studies of social welfare in Philadelphia, the condition of railroad workers, education in Puerto Rico, and public finance in Great Britain. He would help build ecumenical support for worker rights, collaborating with Father John Ryan and F. Ernest Johnson of the Federal Council of Churches. Lindsay lived until 1959 and participated in most major policy debates related to labor standards through the post–World War II era.[71]

The exceptional competence, academic and public service leadership, and religious commitment of the Consumers' League advisors gave both a special distinction and direction to the league's research. Such distinction and direction would prove difficult to sustain during the many controversies of the next decades. The league's campaign in the 1920s for a child labor amendment threatened to destroy the ecumenical unity of the league's allies. In that campaign, many Catholic leaders deserted the league, not including John Ryan, in fear of the family consequences of the amendment. A less divisive but still controversial decision in the same period was the opposition of the league's director to the proposed Equal Rights Amendment. Florence Kelley feared its legal impact on women's protective legislation. But those controversies came later.[72]

In fact, the organizational skill of the league's leaders was the fourth strength they brought to their task in the 1890s. That organizational skill included recruiting exceptionally respected academics and ecumenical clergy. Once the league moved beyond its New York base, it managed to build a national federation of strong grassroots state and city affiliates. They barred both workers and employers from leadership. This policy, designed to avoid a conflict of interest, forced local leagues to remain predominantly middle- and upper-class women's organizations. The leadership developed special links to other elite women's groups, especially the General Federation of Women's Clubs. The federation's president, Ellen M. Henrotin, served as a vice president of the national league in the late 1890s.[73]

However, the most important administrative success of the new national league in 1898 was the recruitment of Florence Kelley as secretary, the title for the administrative executive of the national office. Kelley brought many of the same exceptional characteristics to the league as had Lowell, Jacobi, John Brooks, and the academic advisors. Born in 1859 in Philadelphia to a Quaker mother and a successful businessman soon to be elected as a Republican to Congress, she was too young to recall the Civil

War; however, she did correspond with her father about the civil rights issues of the 1870s, before enrolling at Cornell at the age of seventeen. Graduating Phi Beta Kappa, she went to Europe to study and there married a Russian physician, had three children, and became an associate of Friedrich Engels, translating *The Condition of the Working Class in England*.[74]

In 1891, her life changed drastically when, following her divorce, she moved into Hull House. There she worked with Carroll Wright on a study of Chicago slums. Then she graduated from Northwestern University Law School and secured appointment from Governor John Peter Altgeld as the first Illinois factory inspector. Her reports of conditions in the state's manufacturing plants brought her to the attention of John Brooks, who had assumed the presidency of the National Consumers' League in 1898. He made a special trip to Chicago to recruit her to run the league's central office. For the next quarter century, she *was* the Consumers' League. The league already had begun to move beyond department store investigations, but she led it in championing garment workers, generally improved labor standards, especially for women and children, and later the minimum wage.[75]

Under Kelley, the league found new sources of support and created new methods of achieving its goals. For example, the league's research received the backing of the Russell Sage Foundation and the free legal guidance of Louis Brandeis and, after his appointment to the Supreme Court, of Felix Frankfurter. The league also devised a method of informing the public of acceptable manufacturing, allowing approved firms to sew a special league label into garments. Demonstrating the effectiveness of the label campaign, the infamous Triangle Shirtwaist Company was involved in a legal dispute with the league over placing a copycat label in its garments.[76] Most important, the league began a process of seeking court decisions favorable to labor legislation. For example, league attorney Josephine Goldmark did most of the work in the *Mueller v. Oregon* case in 1908, and Goldmark's brother-in-law, Brandeis, argued the case before the Supreme Court.[77]

As the League moved beyond New York, concern for international labor standards could not be far behind. One way of addressing the international issue was the establishment of leagues in other nations. In 1899, Maud Nathan, president of the New York League and an official with the General Federation of Women's Clubs, promoted the formation of consumers' leagues in England, speaking on "The Ethics of Money Making and Money-Spending" at a large public meeting, also addressed by Beatrice Webb. In 1903, Nathan helped launch a French league and a Swiss league,

and in 1904 one in Germany. As with the general labor standards movement, she received special help from the University of Fribourg. Finally, in
1908 Kelley and Nathan traveled to Geneva for the first international
conference of consumers' leagues. A second was held in Antwerp in 1913.
However, Kelley met little success, for the conferences decided not to establish a formal international league structure nor a common agenda. Kelley
and a number of academic advisors to the American league did play a key
role in establishing the American branch of the IALL.[78]

The American Association for Labor Legislation

Given the heavy concentration of German-educated economists
who served as advisors to the Consumers' League, it is not surprising that
the league became involved in establishing an American section of the
IALL. Samuel Lindsay, Jeremiah Jenks, Charles Henderson, and Florence Kelley played early roles in the formation of the American Association for Labor Legislation (AALL) in 1906, two years after the U.S. hosted
the IALL meeting at the St. Louis World's Fair. However, the prime movement for the AALL came from a group of academics associated with
Richard T. Ely at the University of Wisconsin and the American Economics Association.

The outlines of Ely's early life had remarkable parallels to those of
the other labor standard reformers. Born in 1854, of New England parents, including a devout Presbyterian father, Ely graduated from Columbia University and then went off to Germany to study under the historical
economists, graduating from the University of Heidelberg in 1879. He received an appointment at Johns Hopkins in time to teach Woodrow
Wilson and John R. Commons and to distinguish himself as a leading
rebel against the classical economists. He wrote sympathetic studies of
The Labor Movement in America and on related topics.[79] He studied socialism and discovered lessons for social reform. He investigated the labor
market and recognized its negative impact on the most distressed workers. Then he turned from economics to write about the impact of his faith
on life.

Ely especially admired those critics of laissez-faire capitalism whose
opposition originated in their Christian faith.[80] He concluded his 1883
study of *French and German Socialism in Modern Times* with a favorable
account of the work of Bishop Ketteler, the early supporter of international labor standards.[81] His most popular book before 1900 was the *Social
Aspects of Christianity*. One historian of the social gospel called it "the
first influential effort on the part of a prominent American to state 'the

social side of the Church's mission'."[82] The books demonstrated that his studies in Germany had nurtured both his historical methodology and his religious critique of the excesses of capitalism. A chapter in each book praised the socialists of the chair, several of whom had been his teachers. Ely had attended a series of lectures by Adolph Wagner, one of the founders of the Social Policy Association. More than Gustav Schmoller and Lujo Brentano, Wagner favored state socialism and welcomed efforts to develop a Christian-Socialist program. Ely gave especially favorable mention to Wagner in his own books, both to his social concerns and to the powerful methodological attack on laissez-faire economics. Ely insisted that his colleagues reject simple ideology and use the empirical and historical approach of the Germans. A study of the economy should not involve rational theorizing but research into the actual behavior of people. To further both the historical method and the study of the social question resulting from industrialization, Ely helped establish the American Economic Association. Ely's influence on international labor standards in America is both important and brief, for other than founding the AALL, he did little. It was his disciples at Wisconsin, especially John R. Commons, who sustained the AALL and linked it to the Consumers' League.

Commons shared many of the personal characteristics of the earlier labor standards leaders. His parents, a Quaker and a Presbyterian, were ardent abolitionists. Too young to have served in the battle against slavery, Commons applied his faith to labor rights battles. To prepare, he attended his mother's alma mater, Oberlin. From there, he continued his studies under Ely at Johns Hopkins. Before receiving his degree, he secured a position at Wesleyan, and then a succession of academic posts, at each of which his concern with social problems was perceived as radicalism. Copying Ely, he related religion to labor problems, speaking at many churches and writing *Social Reform and the Church* in 1894.[83] Because universities disapproved of his radicalism, he spent ten years working for government and the National Civic Federation. He published numerous studies of labor, immigration, and income distribution. Finally in 1904, Ely, who had moved to the University of Wisconsin for the same reasons that had cost Commons his jobs, invited him to join the Wisconsin faculty. At Wisconsin, Commons led university efforts to reform state government, writing with his students such bills as the civil service law and the worker's compensation act. Meanwhile, he helped the groups that were pioneering support for labor standards. In 1906 he participated in the founding of the AALL and picked its executive secretary. He concluded his involvement in the Consumers' League with a twelve-year presidency beginning in 1923, leading the league through the difficult transition at the time of Florence Kelley's death. At age seventy-three he left the league and turned over the presidency to former New Hampshire Governor John Winant. Winant left the league to be the first American to head the ILO.[84]

Commons's most lasting contribution to the AALL was his pupil John B. Andrews. A Wisconsin native, educated at the University of Wisconsin, Andrews completed his Ph.D. under Commons's direction. Since both Commons and Ely were occupied with other projects, they recommended Andrews's appointment as executive secretary of the AALL. He held that position throughout its thirty-seven-year history. When Andrews needed help, they enlisted another former student, Irene Osgood, as his assistant; she also became his wife. Following the model of his teachers, Andrews made the primary purpose of the AALL sponsorship and dissemination of research. In 1911, Andrews launched *The American Labor Legislation Review* to publish research and news related to labor legislation. Aware of American exceptionalism, the *Review* included regular accounts of labor legislation achievements around the world.

Even before beginning *The Review*, John Andrews interested himself in defining international labor standards. His first research related to phosphorous poisoning in the match industry, an issue of concern since the Bern Conference of the IALL. His report for the U.S. Bureau of Labor not only contributed to the Esch-Hughes Act, which placed a prohibitive tax on phosphorous matches, but also helped conceive the general industrial hygiene movement.[85] While engaged in a variety of social insurance research and policy advocacy in the next decade, he became increasingly aware of the need for international labor standards. Consequently, he was appointed as a U.S. delegate to the first International Labor Conference of the ILO. He also wrote essays promoting U.S. support for the International Labor Organization.[86]

In its early years, the AALL skillfully linked academic economists with experts in the growing American bureaucracy, labor leaders, and social welfare reformers. For example, in 1908, the American delegation to the IALL meeting in Lucerne included Florence Kelley and a representative of the U.S. Department of Commerce and Labor. Given the U.S. refusal to send even an observer to the ILO during the period of intense isolationism, the U.S. government assumed a remarkable role in relationship to the IALL and the first ILO. Not only did it appoint a delegate, the U.S. contributed along with a dozen other countries to the support of the ILO in Basel. Of course, the U.S. supplied only one thousand francs, about 2 percent of the office's annual budget, a small sum considering France, Germany, and Switzerland gave at least ten thousand francs each. Nonetheless, this participation was official and demonstrated the greater willingness of progressive-era national administrations to attend international gatherings. This approach especially contrasted with that after World War I, such as in 1931 when the Hoover Administration not only sent no delegate to the ILO but forbade Mary Anderson of the Children's Bureau to enter Switzerland during the ILO conference.[87]

Sharing international labor statistics and information on legislative innovations in different countries was a valuable contribution of the early AALL. The empiricism of the founders gave credibility to the Association's work, which enabled it to pressure states to modify labor laws discriminating against immigrants. The AALL's use of labor data grew from both the influence of the German historical economists and domestic innovations. Carroll Wright and his disciples, Adna Weber and Henry Farnum, played a pioneering role in labor statistics. Wright was another New Englander, seasoned by volunteer service in the Civil War. After a brief political career, Wright won support for the creation of the Massachusetts Bureau of Statistics of Labor, the first such bureaucracy in the nation. Seeing accurate labor data as essential for justifying economic reform, he not only made exceptional advances in methodology in the state, but he led an effort to develop labor statistics bureaus in every state and in the federal government. In 1885 he launched the national Bureau of Labor Statistics. There he served as chair of special labor dispute investigatory commissions for the U.S. government. The special studies included ones on the Pullman and Anthracite Coal Strikes. At the turn of the century, Wright's methods found supporters both among progressive social scientists and activists in the AFL and the AALL. By the time of the creation of the AALL, Wright had retired from federal service, but his disciple, Weber, emphasized Wright's methods there. In exceptional cases, such as the phosphorous match problem, the AALL used statistics to win U.S. support for international labor conventions.

Yet, that triumph proved to be exceptional in the early years. The AALL's leadership made a fateful decision at the time of the phosphorous match issue, to not push the second international convention proposed by the International Labor Office that limited night work for women. As

President Henry Farnum observed at the AALL's second annual meeting, "[T]he objects of the International Association are of two kinds, scientific and practical, the latter referring mainly to International treaties. For Constitutional reasons the United States cannot be expected to take part in these."[88] The constitutional reasons included court limitations on state economic regulation and the federal structure, which reserved to the states labor protection and regulation. Later at the meeting, Florence Kelley reported on the European assessment of this exceptionalism, saying, "Two striking points were observed. . . . The first was the general assumption by delegates and officials that the laws of the individual states of the United States were not to be taken seriously for two reasons, namely, that they are not enforced or obeyed, and that where they do exist they are so exceptional as not to count in the general view of the state of labor legislation throughout the industrial world."[89] Kelley responded to the criticisms by proposing that the AALL do a better job of advertising the advances of a few American states, such as Illinois and New York. She did not have a solution to the question of how to win national acceptance for substantive labor standards. She and the AALL recognized the twentieth-century pattern of American national government rejection of international conventions on the grounds that they were matters properly for the states. However, as other progressives, they hoped empirical data would spur state reform.

Samuel McCune Lindsay, who was both a key member of the AALL and an advisor to the Consumers' League, proposed more attention be given to the use of interstate compacts to overcome the limitations on national regulation of labor standards. Lindsay's work launched a long effort by lawyers supportive of labor to find innovative strategies to overcome court barriers to labor rights. Until the judicial revolution of 1937 and the acceptance of the Wagner Act and the Fair Labor Standards Act, Lindsay's approach seemed the only one. If he were right, supporters of labor standards in the U.S. had to first give attention to standardizing the laws of forty-eight states before they could turn to international standards. The daunting task of presiding over the negotiation of interstate compacts on each of the many needed labor standards shows why the AALL, with a two-person staff, decided to focus on data collection not legislation. While this approach was realistic given both the American constitutional system in the 1900s and the initial success of the empirical method in bringing reform, it caused frustrations later when a new generation of academics had less applied interests.[90]

The American Federation of Labor

In many ways, the approach of the AALL to labor standards suited that of the American Federation of Labor (AFL). The AALL leadership proudly reached out to labor and included Samuel Gompers as a vice president. Yet, labor by choice remained on the periphery of the AALL. Gompers valued labor statistics because they tended to reinforce the claims of the AFL. However, he did not want to share or relinquish control of labor's agenda to the intellectuals.[91] They welcomed Gompers in an advisory capacity. The problem was that he wanted the roles reversed. American organized labor possessed its own international agenda and, in particular, had its own international network of organizations, which workers controlled. It was to that network that Gompers, his allies, and opponents among the working class gave most attention. And, in it, Gompers laid much of the groundwork for the modern ILO. With the massive immigration in the decades after the Civil War, American labor was inherently international in perspective. Gompers personified that perspective. He had been born in the East End of London and spoke four languages. Even before the AFL, American unions sent representatives to the First International. The AFL appealed successfully to the Second International in 1889 to back the federation's May 1 labor protest on behalf of the eight-hour day. But for all the international contacts, American labor saw little need for close or extensive cooperation with European unions before World War I. Gompers, despite personal radicalism, approached labor issues with exceptional practicality. In the mid-1890s, he led the AFL through a painful split with doctrinaire socialists whom he feared would undermine any real gains possible under the American system. After this experience, the AFL had problems working with their more doctrinaire European compatriots.[92]

In 1901, the AFL discovered the international organization with which it could work—the International Secretariat of Trade Union Centers (ISTUC). While the AFL did not want to join the ISTUC, it cooperated with it to form the International Federation of Trade Unions (IFTU). The IFTU sought the pragmatic goals of the AFL, avoiding political debates and radical rhetoric, in favor of statistical and legal research and mutual support of fellow trade unionists during strikes. Beginning in 1909, the AFL participated in three meetings of the IFTU before the war, in Paris, Budapest, and Zurich. While the AFL resisted making strong commitments to the IFTU, it laid the groundwork for potentially fruitful international cooperation by 1914. The IFTU planned to hold its 1915 conference in San Francisco, but the outbreak of the war prevented its opening. If there had been no war, the organization's long-term success in standardizing labor laws may have been quite notable. As it was, it provided the contacts for postwar labor cooperation, and it demonstrated to the world the type of nonideological international labor organization with which the AFL wished to work.[93]

On reviewing the AFL position regarding international labor cooperation, it is easy to dismiss Gompers as a conservative obstructionist to the more specific and revolutionary goals of his critics in the international labor movement. Yet, Gompers remained an ever-practical man in an extremely hostile world. He was the preeminent American labor leader, both more humble in origins and more arrogant than many of his counterparts and more distrustful of labor supporters from outside the working class. Having witnessed so many labor defeats in the courts and legislative halls, he relied on economic gains negotiated from a position of trade union strength. He distrusted intellectuals, nonwage leaders of the working class, and politicians. They could end their support and abandon labor. When AFL representatives returned from IFTU meetings and other international gatherings, they criticized European radicals and intellectuals as much as the Europeans attacked the AFL.

Clearly, the AFL was an exceptional labor movement in the exceptional American political context. It avoided politics in order to extract a few basic political protections from a largely unsympathetic state. It avoided politics because it was a chronically practical movement. Political power, as ideology, did not matter, only specific economic gains did. This unique approach grew from a variety of factors, including the American constitutional system, which allowed the courts to block most national labor legislation and much state action. But, there were other reasons too. The American working class was ethically and religiously diverse and could be easily divided by any union actions that moved beyond simple economics.

At times, however, Gompers and the AFL leadership revealed that they may not have been so fixated on the practical, if only they could get Americans to accept their ideals. The campaign for the labor provisions in the Clayton Anti-Trust Act hinted at the ideology. One of the few politicians Gompers came to respect and trust was President Wilson, to a great extent because Wilson supported the Clayton Act's exemption of labor from the anti-trust laws.[94] While the courts' interpretation eventually made the exemption meaningless, Gompers believed the 1914 wording incorporated into U.S. law the heart of the labor critique of laissez-faire.[95] The Clayton Act simply declared that "labor was not a commodity."[96] This concept had been repeated throughout the previous century by critics of industrial exploitation of workers. The German economists in the Social Policy Association and Pope Leo XIII had shared this assertion.[97] Richard Ely devoted a major section of *The Labor Movement in America* to it, saying:

> While labor is a commodity, it is an expenditure of human force which involves the welfare of the personality. It is a commodity which is inseparably bound up with the laborer and in this it differs from other commodities. The one who offers other commodities for sale reserves his own person. . . . The laborer, however, has, as a rule, only the service residing in his own person with which to sustain him and his family. Again, a machine . . . and a workingman resemble each other in this: they both render services, and the fate of both depends upon the manner in which these services are extracted. But there is this radical difference: the machine which yields its service to man is itself a commodity, and is only a means to an end, while the laborer who parts with labor is no longer a commodity in civilized lands, but is an end in himself."[98]

Despite Gompers's alleged conservatism, as Ely noted, his support for this doctrine radically departed both from laissez-faire capitalism and from Marxism.

War and Reform

As Congress considered the final wording of the Clayton Bill in 1914, events in Bosnia catapulted the European world into war. While the war caused incomprehensible suffering, death, and destruction, and in many ways ended western progressive reform movements, it also brought the culmination of progressivism, especially in the American movement toward international labor standards. After years of work, supporters of the ILO had succeeded in opening a small office in Basel and in passing two labor conventions ratified by many nations. The U.S. endorsed the white phosphorous convention, contributed a small amount to the Basel office, and participated actively in the IALL. After the war, the movement grew in size and in institutional achievements. As a result of the Versailles Peace Conference, the ILO moved from a tiny Basel office to a large Geneva bureaucracy. The new International Labor Conference met annually and averaged for the next seventy-five years more conventions per year than had been adopted in the first dozen years. As another result of the war, the U.S. advanced from the periphery of the movement to the center, hosting the first ILO conference in Washington. Members of the AALL and the Consumers' League as well as Gompers and his AFL staff served in key positions, incorporating basic American assumptions into its operations, from special rights for women to protecting labor freedom. Yet, just as the war brought unanticipated advances in the movement, American exceptionalism reasserted itself in the end. After controlling the establishment of the ILO, the U.S. did not join it or any other League of Nations institution, as the Senate refused to ratify the Versailles Treaty. This sudden reversal of fortunes teaches much about the structure and function of the American policy process.[99]

Initially, the war seemed unrelated to America or the domestic labor standards movement. The AALL expanded its focus on social insurance during the early war years. In 1914, Henry Seager of the AALL targeted health insurance as "the most urgent of the remaining social insurance problems."[100] By 1916, the association launched a health insurance campaign that continued until 1919. Of the major participants in the labor standards movement, only Samuel Gompers and the AFL leadership gave significant attention to the war's impact on international labor issues. At the annual AFL convention in November 1914, the AFL approved a resolution authorizing "the Executive Council to call a meeting of representatives of organized labor of the different nations to meet at the same time and place [as the Peace Congress]."[101] The AALL and Consumers' League did not have important contacts with their counterparts outside the United States, and therefore showed little interest.

During the first two and a half years of the war, as the U.S. maintained its neutrality, the AFL periodically returned to the theme of labor and the peace process. In 1916, the AFL stepped beyond its 1914 proposal to demand that "representatives of wage earners" be included at the peace conference. Allied labor leaders in 1916 noticed the AFL proposal and began planning their labor agenda for the peace conference. With American entry into the war in April 1917, the relationship of the AFL to the postwar planning process changed in several ways. First, the tenuous relationship with the IFTU, still headquartered in Germany, with a German director, ended. Second, influence within the Allied labor movements greatly increased. Yet, ironically, for an organization that emphasized practical measures and not the political goals of European labor, Gompers and the AFL now avoided purely labor meetings for general political participation.

There were a number of wartime labor conferences that the AFL dismissed. The allied labor movements held a meeting in 1917 at Leeds and proposed a number of specific labor standards that the peace conference should recognize, such as protections for worker health, standardized labor statistics, and protection of migrant workers. The rump IFTU, including labor from the Central Powers and a number of neutrals, met in Stockholm in June 1917 and in Bern in October. These meetings went beyond the Leeds conference and proposed creation of an international legislative body to approve labor standards. The AFL regarded each of these meetings as premature, though it did not refrain from developing goals and asking the next Allied labor conference, in London in 1918, to approve them.[102]

The 1918 AFL goals for postwar labor became the federation's international position for the remainder of the century. Debates about the consistency of the AFL goals, their value for international labor, and their radicalism or lack thereof likewise continued for decades. There have been few defenders of Gompers's approach and at least three schools of critics. First, radicals always have found the AFL and Gompers to be hopelessly conservative and representative of only a fraction of labor.[103] They accused Gompers of doing the bidding of the American government and being dominated by business interests. They suspected the AFL was uncritical of government policy "in the hope that such support would give the working class a share of the great American pie."[104] Second, moderate critics of Gompers noted that American labor had less political will than did unions elsewhere. Perhaps this lack of will came from the more materialistic, less ideological, American culture. Daniel Patrick Moynihan thought it resulted from Gompers's personal decline in vigor.[105] Scholars of comparative Canadian-U.S. labor policy especially emphasized this critique.[106] Finally, there also are those who, while critical of the AFL approach, sympathize with the plight of American labor leaders within the U.S. constitutional system. They pointed out that American organized labor inherently opposed one of the core national values—the sanctity of private property. The AFL did not so much lack political will as demonstrate remarkable realism. In America, labor's goal was to circumvent the law because it could not use it. Consequently, Gompers and his followers did not support establishing a supernational legislative body to pass specific international labor laws. The AFL feared that international labor legislation might restrict labor rights in America, not protect them.[107]

Each of these interpretations assumed that Gompers sought less advanced goals than the Europeans. Gompers himself defended the AFL goals as more progressive than the alternatives. He held, for example, that the objectives of the Leeds conference were too limited compared to what the times required. The Leeds delegates only considered problems specific to labor. Gompers believed the war necessitated that labor address the general problems of the peace. He criticized the rump IFTU for seeking to divide western labor, to undermine the Allies, and restore German autocracy. As reflected in the AFL proposal for the Interallied Labor Conference of September 1918, the priority of international labor should be to defend democracy and freedom. After political reform, good labor laws would follow. The AFL listed seven basic principles "of vital importance to wage-earners," which the signatories of the peace treaty should recognize. The first came from the Clayton Act, declaring that labor is not a commodity or article of commerce, and related to it, that "involuntary servitude should not exist," and specifically for seamen, that they were free to leave their ships when in port. Two others defined the basic personal freedom of association and of free expression and the right to a jury trial that the AFL always treasured as essential to the right to organize. The last two specified essential labor standards: the prohibition in international commerce of products of child labor and the eight-hour day. In addition to these basic protections for labor, Gompers supported the creation of a permanent international institutional structure where labor would work equally with business and government to define labor standards.[108]

For the United States, World War I was a short engagement, with intense military involvement coming only in the last months of hostilities. War planning and production changes provided innumerable, if brief, opportunities for organized labor and social reformers to bring regulation to labor conditions. For a variety of reasons, labor union membership during the war years doubled. More important, progressive administrators of the war effort turned to the elite social scientists and welfare reformers to run or oversee a variety of labor-related programs and policies, from the military draft to public employment offices. The War Department, under future Consumers' League president Newton Baker, appointed Florence Kelley to a committee overseeing manufacturing of uniforms, bringing the league's labor standards to a whole industry. Felix Frankfurter, the Consumers' League attorney, chaired the War Labor Policies Board. However, in the realm of international labor standards, the planning and negotiation of the peace treaty presented the most important opportunity for reform.

In 1917, the Wilson Administration initiated a planning group called the Inquiry, employing the talents of a host of academics and reformers to prepare for the peace. Members and sympathizers with the AALL and the Consumers' League filled key positions that related to international labor standards. These were perfect positions for the experts from such organi-zations, who preferred gaining influence because of their knowledge and competence rather than through popular campaigns. In September 1918, John Andrews of the AALL joined the Economic Section of the Inquiry to work specifically on international labor planning.[109] In the Division of Social History, James Shotwell, a young colleague of the Columbia University social scientists active in the AALL, assumed similar responsibili-ties. Allyn Young of the Inquiry asked Felix Frankfurter to assemble a staff to review the labor conditions and policies of each major country as well as methods for setting labor standards. To this task, Frankfurter brought a number of skilled young social scientists and lawyers, particularly profes-sional women linked to social reform. Included among the group were Amy Hewes and Dorothy Kenyon. Hewes, of the AALL, was another German-educated economist, who chaired the Mount Holyoke econom-ics department for a generation and later led the fight for the minimum wage in New England. Kenyon, who became a famous New York judge and president of the New York Consumers' League, had just graduated from N.Y.U. Law School when the war began. Such women brought to the Inquiry special competence and insight, reflected in the addition of unprecedented protections for women's rights and requirements for a women's role in international labor administration.[110]

While the American preparation for the labor discussions at Ver-sailles played a major role in the form and consequences of the treaty's labor provisions, factors external to the U.S. were also important. First, the leaders in other nations came to Versailles with their own plans for labor standards. Both the British and French had done considerable work on the topic. Stephen Bauer of the existing ILO in Basel had provided a review of the development of labor standards mechanisms, which re-ceived special attention when Royal Meeker, head of the U.S. Bureau of Labor Statistics, published it in the *BLS Bulletin*. A former colleague of Woodrow Wilson at Princeton, Meeker publicized Bauer's ideas. The Germans, excluded from Paris until the negotiations ended, also had input through a Bern Labour Conference scheduled during the Versailles Conference. Then, near-panic gripped European leaders at the start of 1919 as they witnessed the spread of bolshevism. No one expressed sur-prise when French Premier Georges Clemenceau listed labor standards as one of the three goals of the peace conference, right up with his obsession with German war guilt. The shock at the Bela Kun revolt in Hungary in late winter forced reluctant foreign ministers to agree to the ILO struc-ture, about which many were, at best, indifferent. The influence of communism on the creation of the ILO provides a "meta-example" of the theory that the strength of leftist movements best explains the level of social welfare provision.[111]

Acknowledging these foreign influences, the American interest groups that advocated labor standards did a remarkable job in directing the creation of the ILO. The two Americans who dominated the negotiations, Samuel Gompers and James Shotwell, reflected the diversity of American goals. Gompers came with his voluntarist principles and desire for labor and employers to control labor policy. Carol Riegelman Lubin, later assistant to John Winant at the ILO, found it ironic that Gompers was elected to head the labor portion of this most political of conferences. In fact, by his election, Gompers frustrated the efforts of those who hoped to create a strong intergovernmental organization to pass world labor legislation.[112] Shotwell sought to check Gompers's efforts, providing an opportunity for the French and British to strengthen the government role at the ILO. Given his adversary, he performed that job well, becoming the inside expert on labor standard history, status, and needs.[113]

There were two complex issues that concerned Gompers: the scheme of representation, and the relationship of the ILO to federal states. The British plan for the ILO, submitted on February 1, 1919, proposed to create an organization in which labor, employers, and government would be represented, and which would be able to pass international labor conventions. Not surprising, Gompers opposed the plan. He wanted the organization to include only representatives of labor and management. Any government representation should equal each of the other interests. The British maintained that government should have two votes, while labor and business possessed one each. Gompers's retort was that since employers controlled government, this scheme would give business three votes to labor's one. Coming from a different tradition, the British considered government as the neutral arbiter.[114]

Gompers also emphasized the problems that international labor conventions posed for a federal state. He accepted the U.S. practice of making labor policy a state responsibility and did not want the national governments controlling state experimentation. Gompers joined the employer representative at the conference in approving only an advisory role for international labor standards. The Europeans did not understand the federal system. Gompers's obstructionism became so extreme during these debates that one of the British delegates, future ILO head Harold Butler, appealed to Shotwell to find someone to control Gompers. Shotwell enlisted the help of Felix Frankfurter. Gompers finally acquiesced to a provision that made ILO labor standards advisory until ratified; and it allowed federal states to urge their subnational units to ratify conventions. Of course, this change turned the ILO into a debating society more than a legislature, exactly the goal of Gompers.

With these issues resolved, the conference incorporated the ILO into Part XIII of the Versailles Treaty. The ILO had the unique tripartite structure suggested by the British, with two representatives selected by each government and one delegate each selected by the most representative employee and employer organization in the country. The latter two delegates were free to vote as individuals and could disagree with their government. The International Labour Office was the permanent bureaucracy of the annual International Labour Conference. The conference would consider and pass on to member nations conventions that would state the ILO's sense of needed minimal labor standards. In forming the ILO, the nations also committed themselves to nine minimal principles of labor policy.

These principles originated with Gompers's proposals, with several additions reflecting the input of women. The first declared that "labour should not be regarded merely as a commodity." Others include Gompers's original guarantees of freedom of association, the eight-hour day, and the abolition of child labor. There was a pledge that wages needed to be "adequate to maintain a reasonable standard of life." A weekly rest of twenty-four hours was to be protected. There was a promise of equal treatment of all workers legally resident in a country. And, for women, there was a guarantee of equal pay for equal work and "provision for a system of inspection in which women should take part, in order to ensure the enforcement of the [labor] laws."[115]

Constitutionally, the inclusion of the ILO in the treaty did not mean the U.S. government had agreed to the organization. The president still needed the advice and consent of the Senate. Pending that ratification, the Allied leaders appointed a committee, headed by Harold Butler of Britain, to plan the first annual ILO conference for Washington in October 1919. James Shotwell represented the United States. When Butler needed assistance, President Wilson sent his friend, Royal Meeker, from the Bureau of Labor Statistics. The secretary of labor ushered a joint resolution through Congress authorizing the conference. Problems only developed when no building or extra funds were available for the meeting. Since the president had suffered a stroke about a month before the conference, the detailed arrangements had to be made by staff, who did not always demonstrate as much interest in the project as had the president. When space for the meeting continued to be a problem, Assistant Secretary of the Navy Franklin Roosevelt intervened and supplied logistical support from his department. This turn of events cemented a lasting affection between FDR and the ILO and of Harold Butler for FDR.[116]

FAILURE AND ITS LESSONS

Quickly, the triumph of creating the ILO and hosting the first conference degenerated into rejection. Events of the summer revealed the possibility of serious problems for the ILO in the United States. The president of the International Seamen's Union, Andrew Furuseth, announced his opposition to the ILO. Gompers and Matthew Woll, an AFL vice president, argued forcefully for its creation. Furuseth typified many later critics who raised clearly invalid reasons out of fear. He opposed the ILO because he worried that its standards might be lower than U.S. standards, forcing the country to decrease its protections for workers. This line of argument turned the ILO's purpose on its head.[117] Furuseth and other anti-British labor leaders also disliked granting one vote to each of the self-governing British dominions. They perceived this as a plot by the English to dominate the organization.[118]

A variety of business groups, including the Conference Board and a number of trade associations, joined in opposition to the ILO. In fact, beyond a small core of supporters, including the president, Gompers, Shotwell, Meeker, and John Andrews of the AALL, few came forward as strong backers. Neither Secretary of Labor Wilson nor Secretary of State Lansing gave enthusiastic support. In the Senate, opponents raised issues such as the British domination and the rights of employers and employees to vote along with the government. Given the large number of union members in Massachusetts, Senator Henry Cabot Lodge did not lead the opposition to the ILO as he did to other key points in the Versailles Treaty. The Senate debated the ILO on November 18, 1919. A strong reservation to the ILO was defeated, with 28 percent of the Republicans joining 80 percent of Democrats. A weak reservation passed. The voting pattern on both was similar, with the primary related factor being party loyalty. Senators from urban states, from states with large amounts of manufacturing, and from states with large numbers of immigrants voted against the ILO. However, the highest correlation of opposition to the organization was party affiliation. Republicans generally opposed the ILO. Overwhelmingly, the senators who backed the ILO came from rural states, especially in the South, the center of the president's party in 1919.[119]

Of course, these votes did not matter, since the overall treaty went down to defeat, and the U.S. did not participate in any of the Versailles structures. Consequently, the U.S. role in international labor standards decreased after 1919. Before the war, the U.S. had sent official delegates to the IALL and had supported, modestly, the ILO in Basel. As a result of the rejection of the Versailles Treaty, the U.S. severed all links to the new ILO and all international labor standards commitments.

The strategy of the people and institutions in the United States that championed international labor standards had come amazingly close to success in 1919, only to face complete defeat. They had to uncover lessons in this reversal of fortune. While their failure could be blamed primarily on the larger treaty, they began to ask what needed to be done to achieve success. The effort to achieve labor standards before 1919 had focused only sporadically on the international dimension. The sudden fixation on the ILO in 1919 resulted far more from the fortunes of war than from a long American effort. From the German historical economists, through various church leaders to foresighted industrialists, European elites had laid the foundations for the ILO. American support derived from these Continental roots and only came to the fore when the U.S. played the decisive role in the war. Both the American rejection of Versailles and of the ILO can be explained as a natural consequence, perhaps an inevitable one, of the limited popular understanding of the new U.S. role in the world.[120]

The decision fifteen years later by the U.S. to join the ILO and neither the League of Nations nor the World Court, the two other international bodies created at Versailles, shows how much the interests supporting labor standards learned from the failure of 1919. Given the often regressive features of American labor policy, how could the labor standards organization become acceptable and not the other two?[121] The answer to that question tells much about American policy making, both foreign and domestic. While the policy process may grant a privileged position to business, the battle to join the ILO shows the potential for diversity in the process. A coalition of individuals and interests committed to the public interest and social justice can utilize a crisis such as the Great Depression to overcome the tendency toward policy restraint in the American system.

THREE

The
Reversal

During the decade between the creation of the ILO on October 29, 1919, at the Washington conference, and the great stock market crash on October 29, 1929, the ILO leadership astutely took advantage of tripartism to build and maintain relations with American business and labor, if not the government. As the organization codified basic labor standards, it also began pioneering studies of comparative labor-management relations, wage rates, and other topics of interest to both American business and labor. For example, two business organizations, the National Bureau of Economic Research and the National Industrial Conference Board, collaborated on several projects with the ILO. However, in the mid-1920s, no one would have predicted that the only Versailles institution the U.S. would ever join would be the ILO. Not only did the U.S. maintain its general tradition of avoiding foreign entanglements during the era, but American social policy exceptionalism raised seemingly insurmountable additional barriers to working with a global labor rights organization.

The ILO's first director, Albert Thomas, deserved much credit for promoting the ILO in the U.S. during its first decade. Thomas, a French socialist who had run the munitions ministry during World War I, effectively presented the ILO as a democratic alternative to bolshevism. Despite his bearded, rotund physique and party affiliation, on several American tours he charmed business leaders, academics, and public officials, even while not withholding his opinions. He sought out Henry Ford to discuss modern industrial relations, yet criticized Ford's anti-Semitism. Thomas's honesty impressed Ford, proven a few years later when the industrialist retained the ILO to investigate the cost of living in European nations and to determine wage rates at Ford plants. Ford brought the U.S. government into cooperating with the ILO by having the Bureau of Labor Statistics do the Detroit portion of the ILO study.[1]

In addition to serving as the ILO ambassador, Thomas modified the role of the ILO. In its first three conferences, the ILO drafted sixteen conventions. This was nearly half of the conventions ratified down to 1933 (see table 3.1). After this initial activity, Thomas urged the delegates to slow the convention process and devote attention to information collection and technical assistance. Strategically, the latter activities provided opportunities to involve the U.S.[2]

Thomas sought links to a variety of global nongovernmental organizations. He worked closely with the revived International Federation of Trade Unions, headquartered in Amsterdam. He developed a special relationship with the Catholic Church, beginning a tradition of having a Jesuit on the staff in Geneva. Like his successors, he recognized the value of forming bonds to American groups that would support the ILO's goals. In 1922, an ILO advisory committee on industrial hygiene included ten Americans, notably Alice Hamilton, later president of the Consumers' League. Three years later, two Americans served on a subcommittee on industrial safety. Thomas recruited a member of the Bureau of Labor Statistics to unofficially attend a 1928 conference on labor statistics.[3] Finally, to assure good American relations, Thomas appointed Royal Meeker, Woodrow Wilson's former colleague at Princeton and former head of the Bureau of Labor Statistics, to head the Washington ILO office.

Consequently, the ILO had either the support or at least the neutral cooperation of the peak business, labor, academic, and philanthropic organizations in the 1920s. The U.S. Chamber of Commerce cooperated, although it stopped short of sending an observer to Geneva. Likewise, the National Industrial Conference Board took a neutral, but not hostile, position of watchful waiting.[4] In addition to visiting Ford while in America, Thomas cultivated the interest, if not support, of J. P. Morgan, Charles Schwab, Edward Filene, and Henry Dennison. Filene and Dennison especially became involved in industrial relations research conducted by the ILO. Filene, through his Twentieth Century Fund, paid for some of the studies. Later, both were selected as employer delegates to the ILO. The Rockefeller, Carnegie, and Russell Sage Foundations helped sustain the ILO research, and key faculty from Harvard and Columbia Universities gave credibility to the ILO by working on its projects. As Daniel Patrick Moynihan observed, in this era American business did not have the nearly pathological fear of the ILO that surfaced after 1945.[5]

TABLE 3.1.   International Labor Conventions 1919–1932

Numbers	Year	Subject
1–6	1919	Hours of work; unemployment; maternity protections; night work of women; minimum age; and night work of minors
7–9	1920	Minimum age, seafarers; unemployment indemnity, shipwreck; employment for seafarers
10–16	1921	Minimum age, agriculture; rights of association, agriculture; worker's compensation; agriculture; use of white lead; weekly rest; minimum age, seafarers; medical examination, young seafarers
17–20	1925	Worker's compensation, accidents; worker's compensation, diseases; eligibility of treatment, accidents; night work in bakeries
21–23	1926	Inspection of immigrants on ships; seafarers articles of agreement; repatriation of seafarers
24–25	1927	Sickness insurance, industry; sickness insurance, agriculture
26	1928	Minimum wage fixing machinery
27	1929	Weight of packages in vessels
28–30	1930	Protections against docker accidents; forced labor; hours of work, commerce and offices
31–33	1932	Hours of work, coal mines; protections against docker accidents; minimum age, nonindustrial employment

Surprisingly, two key AFL leaders, Vice President Matt Woll and Andrew Furuseth, opposed the ILO. They agreed with the vehemently antiunion National Association of Manufacturers (NAM) that foreign interference in the American economy was dangerous. Furuseth, head of the Maritime Union, considered the ILO either a British-controlled tool to destroy the American merchant marine or a means by which American shippers would undermine the protections in the La Follette Seamen's Act.[6] Woll, a Gompers's protege and director of AFL policy making, said in 1930, "From the standpoint of American labor . . . this whole idea is wrong, because [in the ILO] the governmental overshadows or replaces the economic and political functioning of peoples through voluntary associations. . . . American labor . . . does not care to tie itself up in such an organization merely for what would tend to give . . . an undesirable, an overshadowing and a fictitious importance to wholly secondary governmental acts."[7]

It is doubtful that most members of American labor who knew of the ILO's existence shared Woll's perspective. William Green, who beat out Woll for Gompers's old job, did not have much time for the ILO, but refrained from criticizing it. The next generation of labor leaders were prepared to go further in building contacts. The AFL sent an unofficial representative to the ILO in 1925 to explore cooperative efforts. In 1928, John Walker, president of the Illinois Federation of Labor and a member of the League of Nations Association, attended the ILO annual conference. But in a decade with huge membership declines and in a country obsessed with going its own way in the world economy, labor faced more pressing concerns than the ILO.[8]

Empirical Experience with Economic Decline

While American labor had more important concerns than ILO membership during the 1920s, the dislocations of some workers in the era, which intensified during the Great Depression of the 1930s, motivated some creative political leaders and others in the American elite to rediscover the organization after 1930. That rediscovery resulted from a complex set of policy experiments that were designed to address the decline of old industrial centers, especially in the first home of textile manufacturing in New England.

The rapidity of the shift in the fortunes of New England textiles may have been responsible for the creativity of its policy makers. Within a half-

dozen years between 1917 and 1923, communities experienced unprecedented productivity demands and then a near collapse of the market.
During the war, profits soared. Consistent with the spirit of wartime unity,
formerly antilabor textile firms accepted union representation for textile
workers and increased their wages.[9] Even in 1919, when much of the
country experienced an industrial crisis, working conditions continued to
improve.

However, the prosperity only masked or delayed for a short time the
shock and disillusionment reflected in Senate rejection of the Versailles
Treaty. For New England textiles the last boom ended. By the beginning
of 1921, at companies such as Amoskeag Manufacturing, the world's
largest textile mill, in Manchester, New Hampshire, work-week reductions followed piece rate cuts of up to 22.5 percent.[10] Meanwhile, the
plant's managers increased the number of looms that each worker ran, ad-
versely affecting product quality as well as employee morale. The corporation's grievance procedure revealed that one-third of the formal
complaints were about declining quality. However, management worried
more about profits than quality or workers.[11] In 1922, it also had to contend
with a ten-month strike involving over twelve thousand workers that shattered the balance at Amoskeag.[12]

The postwar labor disputes in Manchester came to the attention of
political leaders in the state, particularly a young war hero, John Winant.
In the next dozen years he experimented to find a solution to the problems
of Manchester and similar communities. Those experiments took him
from Concord to Geneva, from state government leadership to the ILO.[13]

Born in New York of well-to-do parents, Winant appeared an unlikely defender of the working class. He came to New Hampshire as a
youth to attend the exclusive St. Paul's School in Concord. Then he left
for Princeton, where he immersed himself in Ruskin, Dickens, and the
English Christian Socialists. He later accepted a standing offer from the
rector at St. Paul's to join the faculty, returning to Concord in time to participate in the Bull Moose campaign. Elected to the legislature in 1916, he
resigned to serve as a reconnaissance pilot in the world war. He had returned to the legislature in 1920 and teamed with former Governor Robert
Bass to create a progressive, prolabor faction in the Republican Party.[14]

Bass, who would later lead the Brookings Institution, had spent the
war as a planner with the U.S. Shipping Board and then under Felix
Frankfurter at the War Labor Policies Board. In these positions Bass
knew a number of individuals who helped nurture the ILO, not only
some of Frankfurter's staff, but also A. N. Hurley and Henry Robinson of

the Shipping Board. They had gone to Versailles to serve as the employer counterparts to Samuel Gompers on the Commission on International Labor Legislation.

By 1920, Bass and Winant had positioned themselves to launch a battle for the New Hampshire Republican leadership.[15] In 1922, partially in response to the failure of the old-guard Republicans to address the crisis in Manchester, New Hampshire voters shocked the establishment by electing a Democrat governor, Fred Brown. Winant and Bass advocated party support for basic labor standard legislation and won control in the bitter primary campaign of 1924, defeating a ticket led by another ex-"Bull Mooser," Frank Knox. A basic issue was support for a state eight-hour law like the one in Massachusetts. Bass and Winant understood the competitive problems inherent in such legislation. In December 1923, O. P. Hussey of the Phillips Rubber Company in Massachusetts warned Bass that the Massachusetts law "works an unfair hardship unless all States unite in such a program."[16] Winant acknowledged the validity of Hussey's concerns but advocated a solution using the example of the Consumers' League's proposed "child labor amendment" to the U.S. Constitution. In a statement sure to appeal to Yankee voters, he noted:

> It is common knowledge that the object of this amendment is to raise the standards of the South to a parity with those of New England. There are still a sufficient number of states unmindful of the abuses of child-labor to keep our national standard lower than that of many other nations. . . . We do demand that the children of the South as well as the children of the North be afforded an unfettered start and a fair chance in the race of life. We recognize that the first door leading to equality of opportunity opens into the country's school rooms and that equality of opportunity is the promise of American life.[17]

Such statements demonstrated that Winant was already moving well beyond state solutions to the downward pressure on New England wages and labor standards coming from the South. Of course, many of his supporters did not appreciate his larger vision.[18] In fact, his first term as governor was something of a disappointment, and he was defeated in the Republican primary when he sought reelection in 1926. However, his vision did receive some national recognition. By 1926, he was on the board of a variety of national reform groups, such as the National Child Welfare Conference, Irving Fisher's Stable Money Association, the National Recreation Congress, the Consumers' League, and the AALL.[19]

In addition, he specifically began work on multistate cooperation to address social problems through the intergovernmental New England Council.[20]

The difficulties at Amoskeag reflected the wider crisis in the textile industry throughout New England. That calamity initiated an empirical test of federal diversity in social policy at the dawn of an era of globalization in textile manufacturing. What began as a state and regional crisis taught lessons in modern economics to those who would see. One of the strengths of leaders like John Winant was an ability to make policy decisions on the basis of observed evidence, rather than ideology. Winant did not begin his tenure as governor in 1925, seeking to head the ILO. Within a decade he was observing the organization as a representative of the U.S., and a few years later he headed it, the first American to hold such an international position. These were not preplanned career steps, but neither were they chance promotions. Winant followed the evidence. And, the evidence clearly proceeded from the mills on the Merrimack through the American South and on to Geneva.

THE TEXTILE CRISIS

New England leaders in the early 1920s realized that the region's textile industry was in danger. First, there were short postwar declines in demand and profits. Then the companies cut wages and hours. Labor unrest followed. Fall River, Lowell, and New Bedford had problems just like Manchester.[21] New England's relative share of cotton consumption peaked in the mid-nineteenth century. A disturbing regional trend came after 1900, however, when absolute growth slowed and the region no longer processed half of the nation's total. When national production rose in the late 1920s, recovering from the postwar depression, New England's share stagnated or fell.

The textile industry in America did not decline. Rather, the New England textile industry experienced rapid decay while the Southern industry expanded. Data from North Carolina and Massachusetts clarify this change. In 1925, Massachusetts remained the leading textile state in the country, as it had for a century, with 96,182 workers. North Carolina had risen to second place with 84,139. Only two years later, North Carolina had 95,786 textile workers to Massachusetts's 90,875.[22] These were not temporary reversals. They continued throughout the twentieth century. By 1977, North Carolina had 219,100 textile workers, Massachusetts 21,400.[23]

Leaders such as Winant faced three related problems when observing their region's dramatic industrial decline and the simultaneous industrial revolution in the South. What caused such changes to take place? Were the two changes related? And, how could New England best respond? The answers to these questions led to renewed American interest in the international labor standards movement. While a number of factors explained the deindustrialization of New England and Southern industrial growth, generally the two trends seemed directly related in the textile industry. A number of factors contributed to the shift in production: ability to adopt technological advances,[24] willingness to use scientific management,[25] union penetration rates,[26] tax differentials, and labor standard variation.[27] Only the last two were primarily political.

In the previous generation, New England state governments adopted progressive policies sustained by the region's industrial leadership. Property taxes, including those on industrial facilities, rose to support the new government services. Taxes per spindle in Massachusetts nearly tripled during the progressive era. In contrast, the South generally had many fewer public services and less state and local taxation. In 1919, the average New England tax per textile spindle stood at about fifty-five cents, compared to thirty-five cents in the South. Once industrial decline set in, the northern textile manufacturers pleaded for relief. In 1929, the treasurer of Amoskeag Manufacturing Company appealed at a Manchester public meeting for reduced tax assessments. Fearing the consequences, the city cut the tax rate significantly. Of course, the treasurer failed to explain that all the cash the company was saving was being reinvested in the South.[28]

While there are different interpretations about which factors primarily caused the textile industry decline in New England, the decline itself could not be denied. Political leaders knew tax cuts meant reductions in public services. Their constituents wanted the services that defined the quality of life in New England, such as exceptional educational facilities. Some adjustment of taxes was possible, as in the case of Amoskeag in 1929, but New England did not wish to become the South, with poor public services and a less-provided-for pariah class, the segregated Afro-Americans. Consequently, responsive Yankee politicians turned to the one factor in production over which they had control—labor standards.

The New England states, especially Massachusetts, had a number of labor protections not found, at least as strictly, in the South. For example, the three southern New England states limited the work week to six days for youth up to sixteen years of age. Massachusetts limited work for adult women to nine hours per day and forty-eight hours per week. The comparable law in North Carolina permitted eleven hours per day and fifty-five hours per week. Georgia and South Carolina fully "liberated" their women by providing no such protection.[29] But the most important difference by region was in wage rates. While no government-mandated minimum wage laws existed in the U.S., except in California, wage rates differed markedly by region for a variety of factors, including the rate of unionization or the fear of it. In textiles, this led to a significant difference in the cost of mill operations in the two regions. New England productivity, or value added per worker, exceeded that in the South in the mid-1920s; yet, New England wage rates exceeded Southern rates more than the value added. Worst for New England firms, the differential between their wage rates and those of their Southern competitors increased from the prewar years down to the 1920s.[30]

Southern politicians faced some demand for labor standards, but they rejected any significant strengthening of their labor regulations. How could they do that, but not their New England counterparts? Enough interest groups supporting improved standards functioned in New England that some politicians built their careers by identifying with the groups' concerns. Unlike the South, New England had a competitive political system. While Democrats seldom won office, they did possess a power base, especially in the immigrant wards of urban centers; and they could win statewide office using labor standards as an issue. Democratic gubernatorial candidate Fred Brown had done just that in 1922 during the textile strike in Manchester. During the strikes in the 1920s, in the four coastal New England states from New Hampshire to Connecticut the average Republican vote fell from 64 percent in 1920 to just under 50 percent in 1922. Republicans lost the Rhode Island governorship as well as the one in New Hampshire.[31] Therefore, the dominant party sought candidates who could undermine the Democratic threat, men like John Winant. This response supports the theory that the more competitive party system of New England made government more responsive to the less privileged classes.[32]

New Hampshire Republicans were so desperate to demonstrate their concern with labor issues at the start of the Great Depression that they welcomed back Winant as governor, and they supported breaking the two-consecutive-term rule in 1932 by reelecting him. During the four years of his consecutive terms, Winant introduced a "little New Deal" to New Hampshire, establishing state aid to mothers and children, financial guarantees to bankrupt local governments, and centralized poor relief. Winant's "new deal" consciously attempted to address the labor standards problem. As one student of Winant's career said, "For a long time, Governor Winant sought to correct the wide variation in protective labor standards in the different states. In these states, contiguous in territory, with similar industrial developments, and with frequent interchange of workers across their borders, there were divergent labor laws affording various degrees of protection to labor and industry. Such a condition, Winant realized, hampered all fair programs and humane standards."[33]

The depression furnished the opportunity in the exceptional American political system to respond to these concerns. Supporters of interstate labor standards had long before established a network to exchange thoughts through the AALL. Like other empirical leaders, Winant's role in the interstate coordination movement evolved as he tried to implement New Hampshire reforms and work with colleagues from outside the state. He demonstrated during this evolution a characteristic that made both him and Franklin Roosevelt effective: the absence of a firm ideology. Early in his administration, Winant bought into an idea promoted by a local engineer called the New Hampshire Plan. He proposed to solve the unemployment crisis by getting workers and employers to agree to reduce hours of work and share labor. The plan required workers to cut hours by 10 percent while employers cut wages by 3 to 6 percent. The employers could use the money saved to hire additional workers. Reflecting succinctly both his empiricism and idealism, Winant endorsed the plan, saying, "It is not a cure-all, it is simply a constructive program. . . . It can be as progressive as scientific management, as conservative as an arithmetical formula, and as humane as the Golden Rule."[34] Although unsuccessful, it remained an interesting experiment. Meanwhile, Winant pushed conventional labor standard reforms, especially a minimum wage law, through the legislative process.

INTERSTATE COMPACTS

In the minimum wage battle and in other relief and reform campaigns, Winant relied on New Hampshire partisans and on an extensive network of scholars, activists, public administrators, and fellow politicians outside of New Hampshire. He especially trusted scholars linked to the AALL and the Consumers' League. They tapped into a rich mine of information previously collected on interstate cooperation and uniformity in law. As early as 1889, the American Bar Association had appointed a committee to study interstate legal uniformity, and in the following year New York passed legislation to appoint commissioners to seek the same goal. Beginning in 1892, the annual Conference of Commissioners on Uniform State Laws met at the site of the ABA convention. By 1912, all the states sent representatives to the conference. Three years earlier the Bar Association had drafted a common child labor law as a way of launching the uniformity process in labor legislation. That same year, Ernest Freund of the University of Chicago Law School and president of the Illinois AALL affiliate published a study in *The Survey* alerting readers to the potential of the "interstate compact" wording in the Constitution.[35] Samuel Lindsay explored the idea further in an article called "Reciprocal Legislation." He emphasized that the states could create common laws to solve social problems when the courts prevented Congress from passing a federal law on the subject.[36]

Various intergovernmental organizations emerged to promote the movement. For example, in 1926, interested officials founded the American Legislators' Association. Closer to the textile problems of New Hampshire, Robert Bass helped create the New England Council in 1912 to address the common economic concerns of the region. Winant described the council as "an example of a useful type of regional organization. . . . Through it the six governors are called together frequently . . . to discuss problems that affect the people of their states." He warned, however:

> We are too prone to imagine that a form of government set up more than a century ago will, without any effort on our part, automatically meet all the changes that have taken place in social and economic conditions. . . . If you want to hand on to posterity more than debt, if you want to maintain the American ideal of government, it will be necessary to do something about this problem of efficiency and coordination and cooperation, this problem of the mechanics of government.[37]

While Winant was not the original or leading thinker on interstate cooperation, he and Bass supplied key political leadership to the effort and were among the first to try to move from theory to practice, and from region to nation and beyond. They began with the New England Council. Then Winant dispatched staff to national groups, such as the Conference of Government Labor Officials.

Others also sponsored interstate meetings to address the labor standards problems in America's industrial heartland. New York Governor Franklin Roosevelt called an informal conference of governors to discuss unemployment, which Winant attended along with the governors of Ohio, Pennsylvania, New Jersey, and other New England states. University of

Chicago economist Paul Douglas provided the expert leadership, while FDR served as host. At that meeting, FDR and Winant began a personal acquaintance that soon blossomed. A few months later, Pennsylvania Governor Gifford Pinchot hosted the Eastern Interstate Conference on Labor Legislation, which adopted a number of specific suggestions for common laws on worker's compensation, child labor, and occupational health. After a delay during the election campaigns of 1932, Governor Joseph Ely of Massachusetts sponsored the next meeting in January 1933.[38]

The Boston meeting in 1933 marked a watershed in the movement in a number of ways. First, Winant took advantage of one of the darkest moments of the Depression to push through a draft interstate compact on minimum wages, the first specific outcome from the gatherings. Second, the meeting brought together officials who would play key American roles in the International Labor Organization. The opening speaker was Edwin Smith, holder of Carroll Wright's old position as Massachusetts commissioner of labor and industry. Six months later, Smith would attend the 1933 annual ILO meeting in Geneva as one of the four unofficial American delegates. At the Boston meeting, Smith explained that the purpose of the interstate conference was "to consider the possibility of United States action to bring about greater uniformity in the laws governing the hours of employment of women and minors." Using the AALL approach, he reminded the governors that the recommendations were "based on the study and experience of experts."[39] He was followed on the podium by Felix Frankfurter, then of Harvard Law School, and still a Consumers' League attorney and former supervisor of the international labor law study for the Inquiry. Amy Hewes of Mount Holyoke spoke after Frankfurter. Also a member of the AALL, she had conducted labor law research for Frankfurter in preparing the ILO constitution. Hewes discussed her evaluation of the effectiveness of the voluntary Massachusetts minimum wage law. Then Frances Perkins addressed the meeting. Still the New York industrial commissioner, she soon would be the secretary of labor who would lead the U.S. into the ILO. The meeting concluded with Henry Dennison, a Massachusetts manufacturer, New England Power executive, and leader of the Chamber of Commerce of the United States. Dennison, who participated in a variety of labor standard activities, would be the U.S. employer delegate to the ILO from the late 1930s until 1944.[40]

With these colleagues, Winant finalized his strategy to get New Hampshire to pass a minimum wage law that would spark a national standardization drive. New York's new governor, Herbert Lehman, pushed a similar bill through his legislature. Perkins dispatched future ILO delegate Mary Anderson from the Women's Bureau to supply Winant with information on model laws. She also assigned another future ILO delegate, Grace Abbott, to advertise among other governors the anticipated success in New Hampshire. Winant's minimum wage coordinator, Ethel Johnson, whom he recruited from the Massachusetts minimum wage office, would later be his aide at the ILO and head of the ILO's Washington office during World War II. It is not coincidental that only one of the identified speakers at the Boston interstate conference and only one of the people working on the New Hampshire minimum wage law promotion did not play a role in either creating the ILO or representing the United States in Geneva.

In April, the strategy to utilize the New York and New Hampshire minimum wage laws to build a national ratification effort was in place, and both legislatures cooperated. The New Hampshire Senate passed the law unanimously. Winant signed it on April 26, 1933. The passage of a New York minimum wage law provided FDR with an excuse to send telegrams on April 11 to all the governors east of the Mississippi and north of the Potomac, plus the governors of Alabama and North Carolina, urging similar action. In early May, Abbott sent a new wave of letters announcing the New Hampshire act. In Massachusetts, Edwin Smith, wrote Perkins a few weeks before leaving for Geneva, saying, "I feel that by next fall when the returns from the New York and New Hampshire experience begin to come in . . . that the chances for successfully putting through a [mandatory] minimum wage law here will be much better."[41] Others agreed, and over the winter most of the remaining northeastern states passed some minimum wage legislation. Then on May 29, 1934, commissioners from those states met in Concord and signed an interstate compact on the minimum wage.[42]

Despite this triumph, Winant and other politicians engaged in the interstate compact effort could not long remain oblivious to two important lessons from this approach. First, it was time-consuming regulating working conditions through interstate compacts. More important, the compacts would be useless if not all states signed on to an agreement. The minimum wage compact of 1934, after several years of extensive preparatory work and the support of the national administration, only included states with relatively high wage rates. North Carolina and Alabama, specifically targeted for inclusion in the compact, did not sign on, nor did other southern states.

Given these problems, Winant and Bass, working through Bass's new organization, the Brookings Institution, tried to improve the mechanism for interstate cooperation. They promoted the merger of intergovernmental interest groups, particularly the Interstate Reference Service and the American Legislators' Association into the Council of State Governments. Winant became its first president in 1934. Meanwhile, Frances Perkins invited national labor standards interest groups to a conference on labor standards in the fall of 1934. That conference expected representatives of labor, the churches, and women's groups to facilitate follow-up meetings. One committee of the conference planned a strategy for ratification of the Child Labor Amendment. Another, including a representative of the AFL, National Catholic Welfare Conference, National Consumers' League, National League of Women Voters, and the National Federation of Business and Professional Women's Clubs, focused on state labor legislation. Meeting in the heart of the opposition, they held their second conference in Asheville, North Carolina, in October 1935.[43] Yet, even with extensive promotion eight states did not attend.[44] Another approach seemed necessary, and for a time this appeared to lie in corporatism.

CORPORATISM

Since the beginning of the progressive era, a number of leaders of government, business, labor, churches, and academic institutions proposed voluntary or private contractual methods to control the worst features of laissez-faire capitalism. To a great extent the sharp divisions between Woodrow Wilson and Theodore Roosevelt in 1912 originated in a debate about the merits of corporatism as an alternative to renewal of laissez-faire. Wilson defended enforcement of laws to assure fair opportunity in a capitalist economy.[45] Roosevelt, believing a return to simple laissez-faire was neither possible nor desirable, endorsed government promotion of a community where business and labor cooperated for mutual benefit. Ironically, a number of Wilson's actual reforms advanced Roosevelt's approach, such as the creation of the Federal Reserve, which relinquished banking regulation to a board of bankers isolated from politics. During the 1920s Herbert Hoover, as secretary of commerce, promoted "associationalist" or "corporatist" business policies. Associationalists urged corporations to collaborate in fields ranging from product design to the provision of employee benefits, in order to ameliorate the worst features of laissez-faire. The most extreme forms of this effort, such as the establishment of open price associations, resulted in adverse court decisions.[46] But cooperative price setting seemed extreme even to some advocates of corporatism.

Others proposed that business cooperation be limited to the inhumane and wasteful features of capitalism. Future ILO delegate Henry Dennison, of the U.S. Chamber of Commerce, worked for years to develop a legally acceptable method of restraining competition. While some scholars have emphasized Dennison's depression-era interest in constructing a new economic order, he had been working with Samuel Lindsay and others in the labor standards movement to define that order for some time. In 1922, he wrote an essay for an issue of *The Annals* focusing on industrial relations and the churches, edited by F. Ernest Johnson of the Federal Council of Churches and John Ryan of the National Catholic Welfare Conference and the AALL.[47] Dennison explained his philosophy of laissez-faire within a democracy as follows:

> It is admitted as a basic theory in all democratic communities that there are somewhere limits to the freedom with which one can control his own property, bounds beyond which he cannot "do what he likes with his own," though the variety of its definite applications obscures the basic unity. Ordinarily we hear that every man's right is to do as he pleases with his own as long as he does not interfere with the rights of others. . . . At best this can cover only the simplest situations and can give no help where rights conflict or where a democratic society must decide to what extent it will guard ownership and protect its transfer. A Christian society which does not go further than this would warrant the few who own material wealth in withholding it to the beggary or death of the rest.[48]

In the same issue of *The Annals*, Sam Lewisohn, of Adolph Lewisohn and Sons, and a predecessor of Dennison as U.S. employer delegate to the ILO, wrote "The Employers' Responsibility to the Community,"[49] and Patrick Callahan, of Louisville Varnish, a good friend of Gifford Pinchot, authored "An Employer's View of the Church's Function in Industry." Callahan placed the corporatist economic philosophy of the 1920s in its historical context, reminding readers:

> Formerly . . . [i]ndustry, we thought, should be free; free not only as a whole, but in all its functions and all its factors. Competition should be free; bargaining should be free; above all, labor should be free. From the greatest to the least let each run his race—"and the de'il take the hindmost." That was our philosophy in the last century. It was the extreme individualism of Herbert Spencer applied to economics, with the doctrine

of the survival of the fittest held up as the last word in theory. . . . Modern industry was largely built on the basis of that philosophy and, needless to say, it has been in numerous instances a grim tragedy.

That is all changed now. The world has lost sympathy with the individualistic idea. . . .[W]e can be sure that the day of unrestricted competition, of unlimited exploitation, of non-interference and *laissez-faire*, is a thing of the past.[50]

W. E. Hotchkiss, an official of one of the new trade associations in the garment industry, described the role of trade associations in implementing the new economic philosophy. The clothing trade association had "a committee to speak for all employers of the market in matters of concern to more than an individual house. . . . The arrangement here briefly sketched has frequently been referred to as industrial government."[51] Samuel Lindsay summarized the consequences of associationalism. "Such cooperation may directly affect unit costs of production and indirectly affect every other economic factor entering into or flowing from the production of economic goods."[52]

In addition to this academic perspective, *The Annals* editors found labor, religious, and social welfare leaders to comment upon the ideas of Dennison, Lewisohn, and Hotchkiss. The Roman Catholic clerics related the new corporatism to the ideas of Leo XIII. Patrick Callahan had praised *Rerum Novarum*, and three of *The Annals* writers pursued such endorsement into a defense of medieval "guild principles." As Joseph Husslein, S.J., editor of *America*, said,

> In carefully studying the statutes of a vast number of medieval guilds, nothing impressed me more strikingly than the paramount consideration everywhere given by them to the public good, and the constant subordination to this of both personal and group interests on the part of guildsmen. . . .
>
> [I]n all [their] regulations, approved by public authorities and firmly enforced by guild courts and officials . . . [t]hey possessed the intelligence to understand that after all they themselves constituted the bulk of the community, and that in safeguarding just prices, fair wages, true weights and measures, and qualities of goods they were ultimately promoting their own interests.[53]

Father Raymond McGowan, John Ryan's assistant and eventual successor at the National Catholic Welfare Conference, held that the church endorsed the approach adopted by Husslein. Referring to Catholic social critics of the last century, like Bishop Ketteler, McGowan pointed out that Catholics had to look back no further than 1919 to find clear guidance on the matter. Immediately after the end of the war, the American bishops issued a detailed *Program of Social Reconstruction* and a follow-up pastoral letter to all Catholics. McGowan asserted, "[These] insist upon a sound and deep reform of private ownership along the lines of the guild system of the Middle Ages."

Protestant and Jewish clergy joined in the fundamental critique of laissez-faire, if with more congregational differences. Rabbi Sidney Goldstein stated explicitly, "We do not admit that the law of supply and demand is the last word in business and industry. It leads to unjust prices and to exploitation. Judaism does not accept the doctrine of competition. It leads to unnecessary and unworthy struggle and strife and suffering in human relationships."[54] F. Ernest Johnson of the Federal Council, who co-edited *The Annals* religious issue with Father Ryan, noted the diverse congregational structure of Protestantism, which also applied to Judaism, as a barrier to simple economic policy making. Nonetheless, during the war, the council produced its statement on *The Church and Industrial Reconstruction*, which among other provisions asked "employers to give new recognition to the spiritual worth of their employees and particularly to the principal of collective bargaining and the sharing of management in industry."[55]

All contributors to *The Annals* issue, except Florence Kelley, detected in the new corporatist thinking a hopeful sign that labor standards might arise from "industrial government." Kelley, appalled by the recent Supreme Court decision overturning the second federal child labor law, could not envision business volunteering to "pay its full costs" by giving workers a living wage and eliminating child labor. Given her emphasis upon empirical examination, the rhetoric of the early 1920s did not blind the Consumers' League director to reality. Speaking like a prophet, she mocked Commerce Secretary Hoover for recommending "to the National Conference of Social Work . . . on June 27, 1922, that they make one more combined effort to deal with child labor state by state. . . . This idea is utterly immoral and wrong. The children according to this, are to go back to their slavery while our nation makes further effort to do the impossible, — to assure to them the equal protection of the law under forty-eight divergent legislatures."[56] Kelley's proposal for a constitutional amendment on child labor represented a minority position in the 1920s. As she asked rhetorically, "Who have helped except the American Association for Labor

Legislation, the Consumers' League, the Child-Labor Committee, and the labor organizations?"[57]

When the Child Labor Amendment went to the states two years later, Kelley proved correct. Enough church leaders came down on the side of voluntarism that the industrialists and agricultural opponents to child protection carried the day. America's constitutional structure not only restrained reform, its leaders would not support amending its constitution even for such an obvious good as abolishing child labor. For Samuel Lindsay, this experience confirmed that only interstate cooperation or corporatism would work. In 1934 Lindsay concluded, "[I]n America the expanding spirit of individual liberty, self-reliance, and the ability of the individual to achieve satisfactory results alone or at least locally in cooperation with his immediate neighbors are factors that have much more to do with the backwardness and meager character of American social legislation than the form of government or the legal and constitutional limitations."[58]

THE NRA

When Lindsay wrote his assessment, the movement to standardize American labor protections through corporatism welcomed the New Deal's National Industrial Recovery Act (NIRA) and the resulting National Recovery Administration (NRA). While some labor standards advocates were beginning to champion other approaches, many had great, if brief, hope in the NRA. When James Shotwell assembled the key documents for his history of the ILO in 1934, he included the text of the NIRA. And in his essay in the Shotwell book, Samuel Lindsay called the NRA "a milestone of the first importance in the history of American legislation."[59]

The NIRA marked the culmination of the previous decade's efforts to implement a corporatist solution to America's economic problems. It fostered a voluntary structure of corporate cooperation sufficiently regulated by the federal government to avoid antitrust problems. The NIRA specifically forbade any practices that violated standards set by the Federal Trade Commission. Furthermore, it gave the president authority to recognize trade groups that could establish codes of fair competition and set standards for an industry. This type of government involvement in private planning fit within the voluntarist tradition. Matthew Woll, who would serve as an AFL delegate to the ILO and who was acting president of the

National Civic Federation in the early 1930s, endorsed the NRA concept in the voluntarist spirit of Samuel Gompers because it had minimal government intervention.[60] Labor considered Section Seven of the law ideal because it defined union rights and then committed the president to afford "every opportunity to employers and employees in any trade or industry . . . to establish by mutual agreement, the standards as to the maximum hours of labor, minimum rates of pay, and such other conditions of employment as may be necessary."[61] With the passage of the NIRA, the difficult task of developing codes for each of over five hundred basic industries began. Because of the long-term crisis in the cotton textile industry, hearings on its code were scheduled as soon as possible. They began a week after the NRA started operation in late June 1933. Several labor issues were expected to complicate the standard development practices. On the first day of hearings, South Carolina Senator James F. Byrnes called for a labor management investigatory board to police the "stretch-out," the process of speeding up machines or making workers run more machines than normal. He correctly warned that with the stretch-out employers could agree to reduce hours of operation and achieve old levels of production, thus frustrating the entire NRA goal. His proposal won quick acceptance by NRA administrators. The second day of hearings was expected to be volatile, since the AFL would testify. Industry representatives already had agreed to minimum wage and other standards, including a minimum wage differential between North and South. Northerners made an effort to get uniformity. Frederick Dumaine of Amoskeag called for major change in the standards, sounding something like a labor leader rather than an owner. He warned:

> Ruthless competition has forced wage rates out of all reason and carried living conditions of workers below American standards. . . .
>
> Unbridled competition has brought this trade to the verge of bankruptcy, destroying 7 million odd spindles with property losses approximating 140 million dollars and taken employment from about 60 thousand persons. . . . It has proven the theory that competition is the life of trade to be fallacy and that in fact unrestricted competition is death to trade. . . .
>
> I'm heartily in accord with the principle here being considered and differ with certain details of the measure's execution.
>
> First—it would be better to have one national shift. . . .
>
> Unless there is rigid control of machinery output and expansion, the whole object of this Act is defeated.

Representing a concern existing for a century and employing some 8,000 workers, I solemnly protest the proposed differential in wages by district. The industry is located in a common country, there should be no difference because of imaginary lines or between states and communities. . . .

With no desire to irritate our very good southern friends, I'm constrained to say no fair person will object to a code providing equally for the worker, the owner and the consumer.[62]

While Dumaine did not achieve all his goals, the differential imposed on the industry by the cotton textile code assisted the North.[63] Leaders of the labor standards movement, like Winant, fully backed the NRA. He quickly instituted state actions to bring New Hampshire into compliance.[64] Labor and church leaders also recognized the NRA as an improvement over predepression laissez-faire.[65] Andrew Desfosses, a young worker at Amoskeag in 1933, recalled that the NRA "cut our hours from fifty-four to forty . . . and increased wages . . . so it was quite an improvement."[66] However, soon problems appeared.

The difficulties surfaced in the summer 1934. Companies resisted dealing with the growing United Textile Workers (UTW), they cheated on the wage code, and they imposed the "stretch-out." The union called a strike for September 1, 1934.[67] That day, the UTW claimed, three hundred thousand textile workers stayed home. Conditions in textile communities in New England and the South quickly deteriorated. Several workers in the South were killed by police. In Georgia, the National Guard set up "a concentration camp" for arrested strikers. In Rhode Island, there were clashes between troops and strikers. On September 5, FDR acted to stop the violence.

He appointed a special mediation board chaired by Winant. On September 17, the board announced a four-point agreement: the appointment of a new Textile Labor Relations Board to serve as neutral arbiter of labor issues; a freeze on the stretch-out; the termination of the strike and reemployment of strikers; and the initiation of two studies to help the TLRB do its job. The two studies were classic examples of the empirical methodology favored by progressives like Winant and his associates in the Consumers' League.[68]

Unfortunately, the textile industry did not feel bound by the settlement. When the closed mills reopened, owners often discriminated against union members. The stretch-out continued, and no one implemented the findings of the studies. Winant had been appointed to the board because he recently had negotiated a successful end to a strike at

Amoskeag; but, in Manchester, he had dealt directly with the worker representatives and Dumaine's staff. Converting that strategy to the national level, where the personal contact was impossible, removed the essential component of success. When the workers returned to the mills in late September, they knew they had lost under the Winant settlement.

Winant learned much from the experience about the weaknesses, if not the failure, of the NRA. He received innumerable letters and telegrams reporting violations of the spirit of the settlement. One South Carolinian wrote, "it seems to be an evident fact that to beet [*sic*] the agreement of the Textile Cod [*sic*], why that they did cahnge [*sic*] Gearing and speading [*sic*] pullys [*sic*], so as to make the machine preduce [*sic*] as much in 8 hours as the same machine prducing [*sic*] before the recovery act."[69] On September 7 an anonymous woman worker in Lawrence, Massachusetts, reported the NRA had failed to increase employment because "[W]orkers are required to do the work of two or three people. *I know*, because I have been doing two men's work for about two years and making less than one man's pay, and I am breaking under the strain. Every woman who works beside me has been doing the same as I . . . each one wishing she could find something else to do and so get away from the slavery."[70] The general manager of a company claiming to comply with the NRA code complained, "We represent 520 employees of the Pyramid Fabrics Inc. . . . We have the most efficient and best managed mill in this section. We know that our mill cannot compete with the chiselling conditions existing in several mills in this locality. . . . Pyramid has no stretchout system."[71]

Reading such communications could not help but undermine confidence in corporatism as a solution to labor standards problems. In a widely quoted opinion, President Roosevelt predicted, "It is probably true that 90 percent of the cotton manufacturers would agree to eliminate starvation wages, would agree to stop long hours of employment, would agree to stop child labor, would agree to prevent an overproduction that would result in unsalable surpluses. But . . . [t]he unfair 10 percent could produce goods so cheaply that the fair 90 percent would be compelled to meet the unfair conditions."[72] Whatever the accuracy of these percentages, the NRA and strike settlement failed to establish a mechanism sufficiently powerful to control the behavior of the "unfair" mills. The mediation board, despite positive public response to its work, could not force the industry to reform. Clearly, industrial government under the NRA had failed. The Supreme Court decision in the *Schecter* case, ruling the NRA unconstitutional, could be welcomed as an appropriate response to the experiment with corporatism.[73]

Joining the ILO

Given the difficulties with interstate compacts and the failure of the NRA, one more alternative existed that could overcome state diversity in labor standards: the ILO. While working on reciprocal state legislation in 1927, Joseph Chamberlain of Columbia University suggested that supporters of labor legislation give attention to the ILO. He reviewed a number of Supreme Court decisions in which treaties gave the U.S. government powers otherwise reserved for the states. He concluded, "If it is within the scope of the treaty power for the United States to enter into a Labor Convention, such a convention will over-ride the laws of any state to the contrary. Treaties have frequently had the effect of over-riding state legislation in fields which without the treaty congress could not have entered."[74] He referred especially to *Missouri v. Holland*, in which the Court upheld in 1920 the constitutionality of federal regulation of migratory birds. Such regulation had been declared unconstitutional earlier, but the courts upheld it, following a 1916 treaty with Britain. If a treaty could change the status of waterfowl regulation, it could do the same for federal labor standards. Consequently, the academic network that long had supported international labor standards inaugurated work to explain what had become obvious to Winant, Frances Perkins, and others seeking national standards.

In the early years of the Great Depression, the ILO underwent three fundamental changes that made it more appealing to Americans. First, the ILO committed itself to an agenda to reduce unemployment and encourage relief for those out of work. This marked a fundamental departure from the simple codification of labor standards and employment research of the first decade. Second, it lost its first director with the sudden death of Albert Thomas. While his demise deprived the organization of a tireless supporter of free labor, in many ways it eased the way for American participation. His replacement, Harold Butler, the quintessential British civil servant, appeared less foreign to Americans than a bearded French socialist. More important, Butler had maintained crucial acquaintances with key Americans, including Franklin Roosevelt. Third, the Hoover Administration, after some embarrassing missteps, inaugurated American contact with the ILO.

Throughout the Harding and Coolidge Administrations, the U.S. had gone to great lengths to avoid the slightest contact with the ILO. In an era when the U.S. could not bring itself to join even the World Court, the administration response to the ILO was to be expected. While there existed some hope that Hoover would modify the "isolationism" of his predecessors, he did not alter ILO policy during his first two years in office, despite a vigorous letter-writing campaign by prominent American ILO backers. The next three years demonstrated that mass campaigns, such as the letter-writing effort, worked less well than did bureaucratic maneuvering to influence political leaders.

In 1930, Harold Butler visited the U.S. and met with DOL officials, including Mary Anderson of the Women's Bureau and Grace Abbott of the Children's Bureau. Then in 1931 Butler sent his assistant, E. J. Phelan, to the U.S. to participate in a University of Chicago conference on unemployment and world problems. Meanwhile, the American consul in Geneva, Prentiss Gilbert, completed a report on the ILO that concluded it was a genuinely objective organization, not a political one. The administration responded slowly to these overtures. It began by authorizing Mary Anderson, who was in Europe for other business, to attend the 1931 ILO annual conference as an observer. Although at the last minute the administration withdrew permission, the flap probably assured U.S. participation the next year.

With Thomas gone and the ILO responsive to American concern with soaring unemployment, the administration relented in 1932 and selected a full but unofficial delegation: the Massachusetts commissioner of labor and a University of Minnesota professor represented the government; Edward Filene, business, and an AFL officer, labor. Still the U.S. was not a member of the ILO. The growing interest, however, stirred the AALL, Consumers' League, various church groups, and the academics at Columbia University to launch a concerted effort to achieve full membership. Even the pope cooperated with the lobbying effort in 1931 by issuing an encyclical on the fortieth anniversary of *Rerum Novarum*, affirming that the ILO consciously followed Christian social policy. The National Catholic Welfare Conference, under Consumers' League Vice President John Ryan, advertised this endorsement and an awareness of the "International Aspects of Unemployment."[75] James Myers of the Federal Council of Churches attended the 1932 ILO conference and the council began to campaign actively for U.S. membership.

The women's social welfare network became actively involved when the ILO created a Commission on Women's Work in 1932. Mary Anderson of the Department of Labor served as an official appointee, joined by Burnita Matthews of the National Association of Women Lawyers, Elizabeth Morrissy of the Catholic Conference of Industrial Problems, Ethel Smith of the National Women's Trade Union League, and Mary van Kleeck of the Russell Sage Foundation. While each of these women brought major constituencies into support of the ILO, the crucial step was the appointment of Anderson.[76]

THE NEW DEAL

Now the network of elite policy makers, driven by the empirical experience of failed alternatives to national labor legislation, moved into high gear to force an unprecedented decision to abandon unilateralism and to join an international organization affiliated with the League of Nations. After the election of President Roosevelt, the American Academy of Political and Social Science invited Alice Cheyney, the ILO's Washington office manager, to edit an issue of *The Annals* on the International Labor Organization. Cheyney had Joseph Chamberlain author the piece on "Legislation in a Changing Economic World," which explicitly linked the need for interstate uniform standards of labor legislation with the work and purposes of the ILO. Cheyney herself had already written on the topic, producing in 1930 under ILO auspices a comprehensive comparison of American state labor laws and ILO conventions. Lest readers become bored with the specialized essays in *The Annals*, Cheyney got James Shotwell to compose an essay on "The International Labor Organization as an Alternative to Violent Revolution."[77] Cheyney herself wrote a shortened version of her 1930 "Comparison of [ILO] Convention Provisions with Labor Legislation in the United States."[78] She found ILO conventions not only forced laggard states to improve labor standards but also raised living standards, creating more consumers. As she said:

> It is commonly assumed that the efforts of the International Labor Organization to effect improvement in working conditions are of only sympathetic interest to the United States. The general belief is that our working conditions are so far superior to those of other nations that any standards internationally applicable will necessarily be lower than our own.
> Comparison of the standards set by our labor laws with those defined in international labor conventions does not confirm this assumption.[79]

She then reviewed types of labor standards, from child labor restrictions through regulations of hours of work, days of rest, forced labor, immigrant labor, minimum wages, employment agencies, unemployment insurance, maternity insurance, and occupational health. She appealed to business, noting two benefits of the ILO. "By requiring the 'foreign' producer to meet certain conditions and assume certain financial burdens, it whittles away at whatever comparative advantage he may have . . . By raising the standard of living . . . , it increases the potential market . . . for the American exporter."[80]

To test the last point, the Rockefeller Foundation earlier dispatched Carl J. Ratzlaff of Harvard to Europe to investigate the impact of ILO labor standards. In 1932 in *The American Economic Review*, he confirmed that ILO conventions did help raise standards in a number of countries. He concluded that therefore the U.S. should participate in the organization.[81] As with *The Annals*, this evidence gave important academic legitimacy to the ILO within the American elite. Finally, James Shotwell completed work on his more substantial two-volume history of *The Origins of the International Labor Organization*. Even before its publication in 1934, Shotwell toured Washington offices to drop off copies of the proofs, overwhelming the recipients with ILO information.

Despite economic crisis and the extensive lobbying by academics, social welfare leaders, and clergy, the American political system did not move quickly or directly to join the ILO. When the administration decided to join in 1934, two years after Hoover first sent unofficial delegates to Geneva, it employed subterfuge to win congressional approval, waiting until the end of the 1934 session. After that victory, FDR delayed requesting an appropriation to support membership. Archisolationist Congressman George Tinkham of Boston fumed:

> [T]his is the hour and this is the time, as we near adjournment in confusion, when legislation is reported to this House which never would be reported if due deliberation could be given it. It is the spawning hour for the propagation of proposals fostered by corruption, by special interests, by foreign intrigue, and by conspirators against the public weal. . . . [T]his resolution is not before the House in accordance with a fair interpretation of the rules. . . . There was no notification of members of the Committee on Foreign Affairs that the resolution was to be considered, a quorum was not present when the resolution was reported, and no witness appeared before the committee.
>
>   A letter signed by the Secretary of Labor . . . was sent to the committee. . . . It contains this wholly false statement: "The organization—" wrote Miss Perkins, referring to the International Labor Organization— "is not even now an integral part of the League of Nations."[82]

TABLE 3.2.   House Vote on ILO Membership

	Yes		No		Abstain	
Place	Dem.	Rep.	Dem.	Rep.	Dem.	Rep.
Connecticut	1	—	1	4	—	—
Massachusetts	2	—	2	7	1	3
New Hampshire	1	—	—	1	—	—
Rhode Island	1	—	1	—	—	—
(subtotal)	5	—	4	12	1	3
Nation	219	13	27	79	64	23

Source: Congressional Record, June 16, 1934, 12241.

The Tinkham speech, while given by one of the most eccentric legislators, identified several facts about the policy process in America.[83] First, opposition to international collaboration, even on economic issues, could be a potent force in the country. If Americans tended to fear too much domestic government, isolationists realized they could be terrified by international government. Second, as Tinkham perceived, the best way to overcome the exceptional fear of world government was to bypass the democratic process. With undisciplined parties and the separation of powers, the executive could not count on victory in such matters. Third, while there does not appear to have been either corruption or conscious conspiracy against the public weal in the ILO membership drive, clearly there was extensive special interest lobbying and not a little foreign intrigue. The academics, foundations, clergy, and social welfare advocates who lobbied for the ILO from 1919 to 1934 did not receive their backing from the mass of Americans; in fact, many had no interest in starting a mass movement. So, yes, narrow interests had prevailed, but they were interests seeking the public good. Likewise there was foreign intrigue, even if by such benign figures as Harold Butler and the pope.

Of course, Congressman Tinkham knew he would lose. Bypassing the hearing and deliberation process works for necessary but not popular decisions. A few minutes after Tinkham's speech, the House voted, with

233 supporting membership, 109 opposed, and 88 abstaining. While only 27 Democrats voted against membership, 64 abstained. Among Republicans, the vote went overwhelmingly against the ILO, with only 13 voting for membership and 79 opposing. Given that the ILO most likely would protect northern industrial workers threatened by low-cost foreign competition, the geographic pattern of support demonstrated party loyalty to be more significant than regional interest. The rural and especially the southern states gave the resolution most of its support. In fact, half of the affirmative Democratic votes came from the border and southern states. In the four New England textile states—Connecticut, Massachusetts, New Hampshire, and Rhode Island—only five of ten Democrats supported membership. Here again party loyalty played a role, for none of the region's fifteen Republicans did so. Table 3.2 shows the New England results and the national totals.

The ILO membership decision taught several lessons about the U.S. policy process, including those noted by Representative Tinkham. First, while the weak American party system makes it extremely difficult for strong leadership to face controversial decisions, party is more important than most other factors in winning controversial victories. Without party loyalty, it is doubtful that Congress would have voted for the ILO. The members of Congress who voted yes did so because they represented secure districts or districts where membership in the ILO did not concern constituents. Party discipline weakened in regions such as New England, where Democrats faced strong competition for reelection. Although party discipline mattered, it was not strong. In the American system a member of Congress cannot expect understanding at election time by arguing, "I voted for the bill because it was the party's position; however, I personally opposed it." Since many public decisions must demand shared sacrifice and be symbolically unpopular, the system encourages either end runs around the democratic process or, as in post–World War II foreign policy making, the commitment to bipartisanship. The exceptional American political process, with its barriers to policy innovation and with its emphasis upon individual accountability in legislative decisions, is inherently conservative, if not fossilized. Yet, bypassing the process to achieve goals, however good, means that the benefits of vigorous debate and other virtues of democracy are lost. The very individualism and system of divided powers that evolved to protect American democracy from abuse of power become barriers to its use. By delaying policy decisions, the process particularly causes Americans with fewer resources to suffer from lack of public support for their needs.

THE END OF AMOSKEAG

Neither the interstate compact process, the NRA experiment with corporatism, nor the decision to join the ILO came soon enough for the workers at Amoskeag. Only states with wage rates comparable to New Hampshire signed on to the Minimum Wage Interstate Compact. Corporate cheating undermined the NRA before the Supreme Court dispatched it to oblivion. The ILO was so weakened, as a result of the structure Gompers imposed on it, that it could not assure minimal world or national labor standards. Before 1988, the U.S. only ratified ILO conventions dealing with labor statistics and seafarers. The latter category excluded textile workers and the former only documented their troubles.

Frederick Dumaine, the Amoskeag president, correctly judged the nature of the American system in the 1920s. While he fought vainly under the NRA for minimal labor standards to protect his productive Manchester workers, he proceeded to save the corporation's investors from ruin long before his NRA testimony. On August 25, 1925, he divided the company in two. The Amoskeag Company of Boston took all the cash and government bonds. The Amoskeag Manufacturing Company received the manufacturing facilities and related assets, such as inventories, and six million dollars in cash from the Amoskeag Company, in exchange for the stock of Amoskeag Manufacturing. This move withdrew eighteen million dollars in accumulated cash from the manufacturing operation for the company to invest elsewhere. It froze for the stockholders the results of 100 years of successful operations. The Amoskeag Manufacturing Company had to survive on its own in the less prosperous postwar world. Investors saw the withdrawal of capital in 1925 as prudent. Workers and other Manchester residents saw it as selfish. It deprived Amoskeag Manufacturing of a massive amount of capital that could have been used to modernize.[84]

Abandoning northern textile manufacturing, the company cut back on maintenance in Manchester. When the plant manager, Parker Straw, objected to the cuts in 1929, Dumaine fired him. In January 1936 the Amoskeag Manufacturing Company filed for bankruptcy, and then "Labor was asked practically to guarantee 'permanent peaceful operations' and to accept wage reductions averaging 15 percent, the rates to be determined on a 'competitive-cost' basis, which means the lower wage scales paid in the South would be matched. By a majority of 536 in a vote of about 7,000 the long lines of grim-faced men and women agreed to the plan."[85] At the time the workers voted on a new contract, Amoskeag Manufacturing filed its first reorganization plan, claiming it could both pay off eleven million dollars of its bonds and operate the plant if given court protection.[86] Every month of additional operations transferred more assets to the bondholders from the city's foregone taxes and the workers' foregone wages.

Then an "act of God" threw these plans into doubt. Record floods, resulting from a broken ice jam up the Merrimack River, inundated the lower floors of the mile-long plant.[87] The reorganization plan had to be withdrawn. Outside bondholders rebelled.[88] In June, the bankruptcy court ordered the liquidation of Amoskeag Manufacturing Company.[89] In the fall of 1936, Representative Adolph Sabath of Chicago held hearings in Manchester, during which Dumaine was grilled by the committee.[90] Noted for his gruff style, Sabath confronted Dumaine with the assessment that "the reorganization proceedings of 1927, in which fourteen million dollars in bonds were issued, were nothing but a milking process."[91] A lesser man might have withered under this assault, but not Dumaine. Six days after his testimony, he held a stockholders meeting of the holding company at the downtown Manchester offices. Without embarrassment, he reported total assets of twenty million dollars, up four million since 1934. Because of the bad publicity surrounding the bankruptcy, stock prices were down to twenty-five dollars per share, but expected to rise, since the liquidation value of the holding company was seventy dollars per share![92]

The fate of the Amoskeag Manufacturing Company exemplifies one consequence of the exceptional American policy process. It acts too slowly to protect the interests of workers, but does allow investors to profit handsomely. Amoskeag Manufacturing never made a product after 1935. By contrast, the Amoskeag Company had annual revenues in the 1990s of $1.2 billion and assets of $934 million. The company had invested heavily in the South and came to control Fieldcrest Cannon in Greensboro, North Carolina, a large towel and linen manufacturer. Sixty years after the manufacturing plant's closure, Fieldcrest bought out the Dumaine family interest in Amoskeag when it became a part of Dallas-based Pillowtex. The only New Hampshire operation of Amoskeag to survive to the end of the century was Westville Homes, a modular home builder in Plaistow, with thirty-nine employees.[93] While the Dumaine family seemed to have done well by this process, on his deathbed in 1951, Frederic Dumaine mumbled, "It wasn't worth it."[94] Clearly, a better process had to be found, and in the mid-1930s the ILO seemed to be it.

The First Decade of Americans at the ILO

Once Congress approved membership in the ILO, U.S. officials needed to define what membership entailed. They sought to determine the legal status of ILO agreements, the structure of the U.S. delegation, and any other changes that would be made to accommodate membership. The ILO was soon to learn the lesson that many other international organizations would: U.S. membership meant U.S. domination. Given American reluctance to abandon unilateral solutions to its international needs, the U.S. has tended to act nearly unilaterally in some international forums. Consequently, soon after it joined the ILO, the U.S. expected to have an American in an important administrative position. By the end of the decade, an American, John Winant, would be the director general.

Before the process could move forward, the U.S. needed to resolve the rather complex relationship between the state and labor departments on ILO policy making. This issue had grown out of the indirect manner by which the administration had brought the U.S. into the ILO in 1934, without full hearings or analysis of interdepartmental relations. When the ILO produced substantive policy decisions, the two departments had to agree which would be responsible for presenting the policy to the proper federal official or institution. Two years after membership, the two departments finally negotiated an agreement sorting out these responsibilities. Typically of the Roosevelt Administration and in many ways of progressive policy making, the U.S. joined the ILO first and later experimented with the bureaucratic details and constitutional relationship.[1]

PERSONNEL SEARCH

While this debate about the U.S. relationship with the ILO continued for years, especially on the status of ILO conventions, the U.S. found
personnel to represent it. Here the president chose Winant, who possessed the knowledge, experience, and style specifically tailored to the
needs of the 1930s. Few others shared the president's experimental approach to progressivism, understood the need for labor standards to avoid
industrial dislocation, especially in textiles, and had executive experience
in government. Significantly, Winant had also participated in the debates
about the treaty power and ILO conventions. This made him a needed
ally for people in the administration, like Isador Lubin, who wanted to
pursue the use of ILO conventions to overcome court barriers to national
labor law.

PROGRESSIVE POLICY STYLE

Although Winant approached public policy making empirically,
not ideologically, he was not without beliefs to guide his empirical findings. The popular media often compared his firm principles to the granite
of his adopted state. How leaders such as Winant could combine firm beliefs and experimentation is one of the important lessons of this era.
Winant repeatedly credited Lincoln and the other Republican leaders
from the battle against slavery with his commitment to equal opportunity
and respect for the dignity of labor. However, unlike later leaders, the
ethics of reformers such as Winant provided policy objectives but did not
limit the methods to achieve their goals. Their beliefs were not an iron
cage to limit policy choices. For Winant, the absence of ideological limits
to policy choice became a burden difficult to sustain in what became a decreasingly empirical and increasingly ideological age.[2]

One of the major advances of the progressive policy maker was the
use of data to help shape agendas.[3] Labor standards reformers had focused
on data collection long before Winant. Carroll Wright exemplified this
approach in the early labor statistics movement.[4] Not surprisingly, one of
Winant's major appointments as governor and later at the ILO was Ethel
Johnson, whom he first recruited away from the Massachusetts Bureau of
Labor Statistics, founded by Wright. Johnson came to Concord and
helped him on the minimum wage battle.[5] The Consumers' League, with
which many of these reformers had collaborated, perfected this approach,

emphasizing the empirical investigation of working conditions, the development of a solution, and then advocacy of policy reform.

Winant's move from Concord to larger fields of policy making grew from this empiricism. Fairly quickly, he saw the experiment with interstate compacts as a failure. Then he experimented with the NRA, and finally the ILO. Since his personal fortune disintegrated while he tested these possible solutions, he did not switch from position to position for financial gain. Rather, he did so to find answers to empirically studied problems.[6] Tragically, at the time that he discovered a solution the world of policy making abandoned progressive empiricism for ideological purity, making Winant an anachronism.[7] New Deal and wartime experiences with planning and the welfare state spawned a neoclassical economic revival that focused on the defense of the free-market process rather than the protection of substantive rights and benefits.

PROGRESSIVE ADMINISTRATION

Winant retired from the governorship of New Hampshire in 1935. In his last term he had become a national figure, a Republican who supported New Deal relief programs.[8] Winant only momentarily retired from politics and social policy leadership. As a Republican supporter of aggressive relief efforts and bipartisan labor mediation, the Roosevelt Administration quickly employed him as a Republican who demonstrated the bipartisan support for New Deal social reforms. Of course, it did not hurt FDR that by compromising Winant's Republican position, he removed the governor from consideration as a Republican national office candidate in 1936.[9] Nevertheless, FDR's needs fit well with Winant's interests in the mid-1930s. Winant wanted to find the answer to the social problems unsolved by the New Hampshire Plan, the National Recovery Administration, and extensive relief programs. FDR controlled key positions that allowed Winant to test other possible directions, seeking simultaneous solutions to unemployment problems, poverty, global pressures to lower labor standards, and the temptation of governments to engage in protective or even retaliatory trade practices. He and the president concurred that the best position was to work with the ILO. Both came to recognize that a possible way to overcome Supreme Court rejection of federal social legislation was to skip beyond the federal government to the ILO.

Two sources of information contributed to Winant's fascination with the ILO in 1935. First, many social welfare reformers with whom he had worked praised the ILO effusively at the time of U.S. entry in 1934. For example, John Gavit, writing in *Survey Graphic*, said,

> This is what makes so momentous on the page of history the entrance of the United States at last into the International Labor Organization; more important and significant if possible than would be its entry into the League itself. For, be it remembered, the ILO was established in a time of crisis even more intense than that prevailing now. Its constitution . . . was written into the peace treaty, and opens with the pregnant statement *that permanent peace can be established and maintained only on the basis of social justice*. . . . No nation can effectively establish decent working and living conditions by itself or within its own borders. As the preamble of the constitution of the ILO puts it: "The failure of any nation to adopt humane conditions of labor is an obstacle in the way of other nations which desire to improve conditions in their own countries."[10]

Whatever the accuracy of Gavit's assessment, it appeared in one of the major periodicals of social welfare. The American Association for Labor Legislation, on whose board Winant served, likewise approved of U.S. membership.[11]

Clearly, the ILO convention ratification process provided one method around the constitutional problems of national welfare and labor legislation. It is important to appreciate how fearful Winant and other progressives were in the mid-1930s that the Supreme Court would never validate such acts. What else could explain how so practical a leader as FDR would propose "court packing" in 1937? It was not until the spring of 1937 that the Court upheld the constitutionality of the Social Security Act.[12] Major labor standards legislation was not passed until the following year with the Fair Labor Standards Act. The Court did not uphold that law, which revolutionized American labor protections, until 1941.[13]

Consequently, as soon as U.S. officials resolved the bureaucratic and personnel issues related to membership, Frances Perkins initiated discussions with the state department about submission of ILO conventions to the Congress. Beginning in late April 1936, Isador Lubin, the commissioner of labor statistics, led an unofficial discussion of treaty policy with James Shotwell, Joseph Chamberlain, other key department of labor officials, and Francis Sayre, Woodrow Wilson's son-in-law, of the state department. They developed three options for treating ILO conventions. They could be submitted to the Senate as treaties. They could be sent to both houses of Congress as regular legislation. Finally, they could be sub-mitted to the governors of the states for state ratification. Lubin and his ad-visors recommended following the treaty option for two reasons:

> (1) We should establish the precedent of submitting conventions to the Senate so that in the event we wish to test out the treaty-making power as a vehicle for securing social legislation a definite precedent will have been established.
> (2) Under the Supreme Court rulings legislation relative to the shorter work week, the prohibition of employment of women in mines and other matters . . . do not come within the legislative competence of the Congress. To be sure, if the Senate should approve a convention and pass it as a treaty, legislation would have to be enacted . . . by both houses.[14]

Winant had been the first to endorse Lubin's position, reinforced no doubt by his secretary, who was to become Lubin's wife and their joint ally in support of the ILO. The American Academy of Political and Social Science had invited Winant to write an essay on the constitutionality of social security for a 1936 edition of *The Annals* on the Constitution in the twentieth century. There Winant put forth his fears that the U.S. courts misunderstood the relationship of the Constitution to changing economic realities, saying of the new law:

> The lawyers will concern themselves with the issue of whether a spe-cific act is in accord with the specific powers with which Congress has been endowed by a written document. But social security is more than a statute, it is a great national necessity; and the Constitution is more than an aggregate of legal commands engrossed on parchment; it is a living instrument of national government. The question is whether a great objective of national policy — the security of a people against the major hazards of modern industrial life — has, by the constitutional Fa-thers, been put beyond the reach of government. Such an issue belongs to public policy . . . upon it a public official, even though unlearned in the law, has a right to be heard.[15]

If ratification of ILO conventions constituted a treaty under the Constitution, then Congress could pass enabling legislation preventing child labor or providing a minimum social security system, so long as the Senate ratified the appropriate international agreement. Given this possible solution to the constitutional deadlock in the U.S., the administration and ILO supporters wanted Winant involved in the organization. Shortly after the U.S. joined, ILO Director General Harold Butler visited Washington in October 1934, seeking FDR's support for appointment of an American to a leadership position in the ILO. Roosevelt, Frances Perkins, and James Shotwell naturally hit upon Winant, who accepted the appointment upon leaving office in Concord in January 1935.

Progressive Issue Experience

Events were unfolding so quickly in the field of labor and welfare legislation that Winant took on his new role as assistant director at the ILO while continuing involvement in the U.S. social policy debate. In 1935, he worked briefly for the ILO, returning home before the end of the year to chair the bipartisan social security board. It was in that role that Winant undertook the constitutional defense of federal social welfare and protective labor legislation. In the fall of 1936, when the Republican ticket of Alf Landon and Frank Knox launched persistent attacks on social security, Winant resigned from the nonpartisan board to campaign for social security, if not FDR.[16] While in the U.S., Winant pursued his ILO involvement in two ways.[17] First, as part of his official role at the board, he shared information from Harold Butler and experts at the ILO on other nations' social insurance systems. His brief experience on the ILO staff in 1935 had made clear that other nations had much to teach the U.S. about social insurance and that the staff at the ILO had abundant information on the topic. He realized the ILO used the same empirical approach to policy development that progressives had followed. Second, Winant served as one of four American delegates to the 1936 ILO conference in Geneva along with Frieda Miller, the New York minimum wage chief; Emile Rieve of the Hosiery Workers, representing labor; and Marion Folsom, of Eastman Kodak, the employer delegate.[18]

The 1936 ILO Conference

The members of the 1936 ILO delegation brought remarkable experience and commitment to the ILO. Miller was an expert on labor statistics with whom Winant had worked closely during the minimum wage discussions of the early 1930s. Miller continued her involvement with the

ILO until she became head of the U.S. Women's Bureau in the 1940s. Rieve had worked with Winant during the textile strike in 1934. Folsom had been a leading advocate of pension systems as a means to employment stability. He had been one of the architects of the Social Security Act and had served as an advisor to Winant's Social Security Board. In the 1940s, he would help found the Committee on Economic Development (CED) and other wartime international planning efforts.[19]

Substantively, the administration wanted ILO support for conventions committing certain industries to the forty-hour week: textiles, iron and steel, mining, civil engineering, and public works. Frances Perkins told Winant and Miller officially, "It is the policy of the Government of the United States to favor adoption of a forty-hour week in as many industries as possible." She emphasized, "Every effort should be made by the delegation to secure adoption of the five proposed conventions."[20] However, from the start of the conference, many countries opposed the effort. Unable to get the full conference to agree on the five industrial standards, the conference assigned the task of reviewing and finalizing recommendations to specialized industrial committees.

Textile employment became the focus of debates. Critics of the forty-hour limitation warned that countries adopting it would be placed at an unfair disadvantage in world markets, since Japan and Germany were unlikely to ratify. Some admitted that even if hours were regulated, wage rates needed to be standardized, lest low-wage producers dominate world markets. Others feared world manufacturers would substitute machines for people if tough hour restrictions were imposed. The Japanese delegates noted the anti-Japanese innuendos inherent in many of the other delegates' comments. Japan, Winant pointed out, had to be efficient in textile trade and run a trade surplus because the nation needed to import many raw materials. The British proposed submitting the whole matter to a technical conference of textile experts. By a vote of fifty-nine to twenty-six, the ILO agreed to call a special world textile conference.[21]

THE TEXTILE WARS

Throughout the depression, textile employers had responded to competitive pressures by moving production to areas with lower wages and from higher-wage workers, such as adult males, to lower-wage employees, namely youth and women. In extreme cases, as at Amoskeag, after workers and the community accepted wage and tax cuts in an effort to retain the industry, the company closed. It seemed that the free market had forced a fruitless "race to the bottom." In New England, cotton textile employment "declined from 194,891 in 1923 to 19,956 in 1933, and . . . even those remaining in the industry . . . suffered heavily from reduced earnings and from unemployment."[22] The textile crisis was not confined to New England but spread around the world, especially in other old centers of the industry. Lancashire in England had been suffering from a textile decline for many years that even the special relationships in the empire could not help. As India increased textile production, moving from 6 million spindles in 1913 to 9.7 million in 1936, exports from the United Kingdom to the subcontinent fell from 3 billion yards to 489 million. Even within India all was not well, with newer regions of production flourishing and the old center in Bombay stagnating.[23] Although the areas where production survived or boomed varied greatly, they shared at least one common feature, comparatively lower labor standards. The American South, for example, had both fewer labor protections and lower wages than did New England. The shift of production, whether out of New England or Bombay, worried local public officials, business owners, and workers in the declining regions. However, what really frightened leaders of many old textile countries was the remarkable growth of the industry in Japan. As ILO economist Lewis Lorwin noted in 1937, "In contrast to the decline of the United Kingdom from its former status as 'workshop of the world,' in so far as cotton goods are concerned, is the spectacular rise of Japan to the status of what might be called 'the workshop of the Far east.'"[24] For example, British exports of cotton cloth to India fell in the mid-thirties to 16 percent of 1913 levels. Although a 60 percent increase in domestic Indian production accounted for a portion of this decline, most was attributable to Japanese exports to India that rose to a phenomenal fifty-eight times the prewar volume.

Since all the major world powers possessed a significant textile industry, political leaders worried about the risks of these developments. They neither welcomed abandonment of production in their nation nor the decay in labor standards necessary to restore production in a free-market system. The major textile nations tested one possible solution, corporatist planning. In the U.S. there was the National Industrial Recovery Act, with textile codes designed to spread production cuts among all producers, while setting minimal labor standards. Likewise, in 1936 the British Parliament passed the Cotton Spinning Industry Act, which required the destruction of 10 million older spindles, or one-quarter of the country's total. Even Japan had sought production limits through its textile trade association, whose members agreed to observe more holidays.[25] While more holidays or other restrictions in the hours of work lightened the burden on some workers during the textile crisis, most workers did not benefit from the changes. A reduction from ten to eight hours of work might increase free time, but such cuts usually caused significant income declines because the piece-rate system common in textile mills paid workers per unit produced and not by the hour. Few employers raised piece rates to compensate for the declining amount of labor. The danger of the textile crisis sprouted when countries began to restrict trade or retaliate against international competitors, especially Japan. As early as 1932, the British Import Duties Act marked the abandonment of a century of British free-trade policy.[26] Subsequently, the British adopted a variety of retaliatory trade policies that soured relations with Japan. In 1934, the Dutch followed suit and imposed a quota on Japanese imports into the East Indies. These targeted restrictions made the Japanese desperate, since they also faced a specialized textile crisis in silk prices. Japan attempted to solve the resulting textile balance-of-payments problem by devaluing the yen and vigorously expanding trade in other textile goods. The textile disputes grew so severe that noneconomic interests concerned with world peace and political stability, such as the interreligious National Peace Conference in the U.S., urged that something be done globally to stop a textile war.

THE WORLD TEXTILE CONFERENCE

In the context of this looming trade war, the 1936 ILO conference called a world textile conference. As soon as the U.S. delegation returned from Geneva, Perkins and Winant laid plans to collect sufficient data on the world textile industry so that the conference would operate from facts, not opinions. Winant's commitment to an empirical policy process and his substantive knowledge of the textile crisis now proved exceptionally timely for the first major ILO experiment under U.S. leadership. Contacts were made with the ILO, and a cooperative planning process launched. Harold Butler, cognizant of the special position of the United States in the ILO, suggested that the conference take place in Washington. Overcoming administration fears of such an overt demonstration of internationalism in an isolationist decade, Perkins not only agreed to play host, but also to pay some of the cost for ILO staff to come to Washington.[27] No doubt the special relationship between FDR and Butler, developed at the first ILO conference in Washington in 1919, helped bring the extraordinary invitation to fruition.[28] Winant's close contacts with both men served to facilitate the cooperation between the former associates. Several students of the ILO at the time believed that Butler not only wanted to promote U.S. protection of the ILO, but already planned to bring Winant into the ILO as his successor.[29]

While Winant and other American leaders initially feared congressional opposition to the textile conference, in fact, members of Congress supported the conference as one way to relieve pressures from cotton textile interests frustrated by the continuing depression. American experts on the industry explained that solutions required expanding the geographic focus of their work. The New England studies had noted the links between northern industrial problems and wage differences with the South.[30] By 1937, astute southern manufacturers saw their future prospects could resemble those of their northern compatriots if labor cost advantages grew overseas.

By the late 1930s, the South clearly faced competition with producers outside Europe and North America. The imposition of various employment taxes under the Social Security Act and of union protections under the Wagner Act already gave comparative labor advantages to many foreign manufacturers. American producers could survive only by restricting trade or through international labor standards. Since southerners traditionally favored minimal trade barriers, labor standard agreements seemed the only acceptable solution.[31] Consequently, Congress approved the conference as a fortuitous opportunity for social welfare advocates, labor leaders, and business leaders to work for a common endeavor. As it received increasing attention, the focus expanded from reaching agreement on world standards for maximum hours to international implementation of a comprehensive set of labor standards regulating hours of work, wages, and child labor.[32]

The membership in the American delegation to the conference demonstrated the extent of the coalition that formed in 1937 to support textile standards. As at all ILO conferences, nations sent tripartite representation, with independent labor and employer delegates joining those from government. The U.S. government delegation included officials with responsibility for agriculture, trade, labor, child labor, women's work, and social security. The Agriculture Department came to protect U.S. interests in marketing of cotton crops, since the U.S. still supplied significant amounts of raw cotton to foreign textile producers.[33] Trade officials, especially Lynn Edminster from the State Department, A. Manuel Fox of the Tariff Commission, and Ernest Draper of the Commerce Department, supported labor standards in lieu of higher tariffs.[34] Isador Lubin and Ford Hinrichs of the Bureau of Labor Statistics defended the Department of Labor (DOL) position on general employment policy, while W. Ellison Chalmers came from the new DOL office at the ILO in Geneva.[35] Katharine Lenroot, from the DOL's Children's Bureau, promoted the abolition of most child labor. Mary Anderson, from the Labor Department's Women's Bureau, defended women's interests. Because of their long bipartisan work in their bureaus of the Labor Department, both Lenroot and Anderson lent credibility to the social welfare interests supporting the conference.[36] Likewise, Thomas Emerson, general counsel of the Social Security Board, promoted social welfare policy standardization with the blessing of Winant, the board's recent chair.[37]

The employer delegation reflected the new geographic center of the American textile industry. O. Max Gardner, former governor of North Carolina, held the equivalent position to Winant's among employers.[38] Of Gardner's advisors, nine came from the South, including Robert West, who had run both New England mills and Dan River Mills in Virginia. Joining West were William Banks of the Georgia Cotton Manufacturers Association and T. Scott Roberts of the Alabama Association.[39] Six of the ten southerners came from North Carolina, with one each from Alabama, Georgia, South Carolina, and Virginia. Despite southern leadership, the delegation included fifteen northerners—six from both Massachusetts and New York, two from New Jersey, and one from Pennsylvania.[40] The diversity of the employer delegation indicated both the growing anxiety in the South with world competition and the predominate locus of concern in the North. Many southern mill owners continued to feel the trend in the industry was not toward offshore production but from higher-wage, more regulated, and more unionized northern centers of production to the South.[41] Others were less sanguine about the long-term prospects of the southern industry.

The labor delegation contrasted with the employers' in both size and centralization. Unlike the more autonomous textile employers, organized labor sent formally elected worker delegates. The challenge was to select representatives of different unions and a mix of locally and nationally elected leaders. Emile Rieve of the Hosiery Workers, who had been at the 1936 ILO conference, served as the chief delegate. Of the eleven other labor representatives, seven came from the United Textile Workers of America, including President Francis Gorman. However, while the labor leaders had the sympathy of people such as Winant, they represented a

severely weakened movement more in search of recognition than international policy reform. Signs of labor weakness abounded everywhere. The
UTW sent three Washington headquarters officials, because its locals had
been on the defensive since the disastrous 1934 general textile strike.[42]
Only one local leader, Paul Christopher, came from the South. Horace
Riviere, from Manchester, New Hampshire, represented a local whose
members had been unemployed for a year after the closing of Amoskeag.[43]

The conference began on April 2, 1937, the twentieth anniversary of
Woodrow Wilson's war message. The significance of the starting date was
not lost on some observers, who saw social crises at the heart of the decaying world situation.[44] In the eighteen years since its founding, Wilson had
become recognized as the ILO's godfather. Now the group worked to ease
tensions, especially between Japan and the remainder of the world. Reflecting this theme, the conference organizers scheduled as a recreational
event a film on Japan that showed the "education, recreation and other
phases of welfare work widely practiced in the Japanese textile industry."
The film also showed "the landscape of the country in different sea-
sons."[45] While the film may have eased tensions, it did not overcome anti-
Japanese feelings.

Western governments and the Japanese remained deadlocked
throughout the conference. On April 6, Japanese labor practices were attacked by the British union representative, Arthur Shaw. He criticized the
failure of Japan to abide by earlier, weaker ILO standards. Reversing the
approach of the Consumers' League, the Japanese employer delegate,
Keinosuke Zen, defended Japanese practices that brought lower textile
costs to consumers, especially in colonial markets. His economic theory
completely rejected fundamental assumptions of the labor standards
movement and made any meaningful agreement impossible. Unlike the
economic theorists of the last part of the twentieth century, social welfare
advocates such as Winant could not condone the exploitation of workers
for the good of consumers.[46]

The Americans tried desperately to put a positive interpretation on
the conference. Ex-Governor Gardner said, "Government, employers and
workers in this country were substantially in agreement." The American
delegates acquiesced in a list of items they wished addressed, including
work hours, opposition to child labor, and protection of collective bargaining. Gardner praised the U.S. experience with the NRA standards,
which had brought a package of worker protections to the textile industry
along with market stability. Essentially, he envisioned expansion of the
NRA to the world.[47]

However, not everyone accepted Gardner's plans. As Robert West of Dan River Mills pointed out, while he supported the conference, most American textile firms scoffed at the ILO. They believed:

> In the first place, [world] textile employers . . . were not prepared to assume the risk of the forty-hour week. . . . In the second place, few of the workers' delegates who supported the [proposed] forty-hour Convention [were] prepared to recognize the corollary of an improved technology to support the shorter week without reducing the standard of living. . . . In the third place, the voting of the government delegates [did] not lend much encouragement. Of the twenty-eight countries whose government delegates voted in favor of the Convention, seven have failed to ratify any international labor Convention, and eighteen have failed to ratify the [existing] forty-eight hour Convention.[48]

West's last observation highlighted the problem with the conference's impact.

The conference did not finalize any policies that were binding on all nations. Isador Lubin emphasized this point when asked by Frances Perkins about the absence of representatives from the Labor Deparment's Division of Labor Standards. He reminded her that they were not included because, "As you no doubt know, it was definitely announced that the Conference was to concern itself with technical problems of the textile industry and that <u>no action would be taken relative to any legislation and that no recommendations along those lines would be submitted</u>. . . . Had the agenda made provision for the discussion of drafting of legislation or recommendations for legislation, the Division of Labor Standards would certainly have been included."[49] The lack of a legislative outcome made the conference meaningless.

Winant, who chaired the conference, expressed disappointment with many participants who sought standards to protect their existing market share and not to achieve justice. Keinosuke Zen had professed his perception of the link between low labor standards and consumer purchasing power. He failed, however, to perceive that ending labor exploitation would allow the poor of the world to consume more goods. Winant had hoped that more delegates would have championed raising worker incomes through labor standards and thus increasing purchasing power and world consumption.

To those who might say his position was naive or idealistic, he could present research he and Ethel Johnson had encouraged during his last term as New Hampshire governor. The New Hampshire Department of Labor study found that as incomes rose modestly, low-income families significantly increased spending on clothing. Lewis Lorwin, who wrote one of the preliminary studies at the conference, summarized this argument, saying, "From a commercial point of view, the textile industry may be described as suffering from over-production in the sense that the effective demand for textiles falls behind potential productive capacity; from a social point of view it is an industry of under-consumption. As in other industries, the solution for the paradox lies in measures and policies which would enlarge real income and the purchasing power of the mass of people in all countries."[50]

Lorwin realized that increased wages could create employees with more money, enabling them to buy the goods that, in the depression, could not be sold. At the ILO, other governments and employers failed to recognize this fact. Governments attempted to use tariffs and other trade policies to protect existing markets. Businesses claimed wages related directly to productivity. However, New Englanders knew productivity had not protected workers in New Hampshire, when their counterparts in other places were exploited. The New England textile workers were the most productive in the world and, consequently, made their employers among the most profitable. But all that profitability ended when producers found that a workforce in the South could be had for a discount. As Robert West of Virginia's Dan River Mills added, "There is no bottom to unrestrained competition for cheaper production."[51]

Although Frances Perkins, Winant, textile labor leaders, and sympathetic manufacturers were disappointed that the World Textile Conference produced no binding agreement, they hoped it set a valuable precedent for holding world conferences of industrial experts.[52] American internationalists praised the conference. George Norlin, president of the University of Colorado, writing for the Carnegie Endowment, while understating the conference's goals, reminded the public, "[It] was not called to adopt conventions or with an immediate objective." Rather, the conference allowed "an exchange of views in regard to competition between Western and Oriental countries."[53] John Andrews, in *The American Labor Legislation Review*, had editorialized on the eve of the conference that "the seventeen years of constant application of the official I.L.O. to such problems of international cooperation has developed a technique that inspires admiration and confidence."[54] In the next issue of the *Review*, E. J. Phelan, who was to head the ILO in the early 1940s, evaluated the conference. Not surprisingly, Phelan concluded, "The International Textile

Conference was an experiment which has proved wholly successful. . . . The real significance of the conference is that the work has been well begun."[55]

In contrast to Phelan, Winant knew that the conference had begun a process in need of conclusion. A few weeks after its close, he explained his position to the Milbank Memorial Fund:

> If you take any single industry, if you go back to the essentials and if you try to understand the welfare of those who are engaged in that industry . . . and I am thinking not only of the worker, but I am thinking of the investor as well . . . you find that if there are those that take an unfair competitive advantage, if there are those who so organize their fellow men for profit as to cut the social well being of the community, every decent employer and all workers, and the communities themselves are adversely affected by that action.

He then admitted he was studying a solution, but did not yet have one. He concluded that, "It is for that reason that some of us have been trying to work out some form of minimum wage, some form of limitation of hours, some provision to insure fair trade practices to protect the rights and well being of workers, owners and communities."[56]

An American Director General

It was to seek that solution that Winant welcomed the opportunity to return to the ILO as assistant director immediately after the textile conference. At the 1937 ILO conference, the U.S. and Latin American states demonstrated that the organization was to become a new world institution. They took the lead in seeking approval for a forty-hour convention while European states resisted. With the European situation deteriorating, Italy withdrew, and rearmament programs in France and Britain reduced their interest in labor standards. The process of Americanization accelerated the next year when Winant succeeded Harold Butler as director. Some believed Butler had resigned under pressure to allow an American to take over.[57] Twenty years after the U.S. rejected the Versailles Treaty, an American directed an organization associated with the League of Nations. With the decline of the League as war approached, the ILO's meetings remained one of the few remaining international political forums, oddly headed by a person from the unilateralist U.S.[58]

At the start of World War II, Winant preserved the ILO by severing its links to the League of Nations and converting it into a tool of the western democracies. The war began less than nine months after Winant took control, but even before the fighting broke out, the organization lost major member states. Two months into the war, when Russia invaded Finland, the ILO expelled the Soviet Union, making the organization even more American. Then, with the fall of France in June 1940, Winant removed the ILO from Geneva to the "New World." Surviving unilateralist thinking precluded the ILO coming to Washington, so Canadian Prime Minister Mackenzie King offered a location on the campus of McGill University in Montreal. Once safe, the staff went into a holding operation for the first years of the war.[59] While Winant soon departed for the ambassadorship to Britain, he had provided inspiring leadership during a time when inspiration more than concrete administrative actions made the difference between survival and dissipation of the organization.[60] Winant could claim in June 1939, as war threatened, that the ILO fulfilled Lincoln's "promise that in due time the weights would be lifted from the shoulders of all men and that all men should have an equal chance."[61] Although Winant supplied encouragement during his tenure as director general, assuring the ILO of a postwar life, he took no concrete steps to develop effective international labor standards. As he departed Montreal for London, he shared the hope of an elite group of Americans interested in the ILO that the postwar world would permit the full flowering of the organization's potential. The ILO survived throughout the early war years as a skeleton of its former self, housed in a chapel on the McGill campus. Irishman Edward Phelan, Winant's deputy, took over as director, and an emergency committee of Allied officials governed the rump organization. The ILO continued its labor research but had to wait for a renewed international role in the postwar world.

WARTIME ECONOMIC PLANNING

Well before the war's end, a number of the former ILO supporters used the organization as a base to design a postwar world economic system without the presumed flaws of the interwar arrangement. To understand the era, it is essential to appreciate how much leaders in the U.S. feared and sought to avoid the problems of the Wilson Administration in bringing a lasting peace. Franklin Roosevelt's selection of Republicans such as Winant for key national security policy positions grew from the perceived failure of Wilson to make his war administration bipartisan. Some worried that the 1944 elections would be similar to those of 1918, when Wilson lost a mandate to participate in international mechanisms that would reduce world conflict.[62]

As bipartisanship developed to address some of Wilson's problems, the approach to postwar economic change was built on the lessons of World War I.[63] Economic planners during World War II identified several related problems of the post–World War I era that needed correction to avoid future conflicts. They believed that Wilson had recognized the problems of economic competition and had hoped to reduce them. He also had planned to define and protect labor standards so that nations with the highest standards of living could welcome global reductions in trade barriers. While agreeing that Wilson correctly had perceived the general problem, however, World War II planners faulted his implementation of a solution. Implementation failed on two basic levels: the postwar planning process and the scope of institutions established to coordinate international economic policy. The fundamental procedural error of Wilson had been to tie his dream of post-Westphalian economic planning to the grand postwar peace conference at Versailles dominated by the leaders of Westphalian nation-states.[64] Consequently, a second or structural flaw of the interwar world was the absence of powerful international financial and trade institutions comparable to the international labor standards structure of the ILO. Such multinational organizations were essential to prevent economic conflicts between self-interested nations and their nationalistic rulers.

Although the post–World War II planners did not assume the ILO would continue, they agreed on the need for multinational institutions to address a range of international economic issues, including banking and finance, aid to war-torn and developing economies, labor standards, and basic trade rules. The planning began with binational discussions between the U.S. and Britain as part of the continuation of the Lend-Lease loan program in 1942. It expanded with proposals to meet the postwar relief needs of other allies.[65] John Winant, as ambassador to Britain, played a key role in these negotiations.[66] The spirit of the planning may be summarized by Secretary of the Treasury Henry Morgenthau's comments in May 1942, "There is urgent need for instruments which will pave the way and make easy a high degree of cooperation and collaboration among the United Nations in economic fields hitherto held too sacrosanct for international action or multilateral sovereignty. A breach must be made and widened in the outmoded and disastrous economic policy of each-country-for-itself-and-the-devil-take-the-weakest."[67]

Morgenthau's primary concern was with currency stabilization and redevelopment funding after the war.

Many others, including Secretary of State Cordell Hull, focused on trade liberalization.[68] Hull had acted as the godfather of tariff reduction in Congress in the 1920s. He had worked for a number years to refine the reciprocal trade agreement approach to tariff reductions. Hull's tariff reduction goal, if not his approach to the goal, had widespread support among American economists. When Congress considered the infamous Smoot-Hawley Tariff during 1929 and 1930, over one thousand economists, signed a petition calling for tariff cuts, including such labor standards leaders as John Andrews at the American Association for Labor Legislation.[69] Andrews and others connected with the labor standards movement saw no threat to such standards from low tariffs, since they assumed international labor legislation would protect workers from competition.

However, James Shotwell warned in the early 1930s of the dangers inherent in the U.S. tariff policy process, in which changes were evaluated by the self-interest of business and not by a search for the common good. Shotwell labeled unregulated trade a form of "economic anarchy." It was "privileged anarchy, feudal and aristocratic by nature and antisocial to the extent that each is led to think in terms of exploitation of his fellows and the increase of his own personal wealth instead of putting the accent first upon the increased prosperity of the country as a whole." Shotwell believed that developing trade policy that would promote the public good faced fundamental problems, for "[t]he execution of the project . . . calls for international action for which few governments are yet adequately prepared. . . . [T]he process would be much facilitated if there were in existence a technical international organization capable of setting forth the varying conditions which must be kept in mind in applying treaties of this sort."[70] He concluded that such a body existed in the ILO, although in 1936 he and IBM President Thomas J. Watson proposed developing a sister organization to the ILO as part of what they called a "House for Economic Relations." They believed that trade and finance deserved an organization equal to the one for labor standards and social justice. They intended this new "house" as a companion to other expanded League of Nations institutions, including a cultural organization like the future UNESCO.[71]

According to Shotwell, the ILO derived its strength from its tripartite structure, composed of two government representatives and independent labor and employer delegates. The employer delegates would pursue the self-interest of business. The labor delegates would defend the working class. The government delegates, torn between the wealthier business class and the more numerous workers, would presumably seek to identify the common good. The expert staff would provide guidance through empirically derived data. The ILO structure could serve as a model for a separate trade and finance organization or it could be expanded to include trade standards.[72] Such ideas continued to circulate for the next decade among advocates of labor.

The wartime planning effort provided an opportunity to try to implement these ideas. The testing ground came in two major Allied socioeconomic conferences in 1944, one the famed meeting at Bretton Woods, the other in Philadelphia.[73] These two conferences, along with one each on food and relief policies, essentially prepared the way for the Geneva round of tariff negotiations in 1947 and the creation of the proposed International Trade Organization (ITO). These mechanisms, the planners hoped, would free the world economy of direct manipulation by politicians of the nation-states, who had twice launched devastating world wars to gain economic advantage.

The importance of the Philadelphia conference was visible in the delegations of government officials, union supporters, and business leaders sent by the U.S., as well as by the unprecedented endorsement given by the president after the deliberations concluded.[74] The two government delegates included Secretary Perkins and the chair of the Senate Committee on Education and Labor, Elbert Thomas of Utah. Perkins remained a firm supporter of the ILO. As her biographer, George Martin, said, "[She] worked steadily to strengthen the ILO and the country's contribution to it. Others in the labor department took it equally seriously."[75] Thomas was an appropriate delegate because of his Senate position. However, even had he not been a senator, he qualified as an academic expert on trade policy. With a Ph.D. from California-Berkeley in Asian studies, Thomas inherently considered policy options in a comparative context. A Wilsonian opponent of trade barriers, he had come to the Senate in 1932 by beating Reed Smoot, cosponsor of the protective tariff passed two years earlier.[76] Joining Thomas as an advisor from the House was Margaret Chase Smith, who brought bipartisanship to the delegation. The other "government advisors" FDR sent to Philadelphia shared the official delegates' support for the ILO.[77] Arthur Altmeyer, a former student of John R. Commons and successor to Winant as head of the Social Security Board, provided expertise in social welfare legislation.[78] A former associate of both Winant and Altmeyer from the Social Security Board, Thomas Blaisdell, a Columbia

University-trained economist, came from the War Production Board. Frieda Miller, who had been serving as Winant's special assistant in London, brought his perspective. After the conference, she left Winant's staff to begin an eight-year career as head of the U.S. Women's Bureau. Other DOL staff included Isador Lubin; assistant labor secretary and former AFL executive Daniel Tracey; and Carter Goodrich, Columbia University economist and chairman of the ILO governing body during the war. Also part of the government delegation were a variety of state, academic, labor, and military officials.

While the government delegation's expertise reflected the importance accorded the ILO in 1944, the labor delegation provided a glimpse of the divisions that would plague U.S. labor during the postwar years and undermine the movement at the point of its greatest power. The governing structure of the ILO permitted only one labor delegate from each country, selected "in consultation with the 'most representative organization of labor.'"[79] Yet, in the U.S. there were two large labor federations, the AFL, the older skilled-worker union federation, and the CIO, created in the 1930s as a federation of unskilled and skilled workers organized together by the industry in which they worked. While the AFL still had the largest membership, the new CIO had been growing more rapidly.

Frances Perkins and Roosevelt wanted the two labor movements to share the delegate seat, an arrangement the ILO leadership welcomed. Perhaps with intentional exaggeration, Perkins conveyed the importance of this compromise in a memo for the president. Under the heading "UNITED FRONT VITAL NOW," she emphasized:

> At the present time we are at the critical stage of the war. We are also on the verge of profound decisions which will determine the nature of the peace and affect labor security and advancement both in this country and in the world. . . . Failure to [get one delegation] may result in a very real setback to our expanding economy which depends in turn on world trade under fair competitive and labor conditions. It may blot out our hopes, not only for improved labor standards, but for a world peace lasting for many generations and based on democratic principles and the concept of the opportunity of the workers and farmers to advance their standard of living in proportion to the improvement in industrial and scientific technology.[80]

Despite Perkins's hopes and concerns, William Green and the AFL would not agree to share the ILO seat. The president, while privately urging Green to split the delegation and the vote with the CIO, did not want a public disagreement with him. In early April, CIO President Phil Murray, thanking FDR for efforts on behalf of the CIO, withdrew the organization's request for representation.[81] While this gesture solved the immediate crisis, it highlighted the continuing division within the labor movement, which weakened the credibility of the American labor voice at the ILO.

Bob Watt of the AFL led the labor delegation to Philadelphia. He had many friends in the CIO, since he had worked with it in his home state of Massachusetts. Joining Green from the AFL was the old international labor expert Matt Woll, as well as future AFL President George Meany. Henry Fraser, from the Order of Railway Conductors, represented the railroad brotherhoods. The CIO perspective was presented by labor relations expert Marion Hedges, Florence Thorne, and Catholic Bishop Francis Haas of Grand Rapids, Michigan. Haas, a disciple of John Ryan, had just completed service as special commissioner for labor conciliation at the Department of Labor and chair of FDR's Fair Employment Practices Committee. Despite his renown as a labor mediator, the AFL-CIO divisions continued during the meetings, and Haas used mediator language to express cautious optimism at the conference's end, saying, "[It] has not done all it set out to do, but I believe that it did do more than it has hoped could be done."[82]

The employer delegation at Philadelphia included many former business supporters of labor standards with a few new faces of the same mold. Former textile machine manufacturer Henry Harriman was the voting member, and he was joined by several other New Englanders, including Henry Dennison of the Dennison Stationary Company and Clarence McDavitt of New England Telephone. Robert West, who had had experience running both northern and southern textile mills, represented textile interests. Other business delegates also came from manufacturing, including once again Marion Folsom of Kodak and Charles Redding of Leeds and Northrup, a Philadelphia instrument manufacturer. New to the ILO was Folsom's associate from the Committee for Economic Development (CED), Studebaker President Paul Hoffman. In contrast to the divided labor delegation, business leaders such as Hoffman, Folsom, and Dennison shared a common concern with promoting liberal and responsible internationalism. In fact, the business delegation appeared as progressive on international labor standards as the members from the AFL. *Business Week* noted that labor standards were of great interest to American business, "because . . . derivatively [they] affect prices and international trade relationships."[83] A week later it noted, "It seemed apparent, therefore, that U.S. policy . . . is to strengthen the I.L.O., and broaden the sphere of its interest. The most significant opposition thus far voiced to proposals for greater I.L.O. sovereignty has come from the worker delegates, notably A.F.L.'s Robert Watt who appealed for avoidance of 'making everyone's business our own.'"[84]

The AFL's struggle with the CIO led to Robert Watt's support for seating the labor delegate sent by the fascist Peron government in Argentina. Vincente Lombardo Toledano, the young Mexican labor delegate, demanded the Argentine's exclusion. Since Lombardo Toledano had befriended the CIO, Watt opposed his resolution, a decision noted critically by the American business press.[85] While the behavior of the labor delegates did not prevent positive action at Philadelphia, it portended many problems once business became less willing to accept the necessity of strong international standards. In 1944, business saw the ILO, according to *Fortune*, as "Revolution Insurance." When postwar revolution did not occur, business would be less fearful of a world without the ILO. Without business, the divided labor delegation would prove a weak reed upon which to maintain American ILO support.[86]

With business apprehensive of social chaos and the administration concerned about a world in which other nations might compete without the added costs of a New Deal safety net, the Philadelphia conference achieved remarkable symbolic achievements. Its accomplishments resulted partly because the most divisive ally did not participate. While the administration sought intensively to have all the Allies attend, the Russians boycotted.[87] The Russian absence undermined the claim that the ILO spoke for the nonfascist world. It presaged the fundamental struggles within the ILO over human rights policies that emerged in the Cold War era.[88] Among those attending, the British added other difficulties by demanding special treatment of dependent territories. These issues likewise were to haunt the organization in the later part of the century, as developing countries maintained that they could not meet the standards of the first world.

The ILO's governing body asked the conference to address five issues at Philadelphia: the effectiveness of its structure, advice for the United Nations on labor standards, the issue of colonial labor standards, and two topics growing out of the depression—the organization of economies to avoid excessive unemployment and the standardization of social security programs.[89] In addressing these issues, the conference developed seven recommendations for member governments as well as a

reaffirmation of the original ILO charter with a new Philadelphia declaration. The seven recommendations included commitments to minimal
income security, health insurance for all workers, social security for members of the armed forces, employment demobilization plans, support for
free public employment services, calls for public works and national planning to relieve unemployment, and a requirement that colonial powers
promote the social development of dependent territories. The American
delegation voted unanimously for all the recommendations except the
first two. While Robert Watt of the AFL backed the income and health security recommendations, the business delegate opposed both, and the
U.S. government delegates abstained on the health insurance plank, "Since
the recommendation called for measures going far beyond present practice
in the United States."[90] The negative business votes indicated the survival, even among progressives, of exceptional American attitudes about
public social welfare. A new generation of business delegates, freed of the
wartime pressures to cooperate with labor, would convert these minor
reservations into major points of disagreement.

Despite the reservations of the American business leaders, they
joined in the nearly universal acceptance of the general declaration of the
conference, which implied a significant limitation on market practices.
The declaration, if implemented in practical policy, called for a revolution in labor and social practice in the United States, as much as in other
members of the United Nations. It reaffirmed in its first principle that
"labor is not a commodity," which was equally anathema to Marxism and
laissez-faire liberalism. It asserted that "freedom of expression and of association are essential to sustained progress," and therefore it demanded
the "effective recognition of the right of collective bargaining." It recognized that "all human beings, irrespective of race, creed or sex, have the
right to pursue both their material well-being and their spiritual development in conditions of freedom and dignity, of economic security, and
equal opportunity." It declared social justice to be the guide for "all national and international . . . economic and financial [policies]" and identified as a key role for the ILO monitoring compliance with this goal. And,
as in the recommendations, it called for "the extension of social security
measures to provide a basic income to all in need of such protection and
comprehensive medical care."[91]

While the Declaration of Philadelphia received widespread positive
media coverage and the endorsement of the president, including a special
reception for the delegates at the White House, critical observers noted
that the results were inherently cries for action, not guarantees it would

occur. A month after the end of the conference, the editors of *Business Week* reminded readers of the vital importance of the conference for the war effort. They claimed that on the brink of D-Day, leaflets being dropped all over Europe described the commitment of the Allies at Philadelphia to international labor standards. They concluded, "[T]here is a temptation to be pleased at the prospect of foreign competitors being asked to operate under many of the same regulations which have been imposed upon our enterprise." However, the editors added a fundamental criticism of the conference, noting many business leaders found "disturbing the obvious intent of the Administration to bulwark its domestic policies in an international treaty."[92] *The Nation* recognized the American business approach as an example of the exceptional American cultivation of "the *mystique* of private enterprise." The editors worried that there could not "be tolerance and cooperation between" American laissez-faire attitudes and the social democracy of Europe or of the developing world, as led by the Mexican government.[93]

Supporters of the ILO knew that the conference resolutions and declaration were vague expressions of hope. As the conference chair, Walter Nash of New Zealand, said, they would "not be worth the paper [they were] printed on unless there is action, positive action, vigorous action, courageous action, to give effect to its principles."[94] A few weeks after critiquing the extreme liberalism of American laissez-faire proponents, *The Nation*'s editors warned that the declaration ran the danger of being "a 'paper' resolution which reactionaries can indorse without fear of being called upon to put principles into practice."[95] The religious press, represented by *The Christian Century* and *Commonweal*, was more positive but also worried about meaningful results. *The Christian Century* emphasized that the president and Congress had to act to implement the declaration.[96] *Commonweal* prophetically noted four ominous problems evident at Philadelphia. First, the AFL and CIO split weakened the impact of free labor in the ILO. Second, Russia was absent. Third, the ILO lacked control over international financial and economic policies, which would restrain labor policy choices. Finally, siding with Bertram Pickard of the Society of Friends, the ILO needed popular participation in the formulation of international economic and social policies.[97]

Generally, planners and observers at the time did not make intimate links between world finance and trade policy and labor and social policy. A few observers did discuss the need to coordinate them. Ruth Anshen brought together a number of foreign policy experts in 1943 to write of postwar plans, and paired John Winant's piece on the ILO with one by

Alvin Hansen on trade and finance policy.[98] Hansen, a long-term New Deal advisor and the major American Keynesian, had been serving as a consultant to the wartime National Resources Planning Board.[99] Carter Goodrich of the Department of Labor, who served on the ILO governing body, also advocated linking the two policy areas. He found support for policy coordination in statements of the president.[100] However, such observations were the exception.

Most policy makers suffered from the myopia inherent in the distinct spheres of policy for which their agency was responsible. Since all governments tended to have distinct finance and labor departments, on the world level the functions became separated. Coordination would come only from interagency cooperation, not from the inherent linkage of the policy process, and interagency cooperation tends to be a peripheral concern in any bureaucracy.[101] Given such structures, the proponents of laissez-faire easily ignored labor policy for a generation, while forcing finance and trade policy into a mold of their design.[102] Yet, in 1944 the seeds were sown for a linkage, if only when global economic justice became a more obvious concern.

POSTWAR DISILLUSIONMENT

As *Commonweal* and *The Nation* had foretold, when the war ended, the ILO faced major problems in realizing the potential of Philadelphia's ideals. Labor was divided in America and less interested in global labor rights than in winning representation rights in American factories. As much as any laissez-faire regime, Russia fundamentally opposed free labor rights, and after initial indifference to the ILO, it sought to join and block coherent policy. Financial and trade policy remained distinct, and the ILO, rather than demand a leadership role in economic policy, began the postwar years fighting to gain formal United Nations recognition. Finally, there was the resurgence in the immediate postwar world of extreme laissez-faire liberalism in America.

John Winant had fought for a generation to keep the Republican Party and American business leadership true to what he saw as founding principles of the party and of the American economic system. He reminded the party that the founders had taught "that human rights must be placed ahead of property rights."[103] That had been the message of the Civil War. A new generation of Republicans viewed the message differently. At the end of the Second World War, the party endorsed an economic system that redefined the Civil War as a triumph of laissez-faire policy over economic traditionalism.[104] In 1947, Winant, despondent in a party and world he no longer knew, committed suicide in Concord.[105] Tragically, he did not appreciate that the postwar labor standards movement would represent more of a triumph of human rights and human empowerment than the elite-dominated movement of the first decade of American involvement.

The renewal implicit in the Declaration of Philadelphia would be important later in the century. In 1947, Winant only saw the potentially exhausting need among ILO advocates to renew individual and institutional support. That would have to be achieved without Winant and without a whole cohort of progressive leaders—Kelley, Commons, and Andrews, not to mention FDR. The organizations that they headed seemed to lose their way or reverse direction. A new ILO coalition was necessary to leap beyond the triumphs of membership in 1934 and the Philadelphia conference a decade later.

FIVE

Leadership Change

After the Philadelphia conference, the editors of *The Nation* observed that the ILO's goals required extensive publicity—even moralizing—to succeed. It was neither in the consumer's nor the employer's self-interest to support labor standards. Since labor increased the cost of production, the competitive advantage always lay with decreasing labor standards to undercut the competition. Consumers benefited from lower labor standards, except when the consumers were also laborers on the goods they wished to purchase. Thus, the success of the labor standards movement depended upon educating the public about the plight of workers and the requirements of social justice. The movement's major successes came during the depression or the closing days of war, when the public and many employers perceived it to be in their self-interest to offer minimal labor reform in order to avoid social revolution and to promote national unity.

Without these threats to survival, the movement had historically relied on the efforts of elite moralists. Josephine Shaw Lowell, who was old enough to remember the first labor standards crusade in America against slavery, had combined elite ties and moral eloquence to attack self-interested indifference. Academics such as James Shotwell had given credibility to the ethical concerns of the movement in a different way. Both he and Lowell had possessed influence because of the institutional base that had adopted their calls for reform: Lowell from the Consumers' League and Shotwell from the Carnegie Endowment and in his position on the faculty of Columbia University.

After the U.S. joined the ILO in the 1930s, institutional support became more crucial. The creation of Social Security and the passage of the Fair Labor Standards Act had raised the stakes for American workers. There were now more standards to defend. In addition, the effort at trade liberalization, which moved forward under the New Deal with the reciprocal trade agreement process, reduced the indirect protection of American labor standards that came from the tariff. Then, contempt for ILO standards existed among a number of major regimes, a problem both in the 1930s and after World War II. Germany did not attend the ILO after 1933, and in 1937 both Italy and the USSR left. The ILO clearly became an agency of the democracies. After 1945, it remained so because the USSR refused to join. Yet, the issues that gave rise to the ILO during the interwar years seemed more pressing after World War II than they had in 1919. No doubt the war left massive dislocations of peoples and destruction that paralyzed economies. In addition, there was no reason to believe the prewar depression would not resume.

In many ways the ILO started anew in 1945. The League of Nations had disappeared and the ILO had to negotiate a new partnership with the United Nations. The postwar economy did not conform to the expectations of many when a boom rather than a depression followed the war, and political conservatism flourished in place of the New Deal progressivism. Yet, most of the founders of the ILO were gone by the late 1940s. The organization faced its postwar future with uncertain leadership and supporters. Fortunately, some institutions continued ILO support after the war, but these were severed from elite control and frequently subjected to mockery. There was neither a Josephine Shaw Lowell to advocate for labor standards nor a Richard Ely or John R. Commons among American economists to defend U.S. involvement in the ILO. Since the change in group advocacy was an evolutionary process, it was hardly noticed except through the indifference of specific organizations and professions formerly involved in the international labor standards policy process.

The National Consumers' League

The changes in the National Consumers' League provide a good example of the evolution of ILO support between the 1930s and 1940s. The league entered the 1930s with remarkable continuity from the progressive era. Despite a frustrating and divisive battle during the 1920s in favor of the failed child labor amendment, it maintained support among a segment of the nation's academic, social welfare, and religious elite, including Florence Kelley as general secretary, and John Graham Brooks as honorary president. Among its honorary vice presidents were academic stars from the social sciences: Irving Fisher, the Yale University founder of econometrics; Jacob Hollander, Hutzler Professor of Political Economy at Johns Hopkins; Roscoe Pound, dean of Harvard Law School; and E. R. A. Seligman, McVickar Professor of Economics at Columbia. Its active vice presidents still included Jane Addams at Hull House; Alice Hamilton, professor of industrial medicine at Harvard Medical School; and Maud Nathan, friend of Josephine Shaw Lowell and women's suffrage leader. John R. Commons had been the league's president since the mid-1920s. Despite the continuity, by the 1930s the league's fundamental weaknesses compared to the strengths in the progressive era became evident.

There were several reasons for this decline. First, there was the split in the women's movement over equal rights. Florence Kelley and many other league leaders, as pioneers in the women's movement, supported a social feminist agenda, including special protections for women and children. In the 1920s, a debilitating split had emerged between the social feminists and a group of feminists advocating an end to all legal distinctions between the sexes.[1] The league had once been among the preeminent groups in a "women's network" of policy organizations.[2] In the 1930s, some in the new generation of feminist leaders saw it as restraining complete equality. Second, the league's finances, dependent upon donations, suffered in a time of declining incomes.[3] Third, the very success of the league's policy advocacy called into question the continued need for the organization. Finally, there were the personnel changes necessitated by the death or retirement of the old leaders and supporters, including its elected president and permanent general secretary.

In 1931, Florence Kelley was seventy-two years old and gravely ill. She died in February 1932. Jane Addams, whose name led the list of vice presidents, was only a year younger and died three years after Kelley. Commons requested retirement in 1934 when he reached seventy-two. While the league replaced each individual with remarkably talented people, several new leaders quickly moved on into new and important public leadership roles created as a result of New Deal policy. These leaders had brought new perspectives and great intensity, but also short-term commitments to the organization.

At the time of Kelley's death, one of the newest members was Lucy Randolph Mason, who came from two of the "fine families of Virginia." Daughter of an Episcopal clergyman, she had led efforts to improve both working conditions and race relations in Richmond as head of the local YWCA. In 1931, at age forty-nine, she toured the South for the league and authored a book, *Standards for Workers in Southern Industry.*[4] It focused particularly on child labor laws and the regulation of the hours of work of women. Mason wrote about a timely topic, of special concern to northerners who considered the South the source of unfair competition. She was the obvious choice for general secretary.[5]

The league also discovered an ideal candidate to replace Commons in one of its guest speakers. In December 1933, the league invited John Winant to deliver its annual luncheon speech. He praised Kelley for her "militant leadership," and then focused on the problems of interstate competition in labor standards, saying:

> It has been my belief for a long time that jungle warfare has no place in modern industry. The exploitation of workers, with hours and wages as weapons in an attempt to capture markets, has been a deep underlying cause of our lack of social advance. . . .
>
> The arguments against labor legislation within industrial states usually come from the manufacturers who argue that since 48 states comprise competing areas of free tariff and communication, it is unfair to set up in one state standards regarding wages, hours of labor and working conditions unless similar standards are set up in the other states. Hence all efforts should be turned toward uniform labor laws.[6]

Later in his address, Winant referred to New Hampshire's troubles with the textile industry and expressed hope that the NRA and interstate compacts would solve these problems.

Two days later, Rosilla Hornblower of the league wrote to Winant, saying:

> It was a privilege to hear your inspiring speech at the Consumers' League luncheon last Wednesday. . . .
>
> I am making a study, for the league, of various outstanding progressive political figures to see how they stood on social and labor legislation in the earlier years of their careers. . . . Our idea is to prove that it is no detriment to a youthful politician to champion such causes as the regulation of hours and wages in industry, old age security, the abolition of child labor, the stabilization of employment, etc.[7]

Thus began the process of moving Winant from "outstanding progressive" to league president. And, given both the concerns of Mason and Winant with interstate competition, it placed the league in the forefront in the battle to win national labor standards.

In 1935, the NRA was declared unconstitutional and interstate compacts were victims of state intransigence. That year the Massachusetts league invited Robert Watt of the AFL, just returned from the ILO conference in Geneva, to discuss the relevance of his experiences there. Watt consciously linked the recent effort to develop interstate agreements to the ILO, saying, "At the present time, the ILO, which I attended as A.F. of L. representative from the United States, is the Inter-State Compacts Commission of the World. It has some of the same merits, some of the faults. By and large, with seventeen years' experience behind it, the ILO seems to function better than the Inter-State Compacts Commission meetings in which I have participated—but it has a much more difficult role to play."[8]

The presentation by Watt and the agendas of Winant and Mason invigorated the Consumers' League in the mid-1930s. Its program for the 1935 meeting demonstrated its concern with labor legislation. The morning session gathered together experts on the "Administration of Labor Laws," half the presenters being public officials. The league no longer relied on academics or clergy to explain what could or should be done. Now public administrators explained their responsibilities and plans. Dorothy Kenyon, who had assisted Felix Frankfurter in preparing information on international labor standards at Versailles, spoke on the courts and labor. She helped members plan strategies to win acceptance of state legislation. Frances Perkins addressed the group at lunch about "Good Administration of Labor Laws." Then participants devoted the afternoon to labor standards, especially the minimum wage and the regulation of the hours of work via interstate compacts.

Although impressive, this agenda reflected problems lying ahead for the league. While extremely relevant in 1935, the league was tying itself to short-term and specific legislative goals that would soon be realized with the Fair Labor Standards Act of 1938. Second, by minimizing the role of academics and clergy, the league diminished its earlier prophetic role in demanding fundamental change in economic thinking and in the behavior of consumers. A new consumer movement was developing, emphasizing the need to locate the cheapest product of the best quality but indifferent to the conditions under which the product was made.[9] Finally, the new leadership of the league brought exceptional talent and new vision but only short-term commitments to the organization. By the time of the passage of the Fair Labor Standards Act (FLSA), both Winant and Mason had left. Winant was in Geneva, and Mason assisted the new CIO in the South. The briefly rededicated Consumers' League had helped its revitalizers move to new leadership positions in the labor standards movement. The seeds had been sown for the decline of the organization. After the passage of the FLSA and the U.S. "takeover" of the ILO, the league yielded leadership of the movement to public sector officials and organized labor.

In the mid-1930s, some at the league urged the board to add or to shift the focus to consumer quality and prices. While the organization's leaders voted to keep consumer responsibility, not consumer rights, as a goal, the debate revealed the old vision was weakening.[10] By the late 1930s, resistance collapsed and the league began working with the newer Consumers' Union.[11] A new definition of consumerism emerged, more attuned to the modern American emphasis on civic rights over civic responsibility.[12] In the same era, the organization began to lose its state base. Following a pattern common to modern interest groups, the league considered moving the headquarters to Washington in 1940. State chapters declined after the 1930s while the central office expanded. Although the league rejected relocation to the capital longer than many groups, it eventually succumbed to the temptation for national centralization as a membership service organization.[13]

To identify the problems and temptations faced by the later Consumers' League is not to criticize the efforts of its 1930s leadership. In 1935, it was not clear that the FLSA would pass in three years or that the Supreme Court would sustain it in 1941. Rather, the attention in 1935 centered on a strategy to standardize labor protections. Organization survival was rightly placed in a secondary position to the achievement of that goal. With the triumph of the FLSA's passage, the league's leadership focused on defining a new role for itself. The league resisted most of these temptations as long as possible, trying to maintain a decentralized base for two decades after the FLSA. Eventually, it assumed a new role as bureaucratic overseer of labor standards, but remained unable to divorce itself from the new consumer movement.[14]

The ILO Committee

The Consumers' League was not alone in the battle for international labor standards during the thirties. When the U.S. joined the ILO, Winant connected the old elite leaders of the AALL to form a special ILO support organization. They wisely did not want to depend solely on the two interest groups formally represented through the tripartite structure: labor and business. Working with the League of Nations Association, they established the National ILO Committee, chaired by Samuel Lindsay. They skillfully built a committee consisting of a few progressive business leaders, the leadership of labor, many competent academics, and social welfare leaders. Academics with long experience studying labor legislation and international law included three Columbia University professors with experience at Versailles—James Shotwell, Joseph Chamberlain, and Leo Wolman—as well as two from Harvard, Manley Hudson and Carl Ratzlaff. Carol Riegelman and Paul Taylor from the Carnegie Endowment for International Peace also had expertise in international relations. John Andrews from the AALL and Lucy Mason from the Consumers' League also participated. Other experts came from the field of industrial relations, such as William Leiserson, head of the National [Labor] Mediation Board, and Elmer Andrews, Frances Perkins's successor as industrial commissioner of New York. Their interest in the ILO grew from the active role it had assumed under Albert Thomas in sharing information on human relations methods. Finally, the committee included a southerner, Charles Pipkin of Louisiana State University, and a religious leader, James Myers of the Federal Council. The Carnegie Endowment headed by Shotwell provided office space at Columbia University.[15]

The National ILO Committee supplied assistance to the ILO at a time when unilateralism threatened to overwhelm any American commitment abroad. To be successful in this atmosphere, Lindsay and Winant made several strategic decisions. The committee was not a mass organization. Rather, it was an elite group that sought a national elite membership and state and local chapters. The inclusion of Charles Pipkin was part of that strategy, although it was hard to hide the overwhelming linkage not merely to New York but to the upper west side. Another strategy endorsed separating the ILO Committee from the League of Nations Association.

The ILO Committee considered the league an albatross around the neck of U.S. internationalism. When Winant addressed the committee in 1935, the minutes reported, "The main point of [his] talk was that the I.L.O. and the League of Nations should be kept separate in the minds of the American people. . . . He felt that there was no question but that [C]ongress approved the resolution on the I.L.O. with the understanding that there would be no commitments with the league."[16] And, of course, he was right. American membership in the ILO was a remarkable achievement, which could be lost with talk of the League of Nations or the World Court.

The committee focused on a cautious public education strategy and not a mass public propaganda campaign. It avoided any publicity that might promote U.S. cooperation with the league. Historians have criticized leaders such as John Andrews for failing to reach out to a wider public, allegedly because of his comfort in working with academic and social welfare experts.[17] Yet, their approach was reasonable, given American social policy exceptionalism. Understanding popular xenophobia, the leaders of the ILO Committee copied Andrews's strategy. Winant called for reaching out to "State Labor Commissioners . . . and educating the proper people."[18] Andrews proposed prioritizing the goals of the Committee to "[F]irst, increase the number of influential citizens who know about [the ILO]."[19] Winant, Lindsay, and Andrews did want eventually to affect the general public, but their strategic priorities probably were correct. Any mass ILO support group in 1935, even if possible, would have been an ephemeral movement among the majority of American workers. Rather, good education extolling the value of labor internationalism could build the solid support for the ILO that would sustain American involvement.

In 1935, support for joining the ILO primarily came from those concerned with the judicial veto of national labor legislation. Therefore, the ILO Committee intensified efforts to understand and promote the use of the treaty power to establish standards. The committee sponsored two efforts to address this need. First, in 1935, Spencer Miller, who served as both labor representative on the committee and as Episcopal Church liaison to the labor movement, chaired a weeklong conference on the ILO at the University of Virginia attended by 350 academics, employers, and labor leaders. Not only did the committee sponsor the conference in the South to extend beyond its base, but it also published under Miller's editorship the key papers, titled *What the International Labor Organization Means to America*.[20] Of course it meant a lot, as summarized in the introduction by Winant. He reminded readers:

> One of the hardest tasks of the International Labor Conference is to build up standards in countries that we might describe as backward. A thing that is of particular interest to all countries of the world is relative standing. That is particularly true when we are dealing with world markets. We find right here in the United States that competition can be so severe that it is destructive of capital, of profit, and of human beings, and just as men here fight to maintain these standards, so it is necessary that we use our influence to maintain world standards. That is the major function of the International Labor Organization.[21]

In addition to the Virginia conference and Miller's book, the committee sponsored specialized studies. The executive secretary of the committee, William Lonsdale Tayler, wrote specifically on the major American problem with ILO standards in *Federal States and Labor Treaties—Relations of Federal States to the International Labor Organization*.[22] As he stated to Winant, "I have come to the conclusion that the treaty-making power of the Federal Government is broad enough to enable the United States to ratify the Labor Conventions, thereby assuming an active role in the I.L.O. Once the Labor Conventions are ratified, it necessarily follows that the Government would have power to pass legislation effectuating the treaties."[23]

While the Virginia conference was a strategic success, the committee faced the problem of finding diversified support for ILO membership. Business decreasingly showed interest, while increasingly only labor and the churches actively backed U.S. participation. Spencer Miller's role in linking the church and labor symbolized what was to become a distinctly American base of support for the movement.

LABOR

Spencer Miller enlisted John L. Lewis when he needed a speaker with a labor perspective on the ILO. Lewis represented labor at the 1934 ILO conference and had been courted successfully by Frances Perkins and the Geneva leadership of the ILO. But, Lewis's support came with a price, his unique policy perspective.[24] Lewis did not sanction the conciliatory or diplomatic approach of the committee leadership. He condemned business for the industrial policies of the 1920s that "constantly sought to maintain an industrial autocracy, and to deny by every means possible, liberty and democracy to American workers. . . . [T]hose in financial control of industry also demonstrated their complete unfitness to direct industrial operations in the public interest."[25] He blamed industry for the failure of the NRA, proving "'industrial self-government' impossible."[26] He claimed the real tripartite leadership of the movement for industrial democracy was not business, government, and labor, but "sponsored by the churches and colleges, and universities, which finds its practical leadership in the organized labor movement."[27] The "academic revolutionaries warn us of impending changes in our economic and social institutions. Liberty . . . must as a rule be conditioned by what is socially desirable and not by what is individually profitable. . . . The churches, on the other hand, urge their enlightened ethics as a substitute for the pagan ethics of the old capitalistic system."[28] He hoped American labor would guide the world to democracy and cooperation through the ILO.

Lewis's complimentary view of the churches was rewarded by Miller's inclusion of Lewis as a commentator on the ILO at the Virginia conference. Academics also praised Lewis's special labor role in foreign policy when William Maddox of Harvard recounted AFL leadership in the condemnation of Nazi suppression of free labor in 1933. He sympathetically explained the apparent conservatism of American labor as pragmatism of the highest order, grounded in the realities labor experienced but also guided by "The humanitarian impulse (strong in labor ranks) . . . to defend the weak against the strong, the peaceful against the belligerent."[29]

The apparent harmony between labor, academics, and the churches, evident in these comments, masked fundamental divisions in each, and a changing relationship between them and other supporters of the international labor standards movement. Soon, the academic supporters faded as major players in the movement, while the role of the churches increased. And as evident at Philadelphia in 1944, a fundamental divide existed within the American labor movement between the craft unions in the AFL and the industrial unions in the CIO. Each claimed the right to represent U.S. labor.

The long-term ILO successor to Lewis, Robert Watt of the Massachusetts Federation of Labor, managed to temper the consequences of the U.S. labor split. With the emergence of the CIO with Lewis as its champion, the battle between the two federations paralyzed the voice of U.S. labor at the ILO. Both groups possessed a good claim to being the most representative labor organization in the country. While the AFL had the larger membership, the CIO's industrial union approach to organization gave it greater potential members and made plausible its claim to speak for the unorganized as well as for its members. Except for Lewis, who had become a vehement opponent of Franklin Roosevelt, the CIO's strong bias in favor of the Democratic Party gave it more members with close links to the Roosevelt Administration. And, of course, the leader of the CIO had been a labor delegate to the ILO. Despite the CIO's claims, the AFL had history on its side in continuing to name the delegate, and Watt was the perfect compromise candidate, one who had a clear view of the long-term interests of labor in the ILO.

The AFL leadership favored sending Matthew Woll to the ILO. A close associate of Gompers, Woll directed the policy-making apparatus of the AFL. Seen as hostile to the CIO in the many jurisdictional disputes between the two federations that surfaced in American factories, Lewis and the CIO refused to accept Woll as the labor delegate at Geneva. In contrast, Watt, while secretary treasurer of the AFL in Massachusetts, had been sympathetic to early CIO efforts. He welcomed the growth of organized labor regardless of the national affiliation of the union. It also helped that he came from a textile state, since much of the ILO agenda related to that industry in the late 1930s. In fact, he succeeded Emile Rieve of the textile workers, who had represented labor in Geneva in 1936.[30]

In the late 1930s, the Roosevelt Administration wanted and needed strong labor support for the ILO in Geneva and Washington. Here Watt filled the bill. In Congress, George Tinkham continued aggressive attacks on the ILO. A Massachusetts labor supporter of the ILO, such as Watt, assisted in the battles against the populist Boston congressman. On the international level, the Roosevelt Administration requested not only participation in the ILO but also leadership within it. He desired an American like Winant to become director. Here also Watt, who liked Winant and the Consumers' League leadership, proved useful. Finally, Watt understood the importance of international labor standards in the developing world economy, especially one in which tariff barriers were lower. Unlike much of the AFL leadership, he declared that "Tariffs afford a very limited protection against importing sweatshop products, and they afford no protection for labor which produces for world markets."[31]

THE CHURCHES

The churches' supportive role in the international labor standards movement increased. The churches filled the void that was left with the departure of the early generation of academics. As Lewis foresaw, the churches tended to have fundamental conflicts with the ethics of capitalism. The depression made this latent disagreement visible and freed many religious leaders from their conventional accommodation with all American institutions. The seeds had been planted by leaders of the earlier generation, if not in the Jewish prophets and the Sermon on the Mount.

In the 1930s, the Catholic Church's role in the labor standards movement expanded. The institutionalization of social justice teaching in the American church facilitated, if it did not cause, this change. In 1919, the National Catholic War Council issued "The Bishop's Program," urging the enactment of U.S. laws to protect nine basic labor standards.[32] The church's position on labor standards received periodic reinforcement from

Rome, particularly in Pius XI's *Quadregesimo Anno*, the 1931 encyclical issued on the fortieth anniversary of *Rerum Novarum*.[33] American Catholic supporters of labor standards with institutional roles in the church spread these ideas. Most important was John Ryan, who began as an activist in Minnesota and later came to Catholic University and a seat on the board of the Consumers' League.

At the turn of the century, American Catholics were considered an alien group and the church leadership adopted a consciously conservative approach to social policy.[34] The primary social policy the church dictated was charity. Subsequently, Ryan guided the church to the forefront of social policy innovation, especially with his writings on the minimum wage. Richard Ely blessed Ryan's work by composing the introduction to *A Living Wage*.[35] The book served as a link between Continental Catholic critics of capitalism, such as de Mun, and American advocates of labor standards, such as Winant. In the late 1930s, Ryan prepared the church for its role as the prime American ILO lobbyist besides labor. Intellectually, he clarified the difference between charity and social justice and the important, yet somewhat distinct, church position in each field. Second, he led or played a key role in a number of Catholic organizations, from the bishop's program, to Catholic Action, and to the Catholic Association for International Peace. This gave the church influence in all levels of the political process, from Washington lobbying to grassroots organizing and education.[36] Third, he attracted proteges to the National Catholic Welfare Conference, which succeeded the War Council. He discovered men like Fathers Raymond McGowan and George Higgins, who would continue his work to the end of the century.[37] Finally, Ryan served as an important link between the church hierarchy, especially Cardinal Mundelein of Chicago, and the Roosevelt Administration, which freed the church from identification with social conservatives such as Al Smith and the proto-fascist corporatism of Father Coughlin.[38]

However, Ryan did not act alone. Cardinal Mundelein in Chicago contributed to the new direction. By promoting patriotism and institutional visibility while fostering understanding of social responsibility in the American church, he produced the institutional mix that gave the church credibility in speaking about "the social question." Mundelein Seminary reflected his effort with its colonial American architecture, massive resources, and its Summer School of Social Action for Priests. Selecting Reynold Hillenbrand, a man of deep piety and intense social concern, as rector of the seminary allowed for this fortuitous merger to bear fruit in a generation of priests, particularly in George Higgins.[39] Hillenbrand brought CIO leaders, public officials, and experts on current policy options, such as the minimum wage, to speak to his seminarians.[40] To reach the laity, the popular Catholic press, such as *Our Sunday Visitor*, filled church magazine racks with pamphlets on social questions while Catholic university students read new "Catholic" social science texts that explained the value of world government and the rights of labor.[41] Francis Haas, the author of one of the most popular of these texts and the head of the social work program at Catholic University, conveyed these teachings directly to the ILO. He not only attended the Philadelphia conference as a U.S. delegate but also earlier participated in the 1939 Inter-American ILO Conference in Havana.[42]

As early as 1938, Raymond McGowan and Albert Le Roy, the Jesuit attached by the Vatican to the ILO in Geneva, arranged with Winant an English translation of Le Roy's book on "The Church and the ILO." They perceived it as a powerful lobbying weapon to make the Catholic segment of the American population supportive of the organization. While the outbreak of the war in 1939 delayed its publication, the joint planning by Winant and the National Catholic Welfare Conference in 1938 and 1939 demonstrated a shrewd perception by both Winant and the NCWC leadership that the churches could supply the core of a new institutional base to sustain American ILO support.[43]

While the Catholic approval for the ILO in the late 1930s was the most remarkable addition to American support for international labor standards in the period, it did not overshadow the continuing efforts for the standards among mainline Protestant churches. As with the ILO and Consumers' League, Winant served as a link. His membership on the advisory council of the Oxford [World] Conference on Church, State, and Society in 1936 and 1937 tied him to the elite of liberal Protestantism at a time when the government was experimenting with the ILO as a possible protector of New Deal labor and social welfare standards.[44] He also worked with the leadership of the Federal Council of the Churches, especially James Myers, the industrial secretary. Myers personally gathered together those with worker sympathies in the church, the academy, and business. His academic credentials included a Columbia University degree and active involvement in the American Academy of Political and Social Sciences. An ordained Presbyterian minister, he collaborated as well with the Society of Friends. In 1918, he left the ministry to work as the personnel manager of a Poughkeepsie-area factory, later to return to church duties with the Federal Council. With Myers's assistance, Winant promoted the education of congregations on their social responsibility as ethical consumers.[45]

In addition to his efforts with individual Federal Council staff, Winant labored with sympathetic officials in the constituent churches, especially Episcopalian Spencer Miller. Another Columbia University graduate, Miller combined interest in education with concern for labor rights and became an early proponent of adult worker education. His interest in internationalism began with his participation in a variety of multinational adult education programs in the 1920s.[46] The relationship between Columbia University and these church leaders eased cooperation not only with Winant but with James Shotwell and his academic associates. Shotwell served as an advisor to the ecumenical National Peace Conference, which included Catholic, Jewish, and Protestant peace organizations and such secular groups as the General Federation of Women's Clubs and Shotwell's own Carnegie Endowment.[47] Because of these institutional ties, the ILO received formal support from organizations with local membership (congregations) spread throughout the country.

The problem inherent in such institutional support, however, was translating it into active understanding and ILO commitment among the millions out in the pews. To help filter hierarchical advocacy down to the local church, the Consumers' League included regional and state pastors in its network. For example, when the national league reached out to the South in the 1930s, it not only hired Lucy Mason with her Episcopal connections as secretary, it also included Mrs. W. A. Newell of the Methodist-Episcopal Church–South on its council.[48] In states such as Massachusetts, which had strong leagues in the 1930s and 1940s, clergy were heavily represented on the league's governing boards.[49]

In the 1920s and 1930s, the league's bruising battle for the Child Labor Amendment cost it official support from Catholic clergy and forced it to depend on Protestant blue bloods such as Revs. Endicott Peabody and Christopher Elliott in the Massachusetts league.[50] Such incidents revealed the recurring difficulty of converting formal church support into mass backing for either ethical consumerism or international labor standards. In 1942, the general secretary of the National Consumers' League wrote to Margaret Wiesman of the Massachusetts league that "All of the Leagues have the problem of getting adequate publicity." She could have applied the lament not only to the leagues, but also to the churches and other organizations that supported the ILO.[51] The elite leadership of mainline churches, the academy, and the ILO worked well together but had a fundamental problem reaching the majority of Americans. With favorable conditions in the 1930s, the inevitable concern with mass understanding of elite goals was not an insurmountable barrier to policy success. However,

the achievements of the 1930s did not prepare the leadership for the challenge of maintaining mass support in less favorable times.[52]

Complicating the challenge of mass education among church
members was an active opposition to church social welfare activities. At
the start of the 1930s, Reinhold Niebuhr and his brother Richard confronted the simple idealism of the social gospel.[53] Richard warned that
"the danger of the social gospel was in its idealism and in its tendency to
deny the [religious] presuppositions on which it was based."[54] If the
Niebuhrs caused self-criticism of the utopian assumptions of the social
gospel, fundamentalists began to organize opposition to the liberal Federal Council. By the early 1940s, the American Council of Christian
Churches and the National Association of Evangelicals provided a structure for Protestant opposition to the liberal politics of the mainline clergy.
It would be many years before evangelical Protestants became involved in
such social policy advocacy.

By the end of the 1930s, these divisions within Protestantism made
unified church policy support more difficult than among Catholics. Until
the war began, issues of pacifism and preparedness also split congregations. Additionally, problems surfaced from the need to work with
Catholic leaders in the labor standards movement. International Catholicism was linked to the ILO from its founding, despite the Geneva location, but liberal Protestants remembered the Catholic role in defeat of the
Child Labor Amendment. As memories of this conflict faded in the 1940s,
the Truman Administration complicated ecumenical cooperation with a
proposal to extend diplomatic recognition to the Vatican.[55] For all of these
reasons, as Catholics came to play a more significant role in ILO policy,
liberal Protestants seemed to lose interest.

BUSINESS

In many ways, the experience of business allies of the ILO mirrored
that of Protestant backers. A core of elite, liberal business leaders contributed symbolic support to the organization, but their enthusiasm was
not shared by the vast majority of their colleagues. While elite church
leaders faced the inevitable problems of mass education of an uninformed
public, elite business supporters of the ILO needed to bring about a mass
conversion experience. The depression may have stunned the business
community and quieted vocal opposition to the ILO, but it did not cause
widespread support for labor standards. Nonetheless, the depression and

subsequent war years allowed progressive business leaders time to educate some of their fellows in the value of, if not the great need for, minimal international economic rules as a means to open world markets to American producers. The elite leaders had amazing success winning grudging backing for the ILO.

From 1934, when the U.S. joined the ILO, to the end of World War II, American business was represented by four people: Henry Dennison, Marion Folsom, Henry Harriman, and Samuel Lewisohn. They shared elite educations and, except for the younger Folsom, involvement in the promotion of predepression welfare capitalism. Dennison, a Harvard graduate and manufacturer from Framingham, Massachusetts, had written on several occasions about the new relationship between business owners and workers in *Profit Sharing and Stock Ownership for Employees* and *Toward Full Employment*.[56] He frequently had offered his management skills to government, including during both world wars. He had served with the Federal Reserve, on the advisory board of the Department of Commerce, and had attended both President Wilson's Industrial Conference in 1919 and Harding's subsequent Conference on Unemployment. In 1934 he became one of the first members of the National Labor Relations Board and chaired the Industrial Advisory Board of the NRA.[57] During the first decade of U.S. membership in the ILO, Dennison frequently shared the delegate role with another Massachusetts manufacturer, Henry Harriman.

Harriman, a Wesleyan graduate, began his business career as a manufacturer of textile machinery and witnessed the major changes in that industry. He also served with Dennison on the board of the Federal Reserve Bank of Boston and at the U.S. Department of Commerce. He founded the New England Power Company and the elevated rail system in Boston and later became president of the U.S. Chamber of Commerce.[58] After becoming U.S. delegate to the ILO, he was elected by member employers to the ILO governing body from 1937 to 1940. With the other three employer representatives of the era, he found, "[T]he International Labor Organization is performing a valuable service for mankind, and through its consideration of vital economic and industrial problems is materially furthering world peace."[59]

Marion Folsom joined Dennison and Harriman as employer representative in 1944 at Philadelphia. The only southerner of the four, Folsom had northern links, holding a Harvard MBA and having built his reputation as a leader of Eastman Kodak and of various civic causes in Rochester, New York. Serving as an appointee of every president from

FDR to Nixon, including a term in the Eisenhower cabinet as secretary of health, education, and welfare, he shared with Winant a role as an ILO pioneer and as one of the founders of Social Security. His close links to Winant likewise included work at the Brookings Institution, where he served with Winant's benefactor Robert Bass. Folsom arrived at the ILO with a reputation as an innovative and brilliant business supporter of social welfare.[60]

The fourth delegate, Sam Lewisohn, was a successful mining investor, writer, and philanthropist. A Princeton graduate, from the era of Woodrow Wilson, Lewisohn had extensive experience in Jewish charities and child welfare, especially working with juvenile offenders. Lewisohn had great interest in the reform of business management and employment policy. In 1925 he coauthored *Can Business Prevent Unemployment*. The next year he wrote *The New Leadership in Industry*. At the end of World War II he completed *Human Leadership in Industry*.[61] In each of these works, he promoted business responsibility for stabilizing employment and assuring minimal wage and hour standards.

A number of other business leaders played an important role in supporting American ILO participation. Many of these people had a special interest in scientific industrial relations. Thomas G. Spates, a private industrial relations counselor from New York, worked with the ILO before the U.S. joined and continued to endorse the benefits of international reform of personnel practices. Like many early business supporters of the ILO, Spates became involved with the ILO in the 1920s when it launched its innovative industrial relations education program. By the 1930s, Spates linked the industrial planning experiments of the ILO and the NRA. In 1936, discussing the benefits of ILO membership, he recalled that, "If the NRA in its brief but intensely energetic life did nothing else, it at least made employers of this country more conscious than ever before of their social responsibility and of their obligations to labor." He reminded American employers that "the ILO performs the unique and unequaled service of bringing together within the scope of a single organization the accumulated experience of the world in the three basic methods of advancing human relationships in industry: namely, social legislation, collective bargaining, and personnel administration."[62] Other business leaders educated in the new management techniques and economics, such as Leland Robinson of American General, also defended the value of ILO membership.[63]

Leaders of business education, such as Joseph Willets, dean of the Wharton School, likewise respected the ILO and its work. During the depression, he concluded that "the work of the Organization [was] of much more significance to the United States than it has been in the past."[64] However, Willets did not fit the mold of a representative American businessman. In addition to his Wharton position, he chaired the Quaker General Conference Committee on Unemployment and was active in the League of Nations Association. As ILO scholar John Tipton commented, these business supporters came "from a small group of employers who had become conscious of their social responsibilities and of their obligations to labor under the impetus of the NRA."[65] Another ILO scholar, Walter Galenson, noted that the Roosevelt Administration found employer delegates and other business supporters not by locating the most representative of U.S. businessmen, as "required" by the ILO charter, but by finding employers who "shared New Deal views on labor matters. . . . It was possible for the administration to choose ILO delegates from such an unrepresentative group only because the antilabor majority of employers lacked the political power to stop it."[66] The disarray within the business community during the depression provided an opportunity for progressive American business leaders to seize the ILO forum to promote their version of good industrial relations and general labor policy. When employers hostile to the ILO appeared in Geneva in the 1940s, the tradition of business support for the ILO mooted their criticisms for many years.

ACADEMICS

Regardless of business interest in the ILO, as long as the U.S. remained a member, business had a constitutional role under the tripartite system of representation. However, there was no guarantee academics would remain involved, and once the U.S. joined in 1934, academics withdrew from their leadership role in supporting the ILO. As the earlier generation of scholars died out, a new generation did not take their place. This change was remarkable in the two academic associations most directly linked to labor standards: the American Economic Association (AEA) and the American Political Science Association (APSA).

Of the first ten AEA presidents, six served as officers of either the Consumers' League or the American Association for Labor Legislation. One other, John Clark, played a key role in the Carnegie Endowment, which nurtured the creation of the ILO. At the APSA, six of the first ten presidents participated in one of the two labor standard organizations and a seventh, Frank Goodnow, worked with the National Civic Federation, an organization that modeled tripartite membership to address industrial problems. The generation of leaders after World War I was noticeably less involved in labor standards organizations. After Henry Seeger's presidency at the AEA in 1922, only Albert Wolfe from Ohio State was a key Consumers' League activist. The American Political Science Association links to the AALL ended earlier.

The final blow to the close relationship between the professional academic organizations and the labor standards movement came with the dislocations of World War II and, in their midst, the death of John Andrews. The AALL had survived the 1930s as the personal fiefdom of John Andrews and his wife, Irene Osgood. Andrews kept the AALL and the academic associations together by holding AALL meetings at the same time and place as the professional groups. Beginning in 1942, the national meetings were curtailed for the duration of the war. If Andrews had outlived the war, he might have resumed the joint meetings, but he died in 1943 and the AALL ceased to operate. *The American Labor Legislation Review* stopped publication at the end of 1942. No institutional sponsor survived to promote concern for international worker protections within the academic social science associations. The loss of linkages to the top echelons of the academy deprived the postwar labor standards movement of key sources of intellectual vigor, credibility, and independent endorsement. The postwar movement found an independent constituency not directly profiting or losing from labor standards decisions only among the churches.

The death of Andrews and the AALL does not fully explain the reasons for the demise of academic involvement in the movement. The professional expectations and training of social scientists had changed. The APSA and the AEA, which had been influenced heavily by practitioners with interest in the conditions of the masses, became the province of people who taught and wrote but did not associate with workers or other less affluent community members. The two wars coincided with a change in the education of academic leaders. As shown in table 5.1, each of the first six academic advisors to the Consumers' League in 1898 were educated in Germany, three at Berlin. These were people who admired the involvement in labor policy of the members of the Social Policy Association. As that generation passed, their successors were not exposed to academic training that emphasized involvement of the privileged in the problems of the less fortunate.[67]

In economics, the post–World War I era completed a long-term trend away from German historical economics. Richard Ely, E. R. A. Seligman, and Henry C. Adams were founders of that school in America and leaders in the fight for international labor standards. Their work, in

TABLE 5.1   Early Leaders of the Consumers' League

Name	Degree	Role
John Graham Brooks	Harvard	President
John R. Commons	Wisconsin	President 1920s, also AALL
Josephine Goldmark	Bryn Mawr	Chair, Legal Defense
Alice Hamilton	Michigan	President 1930s
Ellen Henrotin	none	Board member
Mary Putnam Jacobi	Ecole De Medicine	Founder
Florence Kelley	Cornell	General Secretary (1898–1932)
W. L. McKenzie King	Harvard	Boston League researcher
Josephine S. Lowell	Brook Farm	League founder
John Winant	Princeton	President 1930s, director ILO

Consumers' League Advisors, 1898

Name	University	Employer	Organization
Henry Adams	Berlin, Paris	Michigan	AEA, president 1896–97
Arthur Hadley	Berlin	Yale	AEA, president 1898–99
Charles Henderson	Leipzig	Chicago	Editor, *Am. Jrnl. Soc.*
Jeremiah Jenks	Halle	Cornell	AEA, president 1906–07
Samuel Lindsay	Halle	Penn	President, Am. Acad. Pol. and S.S.
E. R. A. Seligman	Berlin, Paris	Columbia	AEA, president 1902–03

Sources: Biographical information taken from various reference works, primarily *The Dictionary of American Biography.*

turn, spawned a related institutional school within the American economics profession, led by scholars such as John R. Commons and Thorsten Veblen. Commons continued as leader of both the AALL and Consumers' League until the 1930s, and Veblen's students, especially Isador Lubin, persisted in the battle for labor standards. Henry Dennison, the longtime employer delegate to the ILO, also shared the institutional approach, having worked with the young John Kenneth Galbraith in the late 1930s on critiques of "modern competition." While Keynesian economists of the next generation, such as Alvin Hansen, had some interest in the ILO, they focused on the macroeconomic policy process. They opened the door to reorienting the discipline to modeling the economic system rather than concentrating on the impact of economic institutions and policies on real people and communities.

More hostile to the institutionalists was the next generation of neoclassical economists. They converted the free market from an institution to a goal, perceiving labor standards as mistaken interference with the natural market laws of their perfect world. As one historian of economics said, "[Neoclassicists saw the central problem to be the] allocation of resources, the distribution of income, and the determination of levels of income, output and prices, institutional economists assert the primacy of the problem of the organization and control of the economic system, that is, its structure of power." Institutionalists questioned the very structure of the market, seeing it as a creation of the cultural and political power structure, not a mere abstraction ideally the same in all societies. The institutionalists found the "[p]ower structure in turn is related to legal rights, thence to the use of government in forming legal rights . . . and thereby influencing the allocation of resources."[68]

Another difference between the two schools related to the source and place of values in the economic system. Neoclassicists minimized the role of values in defining market decisions, while the institutionalists emphasized the need to comprehend the values of a culture to understand its economy. One of the leading institutionalists, John M. Clark, whose father had helped Ely found the American Economic Association, "drew a distinction between social and market values and social and market costs. Social values are those that the private market system ignores, such as clean air, scenic beauty, public health, and community welfare. Social costs, such as unused productive capacity, unemployment, destruction of worker morale, and resource spoliation, are also ignored by the private market mechanism."[69] Given such assumptions, institutionalists naturally supported labor standards that controlled the social costs of the global economic market.

After World War II, the neoclassical economists gained more influence in the field than the institutionalists, changing significantly the subject of economic interest and the involvement of economists in social reform. While not necessarily becoming politically conservative, neoclassicism tended to limit the subjects open to academic study, and this limitation made the new generation of economists less interested in venturing outside their specialized fields of research. Writing in 1959, George Stigler, future AEA president, concluded, "More broadly, one can say that economists have not been among the leaders of any important movement for the adoption of policies incompatible with the conservative position." Looking for the cause of this tendency, Stigler, perhaps tongue-in-cheek, concluded:

> The conservatism of the economists cannot be explained by the vulgar argument of venality: that economists have sold their souls to the capitalists. The current rates of pay for good economists are much below what I would assume to be the going rate for a soul.
>
> The main reason for the conservatism surely lies in the effect of the scientific training the economist receives. He is drilled in the problems of *all* economic systems and in the methods by which a price system solves these problems.[70]

Since the support of labor standards called for definition and defense of social values, the movement lost the intense support of the academic field, which a century earlier had helped create it.

Likewise, scholars in political science and history altered their approach to the study of international affairs and labor issues. The change came earliest among scholars of foreign policy. First, several prominent historians, such as the old progressive Charles Beard, attacked the political leadership of Wilson and FDR. In 1934, in *The Idea of National Interest*, Beard emphasized the theme of self-interest in the analysis of foreign policy. Using this approach, he attacked Wilson's idealistic crusade during and after the world war and Wilsonian ignorance of the limits of U.S. power.[71] By the end of the second war, Beard resumed his attack on the failure of Wilsonians, including James Shotwell. He criticized those who said joining the ILO was a major step toward U.S. involvement in the world. He concluded, "The United States had joined the International Labor Office (but that meant little more than participation in endless discussions, the collection of statistics, research, and the publication of reports; certainly it involved no commitments whatever to internationalism or collective security)."[72]

Not all critics of the failure of World War I policies and postwar institutions opposed Wilsonianism. In Thomas Bailey's various studies of the First World War, published at the end of the second war to educate Americans on what mistakes to avoid, he defended Wilson's goals while criticizing the failure of the process.[73] Still, his work weakened support for the leaders of 1919 and any surviving products of their labors, such as the ILO. While Wilsonians experienced a brief return to popularity during World War II, they soon were discredited again by a new group of supporters of self-interest—the realist school.[74] Led by Hans J. Morgenthau, and supported powerfully by journalist Walter Lippmann and diplomat George F. Kennan, the realist minimized the normative concerns in international relations, such as protection of worker rights. Kennan particularly attacked "legalistic-moralistic" American foreign policy making in his *American Diplomacy: 1900–1950*.[75] Morgenthau joined him, praising the "brilliant analysis" of Lippmann's attack on Wilson's fourteen points.[76]

Lippmann's role is ironic, given his service with James Shotwell on the Inquiry. Shotwell fought after 1919 to build a world order based upon global economic integration and global responsibility beyond the nation-state. He hoped to create international relations based upon the scientific analysis of data but with the ultimate goal of peace and social justice.[77] This effort to join ethics to social science made Shotwell popular with church leaders as well as with his generation of social scientists. His essays were published in journals as varied as "*Foreign Affairs* and *The Christian-Evangelist*."[78] It was difficult to imagine the latter publishing anything by Morgenthau.

Morgenthau, Lippmann, and their associates undermined academic interest in the ILO primarily in their critiques of Wilson at Versailles, of the league, and, by analogy, the U.N. and its international agencies.[79] For example, Robert E. Osgood's *Ideals and Self-Interest in American Foreign Relations* praised Teddy Roosevelt's realism and blamed the unrealistic idealism of Wilson for subsequent world problems.[80] Osgood concluded his assessment of World War I:

> [I]n one form, at least, the moral paralysis of the [post–World War I era] seized almost all groups, . . . Americans, in general, were embarrassed by their exhibition of moral fervor during World War I. . . . The response to this experience was a well-nigh unanimous "Never again!" Thereafter, every national move was measured against the possibility of

its dragging America into another war; and since it was believed that the nation had entered the last war on idealistic grounds, Americans were on their guard against undertaking commitments on the basis of strong moral positions toward the affairs of other nations.[81]

Osgood did not want to abandon a moral voice in foreign policy; he sought to explain that creating moral policy was not enough, more important was the implementation of the policy. He faulted the Wilsonian focus on intentions and the tendency to ignore the consequences of policy. The Wilsonians erred not in their morality but because they recklessly confused intentions with application. The realists who admired his work, however, made a mistake analogous to the one Osgood blamed on Wilsonians.

The realists tended to move from the rejection of the methods of the Wilsonians to their products, such as the ILO, which was developed to address real problems. As a Shotwell biographer summarized the consequences of realism:

> Once Washington equated its security with an indivisible global order, "realism" demanded neglect of those independent agencies that had already proven their incapacity to maintain order after Versailles. . . . The essential spirit of Shotwell's contribution to the American diplomatic tradition was contrary to the unbending unilateralism that successive liberal interventionists, running in a bipartisan line from Henry Stimson to Dean Acheson to Richard Nixon, have tried to disguise as the fulfillment of the nation's commitment to the ideals of collective security and international cooperation.[82]

Tragically for the ILO, this simplified "liberal interventionist" version of realism became the vogue in the postwar academic world, not the subtle approach called for by Osgood. As economists became lost in the wilderness of arcane market studies, political scientists and historians abandoned interest in institutions in favor of detailed studies of power processes and human behavior.

Although Shotwell lived until 1965, his influence waned. He had no successor as an activist among historians or political scientists. When his biographer, Harold Jacobson, discussed the ILO as a subject of academic inquiry, his writing contrasted sharply to that of Shotwell. Shotwell had been noted for being "A smooth writer with a convincing style." Jacobson, in vogue with postwar academics, stated that his purpose in studying the

ILO was "to generalize knowledge from comparative experience rather than to diagnose the problems confronting particular organizations."[83] Jacobson, as most of his colleagues, had little interest in writing for the general public, in advocating better policy, or in constructively criticizing a major institution. Rather, he described esoteric research about behavior for other detached academics.

Jacobson's approach mirrored another trend after the war in academic political science, one that paralleled the developments in economics. Behaviorism became the fashion, especially at leading institutions such as Jacobson's University of Michigan. Developing out of a move toward scientism in the interwar years, behaviorism brought to the discipline a demand that more time be given to data analysis and other empirical measures and less to advocacy.[84] As early as 1929, the Wilsonian future president of the APSA, Edward S. Corwin, criticized this trend. "What troubled Corwin most of all was the question of ethical and normative neutrality. Should the discipline actually turn in this direction . . . it would abandon its worthy objectives for a 'mess of pottage.'"[85] The failure of the traditionalists to anticipate and prepare for the foreign policy disasters of the 1930s opened the way for behaviorism's pottage.

Behaviorists inevitably answered foreign policy questions in realist terms. One study found that over 90 percent of the hypotheses tested by behaviorists were realist in origins.[86] Of course, hypotheses defined where scholars placed their attention. Political scientists focused on methodological questions and measuring relationships. What was good policy? What was the value of protecting worker rights? These were normative or value-laden subjects not appropriate for social scientists. Furthermore, labor standard studies faced the barrier of being inherently interdisciplinary. With increasing academic specialization, behaviorists in political science and neoclassicists in economics were forced to focus on questions lying fully in their fields.[87] Consequently, economists, political scientists, and political historians deserted the ILO.

However, the new social scientists did not abandon all political activity after the war. In fact, they probably increased involvement in public affairs. They abandoned neutral normative analysis and criticism for technical assistance and partisan participation. Shotwell had been careful to keep his distance from the partisan policy process even when working for administrations. He served as an outside academic expert guiding policy for the good of all, not for particular groups. He knew a social scientist could answer normative questions and remain politically nonpartisan.

When the later generation abandoned this approach, selling their services to the highest bidder, they would not have any interest in the welfare of the working class. They could neither understand that class by birth nor could the workers pay for their services.[88]

Another academic trend within political science undermined the vitality of the labor standards movement in the postwar years. It grew from the successful rise of the discipline of public administration. The era witnessed the blossoming of the science of administration, the seeds of which had been nurtured before the war by groups such as Henry Dennison's Taylor Society.[89] Shotwell and other supporters of the ILO, including Commons and Lubin, shared the commitment to resolving social problems through the application of scientific expertise by rational experts. Charles DeBenedetti observed:

> Shotwell devoted his life to organizing international experts in the work of rationalizing institutions of world order. He believed experts were best prepared to organize peace . . . [for] they were trained to analyze and resolve problems through the rigorous application of the scientific method, which served (1) to minimize personal prejudices; and (2) as directing force which lights up this otherwise so irrational world and gives us our bearings as we move in what we call progress.[90]

Yet, the emphasis upon expertise risked severing the staff of the ILO from the realm of popular civic relations. ILO officials moved into the obscure universe of highly trained international bureaucrats. Shotwell, Commons, and other early supporters of the labor standards movement had balanced expertise with passionate advocacy and persistent use of the democratic policy process. They welcomed to the leadership of the ILO charismatic politicians such as Albert Thomas and John Winant. But in the postwar years they turned to international labor experts.

Within sociology, a related set of trends severed ties between academia and the labor standards movement. While sociologists had not played a leading role in support for the ILO in the interwar years, they participated in the founding of the movement at the turn of the century. Charles Henderson of the University of Chicago helped create both the Consumers' League and the discipline of sociology. Like other early sociologists, Henderson found his inspiration for nurturing the early social sciences in the social gospel movement. Later in the century, the links of the social gospel and sociology were severed as a result of changes both in the movement and the discipline. As one historian of sociology concluded:

[T]he 1920s were a period of decline for the social gospel. Its theology came under attack from a variety of sources and went through a series of transformations that undermined its implications for sociology. With the decline of the social gospel, Christian sociology was cut off from its theological base. Social gospel sociology also lost one of its key allies, social work. . . .

[S]ociology itself rejected its initial link to social gospel theology and missions. Led by William F. Ogburn and other positivists, sociology was exhorted to divorce itself from social reform, become objective and value free, and base its findings on mathematical research.[91]

SURVIVING INTERESTS

With academics disappearing into the world of specialized empiricism and without political allies such as Winant, ILO support after the war rested on a few surviving business backers, a divided labor movement, some church support, and a staff of skilled international civil servants. For nearly a decade these groups helped the organization adjust to the new world order, one surprisingly different from that anticipated at Philadelphia in 1944. After a brief period of economic dislocation, the postwar western economies, and especially that in the United States, experienced a quarter century of seemingly unrestrained growth, not a return to depression. If the news from the economic front was better than anticipated, international relations quickly turned from tense to worse with the emergence of the Cold War.

As these unanticipated consequences crystallized, the surviving ILO advocates often changed their roles. In the postwar years, new representatives of the business community appeared who tended to be hostile to the social welfare interests of most delegates. Without positive employer delegates, the defense of the ILO fell more to labor. Unfortunately, the labor movement faced other pressing problems, from the continuing AFL rivalry with the CIO that would last until 1955 to the conflicts with various international unions. Frances Perkins had observed during her tenure that the labor and employer delegates to some ILO conferences considered the meetings opportunities more for vacations than for meaningful work.[92] Now that the employers turned from holidays to hostility, labor needed to get its house in order. It largely failed as it fixated on confronting the World Federation of Trade Unions, which the AFL leadership viewed as communist-dominated. By 1949, the AFL and CIO cooperated with free west European labor leaders in establishing the International Confederation of Free Trade Unions (ICFTU). The next year the ICFTU became the primary world labor federation recognized by the ILO, while the WFTU continued to share special status at the UN with the ICFTU. American labor interest in destroying the WFTU because of its links to "the Totalitarian Menace," as George Meany referred to the Soviet Union, marked the beginning of a long postwar battle between American labor and communist unions for the soul of the ILO. It forced the ILO to engage in a two-front war for the next decade, one against hostile American business and the other against the left. Peace would come on the first front long before the second; the struggle nearly destroyed the ILO.[93]

This fight was increasingly led by George Meany. Meany became president of the AFL in 1952 and brought about the merger with the CIO in 1955. A New York plumber, Meany's worldview, at least as revealed in ILO debates, was defined by twin influences: the tough politics of unions and his Catholic faith. He combined the old AFL commitment to voluntarism and collective bargaining with church interest in social harmony and later, social justice. Meany attacked other union leaders without fear, whether from the U.S. or abroad. He was a formidable opponent for those in the international labor movement with sympathies for leftists. At the ILO he was prepared to take on the world with his ICFTU and church friends. The stage was set for a tumultuous era of economic debate at Geneva, defining a vitally important theory of political economy, neither free market nor Marxist.[94] Most important, the postwar labor standards de-

FIGURE 5.1. The Classic Cozy Triangle

Global Business

Congressional Subcommittees   Executive Departments

bates demonstrated that when populist institutions participate vigorously in the American policy process, it can work exceptionally well and even succeed.

Despite a decline in union membership that began in the 1950s, the tripartite structure of ILO policy making, requiring a labor seat at the table, kept the ILO responsive to the needs of the world's workers, especially those in Eastern Europe and in developing countries. Figure 5.1 shows the classic cozy triangle model of policy making, which favors the privileged position of affluent special interests, such as business. Tripartism forced a modification of the classic policy process. Despite its late-twentieth-century membership problems, labor had to be included in the ILO issue network. Essentially, the triangle became a polygon, as reflected in figure 5.2, with labor's large membership giving it not only a seat, but preeminence. While many scholars maintain the cozy triangle is too simple a diagram for the American process, the differences between figures 5.1 and 5.2 capture, however simply, the core differences between ILO policy making and the American norm. The academics, church leaders, and consumer organizations, as well as the variety of business interests in ILO policy, would not alter the fundamental distinctiveness of the process resulting from tripartism. Despite the great growth in multinational business wealth and influence at the end of the twentieth century, the labor standards process demonstrated one method for assuring that international government not lose sight of the need to seek justice under law. At least partially because of tripartism, American labor, abandoned by its allies except the churches, was able to preserve the integrity of the ILO

FIGURE 5.2. Tripartite ILO Policy Polygon

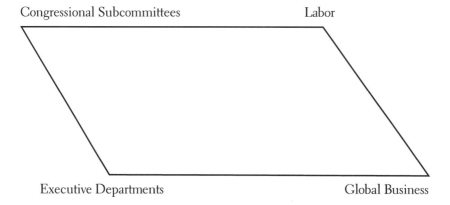

Congressional Subcommittees   Labor

Executive Departments   Global Business

until a new powerful group of human rights attorneys organized support for the labor standards struggle at the dawn of the new millennium.

Early in the postwar years, the realist Hans Morgenthau considered the success of the ILO and other specialized international agencies as one model for creating a world community. He identified the ILO's strength as its specialization, which allowed it to address issues that did not divide nations but were of global concern.[95] Yet, in the Cold War era and beyond, the ILO did not have that luxury. Rather, in debates about defining global social welfare standards, freedom of association, and core labor standards, the ILO did not get a free ride around the major power divisions. Quite the contrary, the ILO became one of the prime battlegrounds between supporters of social democracy and laissez-faire, between the U.S. and the Soviet Union, and, at the start of the new millennium, between multinational business and a global human rights coalition. The ILO successes came not because of specialization but because tripartism encouraged and assured that a variety of perspectives beyond those of nation-states and privileged elites were heard. As early as the late 1940s, conflicts between a new generation of American business leaders and the majority at the ILO tested this theory. On several occasions before the end of the millennium when justice was at stake, the special role of nongovernmental public interest institutions at the ILO proved the value of tripartite pluralism in international relations.[96]

SIX

An Alternate Vision

The quarter century after the end of World War II witnessed international economic and political relations different from those anticipated by the wartime planners. First, the depression did not return. America experienced unprecedented economic growth and world economic preeminence. The prosperity of the era undermined American interest in the ILO. Second, the members of the wartime United Nations quickly split into a bipolar world, pitting the western liberal democracies against communist regimes. Meanwhile, the ending of colonial empires and the emergence of third world countries complicated simple bipolarity. The Cold War and the differences between developed and developing nations made for sharply divisive debates in Geneva and at other international forums. At the ILO, the international disagreements highlighted the organization's weakness. Soon, American business leaders called for curbing or ending American participation. Debates about the membership of totalitarian and authoritarian regimes particularly tested the commitment and contributions of many groups and institutions long involved in the labor standard policy process. This membership crisis forced key western supporters of the ILO to define populist international economic theories as an alternative to both neoliberal and Marxist materialism. By 1980, populist labor organizations and religious institutions, with new allies from the legal profession, began to demonstrate their vital role in bringing integrity, justice, and restraint to the international policy process.

Generally, theorists of the American policy process, especially those focusing upon Cold War foreign relations, have proposed alternatively elite or pluralist interpretations. According to elite theorists, such as C. Wright Mills, specific circumstances in the postwar era served to produce an elite composed of political leaders, corporate executives, and high military leaders who achieved unprecedented control of American policy. According to Mills, the members of the elite came from the same social class and shared the same worldview.[1] They often moved from one branch of the elite to another. This interpretation was given credibility by President Eisenhower, who not only exemplified it for Mills, but warned of its dangers in his farewell address.[2] Other, more recent social scientists accepted this elite theory.[3]

In contrast to the elite model, other students of American policy identified more complexity in the process, finding a variety of interests with some influence. Writing in 1950, Gabriel Almond maintained that instead of one elite, a number of small interest groups battled for policies over the heads of an indifferent public.[4] Roger Hilsman, more than Almond, found the process highly complex and political. Hilsman identified three levels or circles of decision making: an inner one of national security officials, an intermediate group of less important public officials and their advisors, and a third circle that included Congress, the press, interest groups, and the attentive public.[5] Some, such as Robert Dahl, saw the pluralist systems of Almond and Hilsman as reasonably successful in identifying the American public interest. Others, like Kenneth Dolbeare and Murray Edelman, believed that while a foreign policy elite with shared economic interest and beliefs dominated the policy process, the public had free access to it. However, usually the masses accepted the beliefs and even shared the interests of the elite or through apathy or fear gave acquiescence to its wishes.[6] Dolbeare and Edelman added that there were times when nonelites became sufficiently involved to shock the system into a new course. Otherwise, the leaders of the various dominant factions set policy without public input.

The study of ILO policy in the postwar era is too specialized to prove conclusively which policy theory best fits all circumstances. However, it does verify that Dolbeare and Edelman were closer to describing the circumstances of ILO policy making than were pure elite theorists. On several occasions key institutions and actors from outside the elite, especially from populist labor and religious institutions, brought significant policy change. They fought to protect human rights when elite leaders rushed to withdraw from battles or ignored problems. Consequently, the ILO experience shows the importance of nonelite institutions if the process is to produce just and restrained policy. Without the intrusion of such populist institutions, the elite policy makers clearly would have persisted in a direction that minimized conflict and condoned human rights abuse.

While some students of the policy process place labor and religious interest groups with others trying to influence the policy process, the ILO experience demonstrates the distinctiveness of these two types of institutions.[7] Except for the smallest churches and unions, they have memberships larger than interest groups like trade associations or peak business organizations.[8] Also, they are institutions with functioning local structures scattered widely throughout the country. In contrast to most national interest groups, unions and churches have members with modest incomes and average educational attainment. Because of these differences they are populist institutions.[9] For example, no matter how bureaucratic the AFL-CIO is or how hierarchical the Catholic Church, each depends for success on sustaining a large membership of the less affluent, of women, and of the working class. And, each, to some extent, hear and represent the hopes and wishes of the membership. Even religious denominations that are smaller and more homogeneous than the Catholic Church tend to have more class and education diversity than do similar-sized business interests, and they have near gender balance, which seldom is the case in business and professional groups. The ILO policy process, even if exceptional, contradicts the assumptions of many theorists who maintain that the U.S. interest group process only permits populist interests to succeed if they seek small or incremental changes.[10]

In the immediate postwar years, the populist interests combined with many elite policy makers to block the goals of business leaders. Toward the end of the era, the legal profession assumed an important role in supporting populist interests. The success of this coalition demonstrated the limits of the arguments that business inherently occupied a privileged position in American policy making.[11] The experiences of the 1950s did not prove that business had no special advantages in policy making. It showed, however, that popular interests could thwart economic interests if effectively organized and guided by clear and just goals. In the latter part of the era, especially in the mid-1970s, by all accounts the policy deck was completely stacked in favor of economic elites. Both the business and foreign policy establishment favored detente and compromise on human rights, especially at the ILO. Even those elites sympathetic to labor rights cautioned that confrontation would bring disaster, not victory. Yet, the success of labor, working nearly alone, demonstrated not only that populists could win, but that they could be right in assessing means as well as ends.

THE DECADE AFTER THE WAR

In the postwar years, the ILO confronted four major challenges: its relationship to the UN, the need for stable leadership, the necessity for a defined role and public support, and the problem of Soviet membership.[12] Each of these issues, if addressed poorly, would have undermined if not destroyed the organization. The first was most fundamental, since failure to be linked to the UN would have doomed the organization. Unfortunately, rival UN structures existed, such as the Economic and Social Council, which made the ILO potentially redundant. The ILO's recent patron, the U.S., was preoccupied with other issues, and the other major power, the Soviet Union, was hostile. Nevertheless, the old elite supporters of the ILO worked with their handpicked bureaucrats and negotiated a juridical relationship with the UN.[13] However, this was the last time that elite would be available to assist the organization.

The ILO faced a leadership void in 1945. Death and the war had removed the first generation of leaders. There was no Albert Thomas or John Winant in the immediate postwar staff. The appointment of typical international bureaucrats threatened to constrain institutional initiative, which might have brought irrelevancy and extinction. Then in 1948 the U.S. secured the selection of David Morse, acting secretary of labor, as the ILO's new director general. Morse proved to be a brilliant choice, possessing remarkable diplomatic and legal skills as well as a commitment to social justice. He remained at the helm until 1970, except for a brief strategic resignation in 1961. His commitment to human rights originated as much from his family background as from his formal training as an attorney. Not a practicing labor leader like Thomas, nor a successful politician like Winant, he symbolized in his commitment to the law one of the institutional supports that saved the ILO from its own bureaucratization and from its opponents in both western business and eastern totalitarianism.

The child of immigrants to New York, he managed to earn a Harvard law degree and brought a unique blend of toughness and charm to the ILO. Beginning his law practice in 1933 at the start of the New Deal, he secured several federal labor relations assignments that earned him recognition as an expert on labor law. When the war came, he volunteered for the army, in which he had the good fortune to gain experience related to international labor standards and the need for free labor unions. First in Italy and later in Germany, he organized the occupation labor relations program. He found and nurtured surviving democratic labor leaders and with the Allies established harmonious and fair labor-management relations. When the war ended, he returned to civilian government service, eventually supervising the international relations of the Department of Labor. There he served as U.S. delegate to the ILO.[14]

Morse's first election as chief of the ILO was not remarkable, since in 1948 the Soviet Union boycotted the ILO and the U.S. dominated the world economy. However, his reelections in 1957, 1962, and 1967, when the organization had expanded to include not only Russia and its allies but also a new majority of developing nations, proved his exceptional diplomatic skill. This skill resulted less from a simple willingness to work with all members and more from a tenacity and even deviousness in pursuing a vision of the ILO role in the world. Most remarkably, for all his ability to serve major constituencies and build support for the organization at any cost, he did not lose the focus on the organization's ideals. As he reminded delegates in his 1949 report:

> [T]he ILO must play more effectively the role set out for it. That is why I stress participation in world reconstruction, technical assistance, freedom of association, regional activity. That is why I stress the need for human dignity, universality, elimination of unemployment, . . . and a greater effort to have our work applied directly and more vigorously to the immediate as well as to the long-range needs of those we serve — who are, after all, the peoples of the world.[15]

While Morse enunciated the ILO's ideals, he focused on technical services that most members supported and avoided substantive battles over implementing ideals, such as freedom of association.[16]

Like many powerful public administrators, Morse combined vision with skill in expanding the role of the ILO beyond its formal mandate.[17] During the 1950s he increased the ILO's training programs in human resources, especially through technical industrial training in Asia and Africa.[18] In addition to the presumed benefits individuals and their nations experienced from the training, the new focus had several organizational benefits for the ILO. First, the training programs were funded separately from the per-country assessments upon which the organization was dependent. These country assessments were a precarious basis for support, especially when major nations could withdraw, as had Germany, Italy, Japan, and the Soviet Union before the war.[19] Regular assessments declined from 86 percent of the budget in 1950 to less than half in the late 1960s. Money on human resource development grew from one-fifth in 1950 to 84 percent of the budget in 1967.[20]

With this spending came an international constituency intensely committed to Morse and the ILO. Morse realized that the key to survival for specialized agencies like the ILO was not mass public support, which was unlikely to materialize. Rather, the survival of the ILO depended upon intense support from a small group of institutions and interests with special knowledge of world labor issues. He successfully maintained the ILO's natural base within the labor movement, nurtured backing by the Catholic Church and other religious institutions, and fostered an alliance with a new network of development professionals.[21]

The ultimate test of Morse's institutional success appeared in the first major crisis of the postwar years. In 1954, the Soviet Union and its allies, as UN members, applied for the ILO membership to which they were entitled. Many Western leaders complained that the Soviet system of state employers and state-controlled unions could not fit into the ILO tripartite structure. That structure assumed each country's government delegates would be joined by independent employer and labor representatives. The Soviets would send four government delegates, with one disguised as an industrial manager and one as a union official. While some former ILO supporters, especially in the United States, urged withdrawal, Morse had built sufficient ILO strength that the organization weathered the crisis. A well-timed papal audience for the ILO governing body especially demonstrated Morse's success in constituency building. If the staunchly anticommunist Vatican respected the ILO, who in the West could attack it?[22]

By 1955, then, the ILO had addressed each of the major issues from 1945. This success has been overshadowed by the controversies that raged as a result of its decisions. For the remainder of the Cold War, the ILO survived as a remarkable barometer, if not forum, for measuring the conflicting visions of the liberal, communist, and developing world. The award of the Nobel Peace Prize to the ILO in 1969 was much deserved, for forums that resolve seemingly intractable disputes are truly important instruments of peace.[23] What was not included in the consideration of the Nobel Committee was the failure of the organization to effectively implement its human and labor rights ideals in totalitarian and one-party member states. That was a crucial issue at the close of the era, raised as a result of a remarkable change in patterns of American support.

The American policy process, which often blocked innovation, now displayed one of its virtues, the nurturing of independent populist institutions. Such institutions represented visions of justice that were not clouded by the opportunity to share power. The extreme antilabor bias in the U.S. and extreme separation of the church from the state in the U.S. constitutional system guaranteed that neither institution would be effectively co-opted.[24] Both spoke forcefully to correct policy failure on the national and international level.

NEW BUSINESS LEADERSHIP

One of the difficult transitions faced by the ILO after the war came with the arrival from the U.S. of a new group of employer delegates, prepared to defend classical liberalism without reservation. Even before the admission of the Soviet Union in 1954, American employer delegates expressed extreme hostility to the ILO's acceptance of a social welfare ideology. They feared the majority of members from Western European democracies as dangerous social democrats and feminists. Given this hostility at a time when the U.S. and Western Europe controlled the ILO, American business representatives became apoplectic when paired with Soviet "employers" after 1954. They only tempered their antagonism later when they perceived the possibility of a world economy dominated by free-market principles.

With the end of World War II, American business launched a comprehensive assault on labor rights and social welfare ideas. In America it included public education and employee training in free-market liberalism.[25] The assault also was aimed at new welfare protections, such as national health insurance. It fought for the repeal of some labor rights, especially in the Taft-Hartley Act. Finally, it featured an aggressive use of the courts to restrict through interpretation the rights of workers in existing laws.[26] Added to the general mobility of capital to the American South in the early postwar years and offshore much later, the strategy halted the expansion of the New Deal welfare state and of organized labor and began to turn back both. Politically, this process originated with conservative victories in the 1946 elections. It continued in the McCarthy-era charges of widespread communist influence in unions. More significant, union vigor suffered from economic complacency during the postwar economic boom and indifference to trade issues in an era of American economic supremacy. Despite the recent depression, the postwar years witnessed a victorious return to popularity of classical liberalism.[27] This triumph was especially evident among employers involved with the ILO.

The postwar attitude of business leaders toward the ILO changed not merely as a result of organized attacks upon the ILO in the business press

and among academics linked to business, but initially as a result of inevitable personnel retirements. Longtime ILO business delegates Henry
Dennison and Henry Harriman both reached the age of seventy in the
1940s and were dead by 1952. Their immediate replacement, from 1945 to
1948, James Zellerbach of San Francisco, the president of Crown Zellerbach, continued their supportive work with the ILO. In addition to being
the U.S. employer delegate, Zellerbach served as the vice chairman of the
governing body of the ILO. An associate of Dennison on the National
Manpower Council and member of Paul Hoffman's Committee for Economic Development, Zellerbach saw the ILO's conventions as a way to
encourage all nations "to march in step toward the objective of prosperity."
Writing in the *Public Relations Journal* in 1947, he said, "I wish that American businessmen from every corner of the nation could have attended that
Conference. They would have witnessed the general acceptance of the
point of view of American labor and industry." He added that in Geneva,
American employers and union leaders realized their differences were
minor and shared a general defense of free enterprise. Zellerbach's replacement would not be so sanguine.[28] Amidst these positive assessments,
Zellerbach noted an ominous trend among some delegations at the ILO—
their routine support for leftist economic agendas. From his perspective, that
was more reason for the U.S. employers to remain informed and active.[29]

The National Economic Council, a well-funded right-wing business lobbying group, took a different perspective.[30] Especially under the
leadership of Merwin Hart in the late 1940s, the council approached the
ILO as a threat to free enterprise. Hart, who had been a leader of right-
wing causes in the 1930s and early 1940s, used his *Economic Council
Letter* to attack the ILO. In October 1948, for example, he devoted an
issue to the ILO as "World Government—By the Back Door." He warned
readers that "This Letter is one of the most important NEC has ever published. We therefore offer to send each subscriber up to five copies upon
request."[31] The following month, at the brink of the Truman-Dewey
presidential election, the letter specifically attacked the general leftward
trend of the labor movement and the ILO "since 1919." Hart warned,
"[The] ILO has aptly been described as 'the "UN" of all do-gooder activities pertaining to world totalitarianism.'" In a cover story called "ILO
Rides Again: For More World Government over USA," he described the
use of the ILO to override Supreme Court opinions. Turning to David
Morse, he accused him of having presided over the American Military
Government (AMG) in Germany at precisely the time "of the Stalinist
influx into AMG."[32]

What especially disturbed Hart and his allies was the very issue that had made Winant and others first interested in the ILO — the treaty power. He warned that if ILO conventions were ratified as treaties, they would supersede constitutional barriers to federal social policy. Hart saw, "The cloak of legality for this conspiracy is a clause in the Constitution . . . which obviously was never intended to be used as the international leftists are attempting to use it now."[33] The rightists had to respond.

Whatever the influence of the National Council, soon its view of the ILO prevailed among mainstream employer groups. Accordingly, in 1948, the U.S. Chamber of Commerce and the National Association of Manufacturers (NAM) implemented a new joint selection process for the employer delegate.[34] This process potentially would moderate the internationalism of the chamber with the more conservative, antilabor bias of the NAM. When Zellerbach accepted a role advising the Italian government on economic development in 1949, the two organizations picked Charles McCormick of the Baltimore spice company as his successor. Superficially, McCormick appeared to be another progressive internationalist. The son of a Baptist missionary, with experience in Mexico and France and administering a company involved in world trade, he brought more international contacts to the job than any of his predecessors. Likewise, he had a reputation as a progressive in labor management relations, "a rare combination of prophet and practical thinker."[35] Taking over McCormick and Company from his uncle in the midst of the depression, McCormick gained fame for raising wages in early 1933 to encourage employees to forget about the depression and focus on the business. He installed "Multiple Management," a procedure that welcomed employee participation in decision making. Symbolically, McCormick had a doorless office at the end of a public hall.[36] McCormick led the company from four years of red ink to profitability and became a new Henry Ford; but McCormick was no Zellerbach. At best, he served as a transition to a new breed of employer delegate.

McCormick criticized the ILO as "hostile to American free competitive enterprise" and demanded procedural reforms to assure that passage of conventions would be enforced. He opposed the "sham" ratification of conventions that were not enforced but used for "vote-getting at home."[37] McCormick's attitude hinted at future business attacks in the next decade. He traced the changed business attitude to the work of "a joint committee of the U.S. Chamber of Commerce and National Association of Manufacturers — [which] discovered that the ILO was no longer simply a standard-bearer for the smaller, underdeveloped nations. It had emerged as a gushing fountain of statist social and economic schemes, which aimed at higher living standards through more and more government decree rather than by more and more production."[38]

The revised procedures for selecting McCormick grew out of complaints by the newly invigorated neoliberal leaders in the business community. This new breed of business leader shared the NEC's condemnations of ILO conventions as steps toward a Western European welfare state. With the Soviet Union condemning the ILO as a capitalistic tool, it appeared contradictory that American business leaders would be condemning the same institution as "a gushing fountain of statist social and economic schemes." McCormick complained for his colleagues that virtually all of the delegates, especially the government representatives from Western Europe, sided with labor. Even the employer delegate from Britain, sent by the Labor Government, represented a nationalized industry. How could a classical liberal, believing in an unregulated free market, function in such a place?

Three factors became the focus of business opposition to the ILO. First, U.S. business disliked specific ILO conventions, especially those related to labor unions, women's work, forced labor, and health insurance. Second, it feared the impact of ratified conventions on American law. Third, after 1954, the admission of the Soviet Union and its allies to the organization increased the feeling of business isolation.

In the postwar years, the ILO submitted several conventions to member nations that defined fundamental labor rights implicit since the organization's founding. With social democracy triumphant in Western Europe and no major opposition among the labor delegates from any country, the ILO succeeded in converting general principles into explicit conventions, sent to the members for ratification and implementation. The American business delegate seemed the only person who did not take these principles for granted. America's exceptionalism in social policy clearly increased in the era. Business leaders like McCormick could not believe their government, which had just passed the Taft-Hartley Act, would be a party to conventions guaranteeing the right of association. In a country that had sent "Rosie the Riveter" home to have babies, passing conventions requiring equal pay for equal work seemed absurd, and maternity and child allowances positively radical. Then the social security convention demanded guaranteed health insurance — hardly a government responsibility in voluntarist America. McCormick even worried about the implication of the proposed convention outlawing forced labor.[39]

From its founding the ILO had championed many of these issues. It always had supported equal pay for equal work. The first ILO conference in 1919 added maternity leave and medical protections. The difference after World War II, however, was that the ILO went beyond general principles to define the specifics. In 1946, three conventions dealt with the medical examination of youthful workers and restricted night work for minors. In 1948, conventions placed restrictions on night work for women too. While the U.S. did not ratify these conventions, they did not cause as much of a stir among business leaders as what was to come. In 1951, Convention 100 called for equal remuneration for equal jobs. The following year, Convention 103 guaranteed pregnant women twelve weeks of maternity leave and at least six weeks of postmaternity leave. While on leave, women were "entitled to receive cash and medical benefits"; the cash should be "sufficient for the full and healthy maintenance of herself and her child in accordance with a suitable standard of living."[40] As with all the conventions of the era, the U.S. refrained from ratification. But, a vocal segment of the business community expressed outrage at the ideas implicit in these conventions and fear that someday they might be approved.

To make matters worse, Conventions 87 and 98, passed in 1948 and 1949, asserted the right of workers to free association and to organize. These seemed direct assaults on the Taft-Hartley law, forcing reduced regulation of organized labor at the very time the U.S. wanted to increase it. McCormick said of Convention 98, "If this convention had been submitted to the Senate and ratified, the conflicting sections of the Taft-Hartley law would have been nullified automatically (as would many state statutes). The House of Representatives, in which support for the Taft-Hartley law is especially strong would have had no voice in the matter."[41] Finally, the social security convention, passed in 1952, committed any signatory to minimum universal health benefits. Obviously, the AMA and U.S. insurance industry joined with other business lobbyists to oppose this commitment.[42]

McCormick was so upset that he argued about the fairness of the ILO convention process with David Morse and the U.S. government delegates.[43] He observed, "[T]he two most influential delegates in the conference, our government delegates, voted along with the U.S. worker delegate and the Socialist majority."[44] Recalling that this was the era before Soviet admission, when McCormick said "Socialist," he referred to the delegates from Western Europe. He claimed, "[A]s the ILO has pushed further and further into controversial economic and social matters, the sessions have become more and more a battleground for a continuing struggle between the two powerful ideologies of the West—free enterprise, and

Western European Socialism."[45] Writing in the *Nation's Business*, he complained that "the ILO has yet to show genuine admiration for the way of life which has given America's 150,000,000 citizens the highest standard of living the world has ever known."[46]

The hostility of American business to the ILO influenced the decision to define a business ideology hostile to labor and social welfare. In the first decade of U.S. membership, business leaders and labor shared many policy goals at the ILO. Now, business marked out a rigidly free-market ideology of its own. Anyone not favoring market determination of value was the enemy, and given the spirit of the McCarthy era, implicitly a Communist ally. American business not only opposed Communism in its effort to build a liberal free-enterprise system, it considered social democracy as much the enemy as Soviet totalitarianism.

McCormick also articulated the business fear that social welfare reformers would seek to bring a social policy revolution to America through the treaty power. Writing in 1952 in the *Nation's Business*, he joined those who feared "a vote-conscious pro-labor administration might seek to bypass an unsympathetic Supreme Court with an ILO convention."[47] As this argument circulated among other business critics of the "socialistic ILO," it became linked to efforts to ratify the Bricker Amendment. Congressman John Bricker of Ohio proposed the amendment to weaken the president's foreign policy powers. It required treaties be effective only when in full accord with existing U.S. law.[48] The issue received thorough legal consideration in a research report sponsored by the American Enterprise Association (AEA). The AEA specifically related support for the Bricker Amendment to the ILO, concluding in the words of future Secretary of State John Foster Dulles that the amendment was necessary to protect "the rights given the people by their Constitutional Bill of Rights."[49]

The role of the American Enterprise Association in the ILO debates marked a fundamental shift in academic research related to the ILO. At the turn of the century, when social scientists showed interest in international labor standards, they generally supported them. Now there were a number of critics linked to the neoclassical revival in economics. An example was John Van Sickle, an economist at Vanderbilt in the 1940s, at Wabash College in the 1950s, and a board member of the AEA. As early as 1946 he attacked the ILO in the *Southern Economic Journal*.[50] The board of the AEA included and nurtured a new generation of academics, especially from business schools and among economists. The AEA provided a forum for academics to join with business leaders in an attack on the effectiveness and danger of the ILO.

In the midst of the debate over the Bricker Amendment, another issue surfaced that incensed business leaders. In 1953, Russia and its allies decided to take their seats at the ILO. Typical of the bumbling Soviets in that era, they announced their decision with three reservations, including not being bound by the International Court of Justice in ILO matters.[51] Throughout 1954, the U.S. and its allies debated a tactical response to the Russian move. *The New York Times* editorialized that "Instead of serving as a forum for the exchange of views by workers, employers and Government, the Geneva meetings would be corrupted into sounding boards for Soviet delegates, masquerading as spokesmen for all three groups and yet responsible to a single master."[52] The new American employer delegate, William McGrath, recommended withdrawal if the USSR was seated. While calmer heads prevailed, including *Business Week* and McGrath's sponsoring organizations, the U.S. Chamber and the NAM, the addition of the Soviets became the last straw for business leaders such as McGrath.[53]

The Rise of Weberian Capitalists

If McCormick brought an aggressively critical approach to employer representation at the ILO, his friend and successor, McGrath, elevated complaints to confrontation. A Cincinnati furnace manufacturer, who considered himself a self-made man, McGrath shared McCormick's reputation as a management reformer. On a monthly basis he informed all employees of the company's financial status. At least annually he met with each employee and maintained a close relationship with shop-floor managers. While business leaders considered McGrath the father of model employee relations, the reality of the Williamson Company's labor relations was less positive. In the immediate postwar era of labor unrest, McGrath had fundamental conflicts with the CIO and the NLRB over alleged company tampering with representation elections. In 1946, there was a sixty-one-day strike at Williamson.[54] Then in the late 1940s, McGrath battled with the national unions to convert the Williamson local into an independent union.[55] Later, the company had disputes with employees over asbestos exposure and the conversion of the company from a manufacturer of heating and air-conditioning equipment into a supplier.[56] While the final decline and closure came in 1975 after McGrath's death, the corporate culture established by McGrath fit with its history. McGrath had worked as a young man for a firm that had gone out of business. He was said to regard business failure as a virtue of the American system: "It is through these failures that astute men learn what not to do."[57]

McGrath was an example of the triumph of neoclassical materialism within American business in the postwar years. He represented a group whose highest values were production and consumption. McGrath recalled with reverence the beliefs of an early Taylor Society leader, who framed over his desk the assertion, "Only when man's genius for profit went into partnership with engineering . . . were men and materials, the raw stuff of Nature, turned into civilization." Confident of this approach to civilization, McGrath became leader of the Society for the Advancement of Management, the new name for the Taylor Society. McGrath went to churches and civic groups, as well as business organizations, to extend support for reinvigorated, Taylorized classical liberalism.

McGrath's success reinforced the assertion first explained by Max Weber that Protestantism, especially in its American form, inherently endorsed capitalist values. McGrath modified the Protestant ethic's emphasis on saving and hard work by incorporating the newer efficiency sanctions from Frederick Taylor. His reconciliation of the Protestant ethic with Taylor received the blessing of the high priest of the revival of classical liberalism, Norman Vincent Peale. In 1957, Peale awarded McGrath the Guide Post Award for the Cincinnatian's defense of the theology they shared. Peale pointed out that one of the objectives of the award was promoting free enterprise. The plaque handed to McGrath read, "For distinguished service to the nation through support of spiritual principles as the basis of American Freedom."[58] Since McGrath's principles were primarily materialistic, related to hard work, saving, and consuming, the citation was something of an oxymoron.[59]

At the ceremony in 1957, McGrath and Peale condemned the role of the ILO in "spreading poison about the United States all over the world."[60] In another attack, McGrath warned, "If things keep on getting rougher, I would not be surprised if some day the ILO blew up with a bang. And I must say that I, for one, would not be disappointed."[61] These violent wishes, of course, seemed no more contradictory of Christian principles than the materialism that Peale labeled spiritual. What Peale especially appreciated was McGrath's willingness to lecture other clergy on the proper theology. In 1955, for example, McGrath asked "ministers, priests, and rabbis" to observe United States Day, the Sunday closest to United Nations Day. He called on them to remind their congregations that the United States was the leading nation "whose government was based upon rights derived from God."[62]

Peale and McGrath apparently saw no contradictions in linking Christianity to the free market nor in asking rabbis to observe United States Day on a Sunday. Likewise, they seemed unaware that they repudiated the work of a previous generation of business leaders. Yet, clearly their philosophy marked a revolutionary break with the recent past, both in its basic ideas and in its hostility to the ILO. While the old business leadership at the ILO disagreed somewhat with the agenda of Western European social democrats, supporting welfare capitalism rather than full government provision of welfare services, McGrath and his colleagues revived faith in a Darwinian campaign for efficiency and hard work at any human cost.[63] Social democrats and communists were equal threats to this restored capitalist morality, as were the American labor leaders and orthodox clergy who found value in activities other than materialist accumulation.

Given his ideology, McGrath hardly needed Soviet entry to spark his anti-ILO tirades. Writing in the National Economic Council's newsletter, he warned, "[A]s state socialism came into ascendancy in Europe, the ILO . . . has put forward a whole series of legislative proposals which . . . would force their governments into a socialistic mold."[64] He then went on to focus on two ILO conventions, the one on social security, which required universal health insurance, and the maternity protection convention. Sounding like later American welfare reformers, he attacked the maternity convention for making "no distinction" between legitimate and illegitimate children. However, unlike more recent "reformers," he criticized the convention because it assumed women with small children would work outside the home and would require employer support for day care. "It will be obvious that the economic base to support these Utopian proposals simply does not exist."[65]

McGrath did not stop with his attacks on the ILO — he developed a plan to block its influence, becoming a leader of the Bricker Amendment movement. "The Bricker Amendment would give Constitutional protection against the possibility of turning our country into a socialistic state by the ratification of 'Conventions' coming from the ILO."[66] A month after the *Economic Council Letter* opposing the ILO, he wrote a more detailed piece in *Advanced Management*, the Taylor organ,[67] and an essay in *The Freeman*.[68] In 1954, with the Bricker Amendment stalled, McGrath began urging American withdrawal from the ILO, at least of the employer delegate. After Soviet entry, he became more insistent. He gave a nationally covered speech on "The Strange Case of the International Labor Organization" in October.[69] He sent letters to business leaders addressed "Dear Fellow Americans."[70] In the December 1955 *Labor Relations Letter* from the U.S. Chamber of Commerce, his call for withdrawal from the ILO went out to all chamber subscribers.[71] In February 1956 he appeared before the House Foreign Affairs Committee, representing the chamber, which had passed a resolution requesting a study of U.S. withdrawal.[72] In the testimony he especially attacked the health insurance and maternity protections defined in ILO conventions.[73] He mailed copies of the testimony to his "Fellow Americans" list. McGrath's importance for the ILO is twofold. First, he showed how a persistent individual can interfere with the policy preferences of elite policy makers. Clearly, the foreign policy establishment did not want to worry about the ILO in this period. Yet, one determined midwestern business leader succeeded in being heard. *Business Week* noted, "Generally, most employers are indifferent to ILO. McGrath and many of ILO's opponents come from traditionally isolationist Ohio, from which came the proposed Bricker Amendment to limit the president's treaty-making power."[74] Progressive business leaders, such as Zellerbach, categorically rejected McGrath's assertions; but now McGrath represented American business, not Zellerbach. The mobilization of opposition had come from outside the U.S. Chamber of Commerce, whose machinery McGrath and his allies had seized. McGrath taught friends and foes alike about the ability of individuals with financial resources to shape the policy debate.

He also was important because he forced committed supporters of the ILO to come forward, build a coalition, and define an alternative American philosophy to laissez-faire. In the mid-1950s, that coalition formed around a few elite academics and foreign policy leaders and populists from labor and the churches. The defense that arose from labor and the churches depended on a populist perception of the role of work in life. Essentially, the populists called for limiting the application of market principles in public policy. Given that labor and the churches had the support of members of the elite in the 1950s, they did not yet have to imitate McGrath's style to gain victory. They did copy his style later, after they better understood the gulf between their perceptions of labor and those of their elite allies.

THE NEW ILO COALITION

McGrath's attacks brought forth a reaction from the American foreign policy elite, especially in the United World Federalists and the American Association for the United Nations. Such groups served to bring together academics like James Shotwell and his followers, progressive business leaders such as James Zellerbach, clergy, artists, and other professionals. James Shotwell still acted as an honorary president of the U.N. Association. Winant's former executive assistant, Carol Riegelman Lubin, was "staff" for the association on matters related to the ILO. They chose David Cole, a former federal labor mediator, to resolve for the elite the withdrawal debate.[75]

Cole's solution to the ILO controversy provides an example of how the old American foreign policy establishment addressed issues of concern to the working class and social reformers. Finding the crass materialism of the neoliberals offensive, the elite banded together to redirect the debate. They engineered the appointment of Cole by the ILO to do a study of ILO operations. Cole dutifully reported back that the ILO needed to emphasize research and de-emphasize labor standard setting. This was a classic elite compromise. Cole suggested the organization give up some of its controversial substance—the effort to enforce labor standards—in exchange for an expansive research focus that would require a budget increase.[76]

Simultaneous with Cole's study, the foreign policy elite had the secretaries of labor, commerce, and state jointly appoint a committee of experts, especially from the field of industrial relations, to study the ILO. The members came from national universities, including Cal Tech, MIT, and Princeton. The chair, Joseph E. Johnson, had succeeded Shotwell at the Carnegie Endowment for International Peace. All members had had key wartime human-resource experience in government. Howard Peterson, the business representative, had drafted the Selective Service Act. While all had participated in the wartime Democratic administration, they had bipartisan credentials. Peterson had served as campaign finance chair for Eisenhower.[77] The Republican members' resumes, which included service as heads of various internationalist organizations such as the World Peace Foundation, must have appalled McGrath. And one, Charles Myers, had written favorably on the ultimate social democracy, Sweden. William McGrath and his petty business allies, however, could not match the Johnson committee's expertise and connections. In contrast to McGrath's lack of a college education, its members had terminal graduate or professional degrees from elite institutions. When its work was done, not surprisingly, the Johnson committee recommended not merely continued ILO membership, but a funding increase to accommodate Cole's recommendations.[78] In addition to the foreign policy elite associated with the Carnegie Endowment, mainline Protestant denominations came to the defense of the ILO, especially the Department of the Church and Economic Life of the National Council of Churches. During the membership controversy, the department circulated information on the ILO's achievements.[79] In groups such as the United World Federalists, individual denomination leaders, including the presiding bishop of the Episcopal Church, played a role. He was joined by a Baptist and a Methodist leader, as well as by three Catholic clergy.[80]

THE LABOR RESPONSE

From a labor perspective, the problem with the elite response was that it preserved the ILO while deemphasizing labor standards. Organized labor consequently both welcomed elite support in putting down McGrath's challenge and learned of the differences between the labor perspective and that of the foreign policy establishment on labor rights. The elite compromises were difficult to face, since organized labor had been the first group to formally confront the arguments of McGrath. George Delaney, the AFL representative at the ILO, unequivocally attacked McGrath in congressional testimony in 1953 and continued to do so throughout the membership battles.[81] Members of Congress sympathetic to labor forwarded to union leaders the various ILO attack letters from McGrath's group. Both the AFL and CIO responded faithfully with critiques of world materialism.

In these responses, labor began to clarify its opposition to the evolving free-market ethic of business. Lumping business with the communists, a conscious reversal of McGrath's effort to identify the AFL-CIO with communism, the unions attacked both the Soviets and McGrath for subverting the freedom of workers. Defining an alternative ideology, labor explained that the materialism of free-market liberals and Russian Marxists denied the intrinsic dignity of workers. Both failed to distinguish between work and life beyond the paid job. Both failed to defend worker freedom as the cornerstone of political freedom. Thomas Burke of the CIO staff said of McGrath's faction, "The boys with the bucks are up to their old tricks aren't they? They never give up their fondest hope that someday they will be able to destroy workingmen's organization. I sometimes wonder if they ever wake up to the fact that when they destroy the worker's right to organize they are well on the way to destroying themselves."[82] Labor leaders at the time especially defended the ILO's first principle that labor was not a commodity. In 1953, when commenting on the appointment of the new labor secretary James Mitchell, one union leader complemented Mitchell's management perspective by saying, "[He] never took a mechanical view of a contract, but was able to realize that it concerned human beings and not just commodities."[83]

More than their elite allies, labor took an aggressively positive approach toward the ILO. George Delaney went into the sanctuary of the business elite, writing in the *Harvard Business Review* that business should see the ILO as an opportunity and not a threat. American business should note that the ILO provided an ideal forum to show the world that private enterprise is not inherently associated with exploitation.[84] After the Soviet Union applied for admission, labor continued this aggressive approach. George Meany issued a statement saying, "Through the years, the ILO has succeeded in bringing agreement on international conventions which have lifted the working and social standards of oppressed peoples in backward nations. Soviet Russia opposes all human progress because her aggressive designs can be promoted only by human misery and degradation."[85] Labor did not want to leave the ILO but hoped to use it to destroy the suppression of labor rights in Eastern Europe. To implement this approach, the 1954 AFL convention adopted a resolution calling for the U.S. to "reinforce and reinvigorate" its participation.[86] In this context, the new AFL-CIO hatched the plan to push for adoption of the proposed forced labor convention.[87] The forced labor debate exposed the shallowness of the elite defenses of the ILO. Ironically, this experience turned labor into greater critics of the ILO than McGrath.

By 1957, the membership issue was resolved and McGrath defeated. Following the Johnson committee's report and that of David Cole, U.S. relations stabilized with the ILO. To maintain that stability, the departments of commerce, state, and labor appointed a joint labor and business advisory panel in 1957 to oversee and avoid future problems. This committee was a triumph of the foreign policy and business elites. The business representatives were moderates with independent links to internationalism. They included several leading laymen with churches sympathetic to the ILO, including Ray Nichols, a Texas newspaper publisher on the board of the National Council of Churches.[88] Yet, while they helped keep the U.S. in the ILO, they did not push for ratification of the substantive conventions, not even the convention outlawing forced labor.

The modern pattern of factional alignments emerged from the debates over forced labor in the mid-1950s. On the one side were powerful business interests, fixated on an unregulated market. In opposition sat two key groups of individuals and institutions excluded from the elite: primarily labor and frequently selected church leaders. Unlike earlier in the century, labor and the churches now largely carried the battle alone. Women social reformers were replaced by professional women, no longer primarily upper-class lobbyists for poor workers.[89] Academics retreated into their esoteric, specialized world or, worse, became champions of the materialism of the business class or of Marxism. An important new alignment formed between populist defenders of fairness and justice in the policy process and those who dismissed claims of justice as rationalizations of material self-interest, best determined by either markets or revolutions.

THE FORCED LABOR DEBATE

The issue of freedom of association clearly differentiated the advocates of human rights and social justice from western neoliberals and eastern totalitarians. This issue first arose in the form of ILO Convention 105. Beginning in the late 1940s, the ILO took up the problem of forced labor, with American labor being especially interested in a convention that condemned practices widespread in Stalinist countries. As with many debates at the ILO, this one became hopelessly entangled in the other agendas of international factions. At first the proposal was forwarded for consideration to the U.N., since it involved more than a labor issue.

By the time it returned to the ILO in the early 1950s, the opposition included both Bricker Amendment supporters gathered around McGrath and the absent Soviets. In fact, the debates about forced labor became one reason the Russians decided to take "their seat" at the ILO conference. When the ILO issued a forced labor report condemning Russian practices, written by Ramaswami Mudalier of India, the Soviets submitted their application for membership.[90] The Bricker forces did not want such a convention either. They feared its ratification would set a precedent for other ILO substantive conventions. To the amazement of forced labor critics, the U.S. government delegates joined in this opposition. Many condemned the U.S. action, including Senator Hubert Humphrey, Catholic leaders, and the AFL-CIO. *Life* magazine editorialized, "Our AFL-CIO representatives, to their credit, have welcomed this chance to show up the Communists in I.L.O. debate and have done so time and again. The N.A.M. and the Chamber of Commerce, however, prefer to sulk or attack the I.L.O. itself as a 'backdoor to socialism.' All of which adds to the State Department's timidity on the slave labor convention."[91] The State Department said it could not authorize government action on any convention dealing with labor policy since that was a state prerogative under the Constitution. In 1957, the ILO agreed on a forced labor convention and forwarded it to the members. The U.S. refused to ratify it.

Critics, especially from the churches, argued that the Civil War was fought to limit state policy over forced labor. The convention advocated a "world wide 13th Amendment."[92] This criticism came loudest from within the Catholic leadership. The Jesuit journal *America* emphasized the Thirteenth Amendment argument, saying, "The State Department is obviously fully aware of this."[93] Catholic Archbishop Robert Lucey of San Antonio criticized the State Department's fear of confronting the Bricker forces on an issue as fundamental as forced labor.[94] The debate on the convention galvanized Catholic supporters of the ILO and united them with labor. McGrath's extremism made clear the immoral implications of the neoclassical economic arguments. Some business leaders declared that their opposition grew from the inability of the ILO to enforce the ban in the communist countries. Church leaders joined ranks with labor and responded that teeth should be added to the convention by banning trade with countries violating the convention. *America* quoted approvingly the ethics of the AFL-CIO delegate at the ILO, George Delaney, who found the U.S. stand on forced labor did not meet "the moral or legal obligations of U.S. Government participation in the ILO."[95] George Higgins, director of the Social Action Department of the National Catholic Welfare Conference, a successor to John Ryan, now stepped forward as a leader among U.S. ILO defenders.

A Church Strategy

McGrath, McCormick, and their supporters perceived a duality of ILO factions—saintly free marketers on one side and diabolical communists and their social democratic dupes on the other. Seeing belief in that duality as a modern form of the ancient Manichean heresy, a small group of key Catholic leaders joined with labor by the mid-1950s to challenge both the neoclassical liberals and Marxists. They worked on clarifying a philosophy of labor and human rights that differed sharply with both the materialism of McGrath and of the communists. They also did much to sustain the ILO during the counterattacks from both enemies.[96]

There was a long history of church involvement in the labor standards movement, but usually in a supporting role, while business reformers, academics, women social welfare advocates, and labor leaders took the lead.[97] After the 1950s, however, all groups except the populist churches and labor accepted either the business or Marxist alternatives. This alliance between labor and populist churches had been unfolding since the end of the war. Gradually, the National Catholic Welfare Conference (NCWC) became one of the major promoters of the ILO. This support surfaced as early as 1944, when Bishop Haas attended the Philadelphia conference.

In the next decade Catholic ties to the ILO greatly increased, ranging from formal church blessings to the informal training of Catholic students in the value of the organization. Bishop Haas referred warmly to the work of the ILO in his widely used Catholic sociology text.[98] When the ILO met in San Francisco in 1948, Linna Bresette of the NCWC arranged for the church hierarchy to formally welcome the conference.[99] The NCWC News Service regularly provided positive news stories about the ILO for inclusion in the Catholic press, and the Catholic Association for International Peace sponsored an endorsement. Concern with protecting the rights of migrant laborers particularly united labor and the church at the ILO.[100] But the move from full support to leadership of that support awaited the conflicts of the mid-1950s.

The first issue that caused increased church lobbying on behalf of the ILO resulted from the hostile American response to Soviet admission. At the time the Russians applied for their seat in late 1953, Archbishop O'Boyle of Washington delivered a pro-ILO speech to the Catholic Association for International Peace.[101] When McGrath demanded U.S. withdrawal, rather than sit with the Russians, *America* praised the opportunity Russian membership provided for direct criticism of communist labor policy.[102] Presaging the long-term conflicts over proper human rights policy, the church criticized the State Department for not aggressively entering into debates with the Russians at the ILO.[103] The ultimate example of church support for the ILO came when the pope addressed the ILO governing body in November 1954, saying, "[It] truly represents the great mass of workers and their cares." Pius XII concluded with a sweeping blessing "to you and all the collaborators of the International Labor Organization."[104]

Meanwhile, David Morse, George Higgins of the National Catholic Welfare Conference, and leaders of American labor planned a more systematic campaign to challenge criticisms of the ILO.[105] Higgins orchestrated the multipronged support and lobbying strategy, especially focused on the Midwest and Cincinnati to undermine McGrath. First, to compensate for the growing void of academic interest in the ILO, Higgins turned to Catholic scholars and universities for support, especially Mark Fitzgerald at Notre Dame. To reach the mass public, he worked to produce and distribute a free book on the ILO. For those Catholics who would not read a book on the ILO, he coordinated a campaign with Catholic editors and the hierarchy to print positive stories about the ILO. Finally, to address the inevitable critics within the church, he targeted Catholic anticommunists, especially those in Cincinnati. On the national level, he worked with congressional leaders and the secretary of labor to project positive views of the international labor standards movement.

Confronting the isolationism of the Midwest and the indifference among academics, Higgins arranged for the Department of Labor to cosponsor with Notre Dame a "regional" academic conference called "The Colleges Look at the I.L.O." While he included McGrath on a panel with the labor and government ILO delegates, the agenda was packed with ILO sympathizers from the DOL, midwestern universities, and from Notre Dame. Labor Secretary James Mitchell gave the luncheon speech. Edwin Witte of Wisconsin, a student of John R. Commons and an associate of Winant from the early days of Social Security, attended along with leading economists from Illinois, Indiana, and Ohio State. The chair of the conference was Higgins's friend Mark Fitzgerald, an economics professor and priest at Notre Dame.

While there was some effort by Higgins to duplicate the conference in other regions, the Midwest was the prime target, being the territory of Bricker and McGrath. A principle benefit of the conference was to get widespread positive ILO news throughout the country's heartland. The economics department at Notre Dame coordinated that effort with the University Press Office. The preconference notices emphasized the "vital role" played by the ILO and said the conference was called by "responsible U.S. officials and educators." The first sentence of the press release stated, "At the invitation of U.S. Secretary of Labor James Mitchell, a meeting of representatives from eighty colleges and universities will . . . discuss the role of the International Labor Organization (ILO) as a vital instrument for promoting better free world understanding and economic betterment."

Obviously, McGrath had a problem spreading criticisms at a meeting requested by "responsible" people to point out the "vital" role of the ILO. When he did attack the organization, the conference responded with an overwhelming rejection of his shrill anticommunism. Of course, the Notre Dame Public Information Office and Higgins retained the last word in regional and national publicity. Within a week of the conference, stories ran in numerous midwestern papers, *The New York Times*, the labor press, and the Catholic press targeted by Higgins and Notre Dame.[106] The Wabash (Indiana) *Plain Dealer*'s headline was typical: "Labor Secretary Defender of ILO."[107] The Charleston, West Virginia, *Labor's Daily* reported that the labor secretary labeled McGrath's arguments "foolish."[108] The Catholic press either reproduced the press release or the regular column, called the *Yardstick*, provided directly by Higgins. In the April 18, 1955, *Yardstick*, Higgins admitted, "In our opinion, the issue [of membership] ought to be resolved in favor of continued, not to say more intensive, United States participation in the I.L.O."[109] The conference received favorable comments in papers reaching millions of Catholics, like *Ave Maria* and diocesan papers such as *The New World* in Chicago.[110]

Church leaders were not oblivious to the challenge of gaining mass understanding of the ILO issue. *Ave Maria* criticized higher education, "The ILO has been diligently ignored by our colleges." While Higgins was unable to reproduce the conference outside Notre Dame, he, Mark Fitzgerald, and the Catholic hierarchy continued to promote study of the ILO among Catholic universities. The Vatican's staff priest in Geneva supplied information to business, economics, and labor management programs at Catholic colleges and universities.[111] Cardinal Stritch of Chicago wrote to Higgins of the need for more efforts, saying, "I think this is a very good thing, because I have the suspicion that many of our Catholics in this country do not realize that the Vatican has a representative at ILO headquarters and that the Pope has expressed his praise of this organization."[112] He knew many Catholics were so obsessed with anticommunism that they were especially susceptible to McGrath's anti-ILO rhetoric.

It is difficult to generalize about the social and political beliefs held by any group as large as the Catholic population in the U.S. Even the church's saints of the 1950s represented a wide spectrum, from urban social welfare advocates like Dorothy Day through right-wing opponents of communism, if not socialism, such as Thomas Dooley. The special challenge for Higgins was reaching the Catholic business leaders and professionals who often imitated the rhetoric of free-enterprise capitalism. The dean of the Notre Dame Law School, Clarence Manion, was an example.

Manion had a weekly anticommunist radio show in the mid-1950s. On January 22, 1956, Manion defended McGrath, blaming "the grim shadow of the Kremlin" for the opposition. Higgins could not let such criticism rest without a rebuttal. The day after the broadcast, he wrote Manion informing him that a Jesuit was on the ILO staff and forwarding him a copy of the pope's 1954 blessing of the ILO governing body. When Manion retorted that McGrath had told him "the situation in [the] I.L.O.

has changed" since the pope's blessing and that now the U.S. "will be hopelessly outvoted," Higgins's staff responded with data showing that the voting strength of the U.S. and its allies still dominated the organization.

To confront McGrath on his home turf, Higgins arranged for Father Joseph Joblin, the ILO's staff Jesuit, to tour the U.S. and make a special presentation at Xavier University in Cincinnati and to otherwise be feted in the city. Higgins ensured the visit received national Catholic press coverage. His press release did not neglect to emphasize that the church had had a priest on staff in Geneva since 1924. Higgins convinced the hierarchy to issue a statement called "Catholics and the International Labor Organization." He also launched an information campaign attacking the Bricker Amendment.

Finally, Higgins arranged for the translation and publication of Albert Le Roy's *The Dignity of Labor* in 1957. The book project overshadowed all of the other press campaigns. Le Roy, who had been the staff Jesuit from the 1930s until the early 1950s, had originally written the book for a French audience in the late 1930s at the behest of Winant. Now, Higgins encouraged him to update it and publish it in the U.S. through the Catholic press. Higgins composed the introduction, which began with a summary of the 1955 Notre Dame conference. To prepare the groundwork for the book, Higgins asked Secretary Mitchell to speak at the 1956 Catholic newspaper conference, endorsing the ILO campaign.[113] With the help of the ILO, Higgins targeted thousands of individuals to receive free copies, paid for by the ILO. To get the church on board, in the fall of 1956 he sent 4,500 copies of an ILO-produced brochure to priests on the mailing list of his *Social Action Notes for Priests*.[114] When the book came off the press in early 1957, all priests on the mailing list received a promotional flyer.[115] Higgins also sent 250 journalists he had identified as interested in labor issues a free copy.[116] Meanwhile the ILO bought another 1,500 copies for distribution "to prominent government and labor officials and to a number of leading newspaper reporters" in Washington.[117]

Simultaneously, Secretary Mitchell began to reinforce the ILO through the Johnson committee. He secured the appointment by the U.S. Chamber of an employer delegate less hostile than McGrath, Charles H. Smith.[118] When the committee issued its positive report on the ILO in January 1957, it served as a one-two punch, when coupled to Le Roy's book, to put down McGrath just before the chamber and NAM were to decide on ILO withdrawal.[119]

Higgins did not ignore the formal congressional policy process. The AFL inserted copies of the pro-ILO *Yardstick*s in the record of congressional hearings and had them read into the record of floor action.[120] Higgins testified before ILO-related congressional hearings.[121] However, he primarily tried to influence public officials through a close relationship with the secretary of labor, James Mitchell, often seen within the narrow sphere of international labor relations as the odd man out of the Eisenhower Administration.[122] Higgins, Mitchell, and the AFL-CIO formed an issue network that was extremely influential in preventing policy change directed against the ILO.[123] While they did not have sufficient power to get ILO conventions ratified, they did block withdrawal and laid the groundwork for more significant achievements in later decades.

Lessons of the Membership Fight

The membership fight in the mid-1950s taught vital lessons to key participants in the labor standards policy process. Business realized that foreign policy stability was in its interest, and disruptive extremists, like McGrath, had to be controlled. Labor learned that the compromise that ended the membership debate undermined defense of its primary concerns. The foreign policy establishment's solution was to commit the ILO to an expansive research program. The AFL-CIO did not need more research. It wanted concrete action from the ILO, but that was unlikely. It took time, however, for that goal to be clarified. Initially, labor and the churches celebrated their triumph over McGrath. Soon enough, labor and its church allies needed to fight a two-front war against Marxists and the free market.

In the late 1950s, they shifted to the communist front. Controversy surrounded efforts to block the seating of the labor and employer delegates from postrevolutionary Hungary. In 1960, in the transition from the Eisenhower to Kennedy Administration, the efforts of ILO bureaucrats to please the Russians sparked a dispute with American labor. Twin reports from ILO studies of labor in the U.S. and the Soviet Union appeared, which contained criticism of U.S. unions and some positive conclusions about Russian labor practices. George Meany and the AFL-CIO were outraged. The ILO bureaucrats, who were more worried about Soviet government disapproval than an American reaction, had not been totally truthful about freedom of association. American labor believed that only extreme measures would force the ILO to return to the defense of basic labor rights.

During the next few years, labor's displeasure grew and signaled a new alignment of group support for the ILO. Once the alignment stabilized, the united labor and church coalition utilized the ILO to defend the principles of labor dignity rejected by modern materialist ideologies. They discovered new friends in the rising legal profession, which offset the departure of some former allies in the academy and business. Due to the groundwork laid in the late 1940s and 1950s, the ILO, often against the will of its leadership, became a focus and forum for some of the great defenses of freedom against capitalist and Marxist materialism. The success of populist interests in confronting the elites from both the centrally planned and free-market regimes, as well as bureaucratic inertia in Geneva, proved the ILO at the end of the millennium might be modeling the way to move beyond the Westphalian world.

Reaffirmation

Ten years after McGrath had been a nuisance as a critic of the ILO, George Meany became the leading gadfly of the organization. However, instead of defending the self-interest of a few affluent business leaders, Meany fought for abstract principles of human rights and justice. Meany's significance in shaping ILO policy in the 1960s and 1970s demonstrated the importance of two characteristics he brought to the process. First, while often portrayed by critics as a labor bureaucrat, Meany possessed many of the qualities of a populist leader. Born into the working class, he understood and articulated well the beliefs and fears of many average people in urban, industrial America. Meany brought to the policy process the goals, especially a hope for economic justice, common among the working class. This assessment is not to ignore the prejudices and errors that can characterize mass opinion, but certainly blue-collar workers have no monopoly on prejudice and mistaken decisions.[1] However, because the working class often has wishes and assumptions that contrast with those of the elite, mass participation enriches policy debates. Second, Meany not only possessed a different perspective from elite business at the ILO, but also he articulated more clearly the need to ground policy on justice. In this achievement, he exemplified the value, even the necessity, for popular participation in policy making.

During the last third of the twentieth century, churches and attorneys who were committed to human rights joined populist labor to preserve the labor standards movement and achieved some notable victories. Eventually, the three groups united to awaken the consciousness of a significant portion of the attentive public to the continuing need to protect labor rights. The churches served as the intermediary institutions in this process. As populist as organized labor, with a diverse base in local congregations, they shared with attorneys a commitment to ascertain timeless definitions of justice.[2] Although disagreements arose in specifics, the common quest for justice held together the coalition throughout the period.

Two injustices, with little direct bearing on AFL-CIO interests, galled Meany. Most important, the ILO failed to confront the suppression of labor rights in the communist block. Second, the ILO tolerated hostility toward Israel. Given that many AFL-CIO members were Catholics and Jews, critics felt Meany's concerns were driven by a wish to satisfy his union constituents incensed by the oppression and criticism of their coreligionists. However, debates among labor leaders in the era demonstrate that his position was not universally popular within the labor movement. Meany persisted in spite of opponents who called for collaboration and conciliation rather than confrontation.

Meany could not collaborate with those who suppressed freedom of association. In the late 1940s and throughout the 1950s, Meany and AFL-CIO allies assumed the lead among critics of labor suppression in the Soviet empire. They were horrified that the ILO dared to treat the Soviet Union and its allies as members in good standing. Meany became incensed in the 1960s when the Russians sought a share in the leadership. Then Russia and allies from countries without independent unions regularly criticized Israel. The Jewish state was one of the few places outside America and Western Europe with free labor unions and a functioning welfare state. From a labor perspective, how could Israel be criticized in an organization devoted to labor rights? Consequently, once labor had defeated the efforts of McGrath to withdraw from the ILO, Meany came to the U.S. Senate and demanded, as firmly as had McGrath, that the U.S. send a message to the ILO. But while McGrath's support came from some right-wing businessmen, Meany led millions from organized labor. McGrath lost; Meany won. His success presented a model to the next millennium of how to reinvigorate entrenched bureaucracies and overturn symbolic compromises to serve the interests of popular classes and social justice.

Disputes of the 1960s

Several factors coincided in the mid-1960s to crystallize the new labor position. Although the conflicts continued annually over the freedom of trade unions in Eastern Europe, the disputes intensified as the Russians sought more influence in ILO governance. Second, Meany was instinctively distrustful of American business motives. In the mid-1960s, the U.S. Chamber of Commerce began to regard favorably increases in East-West trade. To labor leaders like Meany, any friend of business was suspect, especially when it was the traditional communist enemy. Two other developments in the period intensified Meany's hostility toward the Soviets: the Vietnam War and the appointment in 1963 of Jay Lovestone to head the AFL-CIO's International Department.

A former communist, ousted from party leadership for opposing Stalin, Lovestone brought to his work the intensity usually associated with the converted.[3] From the end of World War II until 1963 he headed the anticommunist Free Trade Union Committee, which labored to undermine leftists in west European unions. Then he came to the federation staff to run the department that coordinated ILO relations and worked with the U.S. government's anticommunist foreign affairs efforts. Lovestone would have pushed Meany to oppose the Soviets at the ILO regardless of the atmosphere of the 1960s, but events such as the efforts at detente and the deaths during the Vietnam War prompted a siege mentality to emerge. Meany argued that working-class kids were dying in Vietnam at the hands of communists, while American businesses sought Russian markets and American liberals denounced the war. As Meany and Lovestone emphasized, the communists had imprisoned more trade unionists and socialists than any regime at the time. Furthermore, Meany was not only anticommunist. He also attacked fascist union suppression in Spain and in other dictatorships. However, Spain was not a major power, and Russia was.[4]

Meany's disagreement with the Russians at the ILO mirrored the concerns of William McGrath in the 1950s. Communist government control of unions and economic enterprises contradicted tripartism. As more third-world states with one-party regimes joined the ILO in the early 1960s, they increased the number of nontripartite delegations. Legitimate tripartite delegations became a minority. David Morse, sharing Meany's anxiety, felt his independence restricted by these trends. Furthermore, matters seemed to be worsening as the Soviets insisted on the appointment of a Russian assistant director general. Morse rejected that categorically in November 1961, but accompanied that decision with a refusal to seek reelection as director general in 1962. U.S. officials and Meany explicitly supported Morse's decisions.[5] As the Kennedy Administration hoped, the reaction to Morse's potential departure caused many to fear for the ILO's future. Some, such as labor secretary Arthur Goldberg, pressured him to reconsider. Meany did not. He judged that the growing communist influence at the ILO could best be contained by a director general more like himself. He thought the ILO needed someone experienced in the free trade union movement, not a lawyer.

Meany's first major break with the ILO occurred when Morse returned as director general. After rescinding his withdrawal, Morse was reelected in 1962 with only Russia and Ghana opposed. The reelection angered Meany for two reasons. First, Morse had not consulted with him before rescinding his withdrawal, ignoring the preeminent position of labor in American ILO policy making.[6] But, more important, Meany did not think Morse sufficiently anticommunist. In two meetings with Morse, one in 1962 at the U.N. and another in Geneva the following year, Meany unleashed tirades. Of the Geneva meeting, Morse wrote, "Meany then launched into a personal attack against me stating that what he wanted from me as D.G. and as an American was *bias* against the communists. . . . I then told Meany that I was sick and tired of all of his insinuations that I was soft on communists. . . . I felt that his attack on this issue was motivated by the fact that he hated my guts and that he was also against me because I was a jew [*sic*]."[7]

Despite such extreme bitterness, Meany and Morse repaired their working relationship and, amazingly, something of their earlier friendship. By the summer of 1964 they realized, "We need this strength and solidarity to meet the difficult problems of the future."[8] They advertised word of their rapprochement to the press, warning opponents of their united front as the ILO faced new Russian problems.[9] In 1965, Meany launched his next criticism of the ILO after the governing body agreed to reconsider a vote that had gone against the Soviet Union. This attack marked the estrangement of Meany from the liberal foreign policy establishment on ILO issues. *The New York Times* editorialized, "[G]oing on strike against an organization so important in the worldwide advancement of labor standards is an abysmal way to express . . . dissatisfaction."[10]

The 1965 tirade was the prelude to events in the next decade. In 1966, the International Labor Conference elected, by a one-vote margin, a Polish delegate as president, bypassing a candidate from Holland. Meany directed the AFL-CIO delegate to walk out. There was good reason for doing so. Many delegates voted for the Pole to send a message to Meany and Lovestone.[11] The walkout, in turn, drove Walter Reuther and his CIO allies to break publicly with Meany's foreign policy.[12] Yet, in the long run, the election incident did not undermine Meany's power; it motivated him to send a clearer message to the ILO and to opponents within the AFL-CIO.[13]

It is a mistake to interpret the AFL opposition to Soviet influence as a sign that Meany had joined the American establishment. The Johnson Administration and the U.S. Chamber of Commerce urged coexistence with Russia in Geneva.[14] Shortly after the ILO walkout, Meany insisted that the State Department deny visas to a group of Russian trade unionists who were invited to visit the U.S. The secretary of state made clear he disagreed with Meany's demands. Nor did Meany receive support for his position from the mainstream press.[15] The willingness of the administration to cooperate with the Soviets during the Vietnam War and the desire of business to seek Russian trade deals solidified Meany's opposition to labor rights compromises.

American business had experienced a transition in ILO policy at least as great as Meany's in the previous ten years. As industry globalized, even conservative American business leaders perceived value in ILO standards. One employer delegate to the ILO explained that business needed the ILO to set labor standards with which they could live, for "U.S. executives increasingly are becoming worldwide employers."[16] If employers desired this benefit, Meany knew he had reason to stake out a different position, regardless of the opinions of his liberal former allies.

Given the united front of liberals, international business leaders, and the foreign policy establishment in favor of detente, Meany and Lovestone, and incidently George Higgins, faced an immense task.[17] At first, matters grew bleaker. In 1968, Walter Reuther led the United Auto Workers out of the federation partially over the foreign policy issue.[18] Then the problem of replacing Morse reappeared. After he passed his twentieth year as director general, Morse wanted to leave, his leadership vindicated in 1969 by the award of the Nobel Peace Prize.

In June 1969, the ILO celebrated its fiftieth anniversary in spectacular fashion. The pope made a rare visit outside Italy to congratulate Morse and his staff on a job well done. While sympathetic to Meany, George Higgins worked with Morse to use the papal visit to win a temporary respite in Meany's anti-ILO activities.[19] Their strategy worked, at least in the short run. As a loyal Catholic, Meany supported the mood of celebration in Geneva; but the old Bronx plumber could not resist adding to his address a reference to the organization's "pro-Communist bias." While the media considered this part of his speech a tactless criticism during a grand celebration, it served as a reminder that the AFL-CIO paid careful attention to ILO matters and would watch as the post-Morse era unfolded.[20] In October the Nobel committee made the surprise award to the organization, apparently passing over Morse individually at his own urging.[21] The ILO seemed to have passed from regular world politics to sanctity.

The Ultimatum

When David Morse resigned the director generalship in 1970 at age sixty-two, he had served in the position for more than a third of his life. While he departed in triumph, in fact he left an organization facing immense problems. First, the absence of an American at the helm presented difficulties when much of the criticism and a quarter of the budget came from the U.S. Then there were conflicting views of the organization's primary function. Following the disputes of the previous twenty years, Morse had protected the ILO by emphasizing research and technical assistance while de-emphasizing standard setting, especially of substantive standards.[22] Third, he had presided over a constitutional compromise that ignored tripartism in the name of universality. If some countries did not possess trade unions or employers free of government control, in the name of reaching out to the world, the ILO allowed them to send whomever they wished to sit in union and employer seats. Also, in the name of universality, the delegates raised a cacophony at the annual conference, arguing over Middle Eastern politics, capitalist militarism, and the legacy of colonialism. If some felt better criticizing the war in Vietnam, so be it. Others focused on union problems in Spain or in the colonies of Portugal. The AFL-CIO could attack Russian suppression of labor. In a spirit of universal freedom, all subjects were on the table.[23]

During the early 1970s a small number of critics, especially Americans like Meany, contrasted the ILO's original function with the structure that had evolved under Morse. They found the current organization wanting. At best, it was irrelevant to the real issues facing labor. At worst, it acted as a tool of the very people who suppressed the working class and human freedom. Morse's personal decency and commitment to justice and human rights had minimized confrontation on these issues. With Morse gone, Meany saw the ILO degenerate into a propaganda arm for the world's oppressors of workers.

The event that sparked Meany's first post-Morse explosion occurred quickly in 1970. Morse's successor, Wilfred Jenks, bowed to Russian pressure and appointed Pavel Astapenko as one of five assistant ILO directors. During the last years of Morse's tenure, the Russians demanded one of the top administrative posts at the ILO. In early 1970, Morse began a dialogue with them but avoided a final decision before he resigned. Wilfred Jenks won a close election to succeed Morse largely because he appeared to the U.S. as the candidate least willing to yield to Russian demands. Yet, upon taking office, Jenks appointed Astapenko.[24]

Ominously, on July 31, 1970, Meany came to the House Appropriations Committee hearings on the State Department budget. Representative John Rooney, a Brooklyn democrat, clarified the cause-effect relationship behind the day's hearings. "We are gathered here this morning because of the concern of the head of the AFL-CIO."[25] Meany presented a long review of the history of the ILO and of Soviet suppression of worker freedom. He emphasized that Russian unions "are agencies designed to control workers, not to give expression to the views or the ideals or the aspirations of workers."[26] He reviewed the 1966 election of a Polish conference chair at the very time the ILO had Poland under sanctions for denying freedom of association. He then introduced into the record a long study called *Crisis in the International Labor Organization*, written by Carlos Vela of the Catholic University of Ecuador. It identified two fundamental problems with the ILO, one structural, the other functional. Structurally, tripartism had decayed since the admission of the Soviet Union and other one-party states. The absence of tripartism deprived the ILO of the true insights of workers. The functional problem was summarized as the infiltration into the ILO of "'two' justices." Elsewhere Vela labeled this problem the development of a double standard. The West expected nations to fully observe the human rights of all citizens and, if they did not, face condemnation. By contrast, the ILO permitted the Soviet Union to ignore these same standards. The organization even developed a different language for reports about totalitarian societies. Vela listed a number of examples of reports criticizing human rights violations in western countries, such as one on Venezuela. He contrasted these to the infamous comparative study of Russian and American labor unions in 1960. In the case of Venezuela, the ILO sent the government an advanced copy of the report as a courtesy, but the government was not invited or allowed to make changes. Nor was the U.S. government permitted to alter the study in 1960. By contrast, the ILO allowed the Russians to guide and revise the work of the study group.[27]

While Meany had fumed against the double standard for a long time, the appointment of the Russian assistant director threatened to give the Russians too much control over administrative standards. Meany decided to draw a line. To force a reversal, he demanded that Congress refuse to pay American dues in the second half of 1970. Pulling out all of his lobbying power, Meany had the appropriations rescinded. He continued the boycott in 1971.

These decisions defied the policy preferences of the foreign policy elite. *The Washington Post* attacked Meany and Congressman Rooney. The paper said nonpayment of the American assessment made the nation a "deadbeat." They criticized the State Department for quietly opposing the illegal refusal to pay the dues. Meany annoyed *The Post* more when he refused to back down and insisted on increasing the level of confrontation. When officials at the Department of State responsible for the ILO opposed Meany's position, he responded that if it were illegal to withhold dues, the U.S. should withdraw.[28]

With this argument raging, the elite faced the ILO's problems. In *Foreign Affairs* a 1971 anonymous article, cleared with Morse, discussed "International Labor in Crisis," hardly a topic expected the year after the organization won the Nobel Prize. The only other *Foreign Affairs* article to require anonymity was the 1947 Mr. X essay proposing containment. Clearly, the ILO had risen to the pinnacle of postwar foreign policy debates. When the editors sent a copy of the proofs to Morse, they added a respectful note, "To David Morse—In recognition of his leadership of the ILO, a commentary on what befell that organization when he left. Intended as constructive analysis, but regretfully resented by the successor who might have done something. A tactical failure—consigned to the judgement of history with appreciation."[29]

The essay reviewed the years of compromise that had brought the ILO to the state of paralysis. The constitutional compromises had made the organization timid "before issues on which powerful forces are in conflict. . . . A concept of universality based upon consensus has emptied the program of activities which might have given expression to tripartism, in favor of neutral technical services."[30] With great vision, the essay predicted that world labor faced vital issues that "arise from the development of what can be called the world free market economy." Manufacturers were moving production out of the developed world to take advantage of "cheap labor." Since this movement to developing countries solely took advantage of cheap labor, the essay predicted growing worker exploitation, not greater development.[31] "[T]his method [of development] contains the seeds of its own destruction."[32] Meanwhile, in developed countries organized labor would be forced to turn to protectionism as the only barrier to this movement. In fact, meaningful labor standards could check the trend, but they did not exist because the ILO had become preoccupied with technical services and political posturing.

While providing an insightful critique of the consequences of the compromises of the previous two decades and of the need for an effective ILO, the *Foreign Affairs* article did not see much hope for the organization. Neither the Soviets nor many developing countries supported effective labor organizations. Compelling real tripartism might drive them from the organization. Preserving the organization at all costs had its price, as the essay concluded, "[T]he makers of social policy now find little interest in the ILO. Representation has become formal, often the concern of a handful of ILO professionals, some of them having little or no connection with labor affairs at home. The organization is highly institutionalized, with rich tradition; but participation in it lacks depth. . . . [T]he ILO needs less autonomy and more involvement."[33] While foreign policy professionals could not envision a way to restore depth, Meany and his allies prepared to provide a lesson in involvement and depth during the next four years.[34]

In that period, Meany led the U.S. in an unanticipated form of participation. While the State Department urged reconciliation, the AFL-CIO initiated another attack on the ILO in 1973 when a Russian, with Western European support, ran for chair of the governing body.[35] Meany turned to trade union and employer delegates to block the Russian's election and secured the post for a Mexican. The Soviets were outraged and in 1974 attacked the AFL-CIO delegate as "merely mouthpieces for major American capitalism and monopoly."[36] Meany, who had argued with the government and employers in the U.S. to follow the labor position, knew the error of this accusation. In 1975, the U.S. filed a formal letter of withdrawal with the ILO. As required under ILO rules, the termination of membership took place two years later.

A reading of the record of the withdrawal process demonstrates the leadership provided by Meany and the AFL-CIO, the caution from business, and the reluctance on the part of the foreign policy establishment and others in the elite. Throughout the early 1970s, although business and State Department officials pursued detente, labor insisted on major change at the ILO. In 1971, the government delegate at the annual conference said President Nixon sought "to obtain favorable congressional action . . . to pay [the U.S.] contribution." The labor delegate reminded the conference, however, that the AFL-CIO had conditions for its support. U.S. labor could only advocate funding "if [the ILO] is restored to its original role as defender of the welfare and liberties of workers all over the world."[37] On the brink of withdrawal in 1975, the Department of Labor and the Industrial Relations Research Association sponsored a series of papers on "U.S. Participation in the ILO," which clarified the contrasting positions of ILO interests. Nonlabor participants were ambivalent about withdrawal. John Windmuller of Cornell's School of Industrial and Labor Relations wrote the academic paper. He had been actively involved with ILO policy for two decades, having edited the 1957 volume on international labor issues for the American Academy of Political and Social Science. He minimized the differences between the problems of the 1970s and earlier eras even before the war. While aware that labor could pressure government and employers to withdraw from the organization, he characterized the concerns of the AFL-CIO as excessive. He also doubted that the withdrawal favored by labor could bring much change in the structure or functioning of the ILO. In conclusion, he did not find "sufficient reason to discontinue membership."[38]

Charles Smith, who had been ILO employer delegate at various times from the 1950s until the 1970s and who had risen to chair of the U.S. Chamber of Commerce's board of directors in 1975, echoed the academic assessment. Noting the problems at the ILO, he emphasized, "An important segment of U.S. employers is affected by ILO activities."[39] Since it was the task of the chamber to represent business, he concluded that the chamber should be at the ILO. He blamed the AFL-CIO for being so critical of business at the ILO and added that the federation's criticisms actually aided the communists. In a spirit that worried Meany and other old labor leaders, he ended with a conciliatory note toward the Russians and a critical comment about American labor: "With regard to the Communists, they may change. Their theory is growing old. Their theology is getting thin. They may mature as their leadership changes from generation to generation. As for free trade unions, they may eventually choose to speak up in support of the private enterprise system."[40] Such statements confirmed Meany's fears that the major elite players in the ILO network placed achievement of detente ahead of defense of labor rights.[41]

Labor prepared to fight. Bert Seidman, the labor delegate to the ILO, authored the paper explaining the AFL-CIO perspective. He found the ILO had a "discriminatory record in human rights, the field in which its spokesmen are often most boastful." Labor would have a moderately positive view of the ILO, if it were not "for the dark political shadow which hangs over the organization." The USSR and other communist countries "have successfully kept the ILO from undertaking any action or even investigation of the brutal denial of human rights." Seidman demanded the renewal of tripartism, which guaranteed that independent labor and employer delegations participated at ILO conferences. Without such changes, "[He could not] imagine that the AFL-CIO would continue to support or even participate in the ILO."[42]

A few months after writing these sentiments, labor received one last chance to try to work with the ILO. Preparing for an effort at reform, they sent a high-level delegation to the June 1975 annual conference. Included were future AFL-CIO President Lane Kirkland and representatives of the auto workers. When the conference attacked the U.S. and defended repressive regimes, the reform conference turned into a showdown. When the conference voted to seat a delegation from the PLO, the U.S. labor delegates walked out. Following labor's lead, the other U.S. delegates left, but then returned. Labor stayed away.[43] Showing contempt for the ILO, Meany concluded, "As a practical matter, it doesn't mean anything to us at all."[44] The AFL-CIO did not return until 1980, when the situation at the ILO was different and free labor had appeared in the communist world.

The withdrawal debate now shifted to Washington. Ford Administration documents clarify the contrasting positions of the tripartite institutions in America. In an "ILO Issues Paper" prepared in September 1975 for the president, staff noted, "The AFL-CIO has made it clear that it will not support further dues payments to the ILO until a letter of intent to withdraw is issued. The U.S. Chamber, while showing mixed feelings, largely agrees with sending a letter of intent. In terms of political realities, the U.S. Government cannot continue to participate viably and effectively if future U.S. Worker and/or Employer participation is in doubt."[45] A few weeks earlier, another presidential memo did not refer to State Department or U.S. Chamber initiation of the move, noting only that "The AFL-CIO Executive Council has called on the U.S. Government to give . . . notice."[46]

POLICY PROCESS LESSONS

While many observers of the policy process, especially when it concerns foreign affairs, emphasize elite control or pluralist bargaining, the U.S. decision to withdraw from the ILO in 1975–1977 does not fit that pattern. During the Ford and Carter Administrations, the foreign policy elite opposed withdrawal. Secretaries of state and national security advisers advocated detente and were unwilling to threaten it by defending worker rights. By conventional theory they should have prevailed. They did not, even though their only opponent was a Bronx plumber. What lessons does this teach?

Some alleged that Meany's foreign policy adventures grew mostly from a desire to be consulted by the elite, not from conviction. But mingling with the elite would have been easier if he were more conciliatory. In international labor policy making, Meany exasperated the "more diplomatic" foreign policy professionals. When Joseph Sisco, President Ford's assistant secretary of state for political affairs, contacted the AFL-CIO on behalf of the administration's efforts at detente and urged conciliation, Meany's staff responded abruptly that the administration would not understand "our arguments."[47] Despite the opposition of President Carter's Secretary of State Cyrus Vance and National Security Adviser Zbigniew Brzezinski, Meany insisted on completing withdrawal. Hamilton Jordan, the White House chief of staff, told the foreign policy leadership that Meany's support for the administration was more important than their wishes on international labor standards.[48] Meany had made democratic considerations trump special interest pressure in the policy process.

Meany's efforts built on a long tradition in the labor movement to differentiate public interest from the special interests. Elite interests have benefitted from widespread acceptance of what political scientist Benjamin Barber has called "The Libertarian Perspective," one that pits the private individual and any groups against the state. The presumption in this theory, often linked to James Madison, is that the pursuit of self-interest checks the abuse of power and that all who participate are seeking their self-interest. Barber quoted Samuel Gompers in his explanation of the American alternative to "The Libertarians." Gompers, and later Meany, favored what Barber named "The Strong Democratic Perspective," which assumes a host of voluntary groups, including organized labor, serve as intermediary institutions to check the pursuit of self-interest in the private sector. There is a value in groups that "are neither mere consumers of government services and rights-bearers against government intrusion."[49]

If the American system of democracy is to work, Barber holds, citizen groups, not only special interests, must participate in formulating policy. To participate in policy making, citizens need to do more than vote—they must organize to present their collective vision of the community. As political scientist E. E. Schattschneider said of the interest group system, "The flaw in [the interest group] heaven is that the heavenly chorus sings with a strong upper-class accent. Probably about 90 percent of the people cannot get into the . . . system."[50] Meany, as Gompers, agreed, except he thought populist interests can give voice to the larger public interest if they have an assured place at the policy-making table. The tripartite structure of ILO policy making guaranteed labor a chance to be heard. With tripartism, labor had an opportunity to shape decisions that elite pressure groups normally controlled.

In assessing the withdrawal decision, it is essential to understand that populist criticism of policy can be complex and sophisticated. Labor did not oppose the ILO because of one issue, but because of both structural and substantive problems at the ILO. President Ford's letter of withdrawal reviewed the four reasons supplied by labor.[51] The "erosion of tripartite representation" appeared first. The other structural flaw was the disregard for due process in ILO deliberations, especially evident in the PLO decision. Substantively, the first complaint involved the selective concern for human rights, and the second the politicizing of the organization. As Meany complained, the ILO wasted time on symbolic grievances, while ignoring the "major responsibility, for example, for international action to promote and protect fundamental human rights, particularly in respect of freedom of association."[52] While the president listed labor's problems with the ILO, the AFL-CIO explained them better.

The AFL-CIO focused first on the erosion of tripartism. It was "smothered in the suffocating spirit of accommodation with totalitarianism of the left or right." Labor recognized that tripartism was essential to make the process work with integrity. Without it, policy was formulated through elite bargaining. Weakened tripartism had fundamental substantive consequences. Labor feared national leaders were willing to bargain away those matters about which essential economic interests did not agree. The most important issue on which there would be no action was human and labor rights. The AFL-CIO found that in defense of human rights the ILO had become "an arena of empty rhetorical and ideological warfare."[53] The elites pretended to argue about rights, but they had no intention of protecting them.

As the withdrawal process unfolded, various individuals and institutions came forward to oppose severing ties to the ILO. A number of liberal members of Congress, including Democrats Dick Clark of Iowa, Dale McGee of Wyoming, and Republican Jacob Javits of New York, wrote to the secretary of state and, a month later, to the president, urging delay. In their letter to Secretary Kissinger, they said, "It is apparent the Congress does not support this initiative by the Executive Branch." They presented as proof the defeat by an overwhelming voice vote of a proposal to cut funds for specialized U.N. agencies.[54] The members of Congress did not oppose criticism of the ILO, but they thought Meany misjudged the impact of U.S. withdrawal. They assumed it removed any influence over the ILO and opened the door to Russian dominance. As with the academic supporters, the congressional liberals lacked the confidence to fight for their policy preferences.[55] As Lowi observed of modern policy making, liberals replaced pursuit of justice with bargaining.[56]

The populist Meany did not bring different goals to the process but a different method of pursuing them. Probably few American foreign policy leaders opposed labor rights as abstract principles. For unions, labor rights were not abstract. Labor rights were essential if workers were to impose justice as a check on the materialism of global business. Consequently, Meany entered the process with a willingness to gamble rather than bargain. That willingness destroyed the appeals to incrementalism and resulting inaction at the ILO. Instead of continuing to muddle through, the ILO had to change or face drastic decline or death.

While the administration lacked faith in carrying out the withdrawal, Ford had to seek change at the ILO. He dispatched a high-level envoy, Lawrence Silberman, who had been his deputy attorney general, to get allies to pressure the ILO to alter its structure. During 1976, the National Security Council worked with Western European allies to moderate the ILO.[57] However, all the documentary evidence during the closing months of the Ford Administration shows the foreign policy leaders continued to desperately seek a compromise that would justify canceling withdrawal. By contrast, labor continued to insist on both structural change and a focus on human rights. The only major institution where labor found sympathy during this battle was the church.

Unlike the 1950s when the church officially supported the ILO and opposed the critics, key church supporters of the ILO sympathized with Meany. This time, in place of symbolic endorsement of the organization, the apostolic delegate in Washington asked Meany to meet him to receive an official communication from the pope urging compromise. Demonstrating church diversity, Higgins took a slightly different position. Agreeing with Meany's general foreign policy perspective, Higgins expressed understanding for labor's position. While urging compromise, he shared the AFL-CIO fear that some in the Washington elite were so interested in the economic potential of detente that they would sacrifice human rights in Eastern Europe and China.[58] Some liberal Catholic leaders had become closer to the secular liberals, attacking Meany's approach as a "short-sighted . . . sterile path of withdrawal, a step into isolation."[59] But Joe Holland and Peter Henriot of the Jesuit Center for Concern in Washington, while questioning Meany's abandonment of the forum provided by the ILO, noted, "organized labor supplies ordinary working people with a potential instrument to struggle for justice."[60] They knew other

Washington institutions did not supply that tool to the average worker. Like most other observers, however, they underestimated the judgment and power of the labor position on the ILO. They also could not foresee that the church would be intimately tied again to the ILO in its greatest postwar battle for labor rights.

THE VICTORY LESSONS

The consequences of the ILO withdrawal were not the ones predicted by liberals or the foreign policy establishment. The ILO lost one-quarter of its budget. The Soviet Union did not take over the ILO after 1977. Instead, the ILO leadership attempted to satisfy American concerns. Director General Francis Blanchard said, "[T]he severe ordeal [of U.S. withdrawal] should strengthen ILO's resolution to pursue with renewed fervor its task of promoting justice among men and nations."[61] In 1977, it agreed on a Declaration of Principles Concerning Multinational Enterprises.[62] Directly responding to AFL-CIO complaints, in November 1978 the ILO governing body censured Czechoslovakia and launched an evaluation of worker complaints from Russia. Early in 1979, the organization condemned the Soviet treatment of labor dissidents.[63]

The decisive drama, however, occurred in relations with Poland. Beginning in 1978, Poland entered a social and political crisis, growing partially from long-term grievances but sparked by unprecedented events in two institutions upon which the ILO had come to rely. At the Vatican, a Pole became pope. An independent trade union appeared among Polish workers: Solidarity. It used ILO conventions as one of the justifications for its existence.[64] With repeated complaints of Polish suppression of the Solidarity movement, the ILO launched an assessment of Polish government compliance with the convention on freedom of association. After a negative report, the Polish government pledged to bring its legislation into line with ILO standards.[65]

By the spring of 1981, Solidarity emerged as the second most important institution, after the church, in Polish civil society. The ILO conference welcomed Lech Walesa as the Polish worker delegate to Geneva.[66] The battle over Solidarity took several years, including a brief Polish withdrawal, before it succeeded. The extent of the ILO role in the transition to labor freedom in Poland and subsequently throughout Eastern Europe is too complex an issue to be determined here.[67] However, clearly the ILO supported the transition from suppression to respect for labor rights after the AFL-CIO pressured the U.S. to withdraw. Whatever the cause of the momentous changes in Eastern Europe in 1978-1980, the AFL-CIO knew the right timing in demanding firm, not conciliatory, action. Within a year of withdrawal, the Carter Administration established an office of human rights in the State Department and began publishing reports on national human rights protections. Brought into the department by this new policy was Patricia Derian, who became a long-term supporter of labor and human rights.[68] While other factors and movements contributed to Carter's human rights concerns, the populist labor movement acted before many other institutions to refocus America on human rights as a primary guide to foreign policy.[69]

American labor made the right decision at the ILO and chose that decision against vigorous opposition because it alone of the three constituent elements of ILO policy making brought the perspective of a different class and a different power base—large numbers of locals throughout the country composed of average citizens. Not only did the AFL-CIO force the ILO to face fundamental human rights issues, but the ILO changes also contributed to a renewal of a more general human rights movement.[70]

Beginning at the time of the ILO withdrawal, the U.S. initiated important foreign policy reforms directed at ending the indifference to human rights among those promoting economic development. In the first half of the period, the focus centered on opposition to Marxist materialism. By the end of the century, it shifted to restraining laissez-faire materialists. In both cases, however, the core argument was whether to complicate economic policy making by allowing populist participation. The experiences of the last third of the twentieth century made clear the value of the tripartite process that guaranteed such participation. The era also validated the core substantive labor standards defined in the early years of the ILO.[71]

INSTITUTIONAL CHANGE

As a result of the struggles at the end of the 1970s, several institutional changes prepared the way for reform of ILO policy making. First, on the federal level the ILO policy process was formalized in two structures. The President's Committee on the ILO officially gathered representatives of the three government departments with an interest in the ILO: state, labor, and commerce.[72] To support the committee, the president formed a Tripartite Advisory Panel on International Labor Standards (TAPILS), including the chief legal staff of the three departments, the AFL-CIO, and the U.S. Council for International Business (USCIB). The USCIB assumed the job of designating the U.S. business delegate, a task previously performed by the U.S. Chamber of Commerce. Labor and employers committed themselves to work more closely on the TAPILS, hopefully to avoid another withdrawal crisis.[73]

In addition to these government institutions, a host of private human rights organizations emerged in the period. The legal profession primarily contributed to these changes. In 1978, the Lawyers Committee for Human Rights appeared, one of the new international nongovernmental organizations (NGOs) that became common in the era.[74] In 1979, the University of Cincinnati originated the Urban Morgan Institute, the first human rights program linked to a law school, and began publishing the new *Human Rights Quarterly*.[75] Within a few years, a number of law schools established human rights programs, such as the Orville H. Schnell Center at Yale.[76] Highly trained professionals tended to control such NGOs, people who might be uncomfortable with the working-class leaders from labor and those religious groups that previously lobbied for human rights.[77] The challenge at the end of the century was collaboration among the various supporters of labor rights and the ILO. Another crisis would be needed to cement that bond.

The ILO role in human rights after 1980 can be interpreted in two radically different ways. Some find the ILO became irrelevant, turning inward, unable to enforce the ideals it codified. Conservative Senator Jesse Helms of North Carolina, who came to head the Foreign Relations Committee in 1995, and some human rights scholars shared this view. Helms supported a new U.S. withdrawal, while some critics hoped to bring change through strengthened U.S. involvement.[78] Yet, others perceived that the ILO focused on its human rights role after the withdrawal crisis. Lewis Henkin of Columbia Law School's Human Rights Institute said, "The ILO has awakened from a reasonably deep slumber."[79]

The two perspectives are reconcilable if the era is seen as one in which three changes occurred. First, the new human rights movement clarified its focus, eventually identifying the links between human and labor rights.[80] Second, the Reagan Administration took a more aggressive approach to international labor policy than Carter. Despite ILO criticism of the antilabor domestic policies of Reagan, especially his firing of the air-traffic controllers in 1981, the administration gave the ILO more attention than had its immediate predecessors.[81] Seeing the ILO as one more weapon in its battle with the Soviet Union, the administration launched unprecedented cooperation with the ILO to defend Solidarity.[82] By the mid-1980s the President's Committee on the ILO, which formed at the end of the Carter Administration, succeeded in restarting the ILO convention ratification process, with both the secretaries of state and labor advocating ratification of substantive conventions.[83] Third, the 1980s marked a transition from the Cold War confrontation with Marxism to concerns with globalized capitalism. While in many ways Reagan defended unregulated or hypercapitalism, in fact it was his administration that first applied bilateral trade sanctions over labor rights suppression.[84]

Whether in decline or transition in the 1980s, the labor standards movement became focused on the labor abuses resulting from globalization by 1990 in response to the growth of multinational economic ties.[85] With the establishment of the Generalized System of Preferences (GSP) in the 1970s, Congress showed some interest in the links between trade and labor rights. In the 1980s it renewed the GSP, which the Reagan Administration used in 1987 to pressure Nicaragua, Paraguay, and Romania to correct human rights abuses. While the GSP can be seen as a unilateral means to achieve the purposes of the ILO, and therefore as a sign of American unilateralism, it demonstrated a new awareness of the relationship of offshore manufacturing growth and labor standards.[86]

The impact of this awareness became clear during the Bush Administration. Despite the administration's tilt toward the U.S. Council of International Business, the tripartite process successfully pushed forward the first ratification of a substantive labor standards convention that applied to all workers.[87] Since the creation of TAPILS, efforts had been underway to study if the U.S. might accept a few core labor standard conventions. After a decade, that process reached agreement on ratification of Convention 105, adopted by the ILO in 1957, banning forced labor. Obviously, the U.S. had an exceptional approach to international labor standards if it took thirty-four years to accept a convention that confirmed the core issue settled by the Civil War! However, this progress showed the tripartite process could achieve results despite the indifference of some elected officials.

The Clinton Administration hoped to distinguish its trade policy from that of Bush by linking it to labor and environmental standards. For example, in its efforts to win support for the North American Free Trade Agreement (NAFTA), negotiated initially by the Bush Administration, Clinton added labor and environmental "side agreements." The North American Agreement on Labor Cooperation (NAALC), signed in 1993 at the peak of the NAFTA debates, established a mechanism for monitoring and resolving violations of fair labor practices.[88] Given Clinton's pledge to push trade liberalization, the NAFTA ratification model resulted in repeated efforts to reassure the American public that labor rights would be protected. While the administration ignored the ILO in early economic liberalization talks, it modified its position after the new World Trade Organization (WTO) failed to practice openness or transparency in linking labor and trade policy. Although Clinton's trade representative, Mickey Kantor, responded inconsistently to criticisms that the U.S. tried to hide protectionism behind its defenses of human rights, Assistant Secretary of State for Democracy, Human Rights, and Labor John Shattuck staunchly denied them. The administration also fought for the 1998 ILO Declaration of Fundamental Principles or core labor standards.[89] That declaration identified four principles as "tenets of membership: freedom of association and the related right to bargain collectively; abolition of child labor; elimination of forced labor; and elimination of discrimination in employment and occupation." In addition the ILO reaffirmed the Declaration of Philadelphia, including that labor is not a commodity. Since the U.S. had ratified only the forced labor convention, the commitment in 1998 indicated the U.S. was interested in adopting substantive conventions. This activity did not make the ILO a household acronym, but public opinion polls indicated that a majority was concerned with labor standards by the end of the 1990s.[90] Reflecting this new awareness, the administration and the Senate agreed to ratify the newest child labor convention. Adopted by the ILO a year after the core labor standards, the Senate ratified Convention 182 in record time — three months — and it did so unanimously.[91] It seemed a new era was dawning.

Shortly after Senate ratification, the public concern with trade moved into center stage when the U.S. hosted the World Trade Organization's ministerial meetings in Seattle. As had happened during the NAFTA debate in 1992–1993, the links between trade and labor standards became front-page news in the week after Thanksgiving 1999.[92] A coalition of labor, environmental, and general opponents of multinational enterprises or globalization brought the conference to a halt and forced the WTO leadership to acknowledge the need for change.[93] Ever the astute political leader, President Clinton sided with the critics, at least to the extent of calling for WTO reform. With less conflict and media attention, the Seattle coalition raised significant protests at World Bank meetings in Washington in April and Prague in September 2000.[94]

In March 2000, nine conservative Republicans teamed with two Democrats, an isolationist from Mississippi and an industrial-district maverick from Ohio, and introduced a joint resolution to withdraw U.S. approval for the WTO agreement. In a debate reminiscent of those surrounding the Bricker Amendment in the 1950s, some conservatives now joined by a few labor rights activists worried that U.S. sovereignty needed protection from global financial and trade organizations. While the resolution was defeated, even supporters of the WTO used the committee debate to demand more transparency in trade policy making.[95] Such unrest raised the profile of the ILO as a counterbalance to the WTO and World Bank. *The New York Times*'s Thomas Friedman, a long-term proponent of globalization, called for more funding for the ILO.[96] In April 2000, the International Confederation of Free Trade Unions called for "enforceable labor standards" tied to WTO actions so that the trade policies would "reinforce rather than undermine universal ILO standards."[97] Then in June 2000, the Organization for Economic Cooperation and Development (OECD) revised its *Guidelines for Multinational Enterprises* to state, "The International Labor Organization (ILO) is the competent body to set and deal with international labor standards. . . . The OECD Guidelines and the ILO Tripartite Declaration [on Multinational Enterprises and Social Behavior, adopted in 1977] refer to behavior expected from enterprises and are intended to parallel and not conflict with each other."[98] The dysfunctional nature of globalization that resulted from the failure to keep the Bretton Woods institutions tied to the ILO finally seemed apparent.

THE CONTEMPORARY PRESSURE GROUP PROCESS

The responsiveness of recent administrations to labor rights, especially the U.S. leadership in the 1998 ILO Declaration of Fundamental Principles, reflects the special dynamics of populist and professional groups and institutions in the labor standards policy process. In an era otherwise known for the vast increase in financial, corporate, and other special interests devoted to buying political influence, their success teaches important lessons about achieving justice in the American system.[99] The growth of special interests began in the progressive era and accelerated with the New Deal broker state.[100] Interest group scholars find that at the end of the twentieth century both old and new groups tended to have an organizational structure based in Washington, with little emphasis upon state and local affiliates. Also, the groups held members to the organization by offering specific material benefits, such as discounts on purchases.[101] Several groups that traditionally led the labor standards movement experienced these changes, notably the Consumers' League. However, three important pillars of the labor standards movement did not follow these trends: organized labor, the churches, and the legal profession. Their special strength lay in not being Washington-based institutions united by the material rewards provided by the capital bureaucracy. Their success demonstrates the vital need to prevent the group process from following current centralization trends.

Some recent scholarship identifies three types of groups participating in policy making: nonprofit, self-interest, and educational. These scholars consider organized labor and business as examples of self-interested occupational groups.[102] Nonprofits include human rights, consumer, and environmental groups united by the pursuit of nonmaterial cultural change.[103] Universities and their faculties represent a third category, presumably seeking truth and wise policy choices. Both nonprofits and universities fit a classification of new social movements dominated by well-educated, cross-class activists. Many commentators assume that these new social movements, led by people Robert Reich called "symbolic analysts," perform a special role in checking the power of multinational businesses. Labor, by contrast, is dismissed as a declining, old-style movement based on class divisions and antagonisms.[104] The churches are ignored.

The experience at the ILO since 1975 raises fundamental problems with these theories. The university faculty and the new social movements tend to confirm Madison's worst fears about factions. Guided more often by pursuit of self-interest than the civic good, pursuing research grants, better jobs, or consumer goods for the elite, the beneficiaries of their advocacy are the group's members. Even when such groups have pursued more general human or environmental protections, the focus seldom is on the lower class. The protection of worker rights cannot count on the benevolence of a newly enlarged power elite of affluent professors and the manipulators of symbols whom they have trained. The new social movements may keep military buildups or business complicity in environmental degradation in check. They have not shown as much interest in blocking suppression of the rights of the world's poor.[105] When these groups have been concerned with human rights, they have not learned how to reconcile those rights with economic rights. By 1990, the groups that led the struggle to reconcile those rights came from the old social movements and the much-maligned legal profession.

Organized Labor

The battle against the ILO proved to be one of the last major policy initiatives of George Meany. He was eighty-one years old at the time of the decision to withdraw, and he died five years later in 1980. However, his legacy continued with the selection of his successor, Lane Kirkland. Different in background and temperament from Meany, Kirkland was more comfortable as an insider in the policy process. With a law degree, Kirkland was indistinguishable from corporate executives.[106] While he talked about expanding the labor movement, in the 1980s labor experienced a long-term decline in representing American workers.[107] Although critics held that Kirkland did too little, his administration did succeed in pressuring Congress to resume ILO convention ratification, clearly confronting the resistance of the business community.[108] Taking advantage of the Reagan Administration's Cold War battle, the AFL-CIO won the support of the secretary of state for the effort.[109] Yet, globalization accelerated during Kirkland's watch, and labor standards protection did not keep pace.

As the position of labor deteriorated, the AFL-CIO developed new alliances on labor rights with the churches and dissident parts of the labor movement. In the late 1980s, the federation began working with the more radical United Electrical Workers (UE), Catholic and Methodist leaders, and President Carter's labor secretary, Ray Marshall, in the International Labor Rights Educational and Research Fund. Marshall, who had been criticized by labor in the late 1970s, now wrote some major defenses of international labor standards and their linkage to trade.[110]

By the 1990s, more radical forces in labor arose, replacing Kirkland at the AFL-CIO with John Sweeney and giving more voice to groups like the UE. Sweeney promoted employment of students in a project called "Union Summer." In 1996 he cooperated in the founding of Scholars, Artists and Writers for Social Justice, which organized large teach-ins in university communities, an effort that seemed to have borne fruit for labor in Seattle in 1999. Meanwhile, labor's network began to control some of the labor rights institutions growing out of the trade wars. Lance Compa, a former United Electrical Workers attorney, directed labor law research at the North American Commission for Labor Cooperation, the institution created by the NAFTA "side agreement" to monitor labor rights in Canada, Mexico, and the U.S.[111] By the late 1990s, labor solidified its position and with the 1998 ILO Declaration of Principles achieved a remarkable endorsement of all that it had fought for during the century.[112]

CONSUMER GROUPS

After the passage of the Fair Labor Standards Act in 1938 and its acceptance by the Supreme Court in 1941, the Consumers' League experienced difficulty in defining a new role in the world. By the 1950s, most of the local leagues were closed. The national office floundered, searching for a home. It moved from New York to Washington and then to Cleveland, Ohio, site of one of its strongest locals. It developed an innovative interest in migratory labor issues, and it continued to celebrate its past, especially the twentieth anniversary of the FLSA in 1958. But, its real temptation derived from the word *consumers*.

One of the great symbolic changes in American reform attitudes was the development of the new consumer movement. This movement focused on assuring the integrity of the purchasing process and the quality of goods received. The beneficiary of the effort was the person consuming goods. The Consumers' League of Florence Kelley focused on helping the person producing the consumed goods. In Kelley's organization the consumers were other-directed, trying to help less fortunate workers. In the modern consumer movement the participants sought to help themselves. In the 1970s, new leadership assumed control at the National Consumers' League, largely abandoning the old focus and methods, entering the modern era of mass fund-raising, mass mail communication, and direct help for the members. Gone were a few elite, exceptionally trained women, joined by nationally renowned academic and clerical supporters, nurturing a vibrant local structure, working on tight budgets for the good of lower-class workers. The Consumers' League, as other women's organizations, ceased to be a cross-class movement and now focused on the needs of the modern upper-middle-class consuming women.[113]

The Consumers' League did not fully abandon its roots. As it approached its centennial in 1999, its interest in worker protection resumed, as did its interest in the ILO. It accepted a role in the Rugmark Campaign for eliminating south Asian child labor and sponsored the Child Labor Coalition and the Global March Against Child Labor in 1998.[114] That march terminated in Geneva and embarrassed the ILO into reviewing the world's failure to eradicate the problem. After the passage of ILO Convention 182 against the worst forms of child labor, the league took a lead role once again in the Child Labor Coalition, sponsoring the coalition's June 2000 conference on ILO Convention 182, seeking to move children from "exploitation to education." On the eve of the conference, the NGO

Human Rights Watch issued a report, "Fingers to the Bone: U.S. Failure to Protect Child Farmworkers." That report provided an opportunity to return to a theme that had first interested Consumers' League leaders in the ILO, use of a convention to compel improvements in domestic labor practices.[115]

As the farm worker issue linked the league's older and more recent concerns, so a new effort to promote social labeling, backed by among others the ILO director general, fit perfectly with the league's historic expertise.[116] The league had perfected social labeling in the early twentieth century, and that history provided it with a renewed leadership role in the movement. However, without vigorous local chapters and tied to late-twentieth-century membership-benefit recruitment strategies, it was not clear the league could return to its former dominance. Likewise, as indicated by the proportion of space given to labor issues in the league's publications, the organization may not have prepared to maintain the renewed labor standards effort. Should it manage to tie environmental protection and labor rights together, as did the protest leaders in Seattle in 1999, however, it might model a way to increase significantly the numbers of people informed about and willing to fight for worker protections.

THE CHURCHES

As in the entire postwar period, churches played a major role in the labor standards movement after 1980. As in Solidarity's struggles, the churches often acted as a reliable institutional support for labor. The development of "liberation theology," especially in the Latin American Catholic Church, provided a renewed theoretical justification for religious concern with labor rights. Beginning with the time of a Catholic bishops conference at Medellin, Colombia, in 1968, and usually traced to the Peruvian priest Gustavo Gutierrez, liberation theology reinforced the eighty-year trend starting with *Rerum Novarum*. The church felt called to criticize specific political developments that undermined justice or peace and to practice "a preferential option for the poor," a phrase often linked to liberation theology. While the hierarchy had mixed reactions to liberation theology throughout the last third of the twentieth century, Pope John Paul II repeatedly reinforced the church's fundamental concern with social justice, especially in *Centesimus Annus*, his encyclical on the hundredth anniversary of *Rerum Novarum*.[117] When the American bishops issued a "Pastoral Message" on the same anniversary, they specifically referred to liberation theology's "Option for the Poor and Vulnerable." They also recalled that Leo XIII had been guided in writing the encyclical by the Fribourg Union, which "argued unequivocally that work is far more than a commodity."[118] Not only did liberation theology spread beyond Latin America to the U.S. and Rome, it also extended beyond Catholicism, with one of its most articulate American voices being Robert McAfee Brown, a Protestant theologian.[119]

In the mid-1980s, the Catholic bishops in the U.S. applied this thinking in an assessment of the American economy, issuing a pastoral letter, *Economic Justice for All*. There, they criticized the institutional weakness of the international economic system and called on the U.S. to form "new international partnerships . . . based on mutual respect, cooperation, and a dedication to fundamental justice."[120] According to Thomas Donahue, Kirkland's immediate successor as head of the AFL-CIO, "The . . . pastoral letter . . . is good news to trade unionists of all religions."[121] Donahue specifically reminded the bishops in his comments on the letter that labor cooperated with the ILO in developing labor standards.

However, within the church, a new group of theologically literate business leaders mounted a critique of the bishops' position. No longer was it Dean Manion and his syndicated radio show against George Higgins and several cardinals. Now Michael Novak and Alexander Haig, backed by the American Enterprise Institute, commented on the bishops' work.[122] Yet, revealing the success of earlier teachings, Novak did not defend laissez-faire. In fact, his comments agreed more with the 1920s corporatism quite compatible with the labor standards movement.[123] The debate about the bishops' pastoral, therefore, provided hope that the most pessimistic assessment of the modern role of the churches was exaggerated: "In the end . . . no Jewish or Christian ethical initiative was able to find a social form powerful enough to reinvigorate the sense of the public good to the point where it could confront and alter the increasingly prevalent assumptions of capitalist individualism."[124] In 2000, John Paul II reiterated the church's support for the ILO by celebrating a May Day Workers Jubilee in Rome with ILO Director General Juan Somavia and AFL-CIO President John Sweeney.[125]

Perhaps most encouraging for the movement was the work of Brown and other Protestant defenders of labor standards. After Robert Drinan, the Jesuit former member of Congress, helped launch the International Labor Rights Education and Research Fund (ILRERF) in the mid-1980s, it received major support from the General Board for Global Ministries of the Methodist Church.[126] Rev. Pharis Harvey, a former missionary, became the executive director. Importantly, by the middle of the 1990s, the fastest-growing Christian group, the evangelicals, gave vocal support for global labor standards.[127] Still, a fundamental problem of Protestant Christianity is the link to what Max Weber labeled the "Protestant Ethic." With a focus on individual conversion and stewardship, the ethic tends to sanctify capitalist behavior, making criticism of materialist excesses difficult.[128] Whether the work of leaders such as Robert Brown can bury the Protestant commitment to the Weberian ethic beneath a reformed commitment to social justice can only be known in the next millennium.[129]

Liberation theology reinforced the general commitment within the churches to altruism, which already had led many leaders from Richard Ely to George Higgins to advocate labor standards. The churches questioned the most compelling arguments of business against labor rights, that the standards raised consumer costs or served as protections for the jobs of overpaid union members. The churches, under the influence of liberation theology, perceived labor rights as a defense of powerless workers in the developing world.[130] They spoke with clarity when they emphasized "the preferential option for the poor."[131]

ACADEMICS

In contrast to the continuing, if not growing, role of the churches in the labor standards movement, the last major social science defense of the ILO came in the 1950s with the Johnson committee and the Notre Dame conference, and that conference convened primarily because of church lobbying. Even the Johnson committee appeared as an initiative of the Labor Department and its issue network in the field of industrial relations. Given the postwar growth of higher education, its minor role in ILO debates begs an explanation, especially in contrast to its leadership before the 1930s. Frederick Abbot, chair of the American Association of Law Schools Section on International Law, blamed the lack of interest among academics on three factors: (1) their class differences from labor, (2) their perception that labor leaders were corrupt, and (3) the complexity of many labor standards issues, requiring familiarity with multiple disciplines.

While the first two reasons are matters of understanding and perception, difficult for institutions to change, the latter grows directly from several recent trends within higher education. First, the increasing specialization within disciplines has led scholars, especially discipline leaders, to focus on narrow research within their fields and not on general policy applications of their work. Late-nineteenth-century academics had been inspired by German social scientists to become involved in public affairs. After the 1930s, the influx of large numbers of émigré academics from Europe had the opposite effect.[132] Second, the fear of McCarthyism reinforced discipline-specific trends toward a new research agenda, especially in the social sciences.[133] Third, new funding lured some academics to focus on topics of utility to the industrial economy.[134] The Carnegie Foundation for the Advancement of Teaching warned in the 1960s of a crisis in values in higher education as academics followed research grants to the detriment of independent research.[135] Money for academic research for labor standards never had been significant, and comparatively little was available in other social science fields. Now funds for other areas surfaced, but still none for labor standards.[136]

The Vietnam era complicated these trends for institutions such as the ILO. History, which had produced James Shotwell, did not "suffer" the burden of research dollars attracting scholars to subdisciplines valued by industry. But historians had changed since Shotwell's day. Just as they recovered from postwar realism, the Vietnam era renewed distrust of any institution created by Woodrow Wilson. Wilson was no longer perceived as the great progressive ally of Shotwell whose ideals were destroyed by the cynical isolationists. Radical historians now considered Wilson an imperialist, anti-Marxist, racist.[137]

The next generation of historians mocked male-dominated institutions such as the AFL-CIO and the Catholic Church.[138] Obviously, Meany's AFL-CIO, with its anti-Marxist obsession, did not warrant the favorable attention of the new labor historians. Their heroes were Emma Goldman and Bill Haywood, not Samuel Gompers.[139] The church role in the ILO became a special liability with an increasingly antichurch professorate and their institutions of higher education.[140] Consequently, when Meany, Higgins, and their friends stood up for labor rights in the 1970s, academics were not watching. If they noticed, they likely agreed with the elite press, which regarded such acts as a new form of foolish American chauvinism or prejudice.[141]

THE LEGAL PROFESSION

Compensating for the departure of the social scientists, a new group rose to prominence, largely linked to universities. In the last two decades of the twentieth century, lawyers took increasing interest in human rights, and many of them showed some concern with labor rights. A number of law schools created centers for human rights, and some international law specialists focused on international labor law. Special groups of attorneys, such as the Lawyers Committee for Human Rights organized in 1978, lobbied for labor rights protections in trade laws. By the end of the century, the Lawyers Committee had a nonpartisan board tied to the highest levels of American politics and business. In 2000, for example, the board included Tom Bernstein, a friend and former partner of President George W. Bush; George Vradenburg of America Online, a major backer of John McCain; and Kerry Kennedy Cuomo, tied to two of the major Democratic families. Concerned inherently with defining justice, these elite attorneys provided an exceptionally influential base for labor standards at the dawn of the new millennium.

An example of their power occurred in 1995, when Senator Helms urged U.S. withdrawal from the ILO. The Section of International Law of the ABA responded by preparing an eloquent ILO defense. Led by a prominent international lawyer from Texas, Jay M. Vogelson, a State Department legal advisor during the Reagan presidency, the ABA resolved not only that the U.S. should continue membership, but, "that the American Bar Association . . . urges accelerated progress . . . toward ratification of those ILO conventions on human rights which are consistent with U.S. law and practice."[142] The ABA defense played the same role as that provided by James Shotwell and his academic allies in the early part of the century. Now, however, the economists, political scientists, and sociologists were replaced by lawyers.

BUSINESS GROUPS

The crisis over Eastern European suppression of labor rights not only altered the ILO, but it also led to a new U.S. process for selecting business delegates. Those delegates would no longer come from the U.S. Chamber of Commerce, a mass business organization with many local affiliates, but from a specialized group composed of multinational enterprises. In 1980, the U.S. Chamber relinquished the right to select ILO delegates to the U.S. Council for International Business (USCIB). Begun in 1945, the USCIB was formed to defend the interests of American businesses heavily involved in trade or global manufacturing. The USCIB specialized in trade liberalization, removing barriers to trade, and helping international business enter overseas markets. It included three hundred of the largest businesses operating out of the U.S. trade capital, New York, not Washington. It did not include all sizes and all types of businesses. It was not an organization that represented average American business leaders. It only served the leadership of the biggest multinationals.[143] Its delegate to the ILO at the end of the 1990s, for example, was Thomas Morehead, vice president for Human Resources at Carter-Wallace, a multinational pharmaceutical and consumer toiletries company.

While the USCIB included some firms that supplied earlier ILO employer delegates, such as Kodak, McCormick, and SIFCO, it would not have included businesses like McGrath's Williamson Heater. Of course, ILO supporters were glad to avoid another McGrath, but his company was replaced with multinational firms with expert legal staff, prepared to support exhaustive policy studies. For example, the USCIB published a sophisticated critique of ILO Conventions 87 and 98 on freedom of association and collective bargaining.[144] McGrath may have been gone; the issues remained the same. They no longer were argued by a poorly educated midwestern furnace maker, trained as a salesman. Now, well-trained attorneys, equal to any funded by labor, presented the business perspective.

That perspective was not as confrontational and more subtle. The Business Roundtable, responding to Senator Helms, advocated continued strong U.S. participation in the ILO.[145] International business came to like the ILO, a group that recommended standards but did not enforce them. Business admired voluntarism and favored international codes of conduct endorsed by the ILO.[146] In their statements, USCIB leaders sounded similar to labor. The key difference centered on the issue of enforcement, which business opposed. USCIB did not want labor rights violations to be used as a justification for imposing trade restrictions.[147] They also called for extreme caution, if not inaction, on ratification of additional ILO conventions.[148] Despite their rhetorical similarities in discussing ILO membership, the differences between the USCIB and labor on trade linkage and vigorous adoption of substantive conventions would determine whether the ILO would be either a symbolic or effective institution in the new millennium.

Lessons
and Needs

At the end of the nineteenth century, the first American coalition supporting modern labor standards evolved. It derived its earliest support from former abolitionists, most notably Josephine Shaw Lowell; social scientists blending empirical study of institutions with the social gospel, including Richard Ely and John R. Commons; and church leaders promoting that gospel, such as John Ryan. A few progressive business leaders, like Edward Filene, also joined the movement in search of an alternative to laissez-faire that would solve what they called "the social problem." Less active were Samuel Gompers and other labor leaders, more fearful of government bias than confident in the use of its good offices. This coalition of pressure groups, dominated by middle-class progressives uneasy with industrialization, typified the new-style policy making of the era. Taking advantage of the crisis growing out of World War I, and building on a variety of European traditions, they finally succeeded in institutionalizing the protection of international labor standards at the ILO. Reflecting theories of the era, they gave control to a tripartite structure that balanced the voice of political leaders with delegates selected by leading interests. In the reaction to the war, the U.S. demonstrated its exceptionalism and did not participate further until the 1930s.

The crisis of the Great Depression provided an opportunity to form a new coalition to support the ILO. Created after pragmatic analysis of economic problems of the era, the revived labor standards movement successfully managed to break with isolationism or unilateralism and join the ILO. Still with strong support from the Consumers' League and the academy, the new coalition received key leadership from John Winant and other political figures. The wartime crisis, following shortly after ILO membership, justified a renewal of the original ILO goals at Philadelphia. Yet, no sooner had these goals been reaffirmed than America again lost interest. Postwar prosperity, especially American dominance of the world economy, removed the need for labor standards. The ILO was then used to clarify the struggle with the Soviet Union. The ILO nearly became a casualty of that battle, only to be saved by a coalition of labor and the churches.

Near the end of the twentieth century, with a U.S. victory in the Cold War, the ILO once more seemed relevant. Once again, the reasons given in 1919 and renewed at Philadelphia applied. Americans realized that the lawless global economy feared by Woodrow Wilson and James Shotwell in 1919, and by Robert Owen a century earlier, had arrived. Multinational firms emerged with sufficient resources to influence or even intimidate national governments into suppressing labor.[1] In the period before 1990, multinational investment traveled from one developed nation to another. In the first half of the 1990s, multinationals invested more heavily outside Europe, North America, and Japan.[2] One factor in that investment pattern was aggressive implementation of the "runaway shop" to find the cheapest and least independent labor. The same pattern had destroyed Amoskeag in the 1930s when mill owners headed South.[3] Now the "labor race to the bottom" focused on the developing nations. Countries such as Mexico attracted business because they offered devaluated wages, lax enforcement of labor protections, and government-controlled unions.[4] In this time of need, the coalition that had supported labor standards before World War II had weakened. Only labor and the churches consistently endorsed labor standards. The Consumers' League became schizophrenic, not sure if it was a consumer or labor protection group. Elite academic support faded. Many business leaders, as deterministic and materialistic as any Marxist, wanted to set all labor conditions through the free market. After two generations of ILO debates, they developed a subtly subversive approach. Their front organization, the USCIB, supported basic labor standards, such as banning the most extreme forms of child labor, so long as there were no enforcement mechanisms. When the USCIB feared substantive ILO conventions, like protections of the right to form unions and bargain collectively, they returned to the arguments of McGrath and the Bricker Amendment backers.[5]

In this context, the 1998 ILO reaffirmation of its fundamental principles, especially the 1944 Declaration of Philadelphia, seemed so important. Not that the declaration forced states to do anything. Rather, the significance of 1998 lay in reminding the members of the organization's origins and its founding principles. This time the supporters of the labor standards movement possessed a century of experience upon which to build in seeking to implement the declaration. They still had to take two steps. First, substantive conventions imposing labor standards and not only labor rights needed to be defined. Second, effective enforcement mechanisms had to be developed. While a democratic and tripartite process would choose the substantive standards, suggested conventions included the minimum wage, weekly rest, and maternity protections. The minimum wage needed to be flexible, taking into account the national differences in cost of living and level of development. The weekly rest not only represented a practical humane measure to control materialism, it also recognized the dignity of life outside of paid employment. Finally, the maternity protections became essential if women's work outside the home was to be implemented with respect for family life. The last two of these conventions were good standards to test in the United States, which in the previous generation ruthlessly had abandoned all respect for days of rest and denied the most rudimentary financial support to family values at the heart of the maternity convention. After the 2000 ILO conference, the adoption of tougher maternity protections in Convention 183 provided a new vehicle to test American commitment.[6]

The increasing attention given to the necessity for labor standard enforcement mechanisms at the start of the new millennium seemed to justify a strong ILO. Although the foreign policy elite continued to experience collective amnesia about the 1944 links of the ILO to the Bretton Woods system, the stubborn resistance by the WTO leadership appeared destined to force a review of that history. The fundamental problem with the world trading regime at the turn of the century became its opposition to inclusion of labor rights and environmental protections in trade policy. The WTO even denied human rights NGOs the right to participate in policy making.

The General Agreement on Tariffs and Trade (GATT), negotiated after World War II, envisioned an International Trade Organization (ITO) that would have allowed NGO input into trade policy making. Without the ITO, the GATT evolved into a forum for trade experts with no NGO contact.[7] The more recent World Trade Organization (WTO), at its 1996 Singapore ministerial meeting, did not even permit the ILO director general to address the delegates.[8] Such behavior culminated in the Seattle riots against the WTO and the subsequent escalation of attacks on the older Bretton Woods institutions: the World Bank and the International Monetary Fund.

There were several reasons to hope and several reasons to fear that the ILO would not become a counterweight to the Bretton Woods institutions foreseen in 1944. Repeatedly in the late 1990s, the ILO asserted its right to be the primary protector of substantive labor rights. Its allies in the AFL-CIO, the church, and the legal community labored with renewed commitment to support this assertion. Thus, the 1998 definition of core labor standards was important, including the renewed pledge that labor was not a commodity. While the ILO had never used sanctions in its first eighty years, it seemed about to do so in an effort to protect labor rights in Myanmar. Significantly, the President's Committee on the ILO endorsed such steps. Likewise, the U.S. ratification of Convention 182 on child labor and the willingness of the Congress to link ratification of the convention to trade preferences set an important precedent. The Trade and Development Act of 2000, targeted on helping sub-Saharan Africa and the Caribbean basin, required that the countries ratify Convention 182 before being eligible. Given the atmosphere after the Seattle WTO meetings and IMF and World Bank ministerial meetings in Washington and Prague, the ILO seemed well-positioned to receive renewed support from the United States. American labor also seemed poised to form effective ties to unions in developing countries, especially Mexico and Central America, where the trends toward democratization created more room for independent, American-style unions.

However, it would be naive to think the road to a changed ILO role will be smooth or short. First, trade officials continue to desire to operate out of sight of interest groups and NGOs; they prefer to keep standards for economic matters distinct from labor rights concerns. Those officials may have been shaken in Seattle, but in other places they dismissed labor linkages and sought to exclude an NGO presence. Proponents of a multilateral agreement on investments hoped to forbid any debate about labor rights in investment forums.[9] Despite the new labor standards initiatives of the Clinton Administration, many supporters of labor rights found the opposition, both institutional within the world trade regime and from powerful multinationals, to be overwhelming.[10] If, as some critics claimed, multinationals were prepared to sacrifice national interests for the short-run self-interest of investors, it was highly unlikely they would respect labor interests.[11]

A second reason for concern grew from the persuasive and relentless arguments for voluntarism voiced anytime linkage of financial or trade policy and labor rights appeared on the horizon. The OECD Guidelines for Multinational Enterprises developed in 2000 could be seen as an effort to head off mandatory linkage. Likewise, free marketers, when pressed, supported social labeling or industry-developed standards. The International Standards Organization (ISO) interceded repeatedly to divert demands for various occupational health and safety laws into industry-controlled standards.

Third, the developing world remained persistent in accusing the first world of using labor standards as a form of protectionism. The cases of first world union collaboration with third world labor seemed too few to counter this belief. In the debate about fundamental principles in 1998, the government representatives from Egypt, Mexico, and Pakistan led opposition to any implied linkage of the principles to trade.[12] Obviously, they would reject more specific conventions?

Probably the most significant reason enforceable labor standards seemed problematic at the start of the new millennium was that the U.S. did not support such standards domestically. The very reasons Winant and the other 1930s supporters of labor law turned to the ILO, to overcome U.S. constitutional barriers, remained for a number of specific standards. It seemed doubtful that the exceptional American social policy process would support "cash benefits" to women for fourteen weeks of maternity leave, as required by Convention 183. Thomas Morehead, the USCIB delegate in 2000, lamented the ILO "had adopted a convention which the United States could not ratify."[13] Ever since the passage of Convention 87 on freedom of association in 1948, and Convention 98 on the right to organize and bargain collectively, U.S. labor law and practices regularly were found in contradiction to these core standards.[14] There was slight chance that the obsessively materialistic U.S. economy would reinstitute a law requiring a weekly day of rest, as the ILO demanded since 1921. Despite the rhetorical commitment to child labor prohibition, U.S. agricultural exemptions for child labor allegedly violate basic global standards. Could there be any hope for change?

Without ignoring these reasons for concern, the international group unity evident at places like the WTO Seattle meeting in 1999, as well as the revitalized linkage of labor, the church, and the law, must give room for hope that American exceptionalism can cut two ways. Possibly, American multinationals eager to receive trade breaks may be prepared to accept some minimal substantive standards, which could open the door for more. Henry Drummonds of Northwestern School of Law called this development "The ILO's Trojan Horse strategy." Why would the U.S. and American conservatives accept the ILO's core labor standards and the principle that labor is not a commodity, with the additional threat that U.S. sovereignty has been compromised? Drummonds concluded, "The question generates a simple answer: The effort to broaden and build support for globalization persuaded the Clinton Administration and its business allies that the gains outweigh any losses."[15]

DEFINING EXCEPTIONALISM

The reaffirmation of the Declaration of Philadelphia and of the four core rights in 1998 proved once again that, with timely support from within the U.S. policy process, labor standards advocates could win. This latest victory reinforces the need to identify the historical lessons of labor rights policy in America. At the 1995 meeting of the Section on International Law of the American Association of Law Schools, several labor rights attorneys focused on "[W]hy the United States has such a dismal record regarding the International Labor Organization agreements."[16] Lance Compa, director of International Labor Rights Advocates, blamed such American exceptionalism on John Winthrop's concept that "we're a city on the hill."[17] Nurtured for nearly four centuries, this attitude made Americans confident that the standards for the rest of the world could not apply here. While such a dismal view of American policy may be understandable given the timing of the remarks shortly after creation of the WTO, the history of the process teaches a different lesson about exceptionalism in the tripartite world of international labor standards.

What happened in Geneva, Seattle, Washington, and elsewhere at the turn of the millennium affirmed the work of a century and a half of labor standards policy makers in America. They demonstrated that well-organized groups can force the policy process to consider values, other than economic efficiency, in setting economic policies. Josephine Shaw Lowell, in both her early and later crusades, as well as Richard Ely, John Commons, John Ryan, and Samuel Gompers, understood that labor was more than a commodity. Each considered the concept of a labor market to be an oversimplification of the process of finding work and determining its terms and wages. Despite the materialism of both their capitalist and Marxist opponents, they forced the nation and the world to acknowledge that principle in 1919. Their descendants compelled the victors to reaffirm it in 1944. A half-century later, in 1998, it was reiterated as fundamental to the world of the new millennium. Despite challenges ahead in developing and enforcing substantive standards, this history must be understood and appreciated.

The labor standards process not only succeeded in gaining worldwide acceptance of several fundamental principles, but also won acknowledgement that there are fundamental principles for the world's workers and employers. Speaking against the fundamental principles in 1998, the Mexican government's ILO delegate demanded different standards in different places. He knew that one of the greatest bulwarks against justice for the less affluent is relativism. But the ILO is built on an old and very different eighteenth-century ideology, one it shares with the foundations of the United States—natural law. Unlike Winthrop's concept that America is exceptional and exempt from world standards, this ideology maintains there is a law of nations and, as the Constitution allows, Congress should enforce it. There is an ideal law that should apply to everyone, at all times, and we should constantly seek to discover and apply it. The much maligned former ILO Director General Wilfred Jenks knew it shared this ideology with the U.S. He said of the ILO's philosophy, "Ideology belongs to time and place. We are not captive to time and place. We belong to everywhere and all time. The ILO has no ideology, but it has ideals, and its ideals, which transcend ideologies, are fundamental, universal and eternal."[18]

The U.S. and the ILO are exceptional not only because of these shared ideals, they also share a commitment to participatory democracy. Tripartism is a mechanism that assumes structures and procedures are needed to allow vigorous popular participation in policy making. Participatory democracy does not assume that elites inherently know how to define the ideals. Likewise, as Wilfred Jenks said, those ideals are not defined as part of a rational ideology. Both the tripartism of the ILO and the pressure group process encouraged by the American system assume that the fundamental need of a good system is not an ideology but a process open to all groups, especially those linked to local communities and average citizens.

While there are a variety of groups with links to communities, two of the best are organized labor and the churches. Both institutions have many local affiliates that, despite entrenched hierarchies and often stifling bureaucracies, keep the institutions in touch with the average members. The legal profession likewise is diffused and, like the churches, brings the inherent quest for justice to policy making. Both tend to have faith that timeless principles of fairness exist. They will not always endorse the right policy, but their mission is to do so; that introduces a valuable element into policy making.

Not surprisingly, there are those who wish to curb the goal of these groups, what Michael Clough has called the "reclaiming [of] . . . policy from the 'Wise Men.'"[19] Political leaders regularly criticize the activities of human rights attorneys. The courts have restricted efforts by Congress to assure unrestrained religious freedom.[20] There are constant criticisms of the power of labor bosses.[21] In fact, the history of the labor standards movement demonstrates the need to promote more, not less, freedom for such groups. Specifically, aggressive protection of church participation in the policy process, such as envisioned in the Religious Freedom Restoration Act, is needed. Likewise, the ILO experience should teach the country to treasure tripartism or variants that require a voice for lower-income groups.[22] Such assurances of participation are necessary not because labor, churches, or local communities are always right. They should be privileged because they occasionally will be right and may be the only voice demanding limitations on an elite that can be tragically wrong or terribly unjust. As Norman Gottwald has said of the history of the church:

> In nearly all periods of Christian history, as in nearly all periods of Jewish history, there have been voices criticizing social and economic injustice as distortions of God's creation. . . .
>
> This subversive practice of the Jewish-Christian ethic was, taken as a whole, ineffectual in promoting enduring structural economic change, but it was insistent and tenacious. It forms an unbroken continuum of testimony and example.[23]

The American system, and more so the ILO policy process, have been exceptional in protecting and welcoming such subversive attacks upon established practices.

Fortunately, as the labor standards movement shows, many leaders of churches, unions, the Consumers' League, progressive businesses, and, recently, the legal profession have appreciated the value of this system as well and fought for its extension, as did many of the founders of the social sciences. Rather than seeking benefits from elites and experts, contemporary social scientists would do well to resume their efforts on its behalf. The labor standards movement, with the populist participation of average workers, has shown both domestically and internationally that it is possible to balance materialist economic policy with concern for both political freedom and social justice.[24] It has proven that the liberal policy process need not be dominated by the unlimited pursuit of self-interest. The inability of liberalism to seek justice can be corrected and the Madisonian process made to work reasonably well for all.[25]

The challenge for the labor standards movement in the U.S. is to utilize the positive features of American exceptionalism to again renew the global commitment to transparent labor rights policy and substantive labor protections in the developing world. Free labor unions, abolition of child labor, a meaningful minimum wage, and similar basic protections will allow workers in the world to negotiate and earn meaningful rewards from their work. It will give all workers the hope that they can retain their dignity. It will affirm, again, that labor is not a commodity. As Josephine Shaw Lowell would remind us, it will force the consumers of the developed countries and within the elites in the developing world to pay the fair value, both in money and respect, for the labor included in their goods. Then Matamoros, Ciudad Juarez, and similar communities may become places where workers freely enjoy the just fruits of their labor. Then the workers of Flint or Dayton will know they are not pitted in a hopeless race to the bottom. Within the United States, appreciation and vigorous defense of an open process may even yield work weeks with guaranteed days of rest, protections for family child rearing, and similar worker protections that force Americans to respect the boundaries between economic and human life. While some may doubt that American materialism can ever be made to respect the intrinsic worth of humanity, the past successes of average citizens and supporters of justice in using the labor standards process to erect barriers to our greed give reason for hope.

Notes

1. For a study of Mexican shopping patterns in border cities see Lawrence A. Herzog, *Where North Meets South: Cities, Space, and Politics on the U.S.-Mexico Border* (Austin: Center for Mexican American Studies, University of Texas, 1990), 148–155.

2. *Dayton Daily News*, 29 June 1998, 1B.

3. For an evaluation of the impact of border plants, see Harley Shaiken, *Mexico in the Global Economy: High Technology and Work Organization in Export Industries* (San Diego: Center for U.S.-Mexican Studies, University of California, 1990), 122. Shaiken points out there have not been many benefits to the host communities of high-tech branch plants, such as skill training for local workers; however, he believes such advances may come. Similarly, see Joseph Grunwald, "Opportunity Missed: Mexico and Maquiladoras," *The Brookings Review* 9 (winter 1990/91): 44–48.

4. Mexico has long been involved in efforts to protect its nationals coming to work in the U.S.; as early as the bracero program of the 1940s, Mexico has had formal agreements with the U.S. for such reasons. See, for example, Dianne C. Betts and Daniel Slottje, *Crisis on the Rio Grande: Poverty, Unemployment, and Economic Development on the Texas-Mexico Border* (Boulder, Colo.: Westview Press, 1994), 109–110; on continuing efforts by Mexico, see Howard LaFranchi, "Keeping Mexican Migrants Safer," *The Christian Science Monitor*, 23 June 2000, 8.

5. On turnover see Tom Barry, "Structure of the Economy," in *Mexico: A Country Guide*, ed. Tom Barry (Albuquerque, N.M.: Inter-Hemispheric Education Resource Center, 1992), 142–150; see also the highly critical study of Mexican working conditions by Dan La Botz, *Mask of Democracy: Labor Suppression in Mexico Today* (Boston: South End Press, 1992), 164–166; for a poignant story of the plight of fleeing Mexican border residents, see *The New York Times*, 5 August 1998, 1A, describing undocumented migrants dying in the south Texas heat trying to escape border towns.

6. A fundamental legal disagreement exists regarding the motivation for immigration: while the official policy is that most is economically motivated and therefore properly subject to intense restriction, as on the Mexican

border, others maintain it is motivated more by political, social, and intellectual factors that make it a human rights issue. For a discussion of this approach, see Susanne Jonas, "Rethinking Immigration Policy and Citizenship in the Americas: A Regional Framework," and David Bacon, "For an Immigration Policy Based on Human Rights," in *Immigration: A Civil Rights Issue for the Americas,* ed. Susanne Jonas and Suzie Dod Thomas (Wilmington, Del.: Scholarly Resources, 1999).

7. Herzog, 250–253; on comparative poverty on both sides of the border, see Robert D. Kaplan, "Mexico and the Southwest: Travels into America's Future," *Atlantic Monthly* (July 1998): 54–64; and Betts and Slottje, 5–25.

8. Sarah Hill, "The Political Ecology of Environmental Learning in Ciudad Juarez and El Paso County," in *Shared Space: Rethinking the U.S.-Mexico Border Environment,* ed. Lawrence A. Herzog (LaJolla: Center for U.S.-Mexican Studies, University of California, 2000), 139–143.

9. On the new directions in the PRI, see Tom Barry, *Zapata's Revenge* (Boston: South End Press, 1995), 11–34; and Jorge G. Castaneda, *The Mexican Shock* (New York: The New Press, 1995), 31–61. For a longer-term, more theoretical consideration of this change, see Nora Hamilton, *The Limits of State Autonomy: Post-Revolutionary Mexico* (Princeton: Princeton University Press, 1982), 241–270, which holds that because of Mexico's dependency on the U.S. economy, it was nearly impossible for the progressive alliance of the PRI and workers and farmers to survive. Of relevance to the current study, Hamilton's findings indicate that outside labor standard supports would be fundamental to sustaining such an alliance.

10. On the current status of labor and the church, see James G. Samstad and Ruth Berins Collier, "Mexican Labor and Structural Reform under Salinas: New Unionism or Old Stalemate?" 9–38; and Roberto J. Blancarte, "Reforms of Law on Religion," 109–110, in *The Challenge of Institutional Reform in Mexico,* ed. Riordan Roett (Boulder: Lynne Rienner, 1995), 9–38. On the church, see Roderic A. Camp, *Crossing Swords: Politics and Religion in Mexico* (New York: Oxford University Press, 1997), 26–78; on the complex personal relations of church and political leaders, see 135–153. For more historical accounts of the labor and church relationship to politics, see Hamilton, 77–103; and Ramon Eduardo Ruiz, *The Great Rebellion: Mexico 1905–1924* (New York: Norton, 1980), 410–420. On continuing labor rights violations in Mexico, see Sam Dillon, "Abuses Reported in Mexico at American Owned Plant," *The New York Times,* 5 August 1998, 10A.

11. Justin Brown, "Open Talk of an Open U.S. Border," *The Christian Science Monitor,* 23 August 2000, 1–4.

12. Mary Beth Rogers, *Cold Anger: A Story of Faith and Power Politics* (Denton, Tex.: University of North Texas Press, 1990), 1–9, 24–26, 165–173; Robert H. Wilson, ed., *Public Policy and Community: Activism and Governance*

in Texas (Austin: University of Texas Press, 1997) discusses especially Valley Interfaith and the El Paso Interreligious Sponsoring Organization. For a more general account of Hispanic empowerment in the Southwest, see Amy Bridges, *Morning Glories: Municipal Reform in the Southwest* (Princeton, N.J.: Princeton University Press, 1997).

13. Jorge Castaneda, "The Fear of Americanization," in Robert A. Pastor and Jorge Castaneda, eds., *The Limits to Friendship* (New York: Vintage Books, 1989), 314–341.

14. For studies of Mexican migrants, see essays in David G. Gutierrez, ed., *Between Two Worlds: Mexican Immigrants in the United States* (Wilmington, Del.: Scholarly Resources, 1996).

15. For a typical account of welfare use by immigrants, see Pete Wilson, "Don't Give Me Your Tired, Your Poor . . . ," *The San Diego Union-Tribune*, 9 January 1994, 1G. On social welfare in Mexico and the southwestern U.S., see Linda S. Chan et al., *Maternal and Child Health on the U.S.-Mexico Border* (Austin: Lyndon B. Johnson School of Public Affairs, University of Texas, 1987), 149–200, which found, for example, that twenty-nine married American women went to Mexico for obstetrics services, while eighty-two women (married and unmarried) came from Mexico to Texas for such services. While clearly the U.S. was more attractive for such services, the flow was not simply one way. Furthermore, for the poor, Mexico does provide health services not available in the U.S. to indigent undocumented aliens. For more recent information on Mexican health care, see Organization for Economic Co-operation and Development, *OECD Economic Surveys: 1997–1998 — Mexico* (Paris: OECD Publications, 1998), 88–119.

16. For the common economic conditions, and problems, of the border, see Betts and Slottje, 109–128, which focuses on the economic factors in migration. For detailed study of life in a border city, see Gay Young, ed., *The Social Ecology and Economic Development of Ciudad Juarez* (Boulder, Colo.: Westview, 1986). For a discussion of consumption as a way of life in the U.S. and immigration, see Stuart Ewen and Elizabeth Ewen, *Channels of Desire: Mass Images and the Shaping of American Consciousness* (Minneapolis: University of Minnesota Press, 1992), 32–34; the implication in their work is that immigrants did not come as consumers but were indoctrinated by the Americanization process.

17. For critical accounts of Mexican labor, see La Botz, on the CTM, 39–60; also Augusta Dwyer, *On the Line: Life on the U.S.–Mexican Border* (London: Latin American Bureau, 1994), 9–48.

18. On Mexican academics, see John Maddox and Henry Gee, "Science in Mexico: Mexico's Bid to Join the World," *Nature* 368 (28 April 1994): 789–804; also on co-opting the intelligentsia, see Barbara Belejack, "Education and Student Organizing," in Barry, 239–244.

19. Ronald F. Inglehart, Neil Nevitte, and Miguel Basanez, *The North American Trajectory* (New York: Aldine de Gruyter, 1996), 83–104, present data

that indicate a remarkable lack of confidence in the Mexican government; they interpret the data as showing similarities between the U.S. and Mexico. In 2000 and 2001, immigration across the border dropped greatly after the election of Vicente Fox, see *New York Times*, 3 February 2001, 5A.

20. Glenn Tinder, *Political Thinking: The Perennial Questions*, 5th ed. (New York: Harper Collins, 1991), 157–194.

21. On the complex relation of the church as a check on economic elites, the military, and civil rulers in Mexico, see Ruiz, 199–212, on Emiliano Zapata; Camp, 3–26; for related documents, see *Cross and Sword: An Eyewitness History of Christianity in Latin America*, ed. McKennie Goodpasture (Maryknoll, N.Y.: Orbis, 1989).

22. In *Federalist 51*, James Madison said, "If men were angels no government would be necessary." In *Federalist 21* he has an extensive discussion of the steps that result from "the reason of man [being] fallible," the formation of different opinions, and the linkage of these to factions based in different interests in society. It is important to recall he felt enlightened statesmen could sort out the pressures from interest groups; however, he lamented, "Enlightened statesmen will not always be at the helm."

23. Daniel Patrick Moynihan, "The United States and the International Labor Organization, 1889–1934" (Ph.D. diss., Fletcher School of Law and Diplomacy, 1960), 3.

24. Jeremy Beecher and Tim Costello, *Global Village or Global Pillage* (Boston: South End Press, 1994), 3.

25. For a discussion of efforts to provide a "Good Business Climate," see Barry Bluestone and Bennett Harrison, *The Deindustrialization of America* (New York: Basic Books, 1982), 180–188.

26. Lena Ayoub, "Nike Just Does It—and Why the United States Shouldn't: The United States' International Obligation to Hold MNCs Accountable for Their Labor Rights Violations Abroad," *DePaul Business Law Journal* 11 (spring/summer 1999), 422–423.

27. Louis Hartz, *The Liberal Tradition in America: An Interpretation of American Political Thought since the Revolution* (New York: Harcourt Brace, 1955), 203–255; for a critique of Hartz, see Edward N. Saveth, "A Decade of American Historiography: The 1960s," in *The Reinterpretation of American History and Culture*, ed. William H. Cartwright and Richard L. Watson, Jr. (Washington, D.C.: National Council for the Social Studies, 1973), 21.

28. Robert William Fogel, *Without Consent or Contract: The Rise and Fall of American Slavery* (New York: Norton, 1989), 411–417, concludes, "What the Civil War achieved, then, was more than just inflated wealth for northern capitalists and 'half' freedom for blacks. . . . It preserved and reinforced conditions favorable to continued struggle for the democratic rights of the lower classes, black and white alike, . . . not only in America but everywhere else in the world."

ONE. THE EXCEPTIONAL GROUP PROCESS

1. Quoted in Kenneth A. Swinnerton and Gregory K. Schoepfle, "Labor Standards in the Context of a Global Economy," *Monthly Labor Review* 117 (September 1994): 53.

2. James T. Shotwell, one of the founders of the movement at the start of the century, said in *The Origins of the International Labor Organization*, 2 vols. (New York: Columbia University Press, 1934), I: 15, that international labor legislation served to link "the moral demands of public opinion and the need for legal compulsion."

3. John B. Andrews, "Labor in the Peace Treaty," in *The League of Nations: The Principle and the Practice*, ed. Stephen Pierce Duggan (Boston: Atlantic Monthly Press, 1919), 237.

4. Article I, Section 8, of the U.S. Constitution grants Congress the power "To define and punish . . . Offenses against the Law of Nations."

5. For a contemporary discussion of the need for transformation, see Karl Polanyi, *The Great Transformation* (Boston: Beacon Press, 1944).

6. For good discussions of these models, see Bjorn Hettne, "Introduction: The International Political Economy of Transformation," in *International Political Economy: Understanding Global Disorder* (Halifax: Fernwood Publishing, 1995), 8–10.

7. For a summary of the political economy model, see Robert W. Cox, "Introduction," in *The New Realism: Perspectives on Multilateralism and World Order* (Tokyo: United Nations University Press, 1997), xvi–xix.

8. David B. Truman, *The Governmental Process* (New York: Knopf, 1951).

9. Robert Dahl, *Who Governs?* (New Haven, Conn.: Yale University Press, 1961). For a discussion of how much Dahl meant to praise the group process, see Jack L. Walker, "A Critique of the Elitist Theory of Democracy," *American Political Science Review* 60 (June 1966): 285–295; and Dahl's response, "Further Reflections on Elitist Theory of Democracy," *American Political Science Review* 60 (June 1966): 296–305; see especially the letter to the editor in the same number of *The American Political Science Review* from Walker commenting on Dahl's essay, 391–392.

10. E. E. Schattschneider, *The Semisovereign People: A Realist's View of Democracy in America* (New York: Holt, Rinehart, and Winston, 1960), 35.

11. Robert Michels, *Political Parties: A Sociological Study of Oligarchical Tendencies of Modern Democracies*, trans. Eden Paul and Cedar Paul (Glencoe, Ill.: Free Press, 1942), is the classic discussion of the "iron law."

12. Theodore J. Lowi, *The End of Liberalism: Ideology, Policy, and the Crisis of Public Authority* (New York: W. W. Norton, 1969), 287–297.

13. For the initial explanation of incrementalism see Charles Lindblom, "The Science of Muddling Through," *Public Administration Review* 19 (spring 1959): 79–88; for a summary of incremental theory see Michael Hayes, *Incrementalism and Public Policy* (New York: Longman, 1992) 195–200.

14. Hopefully, the Civil War does not prove that justice can only be achieved in the U.S. through bloody conflict; see Fogel, *Without Consent*, 411–417, for a discussion of the "moral problem" of the Civil War.

15. See Charles E. Lindblom, "The Market as Prison," *Journal of Politics* 44 (May 1982): 324–336, which holds that average citizens have little control over the policy process because of the domination of business and its market ideology.

16. Defenders of incrementalism would disagree that it burdens a search for social justice; for a definition of distributive and other policy types, see Theodore Lowi, "American Business and Public Policy, Case-Studies, and Political Theory," *World Politics* 16 (1964): 677–715.

17. Lowi, *The End of Liberalism*, 191–283, has the standard interpretation of why interest group liberalism does not result in just policies; Robert W. Cox, "ILO: Limited Monarchy," in *The Anatomy of Influence: Decision Making in International Organizations*, ed. Robert W. Cox and Harold K. Jacobson (New Haven, Conn.: Yale University Press, 1974), 116–119, reviews the complexity of interest group behavior at the ILO.

18. Cox, "ILO," 137.

19. Anthony Downs, *Inside Bureaucracy* (Boston: Little Brown and Co., 1967), 5–23, describes the "The Life Cycle of Bureaus," a good summary of the concept of correlating the age of bureaus and the type of staff they attract; see also Hugh Heclo, *A Government of Strangers* (Washington, D.C.: Brookings Institution, 1977), 142–153, for his discussion of bureaucratic dispositions.

20. Alexis de Tocqueville, *Democracy in America*, trans. by Henry Reeve (New York: Vintage Books, 1945), I: 72–73.

21. See, for example, Arnold J. Heidenheimer, Hugh Heclo, and Carolyn Teich Adams, *Comparative Public Policy*, 2nd ed. (New York: St. Martin's Press, 1983), 311–331; and Peter Flora and Jens Alber, "Modernization, Democratization, and the Development of Welfare States in Western Europe," in *The Development of Welfare States in Europe and America*, ed. Peter Flora and Arnold Heidenheimer (New Brunswick: Transaction Press, 1981), 37–80. For a general history of exceptionalism see Daniel Levine, *Poverty and Society: The Growth of the American Welfare State in International Comparison* (New Brunswick, N.J.: Rutgers University Press, 1988), especially 261–285.

22. Theda Skocpol, *Protecting Soldiers and Mothers: The Political Origins of Social Policy in the United States* (Cambridge, Mass.: Belknap Press, 1992), 3–11.

23. William L. McGrath, "ILO: Back Door to Socialism," *Economic Council Letter* 303 (January 15, 1953); in contrast, John Mainwaring, *The International Labor Organization: A Canadian View* (Ottawa: Canadian Government Publishing Centre, 1986), 101–102, shows the Canadian view was that the ILO simply developed international law, but nothing as threatening as world government.

24. For summaries of arguments, see Skocpol, *Protecting Soldiers and Mothers*, 3–62; and David Brian Robertson and Dennis R. Judd, *The Develop-*

ment of American Public Policy: The Structure of Policy Restraint (Glenview, Ill.: Scott, Foresman and Co., 1989), 61–71.

25. On U.S. development, see Martin J. Sklar, *The United States As a Developing Country: Studies in U.S. History in the Progressive Era and the 1920s* (New York: Cambridge University Press, 1992); on the U.S. as a modern nation, see Seymour Martin Lipset, *The First New Nation* (New York: Basic Books, 1963); on the socioeconomic explanation of social welfare provision, see Harold Wilensky, *The Welfare State and Equality* (Berkeley: University of California Press, 1975), 15–28; David R. Cameron, "The Expansion of the Public Economy: A Comparative Analysis," *American Political Science Review* 78 (December 1978): 1243–1261; Howard M. Leichter, *A Comparative Approach to Policy Analysis: Health Care in Four Nations* (Cambridge: Cambridge University Press, 1979), 70–100; Neil Mitchell, "Ideology or the Iron Laws of Industrialization: The Case of Pension Policy in Britain and the Soviet Union," *Comparative Politics* 15 (January 1983): 177–201, which rejects the socioeconomic explanation in favor of an ideological one; and Flora and Alber, 58–73, which finds that the organization and power of labor is the best indicator of policy content.

26. On working-class consumerism, see Alfred D. Chandler, Jr., *The Visible Hand: The Managerial Revolution in American Business* (Cambridge, Mass.: Belknap Press, 1977), chapters 7 and 11; and Stuart Ewen, *Captains of Consciousness: Advertising and the Social Roots of Consumer Culture* (New York: McGraw Hill, 1977), 34–48.

27. There were two congressional votes where this was especially true, one in 1919 in the U.S. Senate on the ILO portion of the Versailles Treaty, see U.S. Congress, 66th Cong., 1st sess., *Congressional Record* (Washington, D.C.: GPO, 1919), 8730; and another in 1934 in the House on the decision to join the ILO, see U.S. Congress, 73rd Cong., 2nd sess., *Congressional Record* (Washington, D.C.: GPO, 1934), 12241.

28. Through 1985, for example, Canada ratified twenty-six ILO conventions, while the U.S. ratified only seven; more significant than the numerical difference was that the U.S. only ratified conventions related to seafarers, while Canada ratified general substantive conventions such as those related to the minimum age of workers and freedom of association. For ratifications, see International Labour Office, *International Labour Conference List of Ratifications of Conventions* (Geneva: International Labour Office, 1986), 72nd Session, 1986, Report III, Part 5.

29. While not true of the congressional vote on joining the ILO in 1934, it was true of the early ILO delegations, which included among the two government delegates in 1932 and 1933 the Massachusetts commissioner of labor; on a number of early delegations the employer representative was Henry Harriman, a former textile executive; a textile union executive was an early labor delegate, and another government delegate and later ILO director was New Hampshire Governor John Winant; Winant also presided at the ILO's 1937 Textile Conference.

30. For example, see John Bruce Tipton, *The Participation of the United States in the International Labor Organization* (Urbana: University of Illinois Institute of Labor and Industrial Relations, 1959), 39.

31. John D. Stephens, *The Transition from Capitalism to Socialism* (London: Macmillan, 1979), 89, said, "the growth of the welfare state is a product of the growing strength of labour in civil society," see generally 89–176; see also Walter Korpi, *The Democratic Class Struggle* (Boston: Routledge and Kegan Paul, 1983), 26–52 and 184–207.

32. On the link of the Russian Revolution to the ILO, see Moynihan, "The United States and the ILO," 204–206; and Mainwaring, 2–3. On the "Red Scare," see Robert K. Murray, *Red Scare: A Study in National Hysteria 1919–1920* (New York: McGraw-Hill Book Co., 1964), 5–17; also William Preston, Jr., *Aliens and Dissenters: Federal Suppression of Radicals, 1903–1933* (Cambridge, Mass.: Harvard University Press, 1965), 238–272, on the general post–1918 impact of the radical fears; and Stuart D. Rochester, *American Liberal Disillusionment in the Wake of World War I* (University Park, Pa.: Penn State University Press, 1977), 64–87 on the peace conference.

33. Seymour Martin Lipset, "North American Labor Movements: A Comparative Perspective," in *Unions in Transition: Entering the Second Century* (San Francisco: Institute for Contemporary Studies, 1986), 421–452.

34. For interesting comparisons of worker cultures, see Ronald Edsforth, "Divergent Traditions: Union Organization in the Automobile Industries of Flint, Michigan, and Coventry, England," *Detroit in Perspective: A Journal of Regional History* 5 (spring 1981); and Alan J. Lee, "Conservatism, Traditionalism and the British Working Class," in *Ideology and the Labour Movement: Essays Presented to John Savile*, ed. David E. Martin and David Rubenstein (London: Croom Helm, 1979), 90–92. On the complex relationship of religion and labor in America, see Herbert G. Gutman, *Work, Culture and Society in Industrializing America* (New York: Vintage Books, 1977), 79–117, who finds in the Gilded Age much similarity between English and American working-class religious practices; also on labor and religion, Marc Karson, *American Labor Unions and Politics, 1900–1918* (Carbondale: Southern Illinois University Press, 1958), 212–284, shows how the Catholic Church permeated the AFL with its views of the social problem by the end of World War I, a point of particular relevance, perhaps, to the ideology imposed on the ILO.

35. Anthony King, "Ideas, Institutions, and the Policies of Governments: A Comparative Analysis," *British Journal of Political Science* 3 (June–October 1973): 291–313, 409–423; Hartz, 203–227; and Lipset, *The First New Nation*, 170–204.

36. Some of the literature on the privileged position of business in the American policy process can result in such a conclusion; see especially Ralph Miliband, *The State in Capitalist Society* (New York: Basic Books, 1969), 164–165.

37. On corporatism in America or its absence, see Robert Salisbury, "Why No Corporatism in America?" in *Trends toward Corporatist Intermediation*, ed.

Phillippe Schmitter and Gerhard Lembruch (Beverly Hills, Calif.: Sage, 1979), 218–219; Robertson and Judd, 66–67; Michael Shalev, "Class Politics and the Western Welfare State," in *Social Policy Evaluation: Social and Political Perspectives*, ed. Shimon Spiro and E. Yuchtmann-Yaar (New York: Academic Press, 1983), 27–50; and Harold Wilensky, *The "New Corporatism": Centralization and the Welfare State* (Beverly Hills, Calif.: Sage, 1976); and on religion and corporatism, Wilensky, "Leftism, Catholicism, and Democratic Corporatism: The Role of Political Parties in Recent Welfare State Development," in *The Development of Welfare States in Europe and America*, ed. Peter Flora and Arnold Heidenheimer (New Brunswick, N.J.: Transaction Books, 1981), 345–382.

38. On general business ideology, see David Vogel, "Why Businessmen Distrust Their State: The Political Consciousness of American Corporate Executives," *British Journal of Political Science* 8 (January 1978): 45–78.

39. Stephen J. Kunitz, "Socialism and Social Insurance in the United States and Canada," in *Canadian Health Care and the State: A Century of Evolution*, ed. C. David Naylor (Montreal: McGill-Queen's University Press, 1992), 124; and George A. Rawlyk, "Politics, Religion, and the Canadian Experience: A Preliminary Probe," in *Religion and American Politics*, ed. Mark A. Noll (New York: Oxford University Press, 1990), 253–277.

40. Of special relevance here is the conclusion to Jeffrey M. Berry, *The Interest Group Society*, 2nd. ed. (New York: Harper Collins Publishers, 1989), 227–231; on American special use of political interest groups, see Tocqueville, 198–205; more recently, see H. G. Nichols, *The Nature of American Politics*, 2nd ed. (Oxford: Oxford University Press, 1986), 52–57.

41. The concept of states as "Laboratories of Democracy" is associated first with Louis Brandeis; for a recent use of the term, see David Osborne, *Laboratories of Democracy* (Boston: Harvard Business School Press, 1988).

42. Robertson and Judd, 12–14.

43. U.S. Bureau of Labor Statistics, *Bulletin* 321 (Washington, D.C.: GPO, 1922); see especially Stephen Skowronek, *Building a New American State: The Expansion of National Administrative Capacities 1877–1920* (Cambridge: Cambridge University Press, 1982), 19–24. On the courts and labor law, see William E. Forbath, *Law and the Shaping of the American Labor Movement* (Cambridge, Mass.: Harvard University Press, 1991), 10–58. On Gompers's response to the state of "courts and parties" and for a somewhat different view that holds the courts did not inevitably limit the state, but chose to do so, see Karen Orren, *Belated Feudalism: Labor, the Law and Liberal Development in the United States* (Cambridge: Cambridge University Press, 1992).

44. For example, many early proponents of interstate compacts were active in the Interstate Compacts Commission; see especially Samuel McCune Lindsay, "The Problem of American Cooperation," in *The Origins of the International Labor Organization*, ed. James T. Shotwell (New York: Columbia University Press, 1934), I: 349–353.

45. Louis Galambos, *Competition and Cooperation* (Baltimore: Johns Hopkins University Press, 1966), focuses on the textile industry's Textile Institute and the NRA, 173–202; and Robert F. Himmelberg, *The Origins of the National Recovery Administration: Business, Government, and the Trade Association Issue 1921–1933* (New York: Fordham University Press, 1976). The case that resulted in overturning the NIRA is *Schechter Poultry Corp. v. United States*, 295 U.S. 495.

46. On reversal of a privy council ruling of "unconstitutionality" in Canada, see Ann Shola Orloff, *The Politics of Pensions* (Madison: University of Wisconsin Press, 1993), 266–267.

47. I have chosen to use the term "pressure groups" rather than "interest groups" here, to make the distinction that some groups enter the policy process for reasons other than simple self-interest. I use the term in the same way Lowi, *The End of Liberalism,* uses it. It is really the same as the concept Berry focused his book on, which he called *The Interest Group Society.*

48. There is a literature on the need of the working class for leadership from among the intellectuals, not only among conservatives but especially among some Marxists; this assumption especially divided Marxists from Georges Sorel, see Charles Tilly, *From Mobilization to Revolution* (Reading, Mass.: Addison Wesley, 1978), who believes workers can mobilize without outside leadership. Michael H. Bernard, *The Origins of Democratization in Poland: Workers, Intellectuals, and Oppositional Politics, 1976–1980* (New York: Columbia University Press, 1993) is a recent example of the contrasting interpretation, emphasizing the intellectuals' role.

49. Elizabeth S. Clemens, *The People's Lobby: Organizational Innovation and the Rise of Interest Group Politics in the United States, 1890–1925* (Chicago: University of Chicago Press, 1997), 316–317, focuses only on "expectations of benefits," not on achievement of normatively good policy. She also ignores the links of labor and the churches.

50. For example, the AFL-CIO, in the midst of its battles for human rights in Eastern Europe, advertised Daniel Patrick Moynihan's acknowledgement of this point in his essay "There's No Country So Poor It Can't Afford Free Speech," *AFL-CIO Free Trade Union News,* November 1975, 9.

51. For general history of international labor relations, see Lewis Lorwin, *The International Labor Movement* (New York: Harper and Brothers, 1953); and John Price, *International Labor Movement* (New York: Oxford University Press, 1948); and more recently Carl Gershman, *The Foreign Policy of American Labor* (Washington, D.C.: Georgetown University Center for Strategic and International Studies, 1974).

52. On the state and local focus, see Foster Rhea Dulles and Melvyn Dubofsky, *Labor in America: A History,* 4th ed. (Arlington Heights, Ill.: Harlan Davidson, 1984), 153–155. There are a number of studies of the role of local labor federations, see, for example, Lizabeth Cohen, *Making a New Deal: Industrial Workers in Chicago, 1919–1939* (New York: Cambridge University Press, 1990), 39–50, 136–142.

53. Forbath, 10–37, argues the courts played a fundamental role in American labor's exceptional support for voluntarism, but Michael Rogin, "Voluntarism: The Political Functions of an Antipolitical Doctrine," *Industrial and Labor Relations Review* 15 (July 1962): 521–535, holds that the focus on voluntarism served the needs of the AFL leadership and was not a pragmatic response to judicial rejection of labor legislation.

54. On Wilson's role in the Clayton Act's labor protection, see Arthur S. Link, *Wilson*, 5 vols. (Princeton, N.J.: Princeton University Press, 1956), II: 158; Dulles and Dubofsky, 194–195, point out how limited the act's protection was; Dallas L. Jones, "The Enigma of the Clayton Act," *Industrial and Labor Relations Review* 10 (January 1957): 201–221, found Wilson deceived labor, knowing the act provided little protection; however, the evidence from the ILO experience indicates the weaknesses of the wording are not so clear.

55. The Clayton Act's protections were greatly limited in *Duplex Printing Press Company v. Deering*, 254 U.S. 443, in 1921.

56. On CIO rivalry with the AFL, see Walter Galenson, *The CIO Challenge to the AFL: A History of the American Labor Movement 1935–1941* (Cambridge, Mass.: Harvard University Press, 1960), 635–636; on AFL quarrels with unions sympathetic to the Soviet Union, see Tipton, 61–62.

57. On the postwar relationship, see William Serrin, *The Company and the Union: The "Civilized" Relationship of the General Motors Corporation and the United Automobile Workers* (New York: Knopf, 1970); on end to this social contract, see Bluestone and Harrison, 164–170.

58. On populism in unions, see Michael Kazin, *The Populist Persuasion: An American History* (New York: Basic Books, 1995), 49–78, which clearly portrays Gompers as a populist, ambivalent about the liberal state; on democracy in unions, see Seymour Martin Lipset, Martin A. Trow, and James S. Coleman, *Union Democracy* (Garden City, N.Y.: Doubleday and Co., 1956), 227–305.

59. Howard D. Samuel, "Social Goals and International Trade: A New Dimension," in *The Internationalization of the U.S. Economy: Its Labor Market Policy Implications*, ed. Vernon M. Briggs, Jr. (Washington, D.C.: National Council on Employment Policy, 1986), 30–33.

60. On the maternalist welfare state, see Skocpol, *Protecting Soldiers and Mothers*, 311–524; and Seth Koven and Sonya Michel, eds., *Mothers of a New World: Maternalist Politics and the Origins of Welfare States* (New York: Routledge, 1993).

61. Kathryn Kish Sklar, "The Historical Foundations of Women's Power in the Creation of the American Welfare State, 1830–1930," in Koven and Michel, 43–93, focuses on class-bridging coalitions and grassroots organizing; see also Skocpol, *Protecting Soldiers and Mothers*, 321–372.

62. See Carol Riegelman Lubin and Anne Winslow, *Social Justice for Women* (Durham, N.C.: Duke University Press, 1990), 82 and 208, on the absence of women as senior ILO staff between 1945 and 1988.

63. Sklar, "Historical Foundations," 74–75; Skocpol, *Protecting Soldiers and Mothers*, 537–539.

64. On the creation of professional social science organizations generally, see Robert Wiebe, *The Search for Order* (New York: Hill and Wang, 1967), 121–123; on the AEA, see A. W. Coats, "The First Two Decades of the American Economic Association," *American Economic Review* 50 (September 1960): 555–74; on Ely specifically, see John R. Everett, *Religion in Economics* (New York: King's Crown Press, 1946) and J. David Hoeveler, Jr., "The University and the Social Gospel: The Intellectual Origins of the 'Wisconsin Idea'," *Wisconsin Magazine of History* 59 (summer 1976): 282–298.

65. Benjamin G. Rader, *The Academic Mind and Reform: The Influence of Richard T. Ely in American Life* (Lexington: University of Kentucky Press, 1966); and Lafayette G. Harter, *John R. Commons and His Assault on Laissez-Faire* (Corvallis: Oregon State University Press, 1962).

66. Shotwell, *The Origins*.

67. James T. Shotwell, "Recollections on the Founding of the ILO," *Monthly Labor Review* 59 (June 1959): 631–636; on the role of this generation of intellectuals, see Leon Fink, *Progressive Intellectuals and the Dilemmas of Democratic Commitment* (Cambridge, Mass.: Harvard University Press, 1997), 214–241 on W. Jett Lauck, and 275–287 for reflections on the post-World War II individual quests of intellectuals, unconnected to other movements.

68. See Leon Fink, *American Labor History* (Washington, D.C.: American Historical Association, 1990), 14–15; see, for example, Dulles and Dubovsky, which gives fifteen pages to Taft-Hartley and eight to Wagner.

69. On the general role of business and reform, see Robert H. Wiebe, *Businessmen and Reform* (Chicago: Ivan R. Dee, Inc., 1989), 157–178; Gabriel Kolko, *The Triumph of Conservatism: A Reinterpretation of American History, 1900–1916* (New York: Free Press of Glencoe, 1963), 158–163, which refers to the "illusion of reform"; and James Weinstein, *The Corporate Ideal in the Liberal State, 1900–1918* (Boston: Beacon Press, 1968), 40–61.

70. On the NCF, see Marguerite Green, *The National Civic Federation and the American Labor Movement, 1900–1925* (Washington, D.C.: Catholic University of America Press, 1956), 347–349, which discusses the NCF attitude toward Florence Kelley and Samuel Lindsay and other labor reformers.

71. On the complex relationship of business and the state during the 1920s, see Martin J. Sklar, *The Corporate Reconstruction of American Capitalism, 1890–1916: The Market, The Law and Politics* (Cambridge: Cambridge University Press, 1988); Guy Alchon, *The Invisible Hand of Planning: Capitalism, Social Science, and the State in the 1920s* (Princeton, N.J.: Princeton University Press, 1985), 51–128; Alan Dawley, *Struggles for Justice: Social Responsibility and the Liberal State* (Cambridge, Mass.: Harvard University Press, 1991), 211–215; Barry Karl, *The Uneasy State: The United States from 1915 to 1945* (Chicago: The University of Chicago Press, 1983), 50–79; and Morton Keller, *Regulating a New Economy:*

Public Policy and Economic Change in America, 1900–1933 (Cambridge, Mass.: Harvard University Press, 1990).

72. See Colin Gordon, *New Deals: Business, Labor, and Politics in America, 1920–1935* (Cambridge, Mass.: Cambridge University Press, 1994); Galambos, 227–256; and Larry Gerber, "The National Industrial Recovery Act in Comparative Perspective: Organized Labor's Role in American and British Efforts at Industrial Planning, 1929–1933," *The Journal of Policy History* 6, (1994): 403–438. For a "liberal" critique of the NRA, see Arthur A. Ekirch, Jr., *The Decline of American Liberalism* (New York: Atheneum, 1969), 268–287.

73. George Norlin, "The United States and World Organization during 1937," *International Conciliation* 341 (June 1938): 267–277, identifies textile-industry leaders who attended the conference.

74. For example, in the 1955–1957 *Readers Guide to Periodical Literature*, 1251, there were seven articles about the ILO in *Business Week*, with titles such as "Pulling Out of the ILO" (23 January 1956); *Fortune* also had one story in the era. In 1953-55, there were four business periodicals on the ILO; interest also declined in 1957-59, during which no articles appeared.

75. See Robert W. Cox, *Production, Power, and World Order* (New York: Columbia University Press, 1987), 244–249, 318–326; and Folker Frobel, Jurgen Heinricks, and Otto Kreye, *The New International Division of Labour* (New York: Cambridge University Press, 1980), 339–361. For an example of current business support, see "Business Roundtable Urges US to 'Upgrade' ILO Participation," *ILO Washington Focus* (spring 1995): 12.

76. Maud Nathan, *The Story of an Epoch-Making Movement* (Garden City, N.Y.: Doubleday, Page, and Co., 1926). Nathan was a vice president of the National Consumers' League.

77. Landon R. Y. Storrs, *Civilizing Capitalism: The National Consumers' League, Women's Activism, and Labor Standards in the New Deal Era* (Chapel Hill: University of North Carolina Press, 2000), 251, disagrees with the interpretation here, saying of the 1960s, "The [National Consumers' League] embrace of consumer rights did not mean that it had abandoned its traditional agenda. To the contrary, the league tackled consumer problems expressly to attract new members who might be won over to labor's cause."

78. For example, David A. Aaker and George S. Day, "Introduction: A Guide to Consumerism," in *Consumerism: Search for the Consumer Interest* (New York: The Free Press, 1971), 2–3, found consumerism was "uniquely associated with the past decade [the 1960s]."

79. Ralph M. Gaedeke, "The Muckraking Era," in *Consumerism*, ed. Ralph M. Gaedeke and Warren W. Etcheson (San Francisco: Canfield Press, 1972), 57–58. Helen Sorenson, *The Consumer Movement: What It Is and What It Means* (New York: Harper and Brothers, 1941), 6–8, written closer to the origins of the consumer movement, correctly described the role of the Consumers' League; however, it, too, misinterpreted the importance of *The Jungle*.

80. Daniel Horowitz, *The Morality of Spending: Attitudes toward the Consumer Society in America, 1875–1940* (Baltimore: Johns Hopkins University Press, 1985), 58–59.

81. See, for example, N. Craig Smith, *Morality and the Market* (New York: Routledge, 1990), 253, 280, 285, on Cesar Chavez's farmworker boycotts; most boycott treatment dealt with Gandhi and traditional labor union organized boycotts, 134–166.

82. See, for example, *NCL Bulletin* 57, September/October 1995, where the National Consumers' League devoted only page seven to traditional labor standards concerns; each of the other eleven pages of the newsletter dealt with consumer product quality and safety issues.

83. For a discussion of the consumer benefits of trade in the economics literature, see, for example, Dennis R. Appleyard and Alfred J. Field, Jr., *International Economics Trade Theory and Policy*, 2nd ed. (Chicago: Irwin, 1995), 36–38. For a critique of the simple consumer-oriented assessment of the benefits of trade, see Robert Fogel's and Stanley L. Engerman's indictment of slavery in *Time on the Cross: The Economics of American Negro Slavery* (New York: W. W. Norton, 1989), 246, which points out, "for every dollar gained by a typical consumer of cotton cloth, there was a slave laboring somewhere under the hot southern sun who would lose at least $400."

84. Ronald Edsforth, *Class Conflict and Cultural Consensus: The Making of a Mass Consumer Society in Flint, Michigan* (New Brunswick, N.J.: Rutgers University Press, 1987), 197–209, 219, has good coverage of the typical decline or suppression of rank-and-file activism.

85. Skocpol, *Protecting Soldiers and Mothers,* 536–539; and Sklar, "Historical Foundations," 74–78. Some interest group scholars simply emphasize the great increase in groups as an example of their vitality—see Berry, 16–43; for criticism of the bias, see Schattschneider, 20–45.

86. On the general social gospel in the nineteenth century, see Henry F. May, *Protestant Churches and Industrial America* (New York: Harper and Brothers, 1949); Robert T. Handy, ed., *The Social Gospel in America, 1870–1920* (New York: Oxford University Press, 1966); Ronald C. White, Jr., and Charles Howard Hopkins, *The Social Gospel: Religion and Reform in Changing America* (Philadelphia: Temple University Press, 1976); and for a more recent period, Paul A. Carter, *The Decline and Revival of the Social Gospel: Social and Political Liberalism in American Protestant Churches 1920–1940*, 2nd ed. (Ithaca, N.Y.: Cornell University Press, 1956). For a comparison of the response of the three religious traditions in one industrial city, see Arthur Mann, *Yankee Reformers in the Urban Age* (Cambridge, Mass.: The Belknap Press, 1954), 24–101.

87. Richard T. Ely, *Ground under Our Feet: An Autobiography* (New York: The Macmillan Company, 1938).

88. Melvin I. Urofsky, *Louis D. Brandeis and the Progressive Tradition* (Boston: Little, Brown and Company, 1981), 62–67; and Alpheus T. Mason, *Brandeis: A Free Man's Life* (New York: The Viking Press, 1946), 289–315.

89. For a good overview of these links, see David J. O'Brien, "The Economic Thought of the American Hierarchy," in *The Catholic Challenge to the American Economy*, ed. Thomas M. Gannon (New York: Macmillan Publishing Co., 1987), 31–37; on Ryan, the church, and labor generally, see Fink, especially 217.

90. Albert Le Roy, *The Dignity of Labor: The Part Played by Catholics in the Work of the International Labor Organization* (Westminster, Md.: The Newman Press, 1957), 67–71.

91. For a good review of the cross-class nature of churches and the recent appreciation of their role in politics, see Lyman A. Kellstedt and Mark A. Noll, "Religion, Voting for President, and Party Identification, 1948–1984" in *Religion and American Politics*, ed. Noll, 355–379; and Stephen D. Johnson and Joseph B. Tamney, eds., *The Political Role of Religion in the United States* (Boulder, Colo.: Westview, 1986).

92. On the complex relations of churches to public policy, see N. J. Demerath, "Religious Capital and Capital Religions, Cross-Cultural and Non-Legal Factors in the Separation of Church and State," *Daedalus* 20 (summer 1991): 21–40, who holds the U.S. is not simply a country where the state is separate from the church; he also finds the U.S. not unique in the relationship of the church with the state, an interpretation challenged by the history of ILO policy.

93. Clarke Chambers, *Seedtime of Reform*, (Ann Arbor: University of Michigan Press, 1967), 39–48.

94. T. J. Jackson Lears, *No Place of Grace: Antimodernism and the Transformation of American Culture 1880–1920* (New York: Pantheon Books, 1981), maintains that Protestants did not maintain a distance between God and mammon; however, Lears's focus is more generally on the churches, and the statement here refers to the leadership involved in social justice.

95. This is similar to the role of the churches in Canada as critics of laissez-faire economics; see Rawlyk, in Noll, *Religion and American Politics*, 266–267; it is in marked contrast to the British experience, see Richard Carwardine, "Religion and Politics in Nineteenth-Century Britain: The Case against American Exceptionalism," in Noll, 244–245, which despite his essay's title finds significant differences between the two nations in the role of religion in politics, though focusing mostly on the comparative role of the religious right; the religious right gets far more attention in the U.S. than the religious critique of the market economy.

96. Despite Kellstedt and Noll, 355, religious interest groups are ignored in some interest group literature; for example, Berry, 113, makes one reference related to the religious right's opposition to Robert Bork's Supreme Court nomina-

tion and three times mentions the moral majority, never mentioning the role of mainline churches.

97. For a good summary of the medieval and modern synthesis in *Rerum Novarum*, see George L. Mosse, *The Culture of Western Europe: The Nineteenth and Twentieth Centuries* (New York: Rand McNally and Company, 1961), 247–254.

98. See Le Roy; also, for example, International Labour Organization, *Mission of Justice and Peace: The Visit of Pope Paul VI to the International Labour Conference* (Geneva: International Labour Office, 1969).

99. For a discussion of incrementalism, see Hayes, 1–10; for a critique, see Lowi, *The End of Liberalism*, 40, where he addresses briefly the role of churches and labor.

100. See, for example, Samuel McCune Lindsay, "Reciprocal Legislation," *Political Science Quarterly* 25 (September 1910): 435–457; and Ernest Freund, "Can the States Cooperate for Labor Legislation," *The Survey* 12 (June 1909): 409–411, for early examples of their roles.

101. *The New York Times*, 30 July 1999, 19A.

102. There is a voluminous literature on leadership of the "Progressive movement"; generally, Richard Hofstadter, *The Age of Reform* (New York: Vintage Books, 1955), 131–173, proposed that progressives were motivated by concern that they were losing status, calling a chapter "The Alienated Professionals"; in agreement is George Mowry, *The California Progressives* (Berkeley: University of California Press, 1951), 86–104; Wiebe focused not on a negative fear of status loss but rather upon a positive, confident movement seeking to impose order on the new industrial-urban world—see especially *Search for Order*, 111–132. While the debate continues about exactly who belongs in a progressive leadership and why, a few have called for dismissal of the term progressive as so all-encompassing as to be meaningless—see Peter G. Filene, "An Obituary for 'The Progressive Movement'," *American Quarterly* 22 (spring 1970): 20–34; this obituary seems premature.

103. There is a vigorous debate about the impact of the war on progressivism; see, for example, William Leuchtenberg, *The Perils of Prosperity* (Chicago: University of Chicago Press, 1958), 120–121, which summarizes one argument about the war and progressivism by saying, "What killed progressivism? The most obvious answer was that progressivism had been killed by the war." While Leuchtenberg believes some forms of progressivism survived and thrived during the war, others more clearly saw the war ending progressivism, such as Hofstadter, 281: "The war purged the pent-up guilts, shattered the ethos of responsibility that had permeated the rhetoric of more than a decade. . . . [The voters] repudiated the Progressive rhetoric and the Progressive mood." Eric Goldman, *Rendezvous with Destiny* (New York: Random House, 1952), 254, said, "Reform stopped dead." Yet, the war brought many progressive reform proposals to completion; see Allen F. Davis, "Welfare, Reform, and World War I," *American Quarterly* 19 (fall 1967): 516–533; and Leuchtenberg's own assessment of the war's

long-term impact, "The New Deal and the Analogue of War," in *Change and Continuity in Twentieth-Century America*, ed. John Braeman, Robert Bremner, and Everett Walters (Columbus: Ohio State University Press, 1964), 81–143. The ILO experience would support the argument that the war helped bring progressive reform to fruition.

104. On the end of Progressivism in the 1920s, see Leuchtenberg, *The Perils of Prosperity*, 120–139. For studies of the continuity between the progressive era and the 1920s and beyond, see Arthur S. Link, "What Happened to the Progressive Movement in the 1920's?" *American Historical Review* 64 (July 1959): 833–851; Paul Glad, "Progressives and the Business Culture of the 1920s," *Journal of American History* 53 (June 1966): 75–89; and especially Chambers, 229–267, which emphasizes the 1920s as "the Seedtime" for New Deal reforms. In contrast, Otis Graham, *An Encore for Reform* (New York: Oxford University Press, 1967), found there were many "progressives" who did not support the New Deal, thus making links between the two eras difficult. The ILO history, because it bridged the 1920s, with the organization created in 1919 but the U.S. joining in 1934, emphasizes the continuity of the eras.

105. On the "sick sectors" of the economy, see George Soule, *Prosperity Decade: From War to Depression: 1917–1929* (New York: Harper and Row Publishers, 1947), 175–182; and Geoffrey Perrett, *America in the Twenties* (New York: Simon and Schuster, 1982). For an interesting linking of the 1920s experience with later America, see, Kevin Phillips, *Boiling Point: Democrats, Republicans and the Decline of Middle Class Prosperity* (New York: Harper Collins, 1993), 89–93.

106. The best symbol of this approach was to be Franklin Roosevelt—see James MacGregor Burns, *Roosevelt the Lion and the Fox* (New York: Harcourt, Brace, and World, 1956), 197–202; and Robertson and Judd, 103–104. Ekirch, 277–287, discusses the various experiments of the New Deal; in addition to the implicit criticism in Ekirch, Graham, 40–43, has a critical assessment of the flexibility of the New Deal and FDR, a flexibility that could be defined as inconsistency. For a current discussion of the possibility of empirical policy making, see Robert Heineman et al., *The World of the Policy Analyst: Rationality, Values, and Politics* (Chatham, N.J.: Chatham House, 1990).

107. On postwar planning, see Ruth Anshen, ed., *Beyond Victory* (New York: Harcourt Brace and Co., 1943), especially essays by Alvin Hansen, "Economic Organization for Peace," 101–106; and John Winant, "International Labor Organization and Future Social Policy," 107–113.

108. See, for example, Robert E. Baldwin, Robert S. Ingersoll, and Woo-choong Kim, "U.S. and Foreign Competition in the Developing Countries of the Asian Pacific Rim," in *The United States in the World Economy*, ed. Martin Feldstein (Chicago: University of Chicago Press, 1988), 79–158. This book included papers presented at a conference sponsored by the National Bureau of Economic Research that appear quite representative of the dominant thinking regarding trade liberalization. Without need for proof, Andrew Berg, in his "Sum-

mary of Discussion," in Feldstein, 159, found that Baldwin, Ingersoll, and Kim show, "Most American companies . . . have increased their competitiveness. . . . [R]ecent economic history teaches that a liberal trade policy leads to rapid growth." Berg's statements are unsubstantiated beliefs, not truths, but they are stated as facts.

109. A recent statement about the goals of social history published by the American Historical Association captures well the absence of a specific reform agenda. See Alice Kessler-Harris, *Social History* (Washington, D.C.: American Historical Association, 1990), 18; the concluding paragraph says, "The best social history attempts to integrate new research in institutional structures and consciousness and ideology in a way that creates understanding of broader political process and of the tensions that ultimately yield change." Earlier referring to two of the radical social historians, Kessler-Harris summarizes their studies, 17, as "'who rides whom and how'," the concern of James Shotwell; what to do about it no longer was appropriate for academic discourse. For a highly critical summary of the late-century state of the educated classes, see Christopher Lasch, *The True and Only Heaven* (New York: W. W. Norton Company, 1991), 465–468, which has a critical commentary on the educated, including some of the social scientists. For a discussion of the dominance of the free market system in policy making, see Lindblom, *Politics and Markets*, 170–188. For a comparative study of American concern with the rights of special groups, see Mary Ann Glendon, *Rights Talk: The Impoverishment of Political Discourse* (New York: The Free Press, 1991), 18–32, which refers to the "Illusion of Absoluteness" in private property rights.

110. On the ERA as a symbolic concern of a small group, see Jane J. Mansbridge, *Why We Lost the ERA* (Chicago: University of Chicago Press, 1986), 8–19. Of course, many writers rejected simply focusing on giving women access to leadership without restructuring the political-economic system; however, these authors do not demonstrate that change has occurred—see Nancy F. Cott, *The Grounding of Modern Feminism* (New Haven: Yale University Press, 1987), 239, who concludes her chapter on professionalism and feminism, "The trend toward individual accomplishments unrelated to womanhood as such . . . might be read to measure the success of feminism's aims—or the exhaustion of its spirit." See also Ethel Klein, *Gender Politics* (Cambridge, Mass.: Harvard University Press, 1984), 108–109, which notes the different perspectives of the women's movement by class; later, 170–172, she calls for employers to place less emphasis on efficiency and more on family values—however, that appears in hindsight as wishful thinking. See Juliet Schor, *The Overworked Americans* (New York: Basic Books, 1991), 20, 28–32, and 101, on the special impact of current work practices on women.

111. On the church, see Stephen L. Carter, *The Culture of Disbelief* (New York: Basic Books, 1993), 44–66; on 43, Carter says, "One way of coping with the fear [of religion influencing policy] is to try to brush off the religiously devout as fanatics, as is done with depressing regularity." See also Linell E. Cady, *Religion,*

Theology, and American Public Life (Albany, N.Y.: State University of New York Press, 1993), 17–29; and Richard John Neuhaus, *The Naked Public Square* (Grand Rapids, Mich.: William B. Eerdmans Publishing Co., 1984), for example, on 79, the treatment of Martin Luther King, Jr. There are critics of the argument that religion is mocked in the public sphere—see Kathleen M. Sullivan, "Religion and Liberal Democracy," *University of Chicago Law Review* 59 (1992): 195–196; on the criticisms of labor, see Michael Goldfield, *The Decline of Organized Labor in the United States* (Chicago: The University of Chicago Press, 1987), 5–37, which includes data on changing public opinions about unions.

112. International Labour Office, *List of Ratifications*, III, 5, shows six of the seven conventions ratified by the U.S. related to protections of seafarers; the only other was a major ILO structural change in 1946.

113. Daniel Patrick Moynihan, *On the Law of Nations* (Cambridge, Mass.: Harvard University Press, 1991), 177; Moynihan incorporated key portions of his dissertation on the ILO into this work, see 55–67.

TWO. THE THREADS

1. "Second Annual Meeting of the American Association for Labor Legislation: December 29–30, 1908," *Proceedings of the Second Annual Meeting, American Association for Labor Legislation* (Princeton, N.J.: Princeton University Press, 1909), 4.

2. Samuel McCune Lindsay, "Reciprocal Legislation," *Political Science Quarterly* 25 (September 1910): 435.

3. Francis Wilson, *Labor in the League System* (Stanford, Calif.: Stanford University Press, 1934), 29; see also Tipton, 18.

4. On the history of indentured servitude, see, for example, Hugh Tinker, *A New System of Slavery: The Export of Indian Labour Overseas: 1830–1920* (New York: Oxford University Press, 1974), 236–366, which reviews the campaign to end indentured servitude in the British Empire, which overlapped the early labor standards movement.

5. Fogel, *Without Consent or Contract*, 410.

6. Ibid., 208–209, discusses the new civility.

7. Fogel minimizes the links between the abolition movement and other free labor initiatives of the time; see also Robert J. Steinfeld, *The Invention of Free Labor: The Employment Relation in English and American Law and Culture, 1350–1870* (Chapel Hill: University of North Carolina Press, 1991), who found the consensus in support of indentured servitude disappeared by about 1830 in the U.S. and probably earlier in England.

8. On Owen, see David A. Morse, *The Origin and Evolution of the ILO and Its Role in the World Community* (Ithaca, N.Y.: New York State School of Industrial and Labor Relations, 1969), 6–7; George N. Barnes, *History of the International Labour Office* (London: Williams and Norgate Ltd., 1926), 29–30;

Harold Butler, *The International Labour Organization* (London: Oxford University Press, 1939), 3–4; and Ernest Mahaim, "The Principles of International Labor Legislation," *The Annals of the American Academy of Political and Social Science* 166 (March 1933): 10–11, which minimizes the role of Owen. Note each of these authors played a key role in the ILO, Butler and Morse as directors and Barnes and Mahaim in organizing it in 1919. More generally on Owen, see Crane Brinton, *English Political Thought* (New York: Harper Torchbooks, 1962), 44–59; and George L. Mosse, *The Culture of Western Europe: The Nineteenth and Twentieth Centuries* (New York: Rand McNally, 1961), 157–163.

9. See Michael Shalev, "The Social Democratic Model and Beyond: Two Generations of Comparative Research on the Welfare State," *Comparative Social Research* 6 (1983): 315–351.

10. For a good biographical sketch of Legrand, see John W. Follows, *Antecedents of the International Labour Organization* (Oxford: Clarendon Press, 1951), 28–42; also Charles Gide and Charles Rist, A *History of Economic Doctrines*, trans. R. Richards (Boston: D.C. Heath, 1913), 483–486, which emphasizes Legrand's links to Christian socialism.

11. Quoted by Abdul-Karim Tikriti, *Tripartism and the International Labor Organization* (Stockholm: Almqvist and Wiksell International, 1982), 20.

12. On Legrand, in addition to Follows, see Tipton, 14; and Boutelle E. Lowe, *The International Protection of Labor* (New York: Macmillan, 1935), 12–13.

13. Price, 4–5, quotes the *Address and Provisional Rules of the International Working Men's Association, London, September 26th, 1964.*

14. Lorwin, 10–13; for more on the International, see Albert S. Lindemann, A *History of European Socialism* (New Haven, Conn.: Yale University Press, 1983), 108, 121–123, 147, which emphasizes that the doctrinal heterogeneity at the First International was seen by the Marxists as the reason to insist on a uniform (Marxist) theoretical base for the international movement.

15. Price, 2–10.

16. Ibid., 10–15. Interpretations of the role of the International in creation of labor standards vary greatly, ranging from Morse, 6–7; Tikriti, 335; and Francis Wilson, 29; each of whom hold the International to be one of the three or four institutions contributing to the movement. By contrast, some of the founders of the ILO ignored the International and emphasized the role of intergovernmental institutions and academics—see, for example, Mahaim, "Principles," 10–13.

17. Boutelle E. Lowe, *The International Protection of Labor* (New York: Macmillan, 1935), xxi–xxiii; Price, 15–19; and Morse, *The Origin*, 7, each emphasized the IFTU more than the two Internationals. Mahaim, while otherwise ignoring the labor role, credits Samuel Gompers with a key role in forming the ILO, "Principles," 13; and gives even more attention to the IFTU—see Ernest Mahaim, "The Historical and Social Importance of International Labor Legislation," in Shotwell, *The Origins*, I: 17–18.

18. Those who ignored religious leaders include Lowe; Mahaim, "The Principles"; Morse, *The Origin*; Barnes; and Butler, *ILO*. For a contrasting interpretation, see Max Turmann, "The Christian Social Movement and International Labor Legislation," *International Labour Review* 6 (July 1922): 3–10; and Follows.

19. Heinrich Thiersch, *On Christian Commonwealth*, trans. John Watkins (Edinburgh: T and T Clark, 1877).

20. Follows, 10–21; Hindley played a key role in the Chartist movement.

21. Follows, 53; on Hahn generally, see 52–57.

22. Lowe, xxviii.

23. For a general review of Leo XIII's role, see Eric O. Hanson, *The Catholic Church in World Politics* (Princeton, N.J.: Princeton University Press, 1987), 40–58. On Leo and the ILO, see Le Roy, 1–5; while clergy such as Le Roy see the church role in creating the ILO as fundamental, most of the histories by government and academic leaders, such as Shotwell's *The Origins of the International Labor Organization*, ignore the churches.

24. Follows, 72. On de Mun, see Benjamin F. Martin, *Count Albert de Mun: Paladin of the Third Republic* (Chapel Hill: University of North Carolina Press, 1978); 90–91 describes de Mun's difficult political path—a conservative, who supported social protections, uncomfortable with both the liberals and the monarchists, he only occasionally was part of the majority in French governments of the era.

25. John A. Ryan, *A Living Wage* (New York: The Macmillan Company, 1920), 167, gave de Mun favorable mention; on de Mun's role in France, see Gordon Wright, *France in Modern Times*, 4th ed. (New York: W. W. Norton, 1987), 245, 281, and 309.

26. On Decurtins, see Follows, 104–106; and Mahaim, "Historical and Social," 5–6. Lowe, 25–27, places the Swiss proposals in the context of many others in the 1880s; Moynihan, "The U.S. and the ILO," 7–8, points out the Swiss were motivated to lead in the movement because they depended on industries with high labor content and thus high labor costs.

27. See Henry J. Browne, *The Catholic Church and the Knights of Labor* (New York: Arno Press, 1976), 313–358.

28. On the impact of *Rerum Novarum*, see Peter N. Stearns, *European Society in Upheaval: Social History since 1800* (New York: The Macmillan Company, 1967), 280–283; on French upper-class reaction to Leo XIII, see Wright, 244–246.

29. For the text of *Rerum Novarum*, see John T. Pawlikowski and David Byers, eds., *Justice in the Marketplace* (Washington, D.C.: U.S. Catholic Conference, 1985); on Leo's move from charity to social reform, see Karl, 20. Aaron I. Abell, *American Catholicism and Social Action* (Notre Dame, Ind.: University of Notre Dame Press, 1963), 72–82, is especially good on the U.S. concern with condemna-

tion of organized labor; Richard L. Camp, *The Papal Ideology of Social Reform* (Leiden: E. J. Brill, 1969), 86–91, covers Leo in the context of other papacies.

30. See Nathan, 23, 89, and 130–131 on the English League; Skocpol, *Protecting Soldiers and Mothers*, 30–38, covers the role of women in U.S. policy; she contrasts her exceptional treatment with that of Koven and Michel, 20–22, who address the comparative role of women, generally seeing U.S. and British experiences as similar.

31. On Villerme, see Stearns, 175; Follows, 22–25; and especially William Coleman, *Death Is a Social Disease: Public Health and Political Economy in Early Modern France* (Madison: University of Wisconsin Press, 1982), 255–274. Gide, 171, says Villerme's great influence came when he wrote [in *Tableau de l'etat Physique et Moral des Ouvriers Employes dans les Manufactures de Coton*, 2 vols. (Paris: J. Renouard, 1840)] the first "complete description of the heartrending life of the workers and the martyrdom of their children."

32. Malcolm Delevingne, "The Pre-War History of International Labor Legislation," in Shotwell, *The Origins*, I: 28–32; John B. Andrews, "Beginnings of International Labor Standards," in *What the International Labor Organization Means to America*, ed. Spencer Miller, Jr. (New York: Columbia University Press, 1936).

33. Gide, 197.

34. On Blanqui, see Priscilla Robertson, *Revolutions of 1848: A Social History* (New York: Harper Torchbooks, 1960), 86–87, 96; for a biographical sketch, see David Longfellow, "Jerome-Adolphe Blanqui," in *Historical Dictionary of France from 1815 Restoration to the Second Empire*, ed. Edgar Newman and Robert Simpson, 2 vols. (New York: Greenwood Press, 1987), I: 110–112.

35. Wolowski, a Pole, came to France and became a leader in the development of economics, founding the *Journal de Economistes* in 1841; during the Revolution of 1848, he served in the government.

36. See, for example, Johann Caspar Bluntschli, *The Theory of the State*, trans. Richard Lodge, David Ritchie, and Percy Matheson, 2nd ed. (Oxford: Clarendon Press, 1985).

37. On von Stein's trade views, see Wesley Mitchell, *Types of Economic Theory: From Mercantilism to Institutionalism*, 2 vols. (New York: Augustus Kelley, 1969), II: 346; Robertson, 109, also describes von Stein's effort to find moderation, calling on the monarchy to mediate between the rich and poor; finally, a fascinating use of von Stein was made by Richard Ely, *French and German Socialism in Modern Times* (New York: Harper and Brothers, 1883), 79–81, 92.

38. Delevingne, 28–32; John B. Andrews, "Beginnings of International Labor Standards," in Miller, *What the ILO Means*. On the German founders, see Fritz K. Ringer, *The Decline of the German Mandarins: The German Academic Community, 1890–1933* (Cambridge, Mass.: Harvard University Press, 1969), 145–146, on academic critiques of laissez-faire by Werner Sombert and Gustav Schmoller; on 146–147, Ringer describes the Social Policy Association.

39. For an interesting account of the Social Policy Association, written by their American disciples, see Ely, *French and German Socialism*, 235–244, where he discusses the *socialist of the chair* and links them to Christian socialism; see also John R. Commons, *Institutional Economics* (New York: Macmillan, 1934), 115, 720–721, where he says the German historical economists before the Social Policy Association led to the ethical or institutional economics of people such as Schmoller.

40. Delevingne, 29–31; Andrews, 11–12; Moynihan, *On the Law of Nations*, 58–59.

41. For a good discussion of the historical economists, see Thomas Bender, *Intellect and Public Life: Essays on the Social History of Academic Intellectuals in the United States* (Baltimore: Johns Hopkins University Press, 1993), 59–65, who emphasizes there were two groups of critics of laissez-faire among the historical school, some radical or utopian elements and a more moderate group, focusing not so much on social policy goals as on empirical and historical analysis.

42. Mahaim, "The Historical," 7–12; Lowe, 36–65; Barnes, 30–32; Moynihan, "The U.S. and the ILO," 27–36. The IALL spawned a number of other specialized research organizations, such as the International Association on Unemployment. Also, some independent international associations continued to function, such as the International Federation for the Observance of Sunday; on these, see Lowe, xxv–xxxii.

43. Moynihan, "The U.S. and the ILO," repeatedly emphasizes the role of academics as one of the key groups in achieving labor standards.

44. For a discussion of the role of a community base, see Skocpol, *Protecting Soldiers and Mothers*, 361–363, where she points out the effective local links of women's groups. In contrast, she points out the AALL had no local affiliates, 183–194. For membership in national sections of IALL see Lowe, 65, which listed fifteen national sections, the largest being in the U.S. with 2,500, the German second at 1,586, the French and the Swiss both had over 500 members, down to the Belgian with 72; the total membership was 7,011.

45. On methods of the Association, see, for example, Andrews's discussion of the American white phosphorous debate in Andrews, "Beginnings," 8–9; Mahaim, "The Principles," 11–12, discusses the IALL efforts under Stephen Bauer to study laboring conditions.

46. On white phosphorous, see Mahaim, "The Historical," 8–12.

47. Levine, 39–62.

48. On Bismarck, see Ely, *French and German Socialism*, 216–220, 235, and 243; Lowe, xxxii–xxxiii; and Levine, 46–60.

49. Josephine Shaw Lowell was the child of Massachusetts utopian reformers of the Jacksonian era. Friends of Lydia Child, Margaret Fuller, and James Russell Lowell, members of Theodore Parker's Unitarian Congregation, and supporters of Brook Farm, the Shaws raised their children to be reformers. They also educated them well. Josephine studied in Europe and learned

German, French, and Italian. Reflecting the reform impulse, her family volunteered when the Civil War came. Her brother gained the greatest fame, volunteering to lead the first Afro-American unit during the Civil War, a unit that won widespread respect for its unwavering attack on Ft. Wagner, South Carolina, in which Col. Shaw died. Josephine married James Russell Lowell's nephew, Charles, who also died as a Union Army colonel. Charles's death came when he led a heroic charge at the Battle of Cedar Creek, Virginia, in 1864, six weeks before his wife gave birth to their daughter. See Robert H. Bremner, "Josephine Shaw Lowell," in *Notable American Women 1607–1950: A Biographical Dictionary*, ed. Edward T. James, Janet Wilson James, and Paul S. Boyer, 3 vols. (Cambridge, Mass.: Belknap Press, 1971), II: 437–439.

50. Nathan, 18–19; for biographical information, see Roy Lubove, "Mary Corinna Putnam," in James, *Notable American Women*, II: 263–265.

51. On Abraham Jacobi, see Richard A Meckel, *Save the Babies: American Public Health Reform and the Prevention of Infant Mortality 1850–1929* (Baltimore: Johns Hopkins University Press, 1990), 41–52, 78–89.

52. Nathan, 21–22; Everett P. Wheeler, could write on topics as varied as *Daniel Webster: The Expounder of the Constitution* (Littleton, Colo.: F. B. Rothman, 1896), *A World Court and International Policy* (Baltimore: American Society for Judicial Settlement of International Disputes, 1916), and *A Lawyer's Study of the Bible* (New York: Fleming H. Revell, 1919), as well as *Wages and Tariffs*, published in 1888. See *Who Was Who in America*, 11 vols. (Chicago: A. N. Marquis, 1943), I: 1328.

53. On Huntington, see *Who Was Who in America*, I: 610; on Faunce, *Who Was Who in America*, I: 388; on Ducey, *Who Was Who in America*, I: 342–343; on Alexander, *Who Was Who in America*, I: 14; and on Mendes, Cecil Roth, ed., *Encyclopedia Judaica*, 16 vols. (New York: Macmillan, 1971), II: 1343.

54. Nathan, 21–22.

55. Josephine Goldmark, *Impatient Crusader* (Urbana: University of Illinois Press, 1953), 53.

56. John Brooks, for example, volunteered for the Union Army though he was only fifteen at the start of the war. After graduating from Harvard Divinity School in the 1870s, he served a prosperous suburban Boston Unitarian church, yet he organized classes for workmen and otherwise became involved in social justice concerns related to the industrial economy. By the time of the creation of the Consumers' League, he had left the ministry to devote his full time to studying and resolving labor-employer problems. When explaining his findings, however, he did not always introduce them with social science skepticism. Rather he would say, as did his fellow reformers, "This is the economic truth. . . ." See Barbara Miller Solomon, "John Graham Brooks," in *Dictionary of American Biography*, ed. Harris E. Starr, Robert Livingston Schuyler, and Edward T. James (New York: Charles Scribner's Sons, 1958), XI: 66–67.

57. Nathan, xii.

58. Samuel Kydd, *The History of the Factory Movement*, 2 vols. (New York: A. M. Kelley, 1966), I: 109.

59. See Robert Russell, *North America, Its Agriculture and Climate* (Edinburgh: Adam and Charles Black, 1857).

60. See Frederick Law Olmsted, *The Cotton Kingdom* (New York: Alfred A. Knopf, 1953); 494 quotes Russell. Olmsted devoted a chapter to refuting Russell.

61. Louis Wolowski, *Le Travail des Enfants dans les Manufactures* (Paris: Conservatoire des Arts et Metiers, 1868), 31; see Follows, 67.

62. See Nathan, 24–26, for the text of the constitution.

63. Ibid.

64. Ibid., xiii. The saying contrasted in its empiricism with the Fabian socialist saying, "Educate, Agitate, Organize"; see Patricia Pugh, *Educate, Agitate, Organize: 100 Years of Fabian Socialism* (New York: Methuen, 1984).

65. For King's interesting economic theories, see Bruce Hutchison, *The Incredible Canadian: A Candid Portrait of Mackenzie King* (New York: Longmans, Green, 1953); 42–43 discuss King's *Industry and Humanity* (Boston: Houghton Mifflin, 1918). On King's work in Massachusetts, see R. MacGregor Dawson, *William Lyon Mackenzie King: A Political Biography* (Toronto: University of Toronto Press, 1958), 70–78.

66. On Hadley, see *Who Was Who in America*, I: 498; his works included *Relations between Freedom and Responsibility in the Evolution of Democratic Government* (New Haven, Yale University Press, 1903); *The Moral Basis of Democracy* (New Haven: Yale University Press, 1919); and *The Conflict between Liberty and Equality* (Boston: Houghton Mifflin, 1925).

67. Seligman is used by Bender, 49–77, as representative of the academic culture of the era, in his efforts to define the proper boundaries for the social sciences; while personally involved in public issues, Seligman began the process of specialized isolation.

68. On Adams, see A. W. Coats, "Henry Carter Adams: A Case Study in the Emergence of the Social Sciences in the United States: 1850–1900," *Journal of American Studies* 2 (October 1968): 177–197, which finds that Adams was more moderate than Richard Ely, but he contributed an important defense of tripartism in labor policy making, assuring a seat to labor in the process.

69. Skocpol, *Protecting Soldiers and Mothers*, 155–176, discusses Henderson, especially his role in the AALL.

70. Charles Foster Kent and Jeremiah Jenks, *Jesus' Principles of Living* (New York: Charles Scribner's Sons, 1920); Jenks, *Personal Problems of Boys Who Work* (New York: Association Press, 1913); Jenks, *The Trust Problem* (Garden City, N.Y.: Doubleday, Page and Co., 1917); see *Who Was Who in America*, I: 632.

71. Chambers, 35–46; Lindsay, "Social Concepts in Economic Theory," in *Industrial Relations and the Churches*, ed. John A. Ryan and F. Ernest Johnson, published in *The Annals of the American Academy of Political and Social Science* 103 (September 1922): 49–53.

72. On the child labor amendment, see Chambers, 33–46; on the ERA, see 77–78.

73. Henrotin played a key role in the women's suffrage movement in the era; see Mildred W. Wells, *Unity in Diversity: The History of the General Federation of Women's Clubs* (Washington, D.C.: General Federation of Women's Clubs, 1953) and *Harper's Weekly*, 4 July 1908, 16.

74. Friedrich Engels, *The Condition of the Working Class in England*, trans. Florence Kelley Wischnewetzky (London: Allen and Unwin, 1952).

75. Nathan, 68–69; for Kelley's early work and thought, see *The Autobiography of Florence Kelley: Notes of Sixty Years* (Chicago: Charles H. Kerr Publishing Co., 1986).

76. "The Consumers' League Label and Its Offspring," *The Survey*, 8 August 1914, 478.

77. See Mason; and Robert H. Bremner, *From the Depths: The Discovery of Poverty in the U.S.* (New York: New York University Press, 1956).

78. On international leagues, see Nathan, 90–101; for example, the league especially argued for an end to what it called cocoa slavery on plantations supplying the Swiss chocolate industry.

79. *The Labor Movement in America* (New York: T. Y. Crowell, 1886).

80. Everett, 75–98.

81. Ely, *French and German Socialism*, 257–260.

82. Hopkins, 106; see *The Social Aspects of Christianity* (Boston: W. L. Greene and Co., 1888).

83. *Social Reform and the Church* (New York: T. Y. Crowell, 1894).

84. On Commons, especially see *Myself: The Autobiography of John R. Commons* (Madison: University of Wisconsin Press, 1963); 7–15 has interesting reflections on his early life. Later, especially 138–139, he discusses John Andrews and the AALL founding, and on 181 the Consumers' League. See also Theda Skocpol, *Social Policy in the United States: Future Possibilities in Historical Perspective* (Princeton: Princeton University Press, 1995), 148–150, on Commons's methodology.

85. Lowe, 91.

86. Chambers, 252–259; Skocpol, *Protecting Soldiers and Mothers*, 177–203.

87. Moynihan, "The U.S. and the ILO," 500, described how Anderson stayed at a hotel in Monnetier, on the French side of Lake Geneva, and received "unofficial" visits from conference delegations; he also has a good summary (19–20) of U.S. appropriations for the ILO, which began in 1902 and lasted until 1920, when the modern ILO replaced the Basel organization.

88. AALL, "Second Annual Meeting," 4.

89. Ibid., 9–10.

90. Lindsay, "Reciprocal," 435–457; see also Ernest Freund, "Can the States Co-operate for Labor Legislation?" *The Survey*, 12 June 1909, 409–411.

91. Roy Lubove, *The Struggle for Social Security 1900–1935*, (Cambridge: Harvard University Press, 1968), 33.

92. See Gershman, 11–12; and Moynihan, "The U.S. and the ILO," 37–44.

93. Ibid., and Simeon Larson, *Labor and Foreign Policy: Gompers, the AFL, and the First World War 1914–1918* (Rutherford, N.J.: Fairleigh Dickinson University Press, 1974), 13–15. Typical of many other historians of the period, Larson sees Gompers as simply reflecting popular American hostility to socialism and acceptance of rugged individualism, an interpretation the study of ILO policy would challenge.

94. On Gompers's trust of Wilson, see Moynihan, "The U.S. and the ILO," 118 and 196–197.

95. Samuel Gompers, *Seventy Years of Life and Labor*, Philip Taft and John A. Session, ed. (New York: E. P. Dutton & Co., Inc., 1957), 257–259.

96. See U.S. Code, Title 15—Commerce and Trade, Section 17, "The labor of a human being is not a commodity or article of commerce."

97. On "labor as a commodity," see James Gray Pope, "Labor's Constitution of Freedom," *Yale Law Journal* 106 (January 1997), where he studies the use of the concept as defense for labor's view of the Constitution, especially linking the right to organize and strike to the abolitionist battle against slavery. For an explanation of the church position on the topic, see John T. Pawlikowski, "Introduction to Rerum Novarum," in National Conference of Catholic Bishops, *Contemporary Catholic Social Teaching* (Washington, D.C.: United States Catholic Conference, 1991), 11–14. For two contemporary discussions of the concept, see Edwin E. Witte, "The Doctrine That Labor Is a Commodity," *Annals of the American Academy of Political and Social Science* 69 (1917): 113, 139; and "Labor Is Not a Commodity," *The New Republic*, 2 December 1916, 112–114.

98. Richard Ely, *The Labor Movement in America* (New York: T. Y. Crowell & Co., 1886), 98–99.

99. In addition to sources cited in chapter 1, a good collection of essays on the topic of the war and reform is John Milton Cooper, Jr., ed., *Causes and Consequences of World War I* (New York: Quadrangle Books, 1972).

100. John B. Andrews, "Outline of Work, 1914," *American Labor Legislation Review* 5 (March 1915): 153.

101. Shotwell, *The Origins*, II: Document 1.

102. Tipton, 19–20; Tikriti, 81; and Carol Riegelman, "War-Time Trade-Union and Socialist Proposals," in Shotwell, *Origins*, I: 55–79.

103. Likewise *The New York Times*, 25 June 1919, 10, pointed out that Gompers only represented 10 percent of American workers.

104. Ronald Radosh, *American Labor and United States Foreign Policy* (New York: Random House, 1969), 452.

105. Moynihan, "The U.S. and the ILO," 136–137.

106. Bryce M. Stewart, "Labor Standards and Competition Between the United States and Canada," *The American Labor Legislation Review* 17, (1927): 176–177; Mainwaring, 15.

107. Selig Perlman, *A Theory of the Labor Movement*, 2nd. ed. (New York: Augustus M. Kelley, 1949), 156–157, emphasized U.S. labor's opposition to private property; Mollie Ray Carroll, *Labor and Politics: The Attitude of the American Federation of Labor toward Legislation and Politics* (Boston: Houghton Mifflin Co., 1923), 167, emphasized that the AFL avoids law and politics, using private voluntary agreements.

108. Shotwell, *The Origins*, II: Document 13, adopted September 1918.

109. See Skocpol on the AALL, *Protecting Soldiers and Mothers*, 176–203.

110. On the Inquiry, see Leifur Magnusson, "American Preparations," in Shotwell, *The Origins*, I: 97–105; on Amy Hewes, see *The New York Times*, 26 March 1970, 47; on Dorothy Kenyon, see *The New York Times*, 14 February 1972, 32; other women members of the staff included Adelaide Hasse, Marion Denman, Laura Thompson, and Elizabeth Wagonette.

111. Robertson and Judd, 64–67, and Skocpol, 23–26, provide summaries of theories regarding the influence of working-class movements on policy making. On Bolsheviks, see Beth Sims, *Workers of the World Undermined: American Labor's Role in U.S. Foreign Policy* (Boston: South End Press, 1992), 62–63; Moynihan, *On the Law*, 59; Mainwaring, 3; see Shotwell, *The Origins*, II: 127; on Bela Kun, see Moynihan, "The U.S. and the ILO," 204–206. However, Lammy Betten, *International Labour Law: Selected Issues* (Deventer, Neth.: Kluwer Law and Taxation Publishers, 1993), 1–11, makes clear the ILO was on the agenda at Versailles even had there been no Russian Revolution.

112. Riegelman, "War-Time," 69–71, discusses Gompers.

113. Moynihan, "The U.S. and the ILO," 178–181, describes how Edward Phelan interceded with Shotwell to get him to control Gompers; Moynihan earlier (147) observed that Gompers was the only delegate at the conference who truly was from the working class.

114. Mainwaring, 13; Tipton, 26; Moynihan, "The U.S. and the ILO," 159–161; Gompers, 301.

115. United States, Department of State, *Treaties and Other International Agreements of the United States of America: 1776–1949*, Charles I. Bevans, ed. (Washington, D.C.: Department of State, 1968–76), II: 254.

116. On the Washington Conference, see Malcolm Delevingne, "The Organizing Committee," in Shotwell, *The Origins*, I: 285–304; Harold Butler, "The Washington Conference," in Shotwell, *The Origins*, I: 305–330; and Moynihan, "The U.S. and the ILO," 310–329, which points out that a number of Americans, especially FDR and Frances Perkins, first had contact with the ILO at the Washington Conference.

117. Shotwell, *The Origins*, has Furuseth's speech and replies; Walter Galenson, *The International Labor Organization: An American View* (Madison:

University of Wisconsin Press, 1981), 25–26, says U.S. labor and management equally opposed the ILO in the 1920s.

118. Gompers argued generally against government delegates at the ILO, wanting business and labor to each have a vote; on these disputes, see Moynihan, "The U.S. and the ILO," 159–161; see also, Gompers, *Seventy Years*, 301.

119. See U.S. Congress, 66th Cong., 1st sess., *Congressional Record* (1919), 8726–8730, for the vote on the King (senator from Utah) reservation to the Versailles Treaty, November 18, 1919, stating that ILO conventions unratified by the U.S. would not be binding on the U.S.; the vote was forty-three for the reservation, and forty-eight against [for the treaty]. Of the yeas, thirty-four were Republicans and nine Democrats. Of those Democrats, four were not from south of the Mason-Dixon Line. Of the nays, thirteen were Republicans and thirty-five Democrats, with ten not from the South. Seventy-two percent of Republicans voted against the ILO and seventy-nine percent of Democrats for it; yet the highest percent of Democrats voting for it came from the South, the region least industrial but most loyal to the president.

120. John Milton Cooper, *Pivotal Decades: The United States, 1900–1920* (New York: Norton, 1990), 355, concludes that because of the nation's public opinion, "an unstinting participation in the League was impossible for the United States."

121. The traditional view of the regressive labor policies was described at the time by such writers as John R. Commons and John B. Andrews, *Principles of Labor Legislation* (New York: Harpers, 1916), 16; for a typical recent comparative account, see Martin Shefter, "Trade Unions and Political Machines: The Organization and Disorganization of the American Working Class in the Late Nineteenth Century," in *Working-Class Formation: Nineteenth Century Patterns in Western Europe and the United States*, ed. Ira Katznelson and Aristide R. Zolberg (Princeton, N.J.: Princeton University Press, 1986), 197–276; however, at the time of the ILO debate Gompers and the AFL could be seen as aggressively stating labor's opposition to both laissez-faire and progressive-era reform efforts, a stance that would explain the ILO breakthrough.

THREE. THE REVERSAL

1. Hugh S. Hanna, "The International Cost-of-Living Inquiry," *The Annals of the American Academy of Political and Social Science* 166 (March 1933): 164–167. On Thomas generally, see E. J. Phelan, *Yes and Albert Thomas* (London: The Cresset Press, Ltd., 1936), especially 161; George F. Slocombe, *Albert Thomas and the International Labor Organization: Mirror to Geneva* (New York: Henry Holt Co., 1937); Mainwaring, 23–25; Morse, *The Origin and Evolution*, 14; and Cox, "ILO: Limited Monarchy," 102–103.

2. Mainwaring, 46–47, discusses how some criticized Thomas for slowing the process of defining labor standards. Yet, Thomas really defined a middle

ground between simple enactment of labor laws and an expansive ILO role as the central world labor rights organization.

3. Moynihan, "The U.S. and the ILO," 247–248.

4. National Industrial Conference Board, *The Work of the ILO* (New York: NICB, 1928), 158–159; and Thomas Spates, "The Employers of the United States and the International Labor Organization," *Annals of the American Academy of Political and Social Science* 164 (March 1933): 151.

5. Moynihan, "The U.S. and the ILO," 335.

6. Mahaim, 439–442; Radosh, 302.

7. Matthew Woll, "The International Labor Office: A Criticism," *Current History*, 31 (January 1930): 687–688.

8. On labor, see Lorwin, *The International Labor Movement*, 130–131; and Moynihan, "The U.S. and the ILO," 414–446.

9. See Tamara K. Hareven and Randolph Langenbach, *Amoskeag: Life and Work in an American Factory City* (New York: Pantheon, 1978), 233, on feudalism; and Tamara K. Hareven, *Family Time and Industrial Time* (New York: Cambridge University Press, 1982), 289, on two features added at the time, a union and scientific management.

10. Daniel Creamer and Charles W. Coulter, *Labor and the Shutdown of the Amoskeag Textile Mills* (Philadelphia: Works Progress Administration, 1939).

11. On grievances about quality, see Hareven, *Family Time*, 302.

12. Herbert A. Jump, "Six Months in a Strike City," *Survey* 48 (August 1, 1922): 555–557; reflecting the collaboration common in labor rights, the exhausted union accepted the mediation of local clergy. However, the 1922 agreement satisfied neither the union nor the company.

13. On the strike, see Elizabeth Morison and Elting Morison, *New Hampshire: A Bicentennial History* (New York: W. W. Norton, 1976), 184–187.

14. There are several good biographies of Winant. See Bernard Bellush, *He Walked Alone: A Biography of John Gilbert Winant* (The Hague: Mouton, 1968); Alvin Knepper, "John Gilbert Winant and International Social Justice," (Ph.D. diss., New York University, 1954); and numerous periodical sketches.

15. Bass sympathized with a group led by Harold Ickes and other "Bull Moosers" that backed James Cox and FDR in 1920 against "the same reactionary bunch of politicians against whom they rebelled in 1912." See, for example, letter from Edwin M. Lee of the "National Headquarters" of the Cox-Roosevelt Progressive-Republican Committee to Robert Bass, 14 October 1920; also see letter from Harold Ickes to Bass, 24 August 1920, in Robert Bass Papers, Baker Library, Dartmouth College, Hanover, New Hampshire.

16. Letter from O. P. Hussey to Bass, 15 December 1923, Bass Papers.

17. Campaign speech in Bass Papers. The phrase "promise of American life" doubtlessly was intended to send a message to the 1912 Progressives, since this was the title of the book by Herbert Croly, published in 1909, that became the blueprint for Roosevelt's campaign. Croly had founded the *New Republic* and

still edited it in the 1920s, see Charles Forcey, *The Crossroads of Liberalism: Croly, Weyl, Lippmann and the Progressive Era, 1900–1925* (New York: Oxford University Press, 1961), 3–51; Forcey found Croly representative of "national liberalism," a form willing to accept comprehensive national government action to address social and economic problems.

18. Such ideas worried even some admirers of Winant; Hugh Moore of the Brown Company, the massive paper mill in northern New Hampshire, wrote to Bass, "Personally, I like John Winant, and believe he is sincere in every respect. I am not, however, impressed by his knowledge of Economics or his attitude on economic issues." Letter to Bass, 10 January 1924, Bass Papers.

19. Arthur M. Schlesinger Jr., *The Age of Roosevelt: The Coming of the New Deal* (Boston: Houghton Mifflin, 1958), 198; on the AALL, see John B. Andrews, "Annual Business Meeting," *The American Labor Legislation Review* 17 (1927): 99.

20. On Winant's state administration in 1925–27, see H. C. Pearson, "The Winant Administration," *The Granite Monthly* 58 (November 1926): 409–413; also Knepper, 30–36; and Bellush, 60–85. Of special interest, Bellush describes Winant's and Bass's leadership effort to support Coolidge's proposal to join the World Court in 1926.

21. Jacob Herbert Burgy, *The New England Cotton Textile Industry: A Study in Industrial Geography* (Baltimore: Waverly Press, 1932), 44.

22. Broadus Mitchell and George Sinclair Mitchell, *The Industrial Revolution in the South* (Baltimore: Johns Hopkins University Press, 1930), 3.

23. Phillip J. Wood, *Southern Capitalism: The Political Economy of North Carolina 1880–1980* (Durham, N.C.: Duke University Press, 1986), 192.

24. William H. Miernyk, "Unemployment in New England Textile Communities," *Monthly Labor Review* 78 (June 1955); and Dumaine in Hareven, *Life and Work*, 333, discuss technological advances, especially the introduction of electric-powered mill machinery, which undercut the great New England water-power advantage. By 1925, 86.7 percent of New England mills were electrified, a sign of modernization to some, yet an example of a technology that freed industry from the rushing rivers of the region. Mills could move anywhere there was electricity, even the South. Worst, the old mills could not easily accommodate the new equipment and faced the temptation to continue running less efficient but still-functioning older machines. In fact, New England textile machinery manufacturers undermined their fellow New England textile businesses by offering cheap credit to, or even building, Southern mills that bought large numbers of their latest machines. Finally, the development of new consumer preferences, particularly for synthetic fibers, reduced demand for the natural fibers processed by the older factories. The exceptional advantages New England once had in technology and experienced personnel ceased to be an advantage. Natural fibers and renewable energy were abandoned in a rush to the artificial and the nonrenewable.

25. See Wood, 59–93; Clarence H. Danhoff, "Four Decades of Thought on the South's Economic Problems," in *Essays in Southern Economic Develop-*

ment, ed. Melvin L. Greenhut and W. Tate Whitman (Chapel Hill: University of North Carolina Press, 1964), 7–68; Harold Marley, "A Southern Textile Epoch," *Survey* 65 (1 October 1930): 17–20, 55–58; and Jacquelyn D. Hall, James Leloudis, and Robert Korstad, "Cotton Mill People: Work, Community, and Protest in the Textile South 1880–1940," *American Historical Review* 91 (April 1986): 245–286. On night work, see Irving Bernstein, *The Lean Years: A History of the American Worker, 1920–1933* (Boston: Houghton Mifflin, 1960), 4–5. See especially Gregory Clark, "Why Isn't the Whole World Developed? Lessons from the Cotton Mills," *Journal of Economic History* 47 (March 1987): 141–173, which holds culture mattered in keeping New England developed earlier, but overlooks new methods of management. Mitchell, *The Industrial Revolution in the South*, 145, discusses the introduction of scientific management in New England as well as the South. Yet, only so much efficiency could be milked out of the old New England factories and their comparatively humane labor traditions. Southern mills began in a later era and did not have to put down a tradition of paternalistic responsibility and familiarity with the workforce. Southern mills could easily operate around the clock and around the year. Also, they always had the threat hanging over the heads of their largely poor white workforce of responding to worker complaints by bringing in the more desperate and despised local blacks.

26. Not that there were no unions and no strikes in the South, but the strikes were less frequent and public officials more helpful in strike suppression than in New England. Also, the new technology that Southern mills installed had ingenious production rate and quality measuring mechanisms that minimized the advantages New Englanders had in worker skill and commitment. See Bernstein, 11–12; on famous Southern strikes, such as Gastonia, see 20–21. See also Hall, *Cotton Mill People*, 270, on pioneering methods of surveillance; Richard L. Rowan and Robert E. Barr, *Employee Relations: Trends and Practices in the Textile Industry* (Philadelphia: Industrial Research Unit Wharton School, University of Pennsylvania, 1987), 113–116; and Burgy, 169–170.

27. Dumaine listed transportation advantages in the South, but those advantages always had been present: see Hareven, *Life and Work*, 333.

28. Burgy, 171–172; Hareven, *Family Time*, 30–31, 350–351. For a sympathetic treatment of the company's dilemma, facing lower-cost Southern competition, see Arthur M. Kenison, *Dumaine's Amoskeag: Let the Record Speak* (Manchester, N.H.: Saint Anselm College Press, 1997), 85–102.

29. Alice S. Cheyney, "International Labor Standards and American Legislation," *International Labor Organization: Geneva Special Studies* 8, August 1931 (Geneva: Geneva Research Information Committee, 1931).

30. A. F. Hinricks, "Historical Review of Wage Rates and Wage Differentials in the Cotton-Textile Industry," *Monthly Labor Review* 40 (May 1935): 1170–1180.

31. Congressional Quarterly, *CQ Guide to U.S. Elections*, 3rd ed. (Washington, D.C.: Congressional Quarterly, 1994).

32. A classic defense of the value of party competition is Schattschneider, 137; for a fuller discussion, see Walter J. Stone, *Republic at Risk: Self-Interest in American Politics* (Pacific Grove, Calif.: Brooks/Cole Publishing, 1990), 90–118.

33. Knepper, 72–73.

34. John G. Winant, "The New Hampshire Plan," *Review of Reviews* 86 (November 1932): 24. See also "The Nation-Wide Drive for the Five-Day Week," *The Literary Digest*, 13 August 1932, 3–4; and Knepper, 55–56.

35. Freund, 409–411.

36. Lindsay, "Reciprocal."

37. John G. Winant, "Perils and Possibilities of Our Government by the People," *State Government* 8 (April 1935): 81–82.

38. On the meetings, see the United States Bureau of Labor Statistics; and Frances Perkins, *The Roosevelt I Knew* (New York: The Viking Press, 1946), 104–106.

39. "Interstate Conference on Labor Laws," *Monthly Labor Review* (March 1933): 537.

40. On Dennison, see Sanford Jacoby, *Modern Manors: Welfare Capitalism Since the New Deal* (Princeton, N.J.: Princeton University Press, 1997), 15–28.

41. Letter from Smith to Perkins, 12 May 1933, General Records of Department of Labor, Office of the Secretary, General Subject File 1933–1941, Minimum Wage to National Emergency Council, Record Group 174, Box 82, National Archives, Washington, D.C.

42. American Legislation Association, *Interstate Compact for Establishing Uniform Standards for Conditions of Employment* (Chicago: American Legislation Association, 1934).

43. On the southern strategy, see letter from John Winant, as president of the Consumers' League, to Evans Clark of the Twentieth-Century Fund, 3 January 1936, in John Winant Papers, National Consumers' League 1936, Box 161, Franklin D. Roosevelt Library, Hyde Park, New York.

44. On the intense effort to get support for interstate compacts, see U.S. Department of Labor, Division of Labor Standards, Agenda of Second Conference of National Organizations on Cooperation in the Improvement of Labor Standards. The membership in the Committee on State Labor Legislation demonstrated the faithful participation of four types of movements: two of the five members were from women's movements—Marguerite Wells of the League of Women Voters and Geline Bowman of the National Federation of Business and Professional Women's Clubs—and other members came from the Consumers' League, the AFL, and the National Catholic Welfare Conference; in General Records of Department of Labor, Record Group 174, Box 48. See also "Seven States in Compact on Labor Legislation," *The Literary Digest*, 23 June 1934, 20; and Winant's speech to the second conference, "Perils and Possibilities," 81–82. On the work of the Massachusetts Consumers' League, see letter to Rep. Christian Herter, 11 October 1935, in Consumers' League of Massachusetts

Papers, Box 9, File 127, Schlesinger Library, Radcliffe College, Cambridge, Massachusetts.

45. John Milton Cooper, Jr., *The Warrior and the Priest: Woodrow Wilson and Theodore Roosevelt* (Cambridge, Mass.: Belknap Press, 1983), 206–221.

46. On 1920s anticompetitive efforts, see Nelson B. Gaskill, *The Regulation of Competition* (New York: Harper and Brothers, 1936), 9–14; and Edward N. Hurley, *Awakening of Business* (New York: Doubleday, Page, 1917), 58–59. Gaskill and Hurley were the first two heads of the Federal Trade Commission; on such efforts, see Himmelberg, *Origins of the NRA.*

47. John A. Ryan and F. Ernest Johnson, "Summary and Afterword," in *Industrial Relations and the Churches, The Annals of the American Academy of Political and Social Science* 103 (September 1922): 141–143.

48. Henry S. Dennison, "An Employer's View of Property," in Ryan and Johnson, *Industrial Relations and the Churches*, 58. On Dennison, see Edward Berkowitz and Kim McQuaid, *Creating the Welfare State: The Political Economy of Twentieth-Century Reform*, rev. ed. (Lawrence: University Press of Kansas, 1992), 26–31; as well as Jacoby, 15–28.

49. Sam A. Lewisohn, "The Employers' Responsibility to the Community," in Ryan and Johnson, *Industrial Relations and the Churches.*

50. Patrick Callahan, "An Employer's View of the Church's Function in Industry," in Ryan and Johnson, *Industrial Relations and the Churches*, 105.

51. W. E. Hotchkiss, "Collective Agreements in the Men's Clothing Industry," in Ryan and Johnson, *Industrial Relations and the Churches*, 30–31; Hotchkiss headed the National Federation of Clothing Manufacturers, which coordinated firms in Baltimore, Chicago, and Rochester.

52. Lindsay, "Social Concepts," 50.

53. Joseph Husslein, "Labor's Responsibility to the Community," in Ryan and Johnson, *Industrial Relations and the Churches*, 70–71.

54. Sidney F. Goldstein, "Judaism and the Industrial Crisis," in Ryan and Johnson, *Industrial Relations and the Churches*, 89.

55. F. Ernest Johnson, "The Teaching of the Protestant Church," in Ryan and Johnson, *Industrial Relations and the Churches*, 84.

56. Florence Kelley, "Industrial Conditions as a Community Problem With Particular Reference to Child Labor," in Ryan and Johnson, *Industrial Relations and the Churches*, 63.

57. Ibid., 64. While the 1920s generally were an era of few new progressive policies, a result many see of the apathy or disillusionment following World War I, Chambers in *Seedtime of Reform* has shown the era nurtured some new progressive initiatives that flowered in the 1930s, yet Chambers points out on page 43 that the 1920s were an era of reaction, quoting Kansas progressive William Allen White on the Child Labor Amendment defeat, "We are in a slough of reaction. It is the height of folly to push humanitarian measures at this time and give their opponents the prestige of defeat."

58. Samuel McCune Lindsay, "The Problem of American Cooperation," in Shotwell, *The Origins*, I: 331.

59. Ibid., 358.

60. On Woll's conservative position and the National Civic Federation in the 1930s, see George Morris, *CIA and American Labor: The Subversion of the AFL-CIO's Foreign Policy* (New York: International Publishers, 1967), 47–48.

61. NIRA, Section 7, (b); on the NIRA and its links to the 1920s corporatism in the textile industry, see Galambos, 173–202.

62. NIRA Hearing No. 1, 28 June 1933, B1-B2, in Records of the National Industrial Recovery Administration, Hearing No. 1, of the Cotton Textile Industry, 28 June 1933, Record Group 9, Box 73, Entry 44, National Archives, Washington, D.C.

63. Instead of a differential of 65 percent in 1924, the code reduced it to 18 percent in 1934. Since the South already had lower value added per worker, and the code reduced both their wage advantage and their savings from utilization of equipment around the clock, the North did well. Even more so, workers benefitted as wages rose. The forty-hour week became standard, and child labor ended.

64. Knepper, 60–61.

65. John L. Lewis, "Significance of American Membership in the I.L.O. to Labor," in Spencer Miller Jr., ed., *What the International Labor Organization Means to America* (New York: Columbia University Press, 1936), 77, for Lewis's view of the NRA; John A. Ryan, *A Better Economic Order* (New York: Harper & Bros. Publishing, 1935); Francis J. Haas "Compulsory Unemployment Insurance," in *Proceedings of the Nineteenth Session of the National Conference of Catholic Charities* (New York: National Conference of Catholic Charities, 1933), 456–459, on the church and the NRA. On people who worked with government under the NRA, including a number of labor leaders, see Perkins, *Roosevelt I Knew*, 208–209; Perkins also assessed the positive impacts on labor.

66. Hareven, *Amoskeag*, 170.

67. See correspondence of Francis J. Gorman, chairman of the strike committee of the United Textile Workers, to John Winant, 9 September 1934, in Records of the National Recovery Administration, Records of the Textile Labor Relations Board, Record Group 9, Box 1, Entry 401, National Archives, Washington, D.C. Responding to the problems with the NRA, in late August 1934 the UTW made four demands of the Cotton National Industrial Relations Board, which governed working conditions in the mills: a thirty-hour work week; a minimum wage of sixteen dollars per week, with no regional differences; a subminimum wage for trainees, but a limit of not more than 5 percent trainees in a plant; and assurances of worker rights to organize. Negotiations led nowhere.

68. On the Winant board, see James A. Hodges, *New Deal Labor Policy and the Southern Cotton Textile Industry* (Knoxville: University of Tennessee Press, 1986), 112–125; Louise Lamphere, *From Working Daughters to Working Mothers: Immigrant Women in a New England Industrial Community* (Ithaca,

N.Y.: Cornell University Press, 1987), 196–200; Hall, Leloudis, and Korstad, 276–280; and Knepper, 79–82; "Industrial Struggles and Politics Grip Nation," *The Literary Digest*, 15 September 1934, 6–7.

69. Letter from W. Conley to President Roosevelt, forwarded to Winant, dated at the Department of Labor, 13 September 1934, in Records of NRA, Record Group 9, Box 1, File 401.

70. Letter dated 7 September 1934 to Winant. Records of NRA, Record Group 9, Box 1, File 401, page 2.

71. Telegram from Joseph P. Ryan to Board of Mediation, 13 September 1934, Records of NRA, Record Group 9, Box 1, File 401.

72. Franklin D. Roosevelt, *On Our Way* (New York: John Day, 1934), 76–77; quoted by writers such as Lindsay, "Problem of American Cooperation," 361.

73. On *Schecter* and the textile industry, see Galambos, 287–293, who points out that the failure to find limits to cutthroat competition had already occurred by the time of *Schecter*, and the industry had begun to live with cutthroat competition; he points out that several of the counts against *Schecter* dealt with violations of labor standards (minimum wage and maximum hours), but the Court did not directly rule on them. It ruled instead on federal regulation of an intrastate business by presidential executive order. See the opinion of Chief Justice Hughes in *A. L. A. Schecter Poultry Corp. v. U.S.*, 295 U.S. 495, 55 S. Ct. 837 (1935); also see Peter N. Irons, *The New Deal Lawyers* (Princeton, N.J.: Princeton University Press, 1982), 290, which points out that the NRA was the only New Deal program not eventually upheld by courts.

74. J. P. Chamberlain, "The United States and the International Labor Organization," *The American Labor Legislation Review* 17 (1927): 173.

75. On the encyclical *Quadregesimo anno*, see Jean-Yves Calvez, "Economic Policy Issues in Roman Catholic Social Teaching: An International Perspective," in Gannon, 18–19.

76. Geneva Research Center, "The United States and the League of Nations during 1932," *Geneva Special Studies* 3 (1932): 12–13.

77. James T. Shotwell, "The International Labor Organization as an Alternative to Violent Revolution," *The Annals of the American Academy of Political and Social Science* 166 (March 1933): 18–25.

78. Alice S. Cheyney, "A Comparison of Convention Provisions with Labor Legislation in the United States," *The Annals of the American Academy of Political and Social Science* 166 (March 1933): 176–189; this was a revision of her 1930 essay on the same topic.

79. Ibid., 176.

80. Ibid., 188–189.

81. C. J. Ratzlaff, "The International Labor Organization of the League of Nations: Its Significance to the United States," *The American Economic Review* 22 (September 1932): 447–461; Tipton, 38, overemphasized the certainty of Ratzlaff's findings, but still it was important to get an ILO endorsement, even if

supported by little evidence, in *The American Economic Review*. For Ratzlaff's biographical information, see *Who Was Who in America*, III (1951–1960), 712.

82. *Congressional Record*, June 16, 1934, 12238–12239.

83. On Tinkham, a big-game hunter, Asian-art collector, and isolationist, see John Galvin, "George Holden Tinkham," in *The Dictionary of American Biography, Supplement Six, 1956–1960*, ed. John A. Garraty (New York: Charles Scribner's Sons, 1980), 635–636.

84. For a sympathetic portrait of Dumaine's efforts, see Kenison, 173–179; more critical is Alan R. Sweezy, "The Amoskeag Manufacturing Company," *The Quarterly Journal of Economics* 52 (May 1938): 495–496, which discusses Amoskeag's next manipulations, in which on 21 November 1927, stockholders of the holding company were offered a deal on the 285,000 shares of Amoskeag Manufacturing Company preferred stock. They would divide $8 million in cash, $14.7 million in twenty-year bonds, and 13,191 common shares issued by Amoskeag Manufacturing. In other words, they received most of the remaining cash of the factory and a commitment to pay them another $14.7 million. As Sweezy said in his 1938 study of Amoskeag, "[T]he bond issue . . . enabled the trustees to turn the remarkable trick of having things both ways at once. For stock holders who wanted to get out, the bond issue was as good as a cash distribution—better, in fact, since it avoided any forced sale of assets. At the same time it made possible continued operation of the mills under circumstances favorable for squeezing a maximum out of the human and material resources employed."

85. *The New York Times*, 15 March 1936, IV, 11.

86. *Amoskeag Manufacturing Company: Plan of Reorganization*, District Court of the United States for the District of Manhattan, Proceedings for the Reorganization of a Corporation, No. 58599, filed 9 March 1936.

87. (New York) *Daily News Record*, 16 March 1936.

88. *Boston Traveler*, 12 June 1936.

89. *The Providence Journal*, 12 June 1936 and 13 June 1936.

90. On Sabath, see Robert Lowitt, "Adolph J. Sabath," in *Dictionary of American Biography, Supplement Five*, 597–599.

91. (New York) *Daily News Record*, 2 October 1936.

92. Ibid., 8 October 1936.

93. For Dumaine's life after Amoskeag, see Thomas Winpenny, "Frederic C. Dumaine," in *Dictionary of American Biography, Supplement Five*, 190–191.

94. *Time*, 4 June 1951, 98; for a more positive assessment of Dumaine than is implied in his final quote, see Kenison, 1–8.

FOUR. The First Decade of Americans at the ILO

1. Letter of 19 May 1936 from Frances Perkins to John Winant, and letter from Cordell Hull to Perkins, 20 March 1936, General Records of the U.S. De-

partment of Labor, Record Group 174, Box 74, ILO Office Files, National Archives, Washington, D.C. [cited henceforth as USDOL Files].

2. For a summary of the New Deal-era acceptance of policy experimentation, see Burns, 234–241; also essays in *New Deal Thought,* Howard Zinn, ed. (Indianapolis: Bobbs-Merrill, 1966), and Gerald Nash, "The Great Experiment in Industrial Self-Government," and Kim McQuaid, "Experiments in Industrial Mobilization," in *Survival of Corporatism during the New Deal Era 1933–1945,* ed. Robert Himmelberg (New York: Garland, 1994).

3. For example, to solve budget problems during the depression, Winant turned to the Brookings Institution of his old patron, Robert Bass. See *New York Times,* 5 February 1933; Brookings Institution, Institute for Government Research, *Report on a Survey of the Organization and Administration of the State, County and Town Governments of New Hampshire* (Concord, N.H.: The Brookings Institution, 1932).

4. On the labor statistics movement, see James Leiby, *Carroll Wright and Labor Reform* (Cambridge, Mass.: Harvard University Press, 1960).

5. On the relationship of Johnson and Winant, see Ethel M. Johnson, "The Mr. Winant I Knew," *South Atlantic Monthly* 43 (January 1947): 24–41.

6. The approach of progressives such as Winant, finding policies pragmatically or experimentally, can explain the apparent contradictions in their disparate movement from before World War I to the New Deal, as described by Otis Graham; however, the experimental approach of people such as Winant is not the same as modern policy empiricism, such as simple cost-benefit analysis, which theoretically is not governed by norms or goals, other than simple mathematics, but is more like Lindblom's incrementalism. See Hayes, 11–25; also see Heineman, 35–67, for a discussion of rationality and cost-benefit analysis.

7. For example, when Winant left the governorship, he turned over leadership of the state Republican party to his former administrative assistant, Styles Bridges, who everyone believed was a "Tory progressive" like Winant. Reflecting the general transition within American parties of the period, Bridges slowly abandoned Tory-style noblesse oblige to become by the late 1940s a free-market ideologue. On Bridges, see *The New York Times,* 27 November 1961, 1A; and George T. Mazuzan, "Henry Styles Bridges," in *Dictionary of American Biography, Supplement Seven 1961–1965,* 73–74.

8. Bellush, 101–102, has a good summary of his policies; for contemporary reaction, see *Newsweek,* 23 December 1933, 15. For example, he received attention for vigorously supporting New Deal relief programs. New Hampshire filled its quota of slots under programs such as the Civilian Conservation Corps; for example, Vermont had no approved Public Works Administration projects in the fall of 1933, while New Hampshire had a dozen and more awaiting approval.

9. See, for example, "Persons and Personalities," *Literary Digest,* 7 September 1935, 27; and George H. Sibley, "John Gilbert Winant," *Princeton Alumni Weekly,* 15 November 1935, 175–176. In 1959, Frances Perkins told Bernard Bel-

lush that she asked Roosevelt about the interest in removing Winant from the list of Republican candidates in 1936 and that FDR said that was not a factor in selecting him for the ILO, rather it was Winant's talents; see Bellush, 110.

10. John Palmer Gavit, "History Missing Its Cues," *Survey Graphic* 23 (September 1934): 439.

11. John Andrews got the famed reformer Grace Abbott to report on U.S. participation at the ILO; see Abbott, "The United States at the 19th International Labor Conference," *The American Labor Legislation Review* 25 (September 1935): 109.

12. *Stewart Machine Co. v. Davis*, 301 U.S. 548 (1937). The 1936 ruling in *U.S. v. Butler* 297 U.S. 1 (1936) seemed to hint that use of the tax power in the Social Security Act would be invalid; see Robert E. Cushman and Robert F. Cushman, *Cases in Constitutional Law*, 2nd ed. (New York: Appleton Century Crofts, 1965), 302–305.

13. The Supreme Court began upholding New Deal social legislation a few days before the Textile Conference, in *West Coast Hotel v. Parrish*, 300 U.S. 379, decided on 29 March 1937; the Social Security case, *Stewart Machine*, was not decided until 24 May 1937, and the Fair Labor Standards Act in *U.S. v. Darby Lumber*, 312 U.S. 100, in 1941.

14. Memo from Isador Lubin to Frances Perkins, 20 May 1936, on "Submission of ILO Conventions," USDOL Files, Record Group 174, Box 74; on strategy, see also letter from Frances Perkins to William Phillips, Under Secretary of State, 5 May 1936.

15. John G. Winant, "The Constitution and Social Security," *The Annals of the American Academy of Political and Social Science* 185 (May 1936): 22–28; Thomas Reed of the University of Michigan edited this volume, which appeared in 1936 during the election campaign.

16. On the Social Security battle in 1936, see Edward D. Berkowitz, *Mr. Social Security: The Life of Wilbur J. Cohen* (Lawrence: University Press of Kansas, 1995), 40–43. An irony in this battle was that Landon, Knox, and Winant had been fellow Bull Moose supporters of Theodore Roosevelt in 1912, and this effort once again pitted Winant in a victorious campaign against his 1924 New Hampshire gubernatorial rival.

17. Winant continued his campaign on behalf of Social Security past election day. On January 6, 1937, he delivered a radio address on "Security for a People," in which he emphasized that providing for the public's welfare was a proper function of American government, whether it was for military or Social Security. As the Supreme Court began to interpret the validity of the Social Security statute, and the country endured the debate about court packing, Winant began to move back to the ILO; see John G. Winant, "Security for a People," *Vital Speeches of the Day*, 1 February 1937, 241–243. An example of earlier speeches is John G. Winant, "The Social Security Act," *Vital Speeches of the Day*, 4 May 1936, 488–491. Bellush, 114–120, especially discusses Winant's role as

Social Security publicist; see also John G. Winant, "An Approach to Social Security," *The Atlantic Monthly* 158 (July 1936): 69–76; and John G. Winant, "Labor and Economic Security," *The Annals of the American Academy of Political and Social Science* 184 (March 1936): 99–106.

18. On the 1936 delegation, see letter from Frances Perkins to the Secretary of State, 1 May 1936, USDOL Files, Record Group 174, Box 74.; here Rieve's first name is given as Emile, *The New York Times* called him Emil.

19. Folsom would go on to advocate Social Security expansion in the 1950s as head of Dwight Eisenhower's Department of Health Education and Welfare. On Folsom, see Joseph Hankin, "Marion Folsom," in *Dictionary of American Biography, Supplement Ten*, 249–251; on Rieve, *Who Was Who 1974–76*, 344; and on Miller, ibid., 284.

20. Letter from Perkins to Winant, 1 May 1936, USDOL Files, Record Group 174, Box 74.

21. W. Ellison Chalmers, "Results of International Labor Conference, June 1936," *Monthly Labor Review* 43 (August 1936): 316–327.

22. Lewis L. Lorwin, *The World Textile Conference* (New York: National Peace Conference, 1937), 39.

23. Lorwin, *World Textile Conference*, 24–27; on British views, see *The New York Times*, 6 April 1937, 42.

24. Lorwin, *World Textile Conference*, 26; reflecting the concern with Japan, see International Labour Office, *The World Textile Industry: Economic and Social Problems* (Geneva: ILO, 1937), 1: 277–333.

25. Lorwin, *World Textile Conference*, 32–33; for an "official" ILO view on the conference, see E. J. Phelan, "The International Tripartite Textile Conference," *American Labor Legislation Review* 27 (June 1937): 87–89.

26. Lorwin, *World Textile Conference*, 28. All reports of the conference emphasized the concern with Japan's unfair advantages, from low wages to alleged imprisonment of women textile workers; see *Newsweek*, 10 April 1937, 8; and *The New York Times*, 14 April 1937, 17.

27. As in 1919, when FDR helped Butler hold the first ILO conference with Department of Navy funds, the correspondence shows the administration prepared to fund the conference in 1937 without congressional appropriations; see memo from Saunders to the Secretary, "Textile Conference of ILO," 15 January 1937, USDOL Files, Record Group 174, Box 46.

28. Knepper, 135, discusses conference planning; finally congressional support was sought, along with borrowed staff and other support from organizations such as the Social Security Board. See letter from Frances Perkins to Arthur Altmeyer, 20 March 1937, USDOL Files, Record Group 174, Box 46.

29. On planning the conference, see memo from Taylor to Perkins, no date [No first name for Taylor is given. In a memo from Richardson Saunders to Perkins, Taylor is identified as a textile engineer in the Textile Division of the Conciliation Service of the Department of Labor.]; W. Ellison Chalmers to Isador

Lubin, 17 August 1936; and letter from Perkins to John N. Garner, vice president, 29 January 1937, USDOL Files, Record Group 174, Box 46.

30. In addition to Burgy, Danhof, Marley, and Wood, see Edmund P. Learned, "The Cotton Textile Situation," *Harvard Business Review* 14 (autumn 1935): 29–44.

31. For the classic study of lobbying and trade policy, see E. E. Schattschneider, *Politics, Pressure and the Tariff* (Hamden, Conn.: Archon Books, 1935); for a discussion of the traditional southern position, see Joanne Reitano, *The Tariff Question in the Gilded Age: The Great Debate of 1888* (University Park: Pennsylvania State University Press, 1994), 95–98.

32. On the coming of the conference, see "International Labor Relations," *Monthly Labor Review* 44 (January 1937): 72–73; "The United States and World Organization during 1936," *International Conciliation* 331 (June 1937): 605–606; and "International Labor Relations," *Monthly Labor Review* 44 (April 1937): 887–889.

33. On cotton exports, see Lorwin, "World Textile."

34. Fox of the Tariff Commission was an expert on the textile industry, as was Edminster of the Trade Agreements Division of the Department of State; on Edminster's position regarding trade policy, see Alfred Eckes, Jr., *Opening America's Market, U.S. Foreign Trade Policy Since 1776* (Chapel Hill: University of North Carolina Press, 1995), 227–232. A memo from Isador Lubin to Frances Perkins, 10 April 1937, in USDOL Files, Record Group 174, Box 46, has an explanation of why government delegates were selected.

35. For Lubin's views of world trade, see *Our Status in World Trade* (New York: Foreign Policy Association, 1954). Hinrichs had academic training and sympathy for organized labor; see his *United Mine Workers of America* (New York: Columbia University Studies in History, Economics, and Public Law, 1923). Likewise Chalmers; see his unpublished study "Collective Bargaining in the Automobile Industry," Harvard Committee on Research in the Social Sciences, 1935.

36. For Anderson's role, see Mary Anderson and Mary N. Winslow, *Women at Work: The Autobiography of Mary Anderson as told to Mary N. Winslow* (Minneapolis: University of Minnesota Press, 1951); for Lenroot's ideas on child labor, see the various reports of the Children's Bureau and especially the *Report of the White House Conference on Children in a Democracy* (Washington, D.C.: Government Printing Office, 1939).

37. Thomas Emerson, *Young Lawyer for the New Deal* (Savage, Md.: Rowman and Littlefield, 1991).

38. Joseph L. Morrison, *Governor O. Max Gardner: A Power in North Carolina and New Deal Washington* (Chapel Hill: University of North Carolina Press, 1971).

39. See Robert R. West, "Why Most Other Employers Opposed the Textile Convention," *The American Labor Legislation Review* 27 (September 1937): 114–115. On West's mills, see Robert S. Smith, *Mill on the Dan* (Durham, N.C.:

Duke University Press, 1960); Banks headed Grantville Mills, and Roberts headed Adelaide Mills in Anniston.

40. One of the delegates from Massachusetts, Robert Amory, who had attended Harvard and MIT, headed the Nashua Manufacturing Company in New Hampshire, Winant's home state; see *Who Was Who 1969–1973*, 13.

41. Following the ILO tripartite structure, there was one delegate each from government (Winant), labor (Emile Rieve), and employers (Governor Gardner), but each of the three could have many advisers. The employer advisers were West, Banks, and Roberts, plus six other southerners and fourteen northerners other than Massachusetts delegate Robert Amory. For identification of delegates, see letter from Frances Perkins to Harold Butler, ILO Director General, 5 April 1937, in USDOL Files, Record Group 174, Box 46.

42. Ibid. On union status in southern industry, see Wood, 59–92; Hall, "Cotton Mill People." On the link between labor's weakness and the textile conference, see *Newsweek* 10 April 1937, 5–8.

43. On Riviere at Amoskeag, see Hareven, *Family Time*, 319–349.

44. Lewis Lorwin, writing a summary of the conference for the National Peace Conference, noted the twentieth anniversary of American entry into World War I; see Lewis L. Lorwin, *The World Textile Conference* (New York: National Peace Conference, 1937), 47. The National Peace Conference was headed by Wilsonians such as James Shotwell and John Sayre, and especially would note the significance of the textile conference's start date.

45. See the program of the conference described in "Tripartite Technical Conference of the Textile Industry," *Daily Bulletin*, 13 April 1937, in USDOL Files, Record Group 174, Box 46.

46. *The New York Times*, 7 April 1937, 7.

47. *The New York Times*, 8 April 1937, 14.

48. West, 114–115.

49. Memo from Frances Perkins to Isador Lubin, 8 April 1937, and response from Lubin to Perkins, 10 April 1937, USDOL Files, Record Group 174, Box 46. Underlining is in original.

50. Lorwin, *The World Textile Conference*, 34–35.

51. On Winant's views, see *The New York Times*, 4 April 1937, 34; also see West, 115.

52. On Perkins's and AFL President William Green's assessment, see *The New York Times*, 18 April 1937, 6.

53. Norlin, 269–270.

54. John B. Andrews, "International Textile Conference," *The American Labor Legislation Review* 27 (March 1937): 4.

55. Phelan, "International Tripartite Textile Conference," 89.

56. Quoted in Knepper, 147–148; speech given 30 April 1937. For other assessments of the textile conference, see Tipton, 65; and Butler, *The International Labour Organization*, 36.

57. Butler officially left to head Nuffield College at Oxford. Later he wrote that he resigned rather than make an undesirable appointment to the ILO staff; see Harold Butler, *The Lost Peace: A Personal Impression* (New York: Harcourt Brace and Company, 1942), 55. Knepper, 154, revealed that the reason for Butler's resignation was the French government's pressure for appointment of an American.

58. On changes at the ILO in 1937–39, see Bellush, 133–140; Knepper, 110–153; and Tipton, 65.

59. Bruno Lasker, "A Cornerstone for World Reconstruction," *Survey Graphic*, October 1941, 522–536.

60. On Winant's role in moving the ILO to Canada, see Bellush, 141–154. On bipartisan foreign policy, see, for example, Arnold A. Offner, *The Origins of the Second World War* (New York: Holt Rinehart and Winston, 1975), 179–181, which describes the simultaneous appointment of Frank Knox and Henry Stimson. With these appointments, Winant's special relationship with Frank Knox resumed; the two New Hampshire Bull Moosers, who had fought each other from 1924 through 1936, now returned to being allies, as symbols of the bipartisan war effort.

61. Radio address over CBS, 4 June 1939, quoted in Knepper, 169.

62. For a discussion of the fears of the wartime leadership of repeating Wilson's problems, see Eckes, 86–88 and 140–167.

63. For an assessment of the charges that Wilson had been hopelessly unwilling to conduct a bipartisan foreign policy in 1919, see Cooper, *Warrior and the Priest*, 338–345.

64. Walter Lippmann, *Public Opinion* (New York: Macmillan, 1922), 214–216, had introduced a particularly critical view of Wilson's failure at an early date; as a former member of the inquiry, his criticisms were especially powerful.

65. On Lend-Lease, see especially U.S. Department of State, *Foreign Relations of the United States, Diplomatic Papers 1942 — General: The British Commonwealth and The Far East* (Washington, D.C.: U.S. Government Printing Office, 1960), 1: 525–537.

66. Ibid., 169–171; also see 89–116 on the United Nations Relief and Rehabilitation Administration (UNRRA).

67. Ibid., 177, memo from Morgenthau to FDR.

68. Warren I. Cohen, *America in the Age of Soviet Power, 1945–1991*, vol. 4 of *The Cambridge History of American Foreign Relations*, ed. Warren I. Cohen (New York: Cambridge University Press, 1993), 3–7, discusses Hull and Morgenthau.

69. U.S. Congress, *Congressional Record*, 71st Cong., 2nd Sess., (Washington, D.C.: U.S. Government Printing Office, 1930), vol. 72, part 8, May 5, 1930, 8327–8330; ominously for late-twentieth-century tariff policy unity, Matt Woll, AFL vice president and head of the ad hoc American Wage Earners' Protective Conference, on 28 May 1930 submitted a pro-tariff petition, pages 9703–9704.

70. James T. Shotwell, "The N.R.A. and the Tariff," *New York Herald Tribune [Magazine]*, 17 September 1933, 4 and 10; for similar views on the compatibility of trade and labor standard protection, see Leifur Magnusson, "International Labor Action," in Miller, *What the International Labor Organization Means*, 34–36.

71. Letter from Thomas Watson to President Roosevelt, 13 November 1936, and accompanying enclosure, in *Franklin D. Roosevelt and Foreign Affairs, September 1935–January 1937*, ed. Edgar B. Nixon (Cambridge, Mass.: Harvard University Press, 1969), 3: 487–489.

72. Shotwell, "N.R.A. and the Tariff," 4 and 10.

73. On planning these conferences, see U.S. Department of State, *Foreign Relations of the United States: Diplomatic Papers 1944 — General: Economic and Social Matters* (Washington, D.C.: U.S. Government Printing Office, 1967), 2: 106–135, 1007–1025. There were four such conferences during the war, including two specialized conferences in 1943, the Hot Springs Conference on Food and Agriculture and the Relief and Rehabilitation Conference at Atlantic City. Compared to these, the 1944 conferences at Philadelphia and Bretton Woods addressed general postwar economic and social relations.

74. *Business Week*, 29 April 1944, 24–26, reported, "Signalizing the importance which Washington attaches to ILO's potentialities as an international instrument for securing broad peace aims was President Roosevelt's communication."

75. George Martin, *Madam Secretary: Frances Perkins* (Boston: Houghton Mifflin, 1976), 429.

76. On Thomas, see William Mulder, "Elbert Thomas," in *Dictionary of American Biography, Supplement Five, 1951–55*, 681–682.

77. For a complete list, see *Press Release, April 15, 1944*, Franklin D. Roosevelt Office Files Box 499, Franklin D. Roosevelt Library, Hyde Park, New York.

78. Martha H. Swain, "Arthur Altmeyer," in *Dictionary of American Biography: Supplement Nine 1971–1975*, 27–29.

79. Memo from Frances Perkins to FDR, 6 March 1944, Franklin D. Roosevelt Office Files 499, DOL Office of the Secretary, FDR Library.

80. Ibid., emphasis in original.

81. Letter from Philip Murray to FDR, 4 April 1944, Franklin D. Roosevelt Office Files 499, FDR Library.

82. "Speech 8 May 1944," Francis J. Haas Papers, Collection 9, Box 2, Folder "Speeches. Grand Rapids," Archives, Catholic University of America, Washington, D.C.

83. *Business Week*, 22 April 1944, 110.

84. *Business Week*, 27 April 1944, 26.

85. "What is the ILO?" *Fortune*, September 1944, 163–164; see also "ILO Fireworks," *Newsweek*, 1 May 1944, 62.

86. "What is the ILO?" *Fortune*, September 1944, 160.

87. On efforts to get the Russians to attend, see, for example, the Secretary of State to the Ambassador in the United Kingdom, 13 November 1943, in U.S. Department of State, *Foreign Relations of the United States: Diplomatic Papers 1944—General: Economic and Social Matters* (Washington, D.C.: Government Printing Office, 1967), 2: 1008–1010.

88. Carol Riegelman, "Labor's Bridgehead: The I.L.O." *Political Science Quarterly* 60 (June 1945): 211–212.

89. See Frieda S. Miller, "A Declaration of Interdependence," *Survey Graphic* 33 (July 1944): 326–327; Miller was special assistant to John Winant and later head of the U.S. Women's Bureau. See also "Twenty-Sixth International Labor Conference," *The Department of State Bulletin* 10 (June 3, 1944): 514–521.

90. Otis E. Mulliken, "The Twenty-Sixth International Labor Conference," *The Department of State Bulletin* 11 (September 3, 1944): 241.

91. For the text of the Declaration of Philadelphia, see U.S. Department of State, *Multilateral: 1946–1949*, vol. 4 of *Treaties and Other International Agreements of the United States of America: 1776–1949*, comp. Charles I. Bevans (Washington, D.C.: U.S. Government Printing Office, 1970), 221–225. It is the "annex" to the constitution of the ILO.

92. *Business Week*, 20 May 1944, 120.

93. Keith Hutchison, "Realism at the I.L.O." *The Nation*, 6 May 1944, 529.

94. Walter Nash, "The International Labor Conference," *Vital Speeches* 10 (June 15, 1944): 543. Nash was deputy prime minister of New Zealand; this statement was taken from a speech given over CBS Radio on 13 May 1944.

95. *The Nation*, 20 May 1944, 584.

96. "ILO Philadelphia Charter May Become a Classic," *The Christian Century*, 24 May 1944, 637.

97. "The ILO Meets," *Commonweal*, 28 April 1944, 27.

98. See John Winant, "International Labor Organization and Future Social Policy," and Alvin Hansen, "Economic Organization for Peace," both in *Beyond Victory*, ed. Ruth Nanda Anshen (New York: Harcourt Brace and Company, 1943), see especially 105–106. Hansen, a leading Harvard economist and promoter of Keynesian theory, linked John R. Commons (his teacher) and late-twentieth-century economics, teaching three Nobel Prize winners: John Kenneth Galbraith, James Tobin, and Robert Solow; he had also worked with Winant on Social Security.

99. "Alvin Hansen," *Current Biography: Who's News and Why 1945*, Anna Rothe, ed. (New York: H. W. Wilson Co., 1945), 264–267.

100. Carter Goodrich, "International Labor Conference of 1944," in *The Monthly Labor Review* 58 (March 1944): 495. More typical was linkage of the ILO to other social policies, such as United Nations food and relief policy; see, for example, John Winant's article, "An International Organization That Works," *The Saturday Evening Post*, 15 April 1944, 89.

101. There is an extensive literature on distinct policy communities. See, for example, John W. Kingdon, *Agendas, Alternatives and Public Policies* (Boston: Little Brown 1984), 123, where he discusses "policy communities"; Gabriel Almond, *The American People and Foreign Policy* (New York: Praeger, 1965), for his discussion of attentive publics; and Hugh Heclo, "Issue Networks and the Executive Establishment," in *The New American Political System*, ed. Anthony King (Washington, D.C.: American Enterprise Institute, 1978), 87–124.

102. Most contemporary comments on Bretton Woods seem to have ignored the ILO and labor policy. See, for example, Henry Morgenthau, Jr., "Bretton Woods and International Cooperation," *Foreign Affairs* 23 (1945): 182–194; and Henry Simons, "The U.S. Holds the Cards," *Fortune*, September 1944, 157–200.

103. Charles Rumford Walker, "Winant of New Hampshire," in *This America*, ed. John D. Kern and Irwin Griggs (New York: Macmillan, 1943), 495.

104. Examples of the dominant interpretation of the war at mid-century were built upon the findings of Ulrich B. Phillips, "The Economic Cost of Slaveholding in the Cotton Belt," *Political Science Quarterly* 20 (June 1905): 257–275; and later Charles W. Ramsdell, "The Natural Limits of Slavery Expansion," *Mississippi Valley Historical Review* 16 (September 1929): 151–171, who argued that slavery had peaked before the war and was economically inferior to the northern free labor system that destroyed it; revisionist historians of the 1930s and 1940s especially criticized the abolition movement and focused on the war as one fought to promote the northern economic triumph. For a review of these interpretations, and what followed, see Merton L. Dillon, "The Abolitionists: A Decade of Historiography, 1959–1969," *Journal of Southern History* 35 (November 1969): 469–481; the most extreme version of the revisionist interpretation came with Eugene Genovese, *The Political Economy of Slavery* (New York: Pantheon, 1965).

105. The most moving of the many reverential tributes to Winant on his death came from Ethel Johnson, his former assistant in Concord and at the ILO; see "The Mr. Winant I Knew," 24–41. See also "John Gilbert Winant," *Recreation* 41 (December 1947): 412–413 (Winant had been an official of the National Recreation Association); "Agonized Man," *Time*, 10 November 1947, 28; and especially Louis Fischer, "The Essence of Gandhiism," *Saturday Review of Literature*, 6 December 1947, 21–22, which concluded, "I cannot help thinking he was . . . a casualty of the peace we have failed to make." In "The Black Face of Death," *The Christian Century*, 19 November 1947, 1390–1391, the conclusion was, "The high hopes he had nurtured, and held forth as promises . . . turned to ashes. . . . [T]here seemed nothing he could do to avert a catastrophe he knew would be beyond all telling. He was baffled, defeated, depressed." See also LaRue Brown, "John G. Winant," *The Nation*, 15 November 1947, 521–522; and Anne Goodman, "Postscript," *The New Republic*, 8 December 1947, 28, which re-

viewed both Winant's recent death and his posthumous book, *Letter from Grosvener Square* (Boston: Houghton Mifflin, 1947), which focused on his concern about the atomic bomb.

FIVE. LEADERSHIP CHANGE

1. See Chambers, 77–78, who is especially good at capturing the frustration with ERA supporters of the leaders of the fight for protective legislation.

2. On the concept of a "women's network," see Susan Ware, *Holding Their Own: American Women in the 1930's* (Boston: Twayne Publishers, 1982), 87–115.

3. On financial problems, see letter from John Winant, league president, to Evans Clark, director of the Twentieth-Century Fund, 14 March 1935, Consumers' League Papers, Container B25 Office Files 1897–1969, Library of Congress, Washington, D.C.; also see Storrs, 23.

4. Lucy R. Mason, *Standards for Workers in Southern Industry* (New York: National Consumers' League, 1931).

5. John A. Salmond, *Miss Lucy of the CIO: The Life and Times of Lucy Randolph Mason, 1882–1959* (Athens: University of Georgia Press, 1988), 49–74; see also her account, Lucy R. Mason, *To Win These Rights: A Personal Story of the CIO in the South* (New York: Harper, 1952).

6. Address Delivered before the Annual Luncheon of the National Consumers' League . . . by Governor John Winant, December 13, 1933, in John Winant Papers, Box 113, National Consumers' League, Franklin D. Roosevelt Library, Hyde Park, New York.

7. Letter from Rosilla Hornblower to Winant, 15 December 1933, Winant Papers, FDR Library.

8. Robert M. Watt, speech text, "At a dinner given in his honor by the Consumers League and the Citizen Fact Finding Committee," chaired by E. A. Filene, in Ethel M. Johnson Papers, Box 1, Folder 17, Schlesinger Library, Radcliffe College, Cambridge, Massachusetts.

9. The best example of the new movement comes from Helen Sorenson, 221, who in her book on the consumer movement ignores the Consumers' League, except in the appendix, which notes that the Miami league fought fraud in adult education programs; for a review of consumerism in the era, see Richard Wightman Fox, "Epitaph for Middletown," in *The Culture of Consumption: Critical Essays in American History, 1880–1890*, ed. Richard Wightman Fox and T. J. Jackson Lears (New York: Pantheon Books, 1983), 103–141, which finds the critical decades for the consumer movement were the 1920s and 1930s.

10. The vote was on January 26, 1934; see Erma Angevin, *History of the Consumers' League* (Washington, D.C.: mimeo, 1979), 43, in the Records of the National Consumers' League, Box J 10, Library of Congress.

11. Angevin, 47.

12. Jean Bethke Elhstain, *Democracy on Trial* (New York: Basic Books, 1995), 13–14, discusses the new consumerism placing civic rights over responsibilities.

13. Studies of interest groups have found a trend toward moving headquarters to Washington and replacing local affiliates with direct mail contact; see for example, Berry, 57–76. On the stagnation of Consumers' League affiliates and discussions of headquarters moves, see Angevin, 49.

14. Jonathan J. Bean, *Beyond the Broker State: Federal Policies Toward Small Business 1936–1991* (Chapel Hill: University of North Carolina Press, 1996), 6–7, has a good discussion of studies of the origins of the broker state.

15. See Minutes of the ILO Committee, 26 September 1935, in John Winant Papers, National ILO Committee, Box 169, FDR Library.

16. Ibid., and Proposed Program of Work for the National ILO Committee 1935–36, also in Winant Papers, Box 169, FDR Library.

17. Skocpol, *Protecting Soldiers and Mothers*, 179–183, is critical of Andrews's and the AALL's willingness to engage in popular political organizing; Robert L. Rothstein, "Consensual Knowledge and International Collaboration: Some Lessons from the Commodity Negotiations," *International Organizations* 38 (autumn 1984): 736, finds experts typically have much knowledge but little political influence; also see Roger Hilsman, *To Move a Nation* (New York: Delta Books, 1967).

18. Minutes of the ILO Committee, 3, Winant Papers, Box 169, FDR Library.

19. Ibid., 4.

20. Spencer Miller, Jr., ed., *What the International Labor Organization Means to America* (New York: Columbia University Press, 1936).

21. John G. Winant, "Forward," in Miller, *What the ILO Means*, xii.

22. William Lonsdale Tayler, *Federal States and Labor Treaties* (New York: Apollo Press, 1935).

23. Letter from Tayler to Winant, 15 January 1936, Winant Papers, Box 169, FDR Library.

24. On Lewis, especially his religious background, see Melvin Dubofsky, *John L. Lewis: A Biography* (New York: Quadrangle, 1977), 6, which says Lewis avoided religious issues, an interpretation somewhat contradicted by his relationship to Miller; on Lewis at the ILO, see page 146. Also see Robert H. Zieger, *John L. Lewis: Labor Leader* (Boston: Twayne, 1988), who shares the interpretation of Dubofsky.

25. John L. Lewis, "Significance of American Membership in the I.L.O. to Labor," in Miller, *What the ILO Means*, 71.

26. Ibid., 74–75.

27. Ibid., 80.

28. Ibid., 77.

29. William Maddox, "Labor's Stake in American Foreign Relations," *Political Science Quarterly* 50 (September 1935): 418, written when the U.S. joined

the ILO; for his more general views on labor and foreign policy in a comparative perspective, see *Foreign Relations in British Labour Politics* (Cambridge, Mass.: Harvard University Press, 1934).

30. On labor divisions of the late 1930s, see Knepper, 157–158; Galenson, *The CIO Challenge*, 635–639; Lorwin, 180–181; and Tipton, 59–64.

31. Robert J. Watt, "An American Worker's Impression of the ILO in Action," *The American Labor Legislation Review* 27 (September 1937): 112; on Watt's role in domestic and international defense of the ILO, see Tipton, 59.

32. Benjamin L. Masse, "ILO and the Bishops," *America*, 19 December 1964, 797–799; for a criticism of the growing role of the bishops in economic policy, see Michael Warner, *Changing Witness: Catholic Bishops and Public Policy, 1917–1994* (Grand Rapids, Mich.: William B. Eerdmans, 1995), 79–116.

33. Camp, *Papal Ideology*, 99–100, points out that Pius XI was the first modern pope to introduce the phrase "social justice" in his writings; also see Pawlikowski. For American popularization of the concept of social justice, see Raymond A. McGowan, *Toward Social Justice* (New York: Paulist Press, 1933).

34. Edward R. Kantowicz, "Cardinal Mundelein of Chicago and the Shaping of Twentieth-Century American Catholicism," *Journal of American History* 68 (June 1981): 67; see especially Mundelein's reversal of position related to labor in the archdiocesan newspaper, *The New World*, 7 January 1938, 1.

35. Richard Ely, "Introduction," Ryan, *Living Wage*, v–vii.

36. See, for example, National Catholic Welfare Conference, *Aids to Catholic Action* (Washington, D.C.: NCWC, 1933), 84.

37. For McGowan's views, see McGowan, *Toward Social Justice*, 73–96; on Higgins's early life, see George G. Higgins and William Bole, *Organized Labor and the Church* (New York: Paulist Press, 1993), 15–40; on McGowan, see George G. Higgins, "Trade Unions, Catholic Teaching and the New World Order," in *Catholic Social Thought and the New World Order*, ed. Oliver F. Williams and John W. Houck (Notre Dame, Ind.: University of Notre Dame Press, 1993), 351–356.

38. On Al Smith and Coughlin, see Kantowicz, 66–67. On fascism, see syllabus for course by Catholic University, Washington, D.C., Catholic Backgrounds and Current Social Thought, taught in second semester, 1937, at St. John's University, Collegeville, Minnesota, 10, which praised the new Portuguese authoritarian regime of Antonio Salazar, though Catholic "liberals" always seemed more interested in the NRA and similar corporatist solutions than did others. See Isador Lubin, "Roundtable Meeting of Committee on Social and Economic Problems," in *Proceedings of the Nineteenth Session of the National Conference of Catholic Charities* (New York: NCCC, 1933), 474, for early interest in the NRA.

39. Kantowicz, 55–59; and Higgins and Bole, 19–24.

40. Saint Mary of the Lake Seminary, Mundelein, Illinois, Summer School of Social Action for Priests, July 18–August 12, 1938—Third Week: Legis-

lation, Partial Means of Economic Morality, mimeo marked "For Private Use," 376, discussed labor standards.

41. Our Sunday Visitor, *The Modern Social and Economic Order* (Huntington, Ind.: Our Sunday Visitor Press, 1939); NCWC, *Aids to Catholic Action.* On college texts, see Wilhelm Schwer, *Catholic Social Theory* (St. Louis: B. Herder Book Co., 1940), 52–57; and Francis J. Haas, *Man and Society* (New York: The Century Co., 1930). For examples of the political ideas of John Noll, editor of *Our Sunday Visitor,* see the collection of editorials in Robert P. Lockwood, ed., *Seventy Years of Our Sunday Visitor: 1912–1982* (Huntington, Ind.: Our Sunday Visitor, 1982), especially 35 and 133.

42. See Mediation Files—9, Havana International Labor Conference Envelope, and Folder Speeches—Grand Rapids, Michigan, Collection 9, Box 2, in [Francis] Joseph Haas Papers, Catholic University Archives, Washington, D.C.; on Haas, see Thomas E. Blantz, *A Priest in Public Service* (Notre Dame, Ind.: University of Notre Dame Press, 1982), 47–65 and 259–265.

43. Letter from Le Roy to McGowan, 22 January 1938, in National Catholic Welfare Conference, Social Action Department (1919–1967), Organization Files A–Z, ILO File, Catholic University Archives, Washington, D.C.

44. See, for example, letter from Henry Van Dusen, secretary, advisory council, Oxford Conference, to Winant, 28 April 1936, in Winant Papers, Churches—Conferences with Religious Leaders, Box 155, FDR Library.

45. Letter from James Myers to Winant, 6 April 1936, Winant Papers, Box 155, FDR Library; also see Myers's interesting discussion of religion and labor in James Myers and Henry W. Laidler, *What Do You Know about Labor?* (New York: J. Day Co., 1956), 247–260; on Myers's life, see *Who Was Who in America, 1961–1968,* 4: 1675.

46. Miller wrote *The Church and Industry* (New York: Longmans, Green and Co., 1930) and edited *The Workers' Education Quarterly.* For his work related to the ILO, see Miller, *What the International Labor Organization Means;* v–xiii explains the cooperation of Miller and Winant. On Miller's life, see *Who's Who in America, 1934–1935,* 18: 1675.

47. On the National Peace Conference role, see Lorwin, *The World Textile Conference.* Winant also worked with Jewish leaders; see, for example, Sidney Goldstein, chair social justice commission, Central Conference of American Rabbis, letter from Goldstein to Winant, 25 March 1936, Winant Papers, Box 155, FDR Library.

48. See Consumers' League Ballot, 1936, Winant Papers, National Consumers' League 1936, Box 161, FDR Library.

49. Storrs shows the religious affiliation of the Consumers' League leadership on 264–270.

50. See records of the Consumers' League of Massachusetts, File 11, Schlesinger Library, Radcliffe College, Cambridge, Massachusetts.

51. Letter from Mrs. Warwick Hobart to Margaret Wiesman, 20 February 1942, in National Consumers' League Papers, Schlesinger Library, Radcliffe College.

52. Martin Marty, *Righteous Empire* (New York: Dial Press, 1970), 177–179, said of the problem of mass acceptance of the appeals of the liberal clergy, there were two parties in American Protestantism, a conservative majority mostly composed of the laity and a liberal minority, mostly clergy.

53. See especially Reinhold Niebuhr, *Moral Man and Immoral Society* (New York: Scribner's, 1932), 200, which began the new self-critical stage in orthodox Protestantism; Niebuhr is also critical of the failure of American labor to form its own party.

54. H. Richard Niebuhr, *The Kingdom of God in America* (Hamden, Conn.: Shoe String Press, 1956), xi.

55. On Catholic-Protestant tension, see Chambers, 40–44, on child labor issues; and Martin Marty, "The Twentieth Century: Protestants and Others," in *Religion and American Politics*, ed. Mark A. Noll (New York: Oxford University Press, 1990), 330–331.

56. His works included Dennison et al., *Restriction of Output among Unorganized Workers* (New York: Viking Press, 1931); *Profit Sharing and Stock Ownership* (New York: Harper, 1926); and *Toward Full Employment* (New York: McGraw Hill, 1938); and with John Kenneth Galbraith, *Modern Competition and Business Policy* (New York: Oxford University Press, 1938).

57. *Who Was Who, 1951–60*, 3: 222.

58. *Who Was Who, 1951–60*, 3: 372.

59. Henry I. Harriman, "An American Employer's View of ILO Conferences," *The American Labor Legislation Review* 27 (1937): 110–111.

60. *Who Was Who, 1977–1981*, 7: 200.

61. *Who Was Who, 1951–1960*, 3: 517; see his *The New Leadership in Industry* (New York: E. P. Dutton and Co., 1926) and *Human Leadership in Industry* (New York: Harper and Brothers, 1945).

62. Thomas G. Spates, "Significance of American Membership in the ILO to Employers," in Miller, *What the ILO Means*, 49–50.

63. Leland Robinson, "Significance of American Membership in the ILO to American Business," in Miller, *What the ILO Means*, 56–67.

64. Joseph H. Willets, "Possibilities of United States Collaboration with the International Labor Organization," Cheyney, ed., *Annals of the American Academy of Political and Social Science* 166 (March 1933): 168.

65. Tipton, 62.

66. Galenson, *International Labor Organization*, 5–6.

67. Skocpol, *Protecting Soldiers and Mothers*, 203–204, describes a related trend among those social scientists involved with the American Association for Labor Legislation; also see Robert L. Church, "Economists as Experts: The Rise of an Aca-

demic Profession in the United States, 1870–1920," in *The University in Society*, ed. Lawrence Stone (Princeton, N.J.: Princeton University Press, 1975), 2: 571–609.

68. Warren Samuels, "Institutional Economics," in *The New Palgrave: A Dictionary of Economics*, ed. John Eatwell, et al. (London: Macmillan, 1987), 2: 864–865; see also Joseph Dorfman, "The Role of the German Historical School in American Economic Thought," *American Economic Review: Papers and Proceedings of the 67th Annual Meeting* 45 (May 1955): 17–28.

69. Allan G. Gruchy, "The Institutional School," in *International Encyclopedia of the Social Sciences*, ed. David I. Silla (New York: Macmillan, 1968), 4: 464.

70. George Stigler, "The Politics of Political Economists," *The Quarterly Journal of Economics* 73 (November 1959): 525 and 528.

71. See especially Charles A. Beard, *A Foreign Policy for America* (New York: A. A. Knopf, 1940), 152.

72. Charles A. Beard, *American Foreign Policy in the Making: 1932–1940: A Study of Responsibilities* (New Haven, Conn.: Yale University Press, 1946), 160.

73. Thomas Bailey, *Woodrow Wilson and the Lost Peace* (New York: Macmillan Company, 1944), 307–325, which while written to show how to avoid the mistakes of 1919 in 1945, and while not fully critical of Wilson's achievements, still served to teach of the problems of Wilson in a way that called into question the Versailles process and its products, such as the ILO.

74. On the Wilsonians and the war, see Robert A. Divine, *Second Chance: The Triumph of Internationalism in America during World War II* (New York: Atheneum, 1967), 167–178; also see his comments on Charles Beard's interpretation of Wilson. For critical accounts of the impact of World War II on postwar foreign policy ideas, see Richard J. Barnet, *Intervention and Revolution: The United States in the Third World* (New York: World Publishing Co., 1968), 77–93; and on Wilson, see Barnet's *Roots of War* (Baltimore: Penguin Books, 1973), 44–47.

75. George F. Kennan, *American Diplomacy, 1900–1950* (Chicago: University of Chicago Press, 1951); Hans J. Morgenthau, *In Defense of the National Interest: A Critical Examination of American Foreign Policy* (New York: Alfred A. Knopf, 1951); and Robert E. Osgood, *Ideals and Self-Interest in America's Foreign Relations: The Great Transformation in the Twentieth Century* (Chicago: University of Chicago Press, 1953). Kennan later explained that his position regarding Wilson changed; see "Comments on the Paper Entitled 'Kennan versus Wilson,'" in *The Wilson Era: Essays in Honor of Arthur S. Link*, ed. John Milton Cooper, Jr. and Charles E. Neu (Arlington Heights, Ill.: Harlan Davidson, 1991).

76. Morgenthau, 284–286, discusses Lippmann's *Public Opinion*, published in 1922; while Morgenthau perceived the normative evil inherent in international relations policy, he had no confidence particular states could rise above their immediate interests to seek policies in accord even with an obvious good, such as avoiding nuclear war.

77. On Shotwell, see Charles DeBenedetti, "Peace Was His Profession," in *Makers of American Diplomacy: From Benjamin Franklin to Henry Kissinger*, ed.

Frank J. Merli (New York: Scribner, 1974), 385–406; and DeBenedetti, "James T. Shotwell and the Science of International Politics," *Political Science Quarterly* 89 (June 1974).

78. DeBenedetti, "Peace Was His Profession," 399.

79. Morgenthau, 547–553, found the ILO and other "functional" agencies as interesting in their ability to move beyond national rivalries to intrude on domestic policy making; however, he did not generalize from this positive note to seeing it as a model for international policy making.

80. Osgood, 309–332; for a review of the idealism-realism debate, see Daniel M. Smith, "National Interest and American Intervention, 1917: An Historical Appraisal," *Journal of American History* 54 (June 1965): 5–24.

81. Osgood, 332.

82. DeBenedetti, "Peace Was His Profession," 404.

83. Robert W. Cox and Harold K. Jacobson, *The Anatomy of Influence: Decision Making in International Organizations* (New Haven, Conn.: Yale University Press, 1974), vii. Jacobson said of Shotwell, "[His] dream of a world order based on collective security was doomed to failure"; in Jacobson, "James Shotwell," in *Dictionary of American Biography, Supplement Seven, 1961–1965*, 688.

84. On the growth of behaviorism and the controversies it spawned, see Alan Isaak, *Scope and Methods of Political Science*, 4th ed. (Homewood, Ill.: The Dorsey Press, 1985), 33–47; Heinz Eulau, ed., *Behavioralism in Political Science* (New York: Lieber-Atherton, 1973); and James C. Charlesworth, ed., *Contemporary Political Analysis* (New York: The Free Press, 1967).

85. Albert Somit and Joseph Tanenhaus, *The Development of American Political Science: From Burgess to Behaviorism* (Boston: Allyn and Bacon, Inc., 1967), 119.

86. John Vasquez, *The Power of Power Politics* (New Brunswick, N.J.: Rutgers University Press, 1983), 162–170.

87. On the developments in the field of international political economy, see James A. Caporaso, "Global Political Economy," in *Political Science: The State of the Discipline II*, ed. Ada W. Finifter (Washington, D.C.: American Political Science Association, 1993), 451–481.

88. The changes in political science did not reduce the involvement of political scientists in public policy, as is described well in Somit and Tanenhaus, 195–202; however, they title their treatment of continuing involvement in the policy process and politics "extra-scientific responsibilities and activities."

89. On the general growth of bureaucracy in the period, see Henry Jacoby, *The Bureaucratization of the World*, trans. Eveline Kanes (Berkeley: University of California Press, 1973), 191–196; and Donald F. Kettl, "Public Administration: The State of the Field," in Finifter, 407–412.

90. DeBenedetti, "James T. Shotwell," 382; DeBenedetti makes clear in "Peace Was His Profession" that Shotwell was not naive in his faith in the ease of bringing scientific solutions to problems, but Shotwell was committed to the effort.

91. Cecil E. Greek, *The Religious Roots of American Sociology* (New York: Garland Publishing Inc., 1992), 193; and William Ogburn, *Recent Social Trends* (New York: McGraw Hill, 1933). On Ogburn, see also Howard W. Odum, *American Sociology* (New York: Longmans, Green, 1951), 152.

92. Martin, 429.

93. On the WFTU, ICFTU, and the AFL, see Lorwin, *The International Labor Movement*, 233–282; Lorwin was not hostile to the American union leadership. For a critique of the AFL and the ICFTU, see Gary K. Busch, *The Political Role of International Trade Unions* (London: Macmillan Press, 1983), 69–72.

94. For a generally positive biography, see Archie Robinson, *George Meany and His Times* (New York: Simon and Schuster, 1981), 123–139, who is supportive of Meany's anticommunism; more critical is Robert H. Zieger, "George Meany: Labor's Organization Man," in *Labor Leaders in America*, ed. Melvyn Dubofsky and Warren Van Tine (Urbana: University of Illinois Press, 1987), 324–349, who sees Meany becoming more critical of government after 1975. Many labor historians have been extremely critical of Meany; for example, see Melvyn Dubofsky, *Imperial Democracy: The United States Since 1945* (Englewood Cliffs, N.J.: Prentice Hall, 1988), 236, who calls Meany an "enthusiast of American capitalism."

95. Morgenthau, 552.

96. Oddly, Morgenthau, 189–192 and 341–346, perceived the value of the American pluralist model for replacing the Westphalian system; however, he did not appreciate the test being provided at the ILO.

SIX. AN ALTERNATE VISION

1. C. Wright Mills, *The Power Elite* (New York: Oxford University Press, 1956), 25–29.

2. *The New York Times*, 18 January 1961, 1a.

3. G. William Domhoff, *Who Rules America Now?* (Englewood Cliffs, N.J.: Prentice Hall, 1983), 1–16, 82–100, 203–225; and Domhoff's *The Higher Circles* (New York: Random House, 1970), 5–8, 309–355. On the Council on Foreign Relations as an elite breeding ground in foreign policy, see J. Anthony Lukas, "The Council on Foreign Relations—Is It a Club? Seminar? Presidium? Invisible Government?" *The New York Times Magazine*, 21 November 1971.

4. Almond, 130–143.

5. Roger Hilsman, *To Move a Nation* (New York: Delta Books, 1964), 542–544; and Hilsman's *The Politics of Policy Making in Defense and Foreign Affairs* (New York: Harper and Row, 1971), 268–318.

6. Kenneth M. Dolbeare and Murray J. Edelman, *American Politics: Policies, Power and Change*, 2nd ed. (Lexington, Mass.: D. C. Heath, 1973), 472.

7. Truman, 14–44, holds all shared interests are interest groups; on the special role of religious groups in support of peace and economic justice, see William Martin, "With God on Their Side," and Bryant Myers, Alan Whaites, and Bruce Wilkinson, "Faith in Development," *Georgetown Journal of International Affairs*, 1 (winter/spring 2000).

8. Some theorists, such as Berry, 18–24, have a category of citizen groups and farm and labor, distinct from business.

9. For this concept of populist, see Kazin.

10. Lindblom, "The Science of Muddling Through."

11. See Lindblom's *Politics and Markets* for the concept of the privileged position of business, and, more recently, James W. Lamare, *What Rules America?* (St. Paul, Minn.: West, 1988); for an interpretation that business power is exaggerated, see David Vogel, *Fluctuating Fortunes: The Political Power of Business in America* (New York: Basic Books, 1989).

12. See Cox, "ILO Limited Monarchy," 102–107; and Tipton, 62–67.

13. Following the prewar strategy of the foreign policy elite, the relations of the ILO and the UN were handled by the elite and reported by two elite staff in political science and economics. See John H. E. Fried, "Relations between the United Nations and the International Labor Organization," *American Political Science Review* 41 (October 1947): 963–977 [Fried worked for the ILO]; and Carter Goodrich, "The I.L.O.: A Going Concern," *Annals of the American Academy of Political and Social Science* 246 (July 1946): 110–116 [Goodrich, a professor of economics at Columbia, chaired the ILO governing body during World War II].

14. On Morse, see Seeley G. Mudd Manuscript Library, *Labor of Love: Selections from the David A. Morse Papers* (Princeton: Mudd Library, 1995); see also the tribute to Morse by the Council on Foreign Relations, David A. Morse Program, May 18, 1994, in David A. Morse Papers, Box 50, File 6, Seeley G. Mudd Manuscript Library, Princeton, N.J., hereafter cited as Morse Papers, Mudd Library.

15. Faith M. Williams, "Thirty-Second Conference of International Labor Organization," *Monthly Labor Review* 69 (September 1949): 275–276.

16. See Ernest B. Haas, *Beyond the Nation-State: Functionalism and International Organization* (Stanford, Calif.: Stanford University Press, 1964).

17. On this style of leadership, see Eugene Lewis, *Public Entrepreneurship: Toward a Theory of Bureaucratic Power* (Bloomington: Indiana University Press, 1986).

18. Actually, the ILO had long struggled with problems of the third world, often being seen as a special protector of rights of indigenous peoples against colonial powers. Even before Morse, the ILO launched a special effort to define a colonial labor policy; see for example, D. H. Rayner, "ILO Recommends Colonial Policy," *The Christian Century*, 6 November 1946, 1353.

19. On the prewar budget crisis, see Tipton, 63–67.

20. See Cox, "ILO Limited Monarchy," 105–106.

21. On the papal audience for the ILO in 1954, see ibid., 118; and *The New York Times*, 21 November 1954, 18.

22. On Soviet admission to the ILO, see Cox, "ILO Limited Monarchy," 106–107. Also see *The New York Times*, 11 June 1954, 4; 23 June 1954, 7; and 25 June 1954, 20.

23. On the pope's visit and Nobel Prize in 1969, see International Labour Office, *Mission of Justice and Peace* (Geneva: ILO, 1969); and *The New York Times*, 11 June 1969, 1; 21 October 1969, 1.

24. On the U.S. hostility even to the concept of freedom of association, see James A. Gross, "A Human Rights Perspective on United States Labor Relations Law: A Violation of the Right of Freedom of Association," *Employment Rights and Employment Policy Journal* 3 (1999): 93–101, which focuses on the employer effort under the Taft-Hartley Act of 1948 and subsequent court challenges of the 1950s, such as *NLRB v. Babcock and Wilcox* (1956).

25. Elizabeth A. Fones-Wolf, *Selling Free Enterprise: The Business Assault on Labor and Liberalism: 1945–1960* (Urbana: University of Illinois Press, 1994); I maintain the assault was from a liberal free-market perspective.

26. Robert M. Smith, "Using Knowledge Rather Than Goons: Modern Antiunion Agencies, 1956–1985," *Michigan Academician* 28 (1996): 401–418.

27. On McCarthy and labor, see, for example, Richard Fried, *Nightmare in Red: The McCarthy Era in Perspective* (New York: Oxford University Press, 1990), 99–103.

28. See James David Zellerbach, "The ILO and American Business," *The Public Relations Journal* 3 (December 1947): 12–36.

29. Ibid., 12–15.

30. On the National Economic Council, see *The New York Times*, 6 June 1954, 55, which reported it among the leading lobbying organizations in Washington, based upon the amount of money spent on lobbying.

31. "World Government—By the Back Door," *Economic Council Letter*, 1 October 1948, 4.

32. The attack on Morse originally appeared in another right-wing journal; see Blair Taylor, "They Knife Gen. Clay," *Plain Talk*, May 1948, 3.

33. "ILO Rides Again, For More World Government over USA," *Economic Council Letter*, 1 November 1948, 1–4.

34. On that agreement, see "Socialistic ILO," *Fortune*, June 1953, 76.

35. "The Cover," *Business Week*, 11 June 1949, 6.

36. On McCormick, see John Lear, "House of a Hundred Bosses," *Saturday Evening Post*, 28 September 1946, 28–29 and 93; and *Business Week*, 11 June 1949, 6.

37. Charles P. McCormick, "We're Using the Socialist Soapbox," *Nation's Business*, March 1952, 45 and 78.

38. Ibid., 44.

39. See, for example, "Socialistic Blueprint for Security to be Supported by U.S. at ILO," *National Chamber Washington Report*, 13 June 1952, in George Gilmary Higgins Papers, International Labor Organization Series, Catholic University of America Archives, Washington, D.C., hereafter cited as Higgins Papers, CUA.

40. Convention 103, adopted 28 June 1952, Art. 3 and Art. 4.

41. Charles P. McCormick, "ILO—A Body That Might Make America's Laws," *USA: The Magazine of American Affairs*, March 1952, 88.

42. Convention 102, adopted 28 June 1952.

43. See letters from McCormick to Morse, 12 March 1951; Morse's response on 16 March 1951 and 14 April 1951; and McCormick's response on 23 April 1951; in David Morse Papers, Box 57, File 2. See also the report of William McGrath at the end of the 1951 ILO conference, in Morse Papers, Box 57, File 5, Mudd Library.

44. McCormick, "ILO—A Body That Might Make Laws," 87; see also the editorial "Can't 'Public Members' Represent the Public?" *Saturday Evening Post*, 12 July 1952, 10.

45. McCormick, "ILO—A Body That Might Make Laws," 86.

46. McCormick, "We're Using the Socialist Soapbox," 43.

47. Ibid.

48. "Let's Look before We Adopt 'em," *Nation's Business*, June 1953, 98, editorialized especially against the maternity protections that might be imposed by the ILO.

49. Leonard J. Calhoun, *The International Labor Organization and United States Domestic Law* (Washington, D.C.: American Enterprise Association, 1953), 48; the American Enterprise Association later became the American Enterprise Institute. For a much later discussion of the Bricker Amendment, see Louis Henkin, "U.S. Ratification of Human Rights Conventions: The Ghost of Senator Bricker," *The American Journal of International Law* 89 (April 1995): 341–350.

50. J. V. Van Sickle, "The International Labor Office: An Appraisal," *The Southern Economic Journal* 12 (April 1946): 357–364.

51. See Arnold Beichman, "Russia Drives for a World 'Labor Front'," *New Republic*, 23 November 1953, 14.

52. 14 June 1954, 20.

53. "Not Too Proud to Fight," *Business Week*, 16 June 1956, 200. See also *The New York Times*, 11 June 1954, 4; and 13 June 1954, 25. *The Chicago Tribune*, 2 August 1955, 16, attacked the Eisenhower Administration and defended McGrath; see also *Business Week*, 29 December 1956, 70, for the positions of the U.S. Chamber and the NAM, as well as the Commerce and Industry Association.

54. *Cincinnati Enquirer*, 21 February 1946, 2; 23 March 1946, 1; and 24 April 1946, 1.

55. *Cincinnati Enquirer*, 8 March 1947, 1–2.

56. On the company's closure, see *Cincinnati Enquirer*, 11 April 1992, d5; *Cincinnati Post*, 2 November 1991, 6a; and 19 August 1991, 6b. As at Amoskeag,

Williamson in its closing years won tax breaks from local government; see *Cincinnati Enquirer*, 30 March 1990, b5. On the asbestos suit, see Cincinnati *Enquirer*, 9 May 1983, c2; and *Cincinnati Post*, 7 May 1983, 8c.

57. George W. Keith, "William Lynn McGrath," *American Business*, November 1954, 30.

58. *Cincinnati Enquirer*, 31 October 1957, 28; award given on 30 October 1957, the week of "Reformation Sunday."

59. Max Weber, *The Protestant Ethic and the Spirit of Capitalism* (London: G. Allen and Unwin, 1930), first published in Germany in 1904, spawned a century-long debate about the links between forms of Christianity and the ethics conducive to capitalism; whatever the general merits of the argument, the collaboration of McGrath and Peale fit the type described by Weber.

60. *Cincinnati Enquirer*, 31 October 1957, 28.

61. William L. McGrath, "Surprising Case of the ILO," *American Mercury*, March 1960, 111.

62. *Cincinnati Enquirer*, 17 October 1955.

63. On welfare capitalism as an alternative to either the welfare state or laissez-faire, see Jacoby, *Modern Manors.*

64. William L. McGrath, "ILO: Back Door to Socialism," 2.

65. Ibid.

66. Ibid., 3.

67. William L. McGrath, "Problems Existing in the International Labor Organization," *Advanced Management* 18 (February 1953): 9–29.

68. William L. McGrath, "What Should We Do about ILO?" *The Freeman*, 1 June 1953, 627–628.

69. William L. McGrath, "The Strange Case of the International Labor Organization," *Vital Speeches*, 15 November 1955, 81–85, given to the National Machine Tool Builders Association, 25 October 1955.

70. Date stamped "9/1/55," in Higgins Papers, International Labor Organization Series, File "The Communist Issue," CUA Archives.

71. "Withdrawal from ILO to be Recommended by United States Employer Delegate," *Labor Relations Letter*, December 1955, 3, this was published by the U.S. Chamber of Commerce, Department of Manufacturers.

72. Throughout the late 1940s and early 1950s, the U.S. Chamber of Commerce took this approach. For example, at the 25–26 January 1953 board of directors meeting they voted to call for a congressional investigation of the ILO and to drastically cut funding; see Minutes of the Board of Directors 1912–1963, Box 1, Papers of the U.S. Chamber of Commerce, Hagley Museum and Library, Wilmington, Delaware.

73. Statement of William L. McGrath for the Chamber of Commerce of the United States, before House Foreign Affairs Committee, 23 February 1956; mailed to his list March 1956, with cover letter in Jay Lovestone Files, Box 28, File 51, International Affairs Department, George Meany Archive, Silver Springs, Maryland.

74. "Now ILO Rows are up to Them," *Business Week*, 19 May 1956, 170.

75. See memo of David Cole to Anrew [*sic*] Biemiller, head of the AFL-CIO department of legislation, 11 September 1957, in Lovestone Files, Box 28, File 51, Meany Archive.

76. On the response to the Cole report, see "Shaping Policy toward ILO," *Business Week*, 15 September 1956, 176; in response to the bipartisan support for the Cole report, the U.S. Chamber board called for the extreme step of U.S. withdrawal from the ILO, and after Congress took no action on its call for hearings to consider withdrawal, the board resolved at its next meeting, on 15 March 1957, "it is apparent that the Congress will not promptly undertake such investigations." The chamber had been outmaneuvered by Higgins and the AFL-CIO; on chamber resolutions, see Board of Directors Minutes, U.S. Chamber Papers, Hagley Library.

77. On the appointments to the committee, see "Shaping Policy," *Business Week*, 173–176.

78. Once again the American Academy of Political and Social Science came to the ILO's defense, publishing an issue of *The Annals* titled "Current Issues in International Labor Relations" (310, March 1957), under the editorship of John P. Windmuller of Cornell's School of Industrial and Labor Relations; in addition to printing the Johnson Committee's report, it had essays by David Morse and Lewis Lorwin.

79. National Council of Churches of Christ in the USA, *Information Service*, 2 June 1956; see also letter from Elma Greenwood, associate executive director, Department of Church and Economic Life of National Council, to National Catholic Welfare Conference, 25 April 1957, and response from Higgins, 9 May 1957, in Higgins Papers, International Labor Organization Series, CUA Archives.

80. For example, in the early 1950s Henry Sherrill, the presiding bishop of the Episcopal Church, was on the National Advisory Board, as was Ralph Sockman of the Methodist Church and John Wesley Raley, president of Oklahoma Baptist University.

81. Delaney testimony before Senate Judiciary Committee, 9 April 1953, and House Foreign Affairs Committee, 29 July 1953, in Lovestone Files, Box 28, File 50, Meany Archive.

82. Letter from Burke to Congressman Jack Shelley of California, 6 August 1953, in Lovestone Files, Box 28, File 53, Meany Archive.

83. *New York World-Telegram and Sun*, 12 October 1953, quoted in *Current Biography Yearbook* (New York: H. W. Wilson Company, 1955), 422.

84. George P. Delaney, "The ILO—Threat or Opportunity," *Harvard Business Review* 31 (November-December 1953): 120.

85. Press release, 28 April 1954, in Lovestone Files, Box 28, File 50, Meany Archive.

86. See letter from George Delaney to Jay Lovestone, 24 August 1954, in Lovestone Files, Box 26, File 6, Meany Archive.

87. See AFL-CIO Executive Council Resolution, 5 February 1957, in Higgins Papers, International Labor Organization Series, CUA Archives; also letter to Theodore Sorenson, aide to Senator John Kennedy, 3 April 1956, in Lovestone Files, Box 28, File 51, Meany Archive.

88. See the press release from the three departments, Advisory Committee on ILO Established, 23 May 1957, in Higgins Papers, International Labor Organization Series, CUA Archives.

89. Skocpol, *Protecting Soldiers and Mothers*, 525–539.

90. For this interpretation, see "Reds Seek Hold on World Labor," *U.S. News and World Report*, 25 June 1954, 125, on the observations of the British employer delegate, Richard Snedden.

91. "Danger: Pettifoggers at Work," *Life*, 14 May 1956, 48; "Labor Faces New Setback on ILO," *Business Week*, 5 May 1956, 171, also criticized the Bricker forces.

92. "Forced Labor," *Commonweal*, 21 June 1957, 294.

93. "ILO and Forced Labor," *America*, 5 November 1955, 148.

94. *Commonweal*, 8 July 1955, 343–346.

95. "ILO Move against Slave Labor," *America*, 23 June 1956, 296.

96. For a good review of the longer-term conflict of the church with liberalism, see Hanson, 19–58.

97. Earlier examples of church roles in labor standards are described in Worth M. Tippy, "Policy and Program of the Protestant Churches," 125–129, and Raymond A. McGowan, "The Program and Activities of the National Catholic Welfare Council," 130–133, in Ryan and Johnson, *Industrial Relations and the Churches*.

98. Francis J. Haas, *Man and Society* (New York: Appleton-Century Crofts, Inc., 1952), 496–497.

99. See letter of 8 June 1948 from Linna Bresette to Archbishop John Mitty and other correspondence related to San Francisco conference, especially letter from Joseph Musier to Linna Bresette, 24 March 1948, in Papers of National Catholic Welfare Conference, Social Action Department, Records of the Field Secretary, ILO Files—1948, CUA Archives.

100. See press release of 5 July 1948 sent by George Higgins to Catholic editors, in Papers of National Catholic Welfare Conference, ILO Files, CUA Archives; to comfort Catholics who feared the radicalism of the migrant labor piece, Higgins encouraged editors in a note to use the migrant story with one of the bishop's greeting to the ILO, when he said, "none of the goals set forth by the International Labor Organization sound strange or radical to the ears of Catholics who are familiar with the social teaching of the Church." Also see Catholic Association for International Peace, *Toward an Integrated World Policy: A Joint Report* (Washington, D.C.: Catholic Association for International Peace, 1950).

101. "Battle over ILO," *Commonweal*, 4 May 1956, 112–123.

102. "Communists Rebuffed at ILO," *Commonweal*, 19 June 1954, 310.

103. *America*, 23 June 1956, 296.

104. "Fifty Years of Economic and Social Progress: Report for European Conference; with Address by Pope Pius XII," *UN Review*, February 1955, 41–42; see also "Pope to the ILO," *America*, 18 December 1954, 314, which said, "The mere fact that the Holy Father cordially received the ILO Governing Board should be enough to allay . . . unfounded suspicions [of American business leaders]."

105. George Delaney and Lewis Hines handled strategy for the AFL-CIO; on Higgins's role, see Gerald M. Costello, *Without Fear or Favor* (Mystic, Conn.: Twenty-Third Publications, 1984), 223–228.

106. A memo from Rev. Thomas J. McDonagh, head, Department of Economics, University of Notre Dame, to James Murphy, Department of Public Information, 7 March 1955, lists thirteen target media, including the New York- and Washington-area papers, the leading Midwest papers, labor and Catholic papers, and business press, and mentions the cooperation of the secretary of labor; in UDIS Collection, Box 10, Folder 7, International Organization of Employers, University of Notre Dame Archives, Notre Dame, Indiana.

107. 4 April 1955, in UDIS Collection, Box 10, File 7, International Organization of Employers, UND Archives.

108. 6 April 1955, in UDIS Collection, Box 10, File 7, International Organization of Employers, UND Archives.

109. *Yardstick*, 18 April 1955.

110. *Ave Maria*, 16 April 1955, 4; *The New World*, 24 April 1955, ran Higgins's column.

111. See Mark Fitzgerald, presentation at Trinity College, Washington, D.C., 9–11 November 1956, in Higgins Papers, International Labor Organization Series, CUA Archives; also in the Higgins papers, see correspondence of J. Joblin, the priest assigned to the ILO in Geneva, and Higgins, 14 October and 19 October 1956.

112. Letter from Stritch to Higgins, 10 July 1955, in Higgins Papers, International Labor Organization Series, CUA Archives.

113. Letter of Higgins to Le Roy, 2 April 1956, in Higgins Papers, International Labor Organization Series, CUA Archives.

114. Letter from Higgins to Peter Straus, ILO staff in Washington, 30 October 1956, in Higgins Papers, International Labor Organization Series, CUA Archives.

115. Letter from Higgins to Clement Ansulewicz of the Newman Press, publisher of the book, 7 December 1956, in Higgins Papers, International Labor Organization Series, CUA Archives.

116. Letter from Ralph Wright of the ILO's Washington staff to Higgins, 24 January 1957, in Higgins Papers, International Labor Organization Series, CUA Archives.

117. Identical letters from Higgins to Archbishops Patrick O'Boyle of Washington, Cardinal Stritch, and Cardinal Mooney of Detroit, 6 May 1957, in Higgins Papers, International Labor Organization Series, CUA Archives.

118. Letter from Higgins to Albert Le Roy, 2 April 1956, in Higgins Papers, International Labor Organization Series, CUA Archives.

119. See U.S. Department of Labor News Release, 17 January 1957, and Higgins News Release, 28 January 1957, in Higgins Papers, International Labor Organization Series, CUA Archives.

120. See memo from Phil Delaney to Andy Biemiller, 20 January 1956, in Lovestone Files, Box 28, File 51, Meany Archive.

121. See Higgins's statement before the Subcommittee of Senate Committee on Labor and Public Welfare, 4 May 1956, in Higgins Papers, International Labor Organization Series, CUA Archives. This hearing was on Senator Hubert Humphrey's resolution to support an ILO forced labor convention. Typically, Higgins released his statement to the press at the time of the hearing; see letter to Senator Paul Douglas, 4 May 1956, and also letter to Senator Theodore Green, 16 April 1957, in Higgins Papers, International Labor Organization Series, CUA Archives.

122. On the special relationship of Higgins and Mitchell, see letter from Higgins to Cardinal Stritch, 12 January 1955, and letter from Higgins to Mitchell, 31 January 1957; in Higgins Papers, International Labor Organization Series, CUA Archives. On Secretary Mitchell and Eisenhower's cabinet generally, see, for example, Elmo Richardson, *The Presidency of Dwight D. Eisenhower* (Lawrence: Regents Press of Kansas, 1979), 32–34.

123. Church leaders had cultivated Mitchell's support astutely, giving him the *Rerum Novarum* Award, as well as celebrating such steps as his speech at Notre Dame at the ILO conference; to one so isolated during the Eisenhower Administration, this had to build goodwill. See USDOL press releases, 21 March and 1 April 1955, in Higgins Papers, International Labor Organization Series, CUA Archives.

SEVEN. REAFFIRMATION

1. David R. Roediger, *The Wages of Whiteness: Race and the Making of the American Working Class* (London: Verso, 1991), is a good example of the leftist attacks on white working-class racism; see 133–163, where Roediger focuses on racism among Irish Catholic workers. Ava Baron, ed., *Work Engendered: Toward a New History of American Labor* (Ithaca, N.Y.: Cornell University Press, 1991) is a collection of essays showing how organized labor, especially "business unionist," undermined its strength by not hearing or supporting issues of concern to women workers. Both Roediger's and Baron's interpretations come from a school of labor historians that tends to be very critical of the leadership of organized labor, blaming the leadership for failures of leadership. The interpretation in this book assumes that in the exceptional American policy environment, labor leader-

ship seldom has such power and usually must make strategic compromises simply to have a slight chance of being heard. This book also assumes labor's racism or sexism, while undeniably present, is no worse than that of other classes.

2. A. James Reichley, *Religion in American Public Life* (Washington, D.C.: The Brookings Institution, 1985), 269–281, discusses the problem of leadership of mainline Protestant churches in finding support from the congregations for reform policies.

3. Ted Morgan, *A Covert Life: Jay Lovestone: Communist, Anti-Communist and Spymaster* (New York: Random House, 1999), provides a fascinating overview of the life and schemes of Lovestone and of his complex position being both extremely prolabor and anticommunist.

4. On this topic generally, see Andrew Levison, *The Working Class Majority* (Baltimore: Penguin Books, 1975), 17–51. For a full explanation of Meany's responses to the developments of the era, see his testimony in U.S. Congress, House of Representatives, Committee on Appropriations, *Departments of State, Justice, and Commerce, the Judiciary, and Related Agencies Appropriations for 1971: Part 5, Additional Testimony on the International Labor Organization*, 91st Cong., 2nd Sess., 31, July 1970, especially the report by Carlos Vela, 38–39.

5. In the fall of 1961, Morse and Meany were cooperating in a campaign to restrict Russian influence in the ILO; see letter from Morse to Meany, 8 November 1961, Morse Papers, Box 6, File 24, Mudd Library, in which Morse says, "I decided that the best approach would be to tell the Russians *straight out* and *directly* that I would not put the proposal forward [for more Soviet staff at the ILO]." On the AFL-CIO's official position on Morse's decision not to run for another term, see *News from the AFL-CIO*, NA 8–3870, 22 November 1961.

6. Morse had fully consulted Meany about his initial decision not to seek reelection, and Meany had urged him to stay; see Secret Report, Reelection of the Director-General—Conversation with George Meany, 21 October 1961, Morse Papers, Box 6, File 24, Mudd Library.

7. Notes on dinner meeting at home of U.S. Ambassador Roger Tubby, in Geneva, 5 June 1963, in Morse Papers, Box 6, File 24, Mudd Library.

8. Letter from Morse to Meany, 6 July 1964, in Morse Papers, Box 57, File 19, Mudd Library, marked personal and addressed "Dear George."

9. *The New York Times*, 24 June 1964, 34a; see also memo from Morse to Ralph Wright, ILO Washington Office Director, 23 June 1964, in Morse Papers, Box 57, File 19, Mudd Library.

10. *The New York Times*, 12 April 1965, 34a.

11. "Adamant Mr. Meany; AFL-CIO Walkout," *The Nation*, 27 June 1966, 764, has this interpretation.

12. "AFL-CIO Foreign Policy: U.S. Delegates Walk-out," *The New Republic*, 25 June 1966, 7; and "Conflicts Shake Labor's House," *Business Week*, 25 June 1966, 110, report on the Reuther-Meany split. See Victor Reuther memo to Walter

Reuther, 6 April 1965, in Reuther Papers, Box 38, File 8, Reuther Library, Wayne State University, Detroit, Michigan, which holds that Meany's position on the ILO was "technically wrong and morally indefensible."

13. Letter from Meany to Reuther, 10 June 1966, in Higgins Papers, International Labor Organization Series, CUA Archives.

14. Meany was conciliatory to the Johnson Administration in a press conference on 19 June 1966, but had veiled criticism of cultural exchanges with the Soviet Union; in Higgins Papers, International Labor Organization Series, CUA Archives.

15. For example in "AFL-CIO Foreign Policy," *The New Republic*, 7, praised Walter and Victor Reuther for "fighting this [Meany's] kind of blindness"; in "Labor Takes a Harder Line Overseas," *Business Week*, 24 April 1965, 139, noted explicitly the conflict over trade that lay at the background of Meany's position, saying "[Meany's] position takes issue not only with the [Johnson] Administration but also the U.S. Chamber of Commerce, which has advocated East-West trade."

16. "Should U.S. Business Support the ILO? 50th Anniversary of World Body," *Business Week*, 14 June 1969, 68; see also Business International, "International Labour Organization," in *The United Nations and the Business World* (New York: Business International, 1967), 83.

17. Higgins served as a mediator here, trying to get Meany and Reuther back together. See letter from Walter Reuther to George Higgins, 17 June 1966, in Box 182, File 1, Reuther Papers, Reuther Library; as well as UAW *Administrative Letter*, 17 June 1966, 1–3.

18. See Radosh, 443–444. Reuther shared Meany's concern with globalization but had faith in voluntary associations to protect labor standards; see "Labor's Cold War," *The Economist*, 18 June 1966, in Reuther Papers, Box 38, File 8, Reuther Library.

19. On Higgins's and Morse's use of the papal visit to return Meany to support of the ILO, see letter from Higgins to Morse, 23 June 1969, and response 30 June 1969, as well as Higgins's letter to Meany, 23 June 1969, in Morse Papers, Box 58, File 35, Mudd Library.

20. See "Deeds of ILO Hailed By Meany," *The Kenosha Labor*, 19 June 1969; and "Worldwide Jobs Effort Draws Meany's Support," [Lafayette, Indiana] *Union Labor News*, June 1969, preserved in David Morse Papers, Box 6, File 24, Mudd Library.

21. On the Nobel Prize, see *The New York Times*, 21 October 1969, 1a and 14a; and Cox, "ILO Limited Monarchy," 111, which discusses how the prize and the earlier papal visit in 1969 obscured the fundamental challenges facing the ILO.

22. The rate of convention adoption increased from 1.6 per year in the 1960s to 2.2 in the 1970s, then fell to 1.5 in the 1980s and 1990s, yet most of these conventions could be classified as technical rather than substantive, in contrast to

the conventions of the late 1940s and early 1950s; an exception was the 1976 Tripartite Convention, Number 144, which was adopted to try to keep the U.S. in the ILO by protecting the right of free representatives of labor and business to their nation's seats.

23. On the development of universalism, see Anthony Alcock, *History of the International Labor Organization* (New York: Octagon Books, 1971), 291–317; Alcock had the support of the ILO to write this book at the time Meany was becoming especially hostile.

24. On the process of appointing the Russian, see Galenson, *International Labor Organization*, 113–115.

25. Congress, Committee on Appropriations, *Departments . . . Appropriations for 1971*, 2.

26. Ibid., 4.

27. Ibid., 6–47.

28. The editorial, titled "Mr. Meany, Mr. Rooney and the ILO," *The Washington Post*, 25 May 1971, said, condescendingly, "Labor chieftain George Meany, long over-agitated by the imagined pro-Communist bias of the International Labor Organization, exploded when the new director general—an Englishman, C. Wilfred Jenks—appointed a Russian as an assistant last year."

29. The letter to Morse from *Foreign Affairs*, signed Bob, is a remarkably mysterious document that ends with the cryptic note "The Church of England catechism begins Q: What is your name? A: N or M"; in Morse Papers, Box 6, File 16, Mudd Library.

30. N. M., "International Labor in Crisis," *Foreign Affairs* 49 (April 1971): 528–529.

31. For a discussion of the trade-off or impact of development on exploitation, see Lena Ayoub, "Nike Does It and Why the United States Shouldn't: The United States' International Obligation to Hold MNCs Accountable for Their Labor Rights Violations Abroad," *DePaul Business Law Journal* 11 (spring/summer 1999): 421–424, which discusses the interpretation of Jeffrey Sachs and Paul Krugman that more sweatshops are good for easing poverty in Africa.

32. N. M., "International Labor," 528.

33. Ibid., 532.

34. Despite Morse's apparent opposition to Meany's criticism of the ILO in the early 1970s, there is remarkably cordial correspondence between the two, such as Morse to Meany letter, 30 November 1971, and a friendly response from Eugenie Meany (Meany's wife), 7 December 1971; in Morse Papers, Box 57, File 19, Mudd Library.

35. See Galenson, *The International Labor Organization*, 118–120, for a good summary.

36. Ibid., 120.

37. Joseph P. Goldberg, "Tripartism Reaffirmed by the 1971 International Labor Conference," *Monthly Labor Review* 94 (September 1971): 30–36.

38. John P. Windmuller, "U.S. Participation in the ILO: A Political Dimension," *U.S. Bureau of Labor Statistics Monthly Labor Review* 98 (May 1975): 35–37.

39. Charles H. Smith, Jr., "ILO Accomplishments—The U.S. Employers' View," *Monthly Labor Review* 98 (May 1975): 41.

40. Ibid.

41. Galenson, *International Labor Organization*, 122, says Smith personally supported withdrawal, while the Department of Commerce backed the ILO because it assisted multinational enterprise.

42. Bert Seidman, "ILO Accomplishments—Organized Labor's View," *Monthly Labor Review* 98 (May 1975): 38–39.

43. "U.S. Delegation to ILO Walks Out," *Monthly Labor Review* 98 (August 1975): 48.

44. "Impact of U.S. Pullout from ILO," *U.S. News and World Report*, 14 November 1977, 102.

45. ILO Issues Paper, 15 September 1975, in Presidential Handwriting File, ILO folder, Gerald Ford Library, Ann Arbor, Michigan.

46. Memorandum, 26 August 1975, Presidential Handwriting File, Folder ILO, Ford Library.

47. Memorandum from Ernest Lee to Meany, 19 June 1975, in Lovestone Files, Box 28, File 52, Meany Archive.

48. See "Leaving the ILO," *Newsweek*, 14 November 1977, 69; also "The Human Rights Dilemma of Leaving the ILO," *Business Week*, 19 September 1977, 130, which lists key members of Congress opposing Meany, including Hubert Humphrey and Jacob Javits. See also "United States Withdraws from the ILO," *Department of State Bulletin*, 26 December 1977, 912–913, for the statements of President Carter and Secretary of Labor Ray Marshall; also "Why the U.S. plans to quit the U.N.'s Labor Arm," *Nation's Business*, October 1977, 28–33; and Barbara Koeppel, "Meany and Business vs. the ILO: Will We Pick Up Our Marbles?" *The Nation*, 29 October 1977, 429–431, which held that while some general accounts of withdrawal said that labor and employers both called for it, documents show business followed labor's lead.

49. Benjamin R. Barber, *A Place for Us: How to Make Society Civil and Democracy Strong* (New York: Hill and Wang, 1998), 12–37.

50. Schattschneider, 34–35.

51. Stephen I. Schlossberg, "United States Participation in the ILO: Redefining the Role," *Comparative Labor Law Journal* 11 (fall 1989): 22–23, classifies these as five distinct reasons: socialism, tripartism, human rights, due process, and politics.

52. See Folder IT 34, White House Central Files, Ford Library.

53. *News from the AFL-CIO*, 6 November 1975.

54. See letter from McGee to Kissinger, 17 September 1975, Folder IT 34, White House Central Files, Ford Library; the letter to President Ford was sent on 21 October 1975.

55. On withdrawal and morality, see Bruce L. Rockwood, "Human Rights and Wrongs, The United States and the I.L.O. — A Modern Morality Play," *Case Western Reserve Journal of International Law* 10 (1978): 359–413; Rockwood sees the withdrawal as bad policy simply driven by an effort to obtain George Meany's political support.

56. Lowi, 289–291.

57. See NSC memo from Hal Horan to Brent Scowcroft, 12 January 1976, in Folder IT 34, White House Central Files, Ford Library; see also the memo from Robert S. Smith to Scowcroft, 5 January 1977, which talked about advising the Carter Administration on withdrawal and took a generally positive view of the ILO's reform efforts in 1976.

58. On Pope and Meany, see *The New York Times*, 5 October 1977, 7a; confirmed in Lorenz interview of George Higgins on 11 October 1995, Catholic University, Washington, D.C. On Higgins and withdrawal, see Costello, 227–228.

59. Joseph A. O'Hara, "Of Many Things," *America*, 12 November 1977, 2.

60. Joe Holland and Peter J. Henriot, "A New Challenge for World Labor," *America*, 8 October 1977, 211.

61. "ILO Body Studies Sanctions for Human Rights Violations," *UN Chronicle*, April 1978, 68.

62. International Labor Organization, Tripartite Declaration of Principles Concerning Multinational Enterprises and Social Policy, adopted November 1977.

63. *The New York Times*, 3 September 1979, 14.

64. *The New York Times*, 31 August 1980, IV: 14, said, "[In] Gadansk . . . shipyard insurgents have had the wit to examine an I.L.O. convention adopted in 1948. It proclaims the freedom of association and the right to organize."

65. See Virginia A. Leary, "The Paradox of Worker's Rights as Human Rights," in *Human Rights, Labor Rights and International Trade*, ed. Lance A. Compa and Stephen F. Diamond (Philadelphia: University of Pennsylvania Press, 1996), 42, who agrees with Galenson, *The International Labor Organization*.

66. *The New York Times*, 6 June 1981, 3a.

67. On the ILO and Solidarity, see Ludwik Florek, "International Labor Law and Polish Legislation," in *The Changing Face of Labour Laws and Industrial Relations*, ed. Roger Blanpain and Manfred Weiss (Baden-Baden: Nomos Verlagsgesellschaft, 1993), 158–161; American Bar Association Section of International Law and Practice "[Report to the House of Delegates] International Labor Organization," *The International Lawyer* 30 (fall 1996); 653–664; and Steve Charnovitz, "Promoting Higher Labor Standards," *The Washington Quarterly* 18 (summer 1995): 178, which especially discusses the Reagan Administration's use of the ILO against the Polish government. On Poland, see also Bridges, 19; and Schlossberg, 18.

68. Derian was also a supporter of the International Labor Rights Education and Research Fund; see ILRERF, *Trade's Hidden Agenda: Worker Rights in a Changing World Economy* (Washington, D.C.: ILRERF, 1988).

69. While the Carter Administration generally is seen as the one to launch the contemporary linkage of human rights and foreign policy, a fact which the AFL-CIO celebrated, see *AFL-CIO Free Trade Union News* 32 (March 1977); the Foreign Assistance Act of 1961 explicitly included such a link, stating "[T]he principal goal of the foreign policy of the United States shall be to promote the increased observance of internationally recognized human rights by all countries." See 22 U.S. Code, Sec. 2304 (a) (1) 1994. Of course, such precedents as the Nuremberg Trials, by implication, also enshrined human rights in foreign policy, although with an especially individualistic focus; see Joy Gordon, "The Concept of Human Rights: The History and Meaning of Its Politicization," *Brooklyn Journal of International Law* 23 (1998): 703–706.

70. While the International Covenant on Economic, Social, and Cultural Rights had been negotiated in 1966 and had taken effect in early 1976, as had the International Covenant on Civil and Political Rights, there seemed to be no new movement related to human rights until the Carter Administration took office the following year; specifically Gross, 4–7, points out the U.S. only gave partial ratification to these covenants.

71. For a review of this development, by a participant, see Seymour J. Rubin, "Recent Development: Transnational Corporations and International Codes of Conduct: A Study of the Relationship between International Legal Cooperation and Economic Development," *The American University Journal of International Law and Policy* 10 (summer 1995): 1275–1284.

72. On Executive Order 12216, 18 June 1980, which created the President's Committee, see Schlossberg, 26.

73. For a brief review of this process, see ABA, 653; for a critical assessment of the commitment of business and labor to collaborate, see Lance Compa's comments in "International Trade and Social Welfare: The New Agenda—Transcript of January 7, 1994, Meeting of the Section on International Law of the American Association of Law Schools," *Comparative Labor Law Journal* 17 (winter 1996): 369–370.

74. Leary, 22–47, discusses the role of the Lawyer's Committee.

75. On the development of *The Human Rights Quarterly* and programs at the University of Cincinnati, see Irvin C. Rutter and Samuel S. Wilson, "The College of Law: An Overview 1833–1983," *University of Cincinnati Law Review* 52 (1983): 327.

76. For example, Lance A. Compa and Stephen F. Diamond, "Introduction," in *Human Rights, Labor Rights and International Trade* (Philadelphia: University of Pennsylvania Press, 1996), 1–9, discuss sponsorship by Schnell.

77. See Alan Scott, *Ideology and the New Social Movements* (London: Unwin Hyman, 1990), 13–35, for this typology.

78. Sara Cleveland of the University of Texas, and formerly associated with the Schnell Center at Yale Law School, sees the ILO as weak in the 1980s but recently rejuvenated; see her review of *Human Rights, Labor Rights and Interna-*

tional Trade, edited by Lance A. Compa and Stephen F. Diamond, in *Texas Law Review* 76 (May 1998): 1539–1541.

79. Louis Henkin, "That 'S' Word: Sovereignty, and Globalization, and Human Rights, et Cetera," *Fordham Law Review* 68 (October 1999): 8.

80. Leary, 23, provides an example of the academic focus on violations of the human rights of students in China, but ignores union victims, the ones who often suffered the greatest punishment.

81. Gross, 84–85.

82. Charnowitz, "Promoting," 178.

83. On the hearings, see Schlossberg, 27.

84. Ruth Colker, *American Law in the Age of Hypercapitalism: The Worker, The Family and The State* (New York: New York University Press, 1998); ILRERF, *Trade's Hidden Agenda,* discusses Reagan Administration application of the Generalized System of Preferences (GSP) enforcement against Paraguay, Nicaragua, and Romania on 2 January 1987; see also Charnowitz, "Promoting," 183–184.

85. Elisabeth Cappuyns, "Linking Labor Standards and Trade Sanctions: An Analysis of Their Current Relationship," *Columbia Journal of Transnational Law* 36 (1998): 680–684; and Emily Yozell, "The *Castro Alfaro* Case: Convenience and Justice-Lessons for Lawyers in Transcultural Litigation," in Compa and Diamond, 273–274, are good examples of studies referring to this growth.

86. Philip Alston, "Labor Rights Provisions in U.S. Trade Law: 'Aggressive Unilateralism'?" in Compa and Diamond, 72; also Schlossberg, 32.

87. Gross, 16, discusses the close links of Bush and the USCIB; the only substantive conventions ratified by the U.S. were numbers 53, 54, 55, 57, 58 (all adopted in 1938), 74 (adopted in 1953), and 147 (adopted in 1988), all of which dealt with conditions of employment of seamen.

88. William A. Orme, Jr., *Understanding NAFTA: Mexico, Free Trade, and the New North America* (Austin: University of Texas Press, 1996), 290–297.

89. For assessments of the Clinton Administration, see transcript of "International Trade and Social Welfare," 352–353; and Charnowitz, "Promoting," 171–173. See also remarks by U.S. Government Delegate Andrew Samet in the debate over the ILO declaration, in ILO, International Labor Conference, *Report of the Committee on the Declaration of Principles: Discussion in Plenary,* 86th sess., June 1998.

90. Poll reported in *Americans on Globalization: A Study of U.S. Public Attitudes,* conducted by Program on International Policy Attitudes at the University of Maryland, conducted 21–29 October 1999; see *ILO Focus,* summer 2000, 6–7.

91. *ILO Focus* (fall/winter 1999): 1–2.

92. See, for example, editorial "Clinton Fumbles on Trade," *The Los Angeles Times,* 6 December 1999, 6b; and Jerome Levinson, "And No: Labor Rights and the Environment First," *The Washington Post,* 6 December 1999, 27a.

93. Henry H. Drummonds, "Transnational Small and Emerging Business in a World of Nikes and Microsofts," *The Journal of Small and Emerging Business Law* 4 (summer 2000): 249–254, has a good review of Seattle and contemporary commentaries on events leading to and resulting from the protests there.

94. Jay Hancock, "Protesters of Seattle Take Aim at D.C. Talks: World Bank, IMF Are Targeted, Policy toward Poor Faulted," *The Baltimore Sun*, 7 April 2000, 1a; *The New York Times*, 27 September 2000, 8a. There also were related protests at an Organization of American States meeting in Windsor, Ontario, in June 2000; see Stuart Laidlaw, "Pepper Spray Flies at OAS Rally, 41 Arrested at Windsor Demonstration," *The Toronto Star*, 5 June 2000, 7a.

95. Mary Dalrymple, "House Likely to Reject U.S. Exit of WTO," *CQ Weekly*, 10 June 2000, 1409; the resolution was HJ Resolution 90, 106th Congress, 2nd Session.

96. Thomas L. Friedman, *The Lexus and the Olive Tree* (New York: Farrar Straus Giroux, 1999), 359.

97. *ILO Focus*, summer 2000, 3.

98. From *OECD Guidelines for Multinational Enterprises, Review 2000*, Commentary on Employment and Industrial Relations, 20, available from http://www.oecd.org/daf/investment/guidelines/mnetext.htm.; Internet accessed 6 June 2000.

99. See, for example, Berry, 121, for data.

100. Philip Shabecoff, *Earth Rising: American Environmentalism in the 21st Century* (Washington, D.C.: Island Press, 2000), 114, discusses what he calls the "new politics of special interests."

101. Often seen as the classic form of the new organization is the American Association for Retired Persons; see Paul Light, *Artful Work* (New York: Random House, 1985), 75–78.

102. See, for example, Christopher Bellman and Richard Gester, "Accountability in the World Trade Organization," *Journal of World Trade* 9 (1996): 35.

103. See Scott, 13–35, for a discussion of "new social movements"; page 19 contrasts these with working-class movements.

104. Robert Reich, *The Work of Nations: Preparing Ourselves for Twenty-first Century Capitalism* (New York: Alfred A. Knopf, 1991), 177–195; Harold J. Perkin, *The Third Revolution: Professional Elites in the Modern World* (New York: Routledge, 1996), 177–201; and see Erik O. Wright, *Class Counts: Comparative Studies in Class Analysis* (New York: Cambridge University Press, 1997), 91–111.

105. Students from higher-education institutions became heavily involved in the anti-sweatshop efforts of the 1990s; however, their efforts seem to result more from the activities of religious figures, such as Charles Kernaghan, trained by the Jesuits, at the National Labor Committee or Pharis Harvey, a

Methodist minister, at the International Labor Rights Fund, see *New York Times*, 9 December 1999, 2B.

106. On Kirkland, see Dulles and Dubovsky, 396–397.

107. For a review of the decline, see Richard Edwards, *Rights at Work: Employment Relations in the Post Union Era* (Washington, D.C.: Brookings Institution, 1993), 77–101. Edwards concludes his review of union decline with an interesting quotation from Lane Kirkland; see Edwards's note 40. For a more positive assessment, see John B. Judis, "Can Labor Come Back?" *The New Republic*, 23 May 1994.

108. See Lance Compa's comments in transcript of "International Trade and Social Welfare," 369–370, on this alliance.

109. Schlossberg, 30; George Schultz and William Brock backed labor versus the USCIB; Alston makes clear labor used the embarrassment argument—communists said the U.S. could not criticize them because the U.S. had not ratified conventions.

110. On ILRERF and Ray Marshall, see Marshall's "The Global Jobs Crisis," *Foreign Affairs* 75 (fall 1995) and his *Unheard Voices: Labor and Economic Policy in a Competitive World* (New York: Basic Books, 1987). For a criticism of the ILRERF as simplistic in its approach, see Alston, 77; more generally, see Benn Steil, "'Social Correctness' in the New Protectionism," *Foreign Affairs* 73 (January–February 1994): 14–20.

111. Compa and Diamond, 309.

112. John Sweeney, "Statement by AFL-CIO President John J. Sweeney on the Adoption of a New ILO Declaration on Workers' Rights," June 18, 1998, available from http://www.aflcio.org; Internet accessed 24 July 1998.

113. Lawrence B. Glickman, *A Living Wage: American Workers and the Making of Consumer Society* (Ithaca, N.Y.: Cornell University Press, 1997), 157–162, sees consumerism linked to labor through debates about a living wage, an interpretation somewhat at odds with that here; on feminist changes, see Skocpol, *Protecting Soldiers and Mothers*, 539, who concludes, "Feminists must work in organizations and networks that tie them to others in very different social circumstances."

114. "CLC Conference Calls for Reality Check," *NCL Bulletin*, May/June 1998, 3.

115. *NCL Bulletin*, May/June 2000, 8–10; still, the majority of stories in this issue of the *NCL Bulletin* did not focus on labor-related issues, addressing the now-classic consumer quality and price concerns. For the link to the ILO, see *ILO Focus*, summer/fall 2000, 12–13.

116. Steve Charnovitz, review of *Trade, Employment and Labour Standards: The OECD Study and Recent Developments in the Trade and Labor Standards Debate*, by the OECD, in *Temple International and Comparative Law Journal* 11 (spring 1997): 151–152.

117. Alfred T. Hennelly, S.J., *Liberation Theologies: The Global Pursuit of*

Justice (Mystic, Conn.: Twenty-Third Publications, 1995), 8–39; on *Centesimus Annus* and labor standards, see Drummonds, 282.

118. National Conference of Catholic Bishops, *Contemporary Catholic Social Teaching* (Washington, D.C.: U.S. Catholic Conference, 1991), 5 and 12.

119. Hennelly, 247–260. Liberation theology also spread beyond Christianity, see 160–233; and, for example, Asghar Ali Engineer, *Islam and Liberation Theology* (New Delhi: Sterling Publishers, 1990).

120. *Economic Justice for All*, sections 322–325, in *The Catholic Challenge to the American Economy*, ed. Thomas M. Gannon (New York: Macmillan, 1987).

121. Thomas R. Donahue and Rudolph A. Oswald, "Labor Views the Pastoral Letter on the Economy," in Gannon, 228.

122. Lay Commission on Catholic Social Teaching and the U.S. Economy, *Toward the Future: Catholic Social Thought and the U.S. Economy* (New York: Lay Commission, 1984); for a discussion, see Hansen, 113–119; for Novak's ideas, see his "Liberty and Social Justice: Rescuing a Virtue," in *Catholic Social Thought and the New World Order*, ed. Oliver F. Williams and John W. Houck (Notre Dame, Ind.: University of Notre Dame Press, 1993), 269–284.

123. *The New York Times*, 5 November 1984, 20a; and 7 November 1984, 16a.

124. Norman Gottwald, "Values and Economic Structures," in *Religion and Economic Justice*, ed. Michael Zweig (Philadelphia: Temple University Press, 1991), 59.

125. *ILO Focus*, summer/fall 2000, 3.

126. Lance Compa, in transcript "International Trade and Social Welfare," 358; see also ILRERF, *Trade's Hidden Costs*, on backing for the ILRERF.

127. *St. Louis Post Dispatch*, 23 April 1997, 7b, discussed the growing interest among evangelical Christians in joining with the Catholic Church in linking labor rights with religious freedom, particularly in China, but also Indonesia, Pakistan, Vietnam, Iran, and Cuba; pointing out the similarity of the position of labor and the evangelicals, Robert William Fogel, *The Fourth Great Awakening and the Future of Egalitarianism* (Chicago: University of Chicago Press, 2000), 25–27 and 176–235, describes the leadership provided after the 1960s by evangelical churches to the rebellion against the antiegalitarian features of globalization; for example, see Tom Sine, *Mustard Seed vs. McWorld: Reinventing Life and Faith for the Future* (Grand Rapids, Mich.: Baker Books, 1999), 105–141.

128. Phillip Berryman, *Liberation Theology* (Philadelphia: Temple University Press, 1987), 43.

129. For a discussion of liberation theology and the "Protestant ethic," see Michael Lowy, *The War of the Gods: Religion and Politics in Latin America* (London: Verso, 1996), 19–31; similarly, Susan Curtis, *A Consuming Faith: The Social Gospel and Modern American Culture* (Baltimore: Johns Hopkins University Press, 1991), 228–243, described the tendency of social gospelers to have become proponents of American consumer culture.

130. Charnowitz, "Book Review," 158–160, discusses the three justifications.

131. In the 1990s, a coalition of church-based labor rights movements evolved called the Campaign for Labor Rights; it was founded by more than a dozen groups, primarily religious, such as the National Interfaith Committee for Worker Justice and the Coalition for Justice in the Maquiladoras.

132. Bender, *Intellect and Public Life*, 140–145, discusses both the signs of academic withdrawal from public affairs and the academic critiques of that withdrawal; see also Bender's "Politics, Intellect, and the American University, 1945–1995," *Daedalus* 126 (winter 1997): 4–24, and other essays in that number of *Daedalus*, which examined "American Academic Culture in Transformation: Fifty Years, Four Disciplines."

133. See Ellen Schrecker, *No Ivory Tower: McCarthyism and the Universities* (New York: Oxford University Press, 1986), 84–125 and 283–337; and more generally Fried, *Nightmare in Red*, 101–111; and David Caute, *The Great Fear: The Anti-Communist Purge under Truman and Eisenhower* (New York: Simon and Schuster, 1977), 403–484.

134. See Robert M. Hutchins, *The Learning Society* (New York: Frederick A. Praeger, 1968), 33–38; also, 105–121 critiques the highly specialized university emerging in the postwar era.

135. Ibid., 35–37.

136. Ibid., 33–38, describes "investment in man" being one watchword of the era.

137. Works in the early postwar years, such as Richard Hofstadter's influential *The American Political Tradition and the Men Who Made It* (New York: Alfred A. Knopf, 1948), 272–275, attacked the fourteen points; William Appleman Williams, *The Tragedy of American Diplomacy*, rev. ed. (New York: Delta Books, 1962), 57–83, had a chapter focusing on Wilson titled "The Imperialism of Idealism," and on page 89 described Wilson not as an idealist, but as a simple promoter of self-interested liberalism; works appearing during the Vietnam War agreed, such as Ross Gregory, *The Origins of American Intervention in the First World War* (New York: W. W. Norton, 1971), 134, which said of Wilson's motives for going to war, "He felt a need and obligation to promote economic interests abroad." Of course the realists Kennan, Morgenthau, and Lippmann launched these attacks during and immediately after the war. Even their critics, while they did not fully blame Wilson, tended to attack the failure of Versailles, as Frank Tannenbaum, "The Balance of Power Versus the Coordinate State," *Political Science Quarterly* 67 (1952): 189–197; on race, see Kathleen Long Wolgemuth, "Woodrow Wilson's Appointment Policy and the Negro," *The Journal of Southern History* 24 (November 1958): 457–471.

138. See, for example, Baron, 129–130, who describes "Gompers' working-class cult of masculinity."

139. In discussing leaders such as Gompers, the new approach, according

to Fink, *American Labor History*, 13, if it did not marginalize Gompers, began "to qualify the very 'conservatism' of AFL figures such as Gompers . . . , emphasizing an abiding Marxist influence on their thought and the pragmatic nature of their political cautiousness." Fink's analysis was part of a series by the AHA on the status of historical scholarship in 1990. See also Fink's "'Intellectuals' versus 'Workers': Academic Requirements and the Creation of Labor History," in his *In Search of the Working Class: Essays in American Labor History and Political Culture* (Urbana: University of Illinois Press, 1994), 201–235.

140. On the general cultural hostility to expressions of faith, see Carter, *Culture of Disbelief*, 3–13; for a study of the evolution of even the denominational colleges away from the churches, see James Tunstead Burtchaell, *The Dying of the Light: The Disengagement of Colleges and Universities from Their Christian Churches* (Grand Rapids, Mich.: William B. Eerdmans, 1998), 823–833.

141. Leary, 23, discusses the human rights focus on students, not workers.

142. Vogelson, 653, lists those preparing recommendations to be, in addition to himself: Virginia Leary, of SUNY Buffalo's Faculty of Law and a founder of the Lawyers Committee; David A. Waugh, of the ILO's Washington office; Frederick Kirgis, former dean of the Washington and Lee University Law School; and Richard O'Connor, of a leading Connecticut labor law firm (which represented management).

143. The USCIB, according to its statement of "Benefits of Membership in the USCIB," is solely focused on "the key international organizations where rules and standards governing business activity today and for the next century are being written." It has three hundred multinational corporations as members. Available from http://www.uscib.org/frame2.htm; Internet accessed 6 June 2000.

144. Edward E. Potter, *Freedom of Association, The Right to Organize and Collective Bargaining: The Impact on U.S. Law and Practice of Ratification of ILO Conventions No. 87 and No. 98* (Washington, D.C.: Labor Policy Association, 1984).

145. Business Roundtable, International Trade and Investment Task Force, *International Trade and Investment and Labor: Constructive Approaches, May 9, 1995,* available from http://www.brtable.org.; Internet accessed 6 June 2000.

146. Charnovitz, "Book Review," 151–153.

147. ILO, "Report of the Committee on the Declaration of Principles," 4–5.

148. Schlossberg, 30, has 1985 testimony.

EIGHT. LESSONS AND NEEDS

1. See John Holloway, "Global Capital and the National State," in *Global Capital, National State and the Politics of Money*, ed. Werner Bonefeld and John

Holloway (New York: St. Martin's Press, 1995), 116–140; and David C. Korten, *When Corporations Rule the World* (San Francisco: Barret-Kohler, 1995), 121–131.

2. U.N. Conference on Trade and Development, *World Investment Report 1997* (New York: United Nations, 1997), 10, 24, and 113.

3. Katherine Van Wenzel Stone, "Labor and the Global Economy: Four Approaches to Transnational Labor Regulation," *Michigan Journal of International Law* 16 (summer 1995): 990–996, discusses the similarities of the southern policy in the textile industry in the 1920s and 1930s to late-twentieth-century globalization.

4. Ibid.; see also Jeffrey Harrod, *Power, Production, and the Unprotected Worker* (New York: Columbia University Press, 1987), 218–221; and Cox, *Production, Power, and World Order*, 281–308.

5. Gross, 80–84, points out the clear opposition of the USCIB to freedom of association protections, which they fear would strengthen labor protections under the National Labor Relations Act; see Potter, 71–77.

6. *ILO Focus*, summer/fall 2000, 14; for earlier comments on this issue, see, for example, *The Washington Post*, 17 February 1998, 41a, referring to an ILO report issued on 16 February 1998; see also *Toronto Star*, 16 February 1998, 3a, which states, "Among the survey's startling findings: the United States, Australia, and New Zealand are among the prosperous nations still refusing to enact laws providing paid maternity leave and health benefits for pregnant women."

7. For a good review of this development, see Robert F. Housman, "Democratizing International Trade Decision-making," *Cornell International Law Journal* 27 (summer 1994): 703–705; see also "Introductory Remarks" of Frederick M. Abbott, in "International Trade and Social Welfare," 338–344.

8. See unpublished paper by Robert O'Brien, "The World Trade Organization and Labour," presented at the 39th Annual International Studies Association Convention, Minneapolis, Minnesota, 17–21 March 1998, 15–23.

9. Paul Rauber, "All Hail the Multinationals," *Sierra*, July–August 1998, 16–17.

10. Writing before the 1998 victory, labor rights supporters were especially negative about the process; see for example, Charnovitz, "Promoting," 170, who said, "In actuality, the Clinton administration's labor rights initiative of early 1994 was more of a breakdown than a breakthrough." Lance Compa, in transcript of "International Trade and Social Welfare," and Cappuyns also are critical of focus on intellectual property rights, rather than human and labor rights: Cappuyns, 677, quotes the phrase, "Mickey Mouse has more rights than workers."

11. Eyal Benvenisti, "Exit and Voice in the Age of Globalization," *Michigan Law Review* 98 (October 1999): 168–212.

12. See John Zarocostas, "Core Labor Standards Divide ILO Members," *Journal of Commerce*, 3 June 1998, 3a.

13. *ILO Focus* (summer/fall 2000): 14.

14. Gross, 70–102, discusses litigation related to the two ILO conventions.

15. Drummonds, 293.

16. Transcript of "International Trade and Social Welfare," 369.

17. Ibid.

18. Cox, "ILO: Limited Monarchy," 122.

19. Michael Clough, "Grass-Roots Policymaking: Say Good-Bye to the 'Wise Men'," *Foreign Affairs* 73 (January–February 1994): 2.

20. Robert F. Drinan, "Reflections on the Demise of the Religious Freedom Restoration Act," *Georgetown Law Journal* 86 (October 1997): 101–121.

21. Rich Lowry, "Married to the Mob," *National Review,* 8 December 1997, 34–38; for another perspective, see Terry Golway, "The Vilification of John Sweeney," *America,* 29 November 1997, 5. Both were written shortly after the AFL-CIO successfully fought to block quick review (or "fast-track") authority in negotiating an expanded NAFTA.

22. For example, under pressure to address environmental racism, the U.S. Environmental Protection Agency allowed low-income communities to create community advisory groups to have a voice in policy making; see U.S. EPA, Office of Emergency and Remedial Response, *Community Advisory Groups: Partners in Decisions at Hazardous Waste Sites—Case Studies* (Washington, D.C.: U.S. EPA, 1996).

23. Gottwald, 58.

24. Housman, 699–747, has a good review of this trend globally.

25. Donald R. Brand, *Corporatism and the Rule of Law: A Study of the National Recovery Administration* (Ithaca, N.Y.: Cornell University Press, 1988), 1–7, has a discussion of alternatives to the problem of liberalism and justice, first described by Lowi.

Index